| USGIF | MONOGRAPH SERIES | VOLUME 1 |

HUMAN GEOGRAPHY

Socio-Cultural Dynamics and
Challenges to Global Security

EDITORS
Robert R. Tomes
and
Christopher K. Tucker

SERIES EDITOR
Darryl G. Murdock

This project was supported by the United States Geospatial Intelligence Foundation.
Opinions expressed are those of the authors and not neccessarily those of the Foundation.

ISBN 978-0-615-89833-9

Editors: Darryl G. Murdock, Robert R. Tomes and Christopher K. Tucker.

Published by United States Geospatial Intelligence Foundation,
2325 Dulles Corner Boulevard, Suite 450, Herndon, Virginia 20171
Phone: 1.888.698.7443

FOREWORD

When the concept of a Monograph series was first introduced to USGIF membership circa 2009, the idea struck a positive chord. Shortly thereafter, a Human Geography working session was planned and carried out during one of USGIF's annual GEOINT Community Week activities. The resulting work product is reflected within this volume. The Monograph Series, Volume 1: Human Geography combines knowledge and ideas from a variety of authors engaged in what has become an important part of the GEOINT discipline—Human Geography. The subsequent refinement and focus on Global Security came about after determining the interests and foci of submissions received. The end result is an organic product that combines the best of a participatory all-volunteer effort.

GEOINT is a team sport—a complicated team sport, but very much a team sport—requiring consistent communication and efforts from its various components. If we were to survey the breadth and depth of the GEOINT discipline (and, periodically, we at USGIF, attempt to do just that), the findings would be vast and compelling. In fact, to call the profession deeply breathtaking based on the shear variety of activities being routinely performed would not be an overstatement. GEOINT, the discipline, encompasses image interpretation, geographic information systems, data management, incorporation of open-source information, all types of geospatially referenced data and, of course, the analysis of all of these data to answer basic questions about what is where and what happened and more challenging questions about what will or might happen in a geographic and temporal context. Human Geography allows the GEOINT analyst to understand deeper context and help predict outcomes for a given time based on knowledge of the human condition at a particular location on the globe.

This volume is the first in what will be an ongoing series of publications designed to engage thought leaders, students and practitioners on a variety of GEOINT-related topics. We at USGIF are continually recruiting USGIF members to take an active role in the next several volumes. I urge each of you to consider what you may have to offer our global community, whether as an author or co-author, editor, member of an editorial review board or simply as a passionate advocate with a point of view or topical idea to share. All are welcome to participate, regardless of affiliation.

USGIF strives to consistently provide the highest quality information products that benefit students, instructors, professors and practitioners. We also aspire to have our collective works used as required or ancillary reading for students studying particular disciplines. To that end, I encourage you to provide us with feedback about what you like, what you would like to see in subsequent volumes and your ideas on how we can improve both content and our method of getting the word out. Please be active and proactive. This is the only way we can all benefit and improve our profession. Get involved. Thanks for reading.

Darryl Murdock,
Series Editor
monograph@usgif.org

ACKNOWLEDGMENTS

In addition to the contributions of our authors and editors, we would like to thank the following individuals who contributed to the creation of this volume. Thanks to Tory Pugliese for her cheerful organizational help, without whom this volume would not have seen the light of day; Justin Franz for his help recreating tables; Dr. Max Baber and our editorial Review Board for helping select the final publications and provide edits and suggestions for improving the final product; Rene, Evan, Scott and Linda from GLC for their guidance, expertise and patience in producing the final product. Thanks to the leadership of Keith Masback and Aimee McGranahan for their support, understanding and willingness to continue down a long, winding and sometimes opaque publishing path. And of course thanks to my lovely and patient wife, Julia, and our respective families who allowed us the freedom and time to create this compilation.

—Darryl Murdock

EDITORIAL REVIEW BOARD

TABLE OF CONTENTS

INTRODUCTION

Robert R. Tomes
Christopher K. Tucker

Since 9/11, increased demand for open, unclassified insights into global cultures, movements and peoples has once again focused attention on the need to integrate untapped resources available in the world's vast social science disciplines. Human dynamics research, analysis and reporting improve both the "baseline" data available to national security decision makers and the in-depth analysis used to inform defense, development and diplomacy missions.

Socio-cultural intelligence is a diverse area of intelligence collection, analysis and reporting that relies heavily on the work of social scientists and methodological approaches adapted from geography, computational mathematics, anthropology, psychology and other disciplines. "Socio-cultural dynamics" is a broader term we use to characterize the range of actions, behaviors and relationships across micro-, meso- and macro-levels of analysis. Social scientists employ many methods across different levels of analysis to provide information relevant to national security decision makers, from the micro- (individual actors to small groups) to the meso- (political parties, larger groups, some social movements) to the macro-level (larger tribal, religious or societal affiliations).

Included in our understanding of socio-cultural dynamics are myriad activities and methods that others might call the human geographic domain, including research done by anthropologists. All of these areas of research and analysis contribute to socio-cultural intelligence, patterns of life, and insights into aspects of human intent, behavior and perception. It is the application of this knowledge that improves our understanding of the events, trends, behaviors and conditions that shape international security affairs.

A dizzying array of terms have been used within the national security community over the past decade to label or define activities that collect data about humans, groups, activities, behavior and perceptions; that describe analysis of that data using methods, tools or techniques; and that report findings or conclusions focused on the actions or behaviors of specific individuals, groups (clans, tribes, sects), entire regions and seemingly non-geographic or global networks. These terms include human terrain, socio-cultural intelligence, human socio-cultural behavioral modeling, social media monitoring, patterns of life analysis and, more recently, activity based intelligence.

All of these terms and associated analytic methods share common elements: when done well, the Geospatial Intelligence (GEOINT) professional focuses on mastering spatio-temporal representations of complex socio-cultural dynamics in a way that empowers analysts, operators and decision makers to effectively prosecute national security strategy. The associated explosion in spatio-temporal discourse across the national security policy community has often served to confuse more than inform audiences. We are sympathetic to arguments for adopting a re-energized and expanded application of the term "human geography" and find value in the coining of new terms like "activity based intelligence" that emphasize innovative approaches worthy of their own label. Our use of the term socio-cultural dynamics to describe this volume appeals to our belief that the community is in need of more synthesis and integration than antithesis and specialization. It also helps us remain above definitional quibbling and embrace as many perspectives as possible.

We can all agree on the continued importance of socio-cultural dynamics and their relevance to national security. During the Cold War, social scientists worked intensely to help national security decision makers understand the human dimensions of that conflict, from understanding Soviet strategic culture and Politburo dynamics to examining the cultures of Warsaw Pact members to analyzing and countering socio-economic underpinnings of communist ideology.

U.S. Cold War socio-cultural intelligence programs supported all dimensions of Cold War grand strategy to contain and defeat the Soviet adversary. These included large-scale, regional influence operations to undermine the legitimacy of the occupation of Eastern Europe and bolster local alternatives like the Polish Solidarity movement and smaller, focused programs to understand the cultural background and ideological leanings of the leadership of each Soviet missile submarine.

Lamentably, we did not sustain the focus on socio-cultural intelligence during the transition to a post-Cold War era. Socio-cultural intelligence collection, analysis and reporting capabilities subsequently atrophied during the 1990s. As documented in various commissions and reports, national security organizations over-emphasized technical collection disciplines after the Cold War and did not adapt analysis and reporting disciplines to address the nuances of many post-Cold War issues, trends and threats.

National security decision makers seeking to understand the human geography of the global war against terrorism in the aftermath of the 9/11 attacks found that the social science disciplines and traditional socio-cultural intelligence areas had been marginalized.

This volume synthesizes multi-disciplinary perspectives on socio-cultural dynamics to inform strategy and planning discussions by demonstrating the richness and diversity of social science contributions to national security decision making.

The power of place: human dynamics and national security decision making

When America went to war in Afghanistan over a decade ago, troops quickly realized they lacked an understanding of the "human terrain" on the ground as they swept away the Taliban and transitioned to nation building. Meanwhile, the broader national security community struggled to grasp the human dimensions underlying the reasons why a small minority of Muslims had declared war on the West and how a gang of radicals hiding in the mountains of South Asia galvanized a larger global network of terrorist affiliates.

An important inflection point occurred in 2005. In November, the publication of Department of Defense Directive 3000.05, Military Support for Stability, Security, Transition, and Reconstruction Operations (often referred to as SSTRO), made stability operations a core military mission. The document codified in Departmental guidance what many strategists had already observed in programming, budgeting and training activities: stability and support operations should not be viewed as secondary activities from the perspective of readiness, doctrine, training and acquisition priorities. Security and stability operations were henceforth to be considered co-equal missions alongside traditional military missions.

In 2006 the U.S. Army published Field Manual (FM 3-24), *Counter-Insurgency*, and updated its foundational doctrine *Operations*, (FM 3-0) in February 2008, defining "full spectrum

operations" as the simultaneous application of offensive and defensive measures in concert with stability operations.

The emergence of a formal doctrine for Humanitarian Assistance Disaster Response (HADR) has also played a powerful role in elevating the importance of socio-cultural dynamics as they are arrayed across geography over time. HADR operations fundamentally require such data and analysis. The expansion of the human terrain team program and the September 2008 publication of a Human Terrain Team Handbook amplified the need for additional understanding about how to integrate socio-cultural dynamics research and methods into national security decision making.

By the end of the 2000s, strategists, planners and policy makers had identified a larger issue out of experiences in both Afghanistan and Iraq: the lack of an institutionalized process for understanding "socio-cultural intelligence" or what more recently has been termed "human factors" analysis or analysis of the human dimensions of conflict.

National security affairs have always been driven by and dominated by human issues and the interaction of regional, physical, environmental and other dynamics that are grounded in spatial and temporal realities, but are too often discussed and analyzed in isolation. These spatio-temporal factors, often loosely framed in "geospatial" and "geographic" terms, are increasingly central to our understanding of the complex socio-cultural phenomena, events, crises and policy dilemmas that shape international security, foreign policy and diplomatic strategy.

In highlighting national security challenges in a location-aware world, this volume aims to inform national security decision makers about the importance of understanding the complex and ever-changing geography of humanity and human behavior—in all of its forms and in much greater detail. Many decision makers are already asking for information that is spatially and temporally organized to both help shape decision making and to facilitate more efficient implementation of programs. Across the national security community, for example, there is increased emphasis on understanding patterns of life; influence channels for strategic communication; the local, regional and global factors influencing stability or instability; and the implications of environmental or other system-level change on people, groups, societies and nations.

As the Defense Department pivots to the

Pacific to address Asian security challenges, and as the national security community continues to promote democracy, open markets and Internet freedom across the globe, the national security community will need additional sources, methods and research to address the human underpinnings of security, governance and economic integration. It is increasingly important to understand how local politics and communal relations are refracted through cultural lenses that endure the pressures of globalization as well as new dynamics that are reactions to globalization. Even if the focus on stability operations and counterinsurgency missions wanes in the coming years, the demand for spatially and temporally organized socio-cultural information to support decision making will continue to grow.

The 2010s are bringing the national security community full circle back to the dilemma faced by post-Cold War planners and strategists. As was the case 20 years ago, as budget reductions force cuts across defense and intelligence community programs, it may be that open source and social cultural intelligence programs are disproportionally reduced. Ongoing strategy and planning efforts, including preparations for the 2014 Quadrennial Defense Review (QDR), must reduce spending across defense and intelligence community programs while sustaining programs and activities crucial to understanding and preparing for an era of persistent conflict. Increasing our understanding of human dynamics in terms of spatio-temporal change over time must remain a priority.

When Director Letitia Long took the helm of the National Geospatial-Intelligence Agency (NGA) and articulated her vision for the National System for Geospatial Intelligence (NSG) at the 2011 GEOINT Symposium, organized by USGIF, her explicit focus on "human geography" in achieving better analytic depth underscored the need for additional resources to educate the broader national security community about the breadth of the human geography community. Her remarks bolstered the decision to produce this volume and remain relevant today.

We believe that, as the 2014 QDR and other planning efforts proceed, strategists and planners seeking measures to preserve efficiency and effectiveness will be well-served to remember the critical importance of geospatially and temporally referenced socio-cultural intelligence.

Volume background and objectives

The idea for this volume emerged from a series of meetings facilitated by the United States Geospatial Intelligence Foundation (USGIF) that began in 2008 and continued after the volume went to print in 2013. Participants in these meetings have included U.S. government and military professionals from over a dozen departments or agencies, scholars representing a diverse range of academic disciplines, and industry practitioners from across the defense, intelligence, diplomatic, homeland security and international development markets.

Since then, USGIF has steadily cultivated a community of interest sharing the following concerns: the need to raise awareness of how the social and behavioral sciences were contributing to national security decision making; reinforcing the development of standards and best practices as analytic methods proliferated across the intelligence and broader national security policy community; and ensuring that solutions and practices developed since the 9/11 attacks continued to mature as troops departed Iraq and Afghanistan and as funding for programs designed to provide "patterns of life" and other "population-centric" information and analysis started to decline.

USGIF recognized the need for a monograph on socio-cultural dynamics from a geospatial perspective written by and for national security professionals, one that canvassed both the formal discipline of human geography and the many related disciplines that focus on the so-called "human terrain." Responding to this request, our contributors put aside academic differences and quibbles about the definition of specific fields of geography or other social science disciplines; they generally accepted that a volume on Socio-Cultural Dynamics and Global Security was necessary to capture what the community had learned during the 2000s about the human dimensions of conflict.

The volume has three objectives. First, it provides a cross-section of proliferating interdisciplinary writings that provide examples of using increasingly sophisticated techniques in which spatial and temporal variables are aggregated and analyzed to understand the socio-cultural, political, economic and regional dynamics at the core of national security studies. Our sampling of interdisciplinary approaches embraces the diverse lexicon and often doctrinaire approaches to defining and describing human dynamics. Some authors are eager to apply the term "human geography" to all of these dynamics, a term we are happy to promote to capture both the diversity of perspectives as well as the near-universal recognition that human behavior and activity as it is arrayed across the global landscape remains at the core of national security studies. The range of interdisciplinary articles and practitioner experience represented in this volume travels far beyond the traditional definition of human geography that dominates the larger profession of geography in mainstream academic writings. And, while some will note that the appreciation of space and time exhibited in all of these essays demonstrates the primacy of geography and the human element, we have designed this volume to let all disciplines express their viewpoints and methodological approaches.

Second, the volume highlights the new challenges faced by national security analysts, operators and decision makers within an increasingly "location aware" global society. It is not just that human society can only be properly understood in terms of its evolving geospatial and temporal dynamics. It is that the explosion in widely available low-cost commercial imagery, the ubiquity of GPS-enabled devices and applications, the widespread adoption of capabilities like Google Earth, the increasing geo-referencing of media and social media content, and other such phenomena are fundamentally reshaping how humans behave and interact. This includes reshaping how location-aware societies perceive and respond to the actions of our national security enterprise and to the actions, inactions and policies of individual nations and international organizations.

The third objective of the volume is to provide a reference for students of national security affairs. After nearly a decade of sustained focus among national security practitioners on the requirement to understand patterns of life, to enable security and stabilization operations, to address human security challenges, and to understand root causes of communal and other identity-related violence, there remains a critical lack of core texts written by and for students of national security policy making. This volume combines perspectives from academics, senior government leaders and practitioners from both government and industry to provide a new resource for educating students of national security affairs.

We are optimistic that the national security community will agree that successfully managing the challenges of the next half century and beyond requires sustained investment in understanding socio-cultural dynamics within a spatial and temporal framework. Without a commitment to constantly renew our understand of these dynamics and adjust our framework accordingly, we will repeatedly find ourselves facing population-centric security challenges in strange geographies where we have inadequate understanding of how these security challenges have evolved. And, if anything changes continually, it is humanity. A one-time investment in building knowledge resources will never work—this activity must always be ongoing.

Section overviews

This volume is an ambitious attempt at several "firsts." It is the first attempt to integrate into one volume different, and sometimes competing, perspectives on the current state of Human Geography research and methods as they might be applied to inform national security challenges. It is also the first volume to synthesize academic, practitioner, and policy-maker perspectives. Finally, it is the first attempt to connect traditional approaches to Human Geography with practitioners who rely on or draw from these approaches, often without knowing it.

The volume includes 23 articles organized into 6 thematic sections:

- Understanding the Story: Thoughts from National Security Leaders
- Administratively Derived Socio-Cultural Data in Human Geography and GEOINT
- Natural Resources, Human Dynamics and Security
- The Socio-Technical Dimensions of Culture and the Modern Geography of Security
- Names and Language in Human Geography
- Policy and Governance in a World of Experts: Harnessing Socio-Cultural Dynamics for Global Security

By no means do these sections illuminate the entirety of the challenge we face in understanding socio-cultural dynamics both spatially and temporally. Yet the articles in each section do provide a representative sample of the socio-cultural dynamics that are too often neglected within the national security decision making community. Accordingly, we have organized the articles from the perspective of how the different sections are intended to come together.

The volume begins with a series of articles

by senior national security leaders and thought leaders framing issues and challenges as they see them. Dr. Lee Schwartz, Dr. Parag Khanna, Dr. Joseph Fontanella, and Patrick O'Neill all highlight the criticality of a geospatial lens on challenging socio-cultural dynamics. Coming from very different backgrounds and experiences, the first section authors paint a collective landscape and offer unique individual perspectives that frame the subsequent sections.

Section Two focuses on administratively derived socio-cultural data—the kind provided by indigenous governmental administrative capacities such as a census, cadastre, the resulting addressing scheme, and a system of identification cards that link identity to individual addresses. This is a far too often overlooked form of geospatial data that simultaneously serves as the key to decrypting a society while also serving as the glue that holds a stable society together.

Excluded from this discussion was a piece about polling and surveying. Polling and surveying are not normally capabilities conducted by government agencies, but are often contracted by them. As polls and surveys have shown utility within the national security space, and have received more funding, they have become focused on much more fine-grained geographies, providing senior national security leaders with a lens on how socio-cultural dynamics have evolved spatially and temporally. Even though this volume did not have the time or space to address polls and surveys properly, we see them as crucial in the effort to showcase many of the novel polling and survey approaches that are bringing power to geospatial analysis of human dynamics. In particular, how these strategies can be used in concert with social-media monitoring strategies and other modes of spatio-temporally enabled analysis must be further explored.

Section Three could have comprised its own volume, or series of volumes, as there are no bounds to the variety of ways in which natural resources and their relationship with the human geography shape the dynamics of global security. No matter how well you understand societies in terms of the data accrued by polls and surveys, one must understand the impact of natural resources on human dynamics— particularly those that sustain life and livelihoods in particular regions. But rather than a section that covers the kitchen sink (e.g., climate change, ecosystem collapse, invasive species,

fossil fuels, fisheries, etc.), we chose to be sparing and provocative, illustrating this critical dynamic through water and diamonds. Water is critical to humanity everywhere on Earth, but in some places, its abundance makes it less of a critical driver for security. Yet, where it is scarce, understanding water is key to understanding human security. Diamonds, and specifically "conflict diamonds," provide a very different set of insights into the ways that natural resources can shape human security. Both are profoundly tied to geography, and shape the narrative in different societies in different ways.

It would take a much larger volume to provide an exhaustive accounting of the security challenges, geographic conflicts and suffering that occur due to the scarcity or even an abundance of particular natural resources. But, it is important that readers at least understand this dynamic in tension with the sovereignty, property rights and the continuous flow of peoples across geographies in conflict.

Density, conflict and hazards loom increasingly large in the future of human security. Just recently, the majority of the world's population found themselves living in urban areas. This new balance, of course, was in the context of a rapidly increasing world population. This pattern of urban development is too often very different from what Westerners might associate with city living. A dense fabric of informal settlements unmapped by the kinds of administrative capabilities described previously offer an interesting challenge to national security professionals seeking to prevent conflicts from breaking out in these population centers. We regret that we could not do more in this section, particularly as it relates to the recent emergence of the use of spatial data within the development community to better understand how societal risks can be understood, mitigated and responded to when we have a thorough understanding of the geographic exposure of societies to natural hazards. But, for the reader, it is important to note that this topic is often difficult to separate from the issues raised in the two prior sections. This is fertile ground for a future volume.

Taking a somewhat different tack into the realm of the technical, Section Four, entitled "The Socio-Technical Dimensions of Culture and the Modern Geography of Security," lets the reader explore how many of today's hot topics collide when we think of them spatially and temporally. While social media, volunteered geographic information, and activity based intelligence are terms often discussed by very different communities within the national security enterprise, it is clear that the domains that these terms represent are quickly crashing into each other. With everything electronic becoming location-enabled and location-aware, analysts, operators and decision makers are demanding that analysis of these data types provide a geographic "lay-down" of the complex socio-cultural phenomena being observed. With every consumer innovation, and the proliferation of commercial sensors within the inevitable emergence of a global location-aware Internet of Things (IoT), it seems clear that complex socio-cultural phenomena, as they are unfolding across complex urban geographies in real-time, will be laid bare by such technologies. Our national security community must become facile in their use. This is not to say that the administratively derived forms of spatially enabled socio-cultural data outlined previously will be any less useful. Instead, they will become a fundamental backdrop for understanding this explosion in socio-technical data.

In Section Five, entitled "Names and Language in Human Geography," we explore the world of toponymy—the study of geographic names, and how such knowledge shapes our ability to understand what is going on in a society. Ignorance of such issues too often leaves the national security professional flat-footed, ill-equipped to navigate both the geography and the society at large. Whether the deluge of such socio-technical data, the steady accumulation of administrative data, or the endless evolution of less well documented vernaculars that identify places of cultural significance, we are always faced with the challenge of language and culture.

Lastly, we offer a brief sixth section entitled "Policy and Governance in a World of Experts: Harnessing Socio-Cultural Dynamics for Global Security" to provide some insights into the policy and governance challenges that leaders will face as they try to help the national security enterprise better deal with the kinds of socio-cultural phenomena discussed in the previous sections. We intentionally steered away from being prescriptive, and sought instead to highlight a few key areas that seemed obvious, uncontroversial, yet chronically overlooked.

Edited volumes are fundamentally about making hard choices on content and focus. We have taken on a broad topic about which there are many competing perspectives. In the end, we hope that it serves as the beginning of a conversation that goes on steadily as this century unfolds. To encourage and provide a voice for continued debate and discussion about terms, approaches, and avenues to connect scholars to the national security community, USGIF will provide a discussion forum on its website at **usgif.org** following the publication of this book.

Dr. Robert R. Tomes is President of The MapStory Foundation, serves as an adjunct professor at Georgetown University and is BAE Systems' Director of Tradecraft Advancement. A former NGA senior manager and founder of Liminal Leadership™, he authored *U.S. Defense Strategy from Vietnam through Operation Iraqi Freedom* and co-edited *Hybrid Warfare and Transnational Threats*. He earned his doctorate from the University of Maryland.

Dr. Christopher K. Tucker thinks and works at the intersection of technology, strategy, geography and national security. Tucker manages a portfolio of social ventures and technology companies across the domains of international affairs, defense/intelligence and academe. He serves on a variety of government, private sector and non-profit boards.

Section 1

Understanding the Story: Thoughts from National Security Leaders

IS (POLITICAL) GEOGRAPHY DESTINY? THE CASE FOR A NEW HUMAN GEOGRAPHY

Parag Khanna

In the two decades since the end of the Cold War, scholars and policy makers have come to appreciate the increasingly multi-polar nature of world order. This realization constitutes a gradual *structural change* by which the world's polarity de-concentrates away from the singular hegemony of one: the United States. Far less appreciated, but equally significant for military strategists, is the more subtly unfolding *systems change*, meaning a transformation in the very nature of the units in the world system. It is not that the state itself is disappearing (though indeed some are), but a host of new authorities and players have come up from within, outside, above and in parallel to states that have to be taken seriously. These entities include cities, religious groups, activist NGOs, terrorist networks, multinational corporations, tribes, organized criminal syndicates, mercenary armies, and labor unions, to name a few. Not all of these groups are territorial actors at all, forcing us to shift our thinking from the simple political geography of bordered states to a new human geography that considers these as operational units despite their sub-state or transnational nature. There are now diverse combinations of power and resources, loyalty and identity, technology and agency beyond the state; the number of unique authorities is growing even as they increasingly overlap.

We are only beginning to grasp these new spatio-temporal patterns, develop the tools to map and assess them, and formulate successful strategies to respond to them. Globalization today is a universal playing field that is increasingly level among various manifestations of what I call the four Cs: countries, cities, companies and communities. It is essential to include all four in our maps of the new human geography.

The bewildering complexity that results from the nexus of globalization, structural change and systems change portends nothing less than the advent of a New Middle Ages, turning back the clock in some ways by almost one thousand years to the last period of history which was multi-polar, multi-civilizational, and multi-actor all at once. A millennium ago, Song Dynasty China was the world's most advanced civilization (having mastered paper-making and gunpowder), India's Chola Empire ruled the Indian Ocean, and Arab and Islamic Caliphates stretched from North Africa to Central Asia.

Europe was weak and divided, with the Holy Roman Empire nearing its terminal fate. The continent's landscape featured agile city-states forming alliances such as the Baltic Sea's Hanseatic League (which was both trade guild and armed defense pact), mercenary groups such as the Italian *Condottieri*, the Vatican and its religious courts, far-flung kingdoms and duchies, powerful merchant families like the Medici of Florence, privates and slave-traders, marauding tribal bands, and respected universities from Oxford to Bologna. The relationship between territory, authority and identity was fluid. Sovereignty mattered less than authority, which varied by region and place. In terms of the variety and fluidity of socio-cultural dynamics, the early 21st century more resembles the Middle Ages than any other historical era.

As governments, companies, militias, drug cartels, terrorists, criminal networks, humanitarians, tribal groups and others interact and form relationships, it becomes imperative to sort out who is doing what with whom (the vectors of activity) and who has influence over whom (the angles of leverage). This analysis will allow us to: 1) more accurately chart the dynamics of authority; 2) reveal what type of actors are actually "calling the shots" (governments, warlords, companies, tribes); 3) establish where these actors have influence (locally, regionally, globally through a diaspora or in cyberspace); and, 4) ultimately provide better maps of the relevant human geography.

Countries

Let us then further delve into the four Cs, beginning with countries. When it comes to states, we must understand two things. First, no two states are the same; rather, there is a diverse typology: States with strong nationhood (America and Brazil); empires veiled as states (China), states acting as empires (Russia and Iran), empires made up of states (the European Union), natural-resource states (Qatar), market-states with more foreigners than citizens (the United Arab Emirates), quasi-states (Palestine), and states that exist mostly in name (the Democratic Republic of the Congo). Some quasi-states like Kurdistan are more functional than other de jure states like Libya.
The number of countries in the world has grown from approximately 80 at the founding of the United Nations just over 60 years ago to more than 200 today. Most of these are fragile post-colonial nations with the same underlying factors of instability that gave rise to the Arab Spring: over-population, crumbling infrastructure,

corrupt governance, and high unemployment. The more new countries that are born out of secessionist movements—East Timor, Kosovo and South Sudan in just the past decade—the more weak states we will have.
Second, state and government are not the same thing. The state is a legal, physical and functional space, and governments are one significant actor within that space. Government capacity, however—the ability of governments to actually do what they are supposed to do—varies as drastically as the type of states does. Ideal-type governments are both regulatory and provisory: they defend national borders, collect taxes widely and fairly, run efficient courts, protect property rights, police equitably, maintain economic stability and provide a social safety net. But most governments are at best *filters* between domestic priorities and international demands. Global commerce trumps their fiscal and monetary levers, trade flows undermine their industries, corporate supply chains co-opt natural resources, and networked activists undermine regimes. Public goods such as security, infrastructure, healthcare and education is delivered by a range of actors including government agencies, civic groups, religious charities, community trusts and companies.
The wide range of sizes and types of states and their forms of governance have tremendous implications for global security. Indeed, most states in the world are not providers or *suppliers* of security and governance but *receivers*. Many no longer hold the monopoly over the use of force within their borders, and instead export instability and violence over their borders

both willingly and unwillingly. Security institutions ranging from UN Peacekeeping to NATO and other alliances are more about creating stability *in* such places rather than regulating security relations *among* them. As much of the post-colonial world continues to decay along the "arc of crisis" from Congo through Yemen to Pakistan, the demand for global security provision will continue to grow. As we have already learned in Somalia and Afghanistan, "state-building" is not necessarily the correct strategy, nor is it even feasible in a reasonable time-scale.

Cities

From a historical standpoint, there is nothing permanent or immutable about states or governments existing as the exclusive units of power or authority. In other words, the state is not a natural state, it is not a foundational principle of geography. Some states will survive while others will give way to new modes of organizing people through technology, resources, ideology and money.
The far more durable locus of authority since the advent of human settlements is the second C: the city. As of 2010, we officially live in a world that is more urban than rural. By 2030, close to 75 percent of the world's population is expected to live in cities. As a result, it is more appropriate and useful to think of the new human geography on the micro-level of cities than the macro-level of states.
Cities are the *islands of governance* in a world more populated by functional cities than dysfunctional national governments. Just 40 city-regions account for two-thirds of the world economy and

most technological innovation. New York City's economy is larger than that of sub-Saharan Africa. As with states, there are many kinds of cities, the most important of which are global financial capitals like New York, London, Tokyo and Hong Kong which are both economic and political hubs, and mega-cities such as Sao Paulo, Istanbul, Cairo, Shanghai or Mumbai which are major population magnets as well as economic engines. Of growing importance are also port cities and city-states such as Dubai and Singapore that efficiently re-export goods across the world. These entrepôts or "free zones" are not only cultural melting pots with residents from over 100 nations, but also crucial gateways to rapidly growing emerging market regions.

However, as cities grow to be the size of countries—both demographically but also physically by merging into endless urban corridors—it becomes clear that mega-cities are as stratified as nations. Within the growing number of megalopolises dotting the planet we also find teeming slums in Rio de Janeiro, Lagos, Nairobi or Dhaka and dozens of other cities of the fragile and over-populated post-colonial world. While these are often called "shadow economies," they are in fact self-organizing ecosystems with their own geographic patterns, political hierarchies, economic models, and social structures. Our current maps of such complex but dense and influential areas are woefully inadequate, as they have to be constantly updated to account for their dynamism.

The power of cities lies in density, money, knowledge and stability. Rich or poor, cities—more than nations—are the building blocks of global

activity today. Over time, the global network of cities will potentially come to matter as much or more than the formal institutions which connect states and governments. Like the medieval Hanseatic League, alliances of agile cities in the Persian Gulf region already use their sovereign wealth funds to acquire the latest technology from the West, buy up tracts of agricultural land in Africa to grow their food, and protect their investments through private armies and intelligence services. We could see the return of urban-corporate-criminal operations such as the Bank of Commerce and Credit International (BCCI) that was a pivotal player in financing both Latin American drug cartels as well as the anti-Soviet mujahedeen in Afghanistan.

Cities, therefore, play a crucial role in defining the new human geography and the future of global security. They will either be the anchors of national and regional economic and political stability or battlegrounds for the control of wealth and resources. In other words, they can either be well-governed or ungoverned spaces. Before the post-9/11 invasion of Afghanistan and subsequent emphasis on counter-insurgency operations in rugged, mountainous terrain, defense experts began to emphasize urban guerrilla warfare due to the Somalia experience. The Iraq war and difficulty in stabilizing Baghdad remind us that looking ahead, we must deepen this focus on training and preparation for urban combat operations. From Mexico City to Karachi to Port Moresby, we can already foresee scenarios for lengthy campaigns directed at targeting drug cartels, radical terrorist

groups, and criminal gangs, respectively.

For policy makers and defense strategists, "city-building" in terms of infrastructure, employment and police forces could become more important than state-building.

Companies

While the cross-border networks of cities are nascent in their development, those of the third C—companies—are very advanced. Multinational corporations own and operate worldwide supply chains, provide foreign investment and tax revenue without which many governments cannot survive, and generate essential employment to maintain social stability. Indeed, the financial crisis of 2008 revealed not only the pervasive power of an increasingly unregulated private sector, but also the dependence of many governments on banks and financial institutions for revenues. Additionally, corporations increasingly fund massive infrastructure projects in both developed and developing countries. In India, industrialist families such as the Tatas or Ambanis sponsor entire city-factories, providing all employment, healthcare and education for hundreds of thousands of workers.

Even after the financial crisis and subsequent global market crash, corporations still represent half of the world's top 100 economic entities. The world's largest corporation, Wal-Mart Inc., represents greater economic size than all but 21 national economies. It has a global workforce of over 2 million employees. Furthermore, emissions from Wal-Mart's supply chain globally are greater than Ireland's national emissions, which makes Wal-Mart a systemically more relevant actor than dozens of countries.

Energy and mineral companies have an even more profound impact on the governance, stability and welfare of many societies around the world. Africa's largest economy and most populous country, Nigeria, depends to a great extent on the extractive work of one multinational oil company, Royal Dutch-Shell. The intricate relationship between the Nigerian government and Shell is much more accurately described as co-dependence and co-governance than the dominance of one by the other.

Other firms are technology and information providers that are indispensable for all other actors as well. Far more than a news organization, Bloomberg has become the world's largest private intelligence service on markets and politics. IBM, Microsoft, Google and Apple provide the essential hardware and software for basic government and economic functioning worldwide.

Corporations have become the tip of the diplomatic spear for many countries. State-owned companies like Russia's Gazprom and China's Sinopec are principal arms of foreign policy for these powers. Even for free-market states like Canada, Brazil, Japan and India, the expansion of their private multinational corporations abroad is the source of their strategic influence and diplomatic leverage. All over the world, private equity funds are taking stakes in farmland, gold and other resources in exchange for building basic services and serving as friendly

intermediaries with Western governments. The writ of the state has become at best hybrid sovereignty over supply chains, special economic zones, and reconstruction projects. Governments can attempt to monitor or regulate corporations, but they cannot control them.

Note that criminal enterprises have grown in lock-step with globalization's advance, preying both on wealthy states with lucrative markets to serve and weak states that cannot regulate their markets and resources. Criminal organizations and networks operate in supply chains eerily similar to those of legitimate corporations, perpetrating the illicit transfer and sale of goods as varied as drugs, weapons, minerals, currencies and people. The ways in which criminal enterprises leverage, insinuate themselves into, and co-opt legal governmental transfer and commercial exchanges makes tracking them a perpetually notorious task—thus requiring ever more sophisticated data mapping tools.

The irreversible rise of the global corporate sector has significant implications for our thinking about global security, particularly in the fiscally constrained environment facing defense planners. One of the principal lessons from both Iraq and Afghanistan has been that the resurrection and growth of the domestic private sector is, alongside the restoration of law and order, the most important factor enabling sufficient stability to take hold and allow for a winding down of foreign occupation. Insufficient resources were provided to those agencies such as

USAID that have the mandate to encourage local private sector development, and experiments such as the U.S. Defense Department's Office of Business and Stability Operations were short-lived. Moving forward, substantially greater resources need to be devoted to promoting foreign investment (through risk insurance and loan guarantees) in post-conflict societies. "Company-building" is at least as important as city-building and state-building.

Community

The community—the fourth C—is the level at which we can best observe all the elements of the new human geography come together. Nationalism is no longer necessarily the dominant identity or motivation for human groups. Cross-border religious and ethnic identities are strengthening around the world (particularly in Africa and the Middle East), as are tribal and indigenous identities within and across states (particularly in Latin America and Asia). The Inuit of Canada, Hausa of Nigeria, Baluchis of Pakistan, and Naxalites of India are some examples of indigenous groups using means ranging from constitutional reforms to armed rebellion to fight for control over local natural resources and assert their independence. There are also non-territorial "cloud communities" forming around political causes such as the hacker movement Anonymous that generated a global firestorm with the release of the WikiLeaks cables.

Information and communications technologies empower all these categories of community to more vocally express their autonomous interests, which can be further propagated and fueled by ever more connected diaspora groups. Technology has also enabled the rise of new kinds of collective ideational activism such as social media organized revolutionaries across the Arab world. While they have not successfully built a new political order in countries such as Egypt, their continuous ability to disrupt the entrenchment of any regime they consider illegitimate or ineffective makes them a permanent pole of power in society.

The rise of community-centric politics must also influence thinking about actors and roles in shaping global security outcomes. The case of Afghanistan demonstrates that successful counter-insurgency must be conducted at the village level by gaining the support of influential tribal elders. The Arab Spring further shows how collectives of youth, workers and other marginalized groups can have a major impact on politics in pivotal states. At the same time, radical terrorist propaganda and recruitment now takes place to a growing degree through online communities and forums, making cyberspace not just a neutral communicative realm but also a battlefield with new kinds of armies, strategies and tactics. As intangible as the legal and material structure of communities may be, they are essential actors either as partners or rivals in establishing security around the world.

Even if America regains its strategic momentum and China more confidently asserts its interests abroad, it is unlikely that the forces of globalization, capitalism, technology and individual empowerment will unwind the power diffusion that has made the four Cs a fundamental presence in the global strategic landscape. Cities, companies and communities long pre-date modern nations, and will outlast many of them. The task before us is therefore to create a dynamic map of the new human geography.

The growing complexity of strategic affairs necessitates more information—both raw data and actionable intelligence—on actors, motivations and relationships. Analytic systems that can quickly filter, process and utilize such data are ever more at a premium. This map must be generated from a wide spectrum of sources from census and surveys to online social media; it must capture the dyads of influence among a wide range of players on multiple levels; and it must be flexible to accommodate the multiple and shifting identities that increasingly characterize connected populations. Policymakers needed such analytical tools yesterday and still need them today. Let us hope they will have them for the world of tomorrow.

Parag Khanna is Director of the Hybrid Reality Institute and is Adjunct Professor at the National University of Singapore. He has authored three books and is a Fellow at the New America Foundation, LSE IDEAS, the European Council on Foreign Relations, Singapore Institute of International Affairs and the Royal Geographical Society.

THE HUMAN LANDSCAPE

Joseph F. Fontanella

Quotations by Clausewitz are often invoked in U.S. Army doctrine, and particularly by Army engineers, as the fates of the maneuver commanders that they support have for millennia been shaped by the physical terrain. In *On War*, Clausewitz declared "geography and the character of the ground bear a close and ever-present relation to warfare. They have a decisive influence on the engagement, both as to its course and to its planning and execution." While this quote in many ways is considered a truism, it betrays an era focused on major combat operations where standing armies from warring states opposed each other on a battlefield. Yet, as we became embroiled in population-centric operations in Iraq and Afghanistan—christened first by major combat operations, Clausewitz's focus on the physical terrain increasingly seemed incomplete.

It became clear that our doctrine as well as our tactics, techniques and procedures (TTPs) fundamentally overlooked the human landscape arrayed across this physical terrain.

Subsequently, we had to change both the operational planning and doctrinal approaches to our national security apparatus (including military services, Special Forces, Coalition partners, diplomats, development professionals and NGOs that were not necessarily in that order) engaged with local populations to achieve national security goals.

Understanding the geographic and historical dimension of the human landscape in a given area of operations (AO), and how its dynamics spill over from beyond that AO, has become essential to operational success. Unfortunately, after nearly a decade of wrestling with how to achieve such an understanding, we still find ourselves without a consensus on how to go about developing an understanding of these socio-cultural dynamics. And, perhaps more unfortunate, we have not demanded of the many academic disciplines that have been brought to bear on this challenge that they develop and convey their understandings of socio-cultural dynamics in geographic and temporal (e.g. historical) terms. The "mapping" of the human terrain has, more often than not, been a metaphor, rather than a literal description of the socio-cultural work being done. This has left operators, analysts and policymakers in the national security community with less than adequate situational awareness, as situational awareness is inherently spatio-temporal in nature.

We are increasingly comfortable with the notion that precision, high-resolution data of both the physical (natural) terrain and human-built terrain are needed to plan, rehearse and execute a diverse array of mission types. Whether conducting major combat operations (MCO), or modes of irregular warfare (IW) such as counter-insurgency (COIN), counter-terrorism (CT), stability operations (SSTRO: Security, Stability, Transition, and Reconstruction Operations), foreign internal defense (FID), and unconventional warfare (UW) or providing critical humanitarian assistance or disaster response, U.S. ground forces and their allies increasingly require human-scale terrain information, particularly when operating over complex and urban terrain. As most national security experts will assert, over the next 50 years or so, our military will likely be involved in population-centric security operations of various types. This places a premium on the collection of high-resolution 3D terrain data wherever we are likely to engage in operations. Still, within the national security dialog, we have not yet achieved a similarly high level of awareness of the need for a precise and high-resolution grasp of the human landscape—the human geography.

Too often, descriptions of human geography have lacked both sufficient spatial resolution and phenomenological articulation to support the prosecution of the mission types outlined previously. We have largely invested in the collection of only a limited set of high-level socio-cultural themes at a very gross scale (say, 1:1 million scale). It may be that by "collection" we actually mean the re-use of socio-cultural data collected administratively by organizations such as the United Nations, the World Bank, and the like. Sometimes, this is because we are extrapolating based upon dated materials, such as those collected long ago by a colonial power or a pioneering academic. Still other times, this is because we have applied only the most limited resources to characterizing the necessary socio-cultural dynamics at a finer geographical scale, resulting in small pockets of clarity scattered across a very large and dangerous Earth. Programs such as the Army's Human Terrain Teams and SOCOM's Civil Affairs teams have done an amazing job of collecting highly articulated characterizations of socio-cultural dynamics at a local scale. However, a quick glimpse at these programs shows that the knowledge garnered from them is not managed geospatially and it only addresses a single snapshot in time.

It is perfectly understandable that these collection methods would supply us with only one view of the socio-cultural dynamics on the ground. These teams are not made up of historians. However, too often, commanders, analysts and policymakers must understand the spatio-temporal dimension of the local social dynamics as they span decades or even centuries. Places have cultural significance rooted in long and revered histories. Peoples have often been displaced or had their patrimony violated by previous powers. This historic memory, which is fundamentally based on their relation to the land, will profoundly shape the ability of our forces to achieve certain effects. Other methods are required to derive these historical social dynamics, as arrayed across the landscape.

The real question becomes: By what means will we be able to collect and manage highly articulated, historically conscious, geospatially enabled socio-cultural data at a sufficiently high resolution that operators, analysts and policymakers can generate an understanding of the "story" of what is going on within their AO?

It is this story that we seek. Since the beginning of mankind, we have used maps to convey a story about what we think is going on. Historians have long used maps to tell their stories. Yet, the (grossly-underinvested) social sciences do not always have the same commitment to the use of spatial and temporal representations of their knowledge. Their disciplines have often not placed a premium on the rigorous anchoring of their observations in place and time. As a result, the social sciences are filled with powerful knowledge about the socio-cultural dynamics around the globe that are far too difficult for national security operators, analysts and policymakers to access within a common operating picture—which is necessarily geospatial. Methodological innovation is needed if this academic knowledge is to be leveraged for the purposes of achieving security and prosperity in many war-torn parts of the world.

But, it is not just the social sciences. Humankind survives and thrives on interaction with its environment, both the natural and human-built. This unavoidable reality forces us to understand the water resources and other environmental contexts as well as the built-up spaces that are so intertwined with the socio-cultural dynamics that define societies, nations, and global affairs. Water and environmental issues are simply components of the larger landscape, and their geography has long shaped human dynamics.

A key part to understanding what makes the human landscape tick within a given AO is understanding the water resources of an area not just as topographic features, but in terms of the dynamics, use, quality, quantity and the manmade structures that control it or help utilize it such as dams, reservoirs, wells, canals, water treatment plants and water towers. In the "built environment," issues related to potable water, storm water, and wastewater are critical to operational success and to improving overall support to the local population. And in any environment, the nature of the physical terrain (whether it be mudslide-prone slopes, flood-prone river basins or low-lying coastal areas) shapes operational realities for every form of combat operations, humanitarian relief, and for infrastructure projects required to achieve stability.

Human, social, cultural and behavioral dynamics lead to rapid change in the built environment as villages and cities wax and wane. These dynamics have enormous impacts on water resources, whether through nefarious action or simply through population growth and expanded water usage. Water resource conflicts have become a persistent theme in today's world, with population explosion, fragile watersheds and their related ecosystems interacting in fundamentally unsustainable ways. But the mapping of socio-cultural dynamics to real-world geography and moments in time—the human geography—is essential for a much wider array of national security missions. Humanitarian relief necessitates having a detailed and accurate grasp of the human dynamics on the ground. Every form of irregular warfare or population-centric operations, almost by definition, requires a good survey of the human terrain. It is such environments that are increasingly demanding engagement from the United States national security community, whether it be ground forces or sister organizations such as the State Department and USAID. Without a detailed and thoughtful grasp of the human dynamics on the ground in such geographies, the United States will be challenged in its formulation of meaningful goals, strategies and tactics.

In order to gather a spatio-temporal understanding of the socio-cultural dynamics in play in an AO, new and emerging collection methods (and sometimes, some old

school methods) will need to be leveraged in concert with each other. Much attention has been paid to the emergence of Activity Based Intelligence (ABI) in support of F3EA (Find, Fix, Finish, Exploit, Analyze) TTPs, with its emphasis on dazzling airborne platforms, exciting new sensors, and new opportunities to enjoy a fine grained "stare" over a geography of concern. The increasing resolution of myriad collection systems makes the monitoring of "dismounts," or pedestrians, more feasible and useful.

Yet, despite the merging of wide area persistent imaging with geo-located signals intelligence, operators and analysts are still at a loss as to the larger social context and the dynamics driving a situation being observed. Administratively collected social information (for instance, census data, land administration data, business directories) is necessary if we are to place these ABI observations in context. Understanding what social memes have gone viral over social media channels such as Facebook or Twitter may be essential to understanding why people are forming unanticipated mass protests. Conducting polls and surveys is necessary to understand what emerging social flashpoints may exist within a given geography. Deep, textured, historically-grounded, academically-derived and field-validated socio-cultural data will be needed in order to tap into the historical memory of the population at risk or the population from which threats emanate. And, crowd sourced information collected by the

likes of the crisis mapping community, or conceivably by future mobile-app empowered operators, will often fill critical gaps in understanding driven by the paucity of investment in collection over particular geographies.

Success in the collection of this mass of spatio-temporally enabled socio-cultural data will pose enormous information management challenges. How will we manage a rapidly growing mass of supple, interrelated and quickly changing socio-cultural data, particularly if it is collected at a high enough resolution to support population-centric operations? And, is it even possible for such data to pool within the .gov and .mil domains, given that the vast majority of such knowledge exists not within the national security community, but within the "real world"?

As we continue to find ourselves embroiled in this era of population-centric operations, operators, analysts and policymakers will increasingly demand a geospatially and temporally enabled understanding of the socio-cultural dynamics wherever there is a crisis and wherever our nations interests and principles are at risk. We must think about how the national security community will organize to meet this increasing and insatiable demand, and invent new business models for applying our constrained resources in the most effective way. But first, we must work to ensure that when we think about the physical and built landscape over which our security operations will be arrayed, we place equal priority on how we master an understanding of the human landscape.

Dr. Joseph F. Fontanella is the Director of the U.S. Army Geospatial Center, the Army's knowledge center for geospatial expertise and reach-back capability. He also serves as the Army's Geospatial Information Officer and is responsible for validating geospatial requirements, formulating policy, setting priorities supporting the Army Geospatial Enterprise and synchronizing geospatial solutions.

HUMAN GEOGRAPHY: BACK TO THE FUTURE

Lee Schwartz

In the search for a new U.S. government approach to gain a better understanding of people and places—and their complex interrelationships—the established tenets and doctrines of the discipline of Human Geography, in both its theoretical and applied practices, are often neglected. Instead, there has been a proliferation of usually invented terms, most of them associated with a specific program, project or budget line, that have served to muddle efforts to develop a "whole of government" approach to what essentially is captured by the dogma, discipline and practice of human geography. This plethora of terms includes: human terrain analysis, human socio-cultural behavior, foundation-based operations, cultural GEOINT, human dimension analysis, socio-cultural dynamics, human terrain mapping, foreign culture analysis, human dimension, human factors, cultural geography modeling, and others. These mask the fact that the discipline of geography already provides an existing framework for understanding and explaining behavior—from more traditional input-output analysis, location theory and population dynamics modeling to experiential analysis, behavioral studies and cognitive mapping. Human Geography, moreover, offers an evolved and always-evolving body of literature on which to anchor predictive analysis and—one could argue— provides the foundation for political geography, cultural geography, economic geography, military geography and neogeographies such as volunteered geographic information.

I hesitate to provide my own definition of precisely what Human Geography is, other than to emphasize that it is an *approach* or a *perspective* to a way of thinking as much as it is a set of rules or tenets to guide you through a morass of data, rich and poor, good or bad. Famous scientists and philosophers over the centuries, from Herodotus to Ibn Khaldun to Immanuel Kant to Carl Sauer have offered their views on what constituted critical geographic inquiry. And scores of geographers far more steeped than me in the scientific and academic discourse have spent decades grappling with defining and redefining our discipline. The Greek geographer Strabo, famous for his 17-volume Geographicus, written at around the dawn of the first millennium, observed even then that "geography subserves the needs of states." He also recognized the importance of scale by writing "the scene is small when activities are of small importance; and large when they are of large importance." Significantly, one can view the history of military geography as capturing the essence of human geography dating as far back as the fourth century writings of the Chinese philosopher Sun Tzu. In the chapter on the use of intelligence in his treatise, *The Art of War*, Sun Tzu wrote, famously, "Know your enemy and know yourself and you can fight a hundred battles without disaster."

And the renowned British geographer, Sir Halford Mackinder, more than a century ago made the keen observation that it was not only *knowledge* or *ignorance* of the world beyond one's ken that rewarded or punished a given state or civilization, but how that knowledge was *perceived* and *interpreted*.

But in many ways, it is more important today to distinguish what Human Geography is *not* than what it *is*. It is *not* about just building a better database, though that is a fundamental requirement for geographic understanding. It is *not* the same as GeoLiteracy, particularly as defined as a GPS-enabled mobile phone application that allows you to navigate your way to the nearest Starbucks. It is *not* simply the mapping of Twitter feeds, crowdsourced SMS messages, or cell phone call locations and proximities (more data does not mean better data!). It is *not* about merely speaking the language of a country in which you are operating; it is *not* about being able to predict an outcome from a given set of inputs; and it is *not* about applying last year's tools and solutions to next year's conflicts.

At its fundamental basis, human geography, as simply but elegantly defined by Rowland Illick, is about "why people do what they do where they do it."[1] At the heart of understanding people and their "socio-cultural-geographic" dynamics is the need for accurate, verifiable, scalable data that can be collected and monitored over time and space. But even with complete and current data at the finest of detail, human behavior is difficult, if not impossible, to predict. Cultures and social structures are built upon complicated sets of relationships steeped in and formed by history, religion, language, proximity, transactions, emotions, psychology, leadership and personalities. Despite the importance of understanding such relationships for decision making in areas ranging from military operations to diplomatic negotiations, we should not be naive enough to

suggest that we can effectively and comprehensively model and predict likely human responses to what for the most part are theoretical inputs. Rather than prediction, an admirable and more likely attainable goal is merely seeking access to data that give us the best chance to understand and explain— anticipate rather than predict— human behavior over time and space. For despite the complexities of trying to make sense of socio-cultural data, there is one basic and essential characteristic available to link disparate variables together: place. All events occur in a place in time, and those locations can be mapped with varying degrees of complexity depending on the richness or paucity of available data.

But unlike collecting digital terrestrial data for elevation, water, land cover, dwellings, roads and other features on the surface of the earth, there are no orbiting satellites that are imaging, modeling and interpreting human behavior. Lacking an array of Human Geography gathering satellites, therefore, how does a government go about first gathering data and then understanding the human behavior and characteristics that are to be mapped? I submit that the best way to do this is *not* to provide a crash course to soldiers or diplomats in a new language, insert them into a foreign territory, contract outside research to a security specialist or a "social scientist" (as if the latter were a strange species that somehow has a deeper innate ability to

understand people than do common folk), and then ask them collectively to predict or model how a people or their authorities will react to a range of possible inputs. Yet this seems to be a common approach practiced throughout government, whether it be part of an effort to provide early warning of atrocities, model possible reactions to an insertion of armed forces, or leverage the goodwill engendered by the construction of a school or a dam.

I would argue for an alternative approach, one that takes advantage of new tools and technologies that effectively allow people to define their own place in time, essentially to map their own human terrain. Or to tell their own stories, recall their histories, reveal their kinship linkages, or identify their personal, cultural and political boundaries. GPS-enabled place-based technologies, participatory mapping combined with volunteered geographic information (VGI), micro-sensors for real-time field analytics, compressed delivery of streamed imagery, and open source mapping software all allow for a greater ability to map and evaluate changes in human behavior over time and space. The key to government success in tapping into this vast army of what Michael Goodchild termed "citizen censors"— volunteered or otherwise—is first to acknowledge that our military and civilian agencies cannot collect or make sense of this type of information on their own.[2] A fresh approach

---

1.   J. Rowland Illick, former Middlebury College professor of geography, as cited by Jerome E. Dobson, 2007, "Bring Back Geography!" *Arc News*, 29 (1): 1-5.
2.   Wilson, M. W. and M. Graham (2013). Neogeography and volunteered geographic information: a conversation with Michael Goodchild and Andrew Turner. *Environment and Planning A, 45*(1), 10-18.

to the analysis of social and cultural information requires a greater need than ever for establishing partnerships and collaborative networks that allow for the discovery of data at a scale appropriate for the analysis required, identifying gaps and mechanisms to fill those gaps in data, and establishing standards for interoperability, verification, cataloguing, transparency and dissemination of both raw and finished products. Only by constructing a "bottom-up approach" can we achieve the means and direction both to build foundation data as well as to direct specific research in order to fill in the gaps in our cultural knowledge and understanding. We gain analytical value by aggregating and disaggregating geographic data according to appropriate scales to enable "sense-making," understand and explain complex circumstances, and, ultimately, contribute to decision making.

Essentially, therefore, we can build a virtual satellite for Human Geography data and analysis that consists of a network of partners rather than an array of orbiting sensors. Much like with imaging satellites, where resolution and scale vary depending on the data and analysis required, the type of partnerships will also be determined by the scale of analysis and the degree of detail that is needed. Furthermore, data gatherers need to be trained, empowered, accessible, and monitored for quality control purposes. Tools

need to be made available for local peoples to define, describe and map their own surroundings. High-resolution satellite imagery has proven to be a great enabler for crowdsourced data, and tools and processes are being developed to "direct" the crowd better so that there is less duplication of effort and more attention paid to filling in critical needs for information. Collection in situ using place-based technologies can be married in real time with digitized vectors derived from satellite imagery to add a richness to spatial databases heretofore unimagined.

One of the challenges to this approach is, of course, quality control. With satellites collecting, for example, digital elevation data, there exists a high degree of confidence in the accuracy of the data, and of whatever products are produced based on that information. Confidence levels are increased even more when remotely sensed data are confirmed with ground truth. Social and cultural information put together largely by the volunteered technical community or community-based mappers, however, need different mechanisms for verification—a means to police the crowd, so to speak. Such measures are difficult, but not impossible, to implement. Experiments to date reveal great promise for the potential effective use of crowdsourced geospatial data. The real challenge does not lie in getting accurate data from the crowd, but getting

it in a timely, prioritized, segmented, useful, and shareable format in order to answer key questions and enable more informed decision making.

The recently formed Human Geography Working Group that I chair, and its Worldwide Human Geography Data Working Group offshoot, decided early on in discussions over its mission to cloak the goal of its efforts under the theme of "Human Security."[3] Given the complexities involved with the challenge of mapping Human Geography data, a focus on human security seemed to make sense as a unifying concept that translated well across the defense, development, and diplomacy communities. This focus allows for an approach that separated itself from Defense Department programs and funding that were geared almost exclusively towards the warfighter. It also fits in well with the recent Quadrennial Diplomacy and Development Review (QDDR) that was launched jointly by the State Department and USAID. As part of the QDDR process, a realigned State Department Under Secretaryship was assigned the portfolio of Civilian Security, Democracy, and Human Rights. That portfolio focuses on, among other issues, food and water security; humanitarian emergencies and human rights; early warning and war crimes prevention and accountability; but also counterterrorism and law enforcement.

---

3. Chartered in November 2010, under the Geospatial Intelligence Standards Working Group (GWG) of the Department of Defense Information Technology Standards Committee (ITSC).

It is hard to argue that the goal of spreading the global human security blanket is not an admirable one that translates well to all sectors of society—government and non-government alike. Moreover, it provided an opportunity for champions of human geography tradecraft in the U.S. government to develop not only a whole of *government* approach, but also a whole of *governments* approach, leveraging and seeking foreign partners as collaborators in a broad community of interest. But one should not be imprudent enough to have more than very modest expectations that the efforts of such a collective will do anything more than perhaps provide a clearer path towards gaining a better understanding of people through access to better information. Nevertheless, the better you can understand people, as well as their adversaries and challenges, the better you can help provide for their security, or help them provide for their own security.

Finally, it is my view that in order for the discipline of Human Geography to provide true value added in our strategic understanding of socio-cultural dynamics throughout the world, the effort requires more trained professional geographers at its core. Or, at the very least, professionals who are well-versed in geographic theory, methodologies and perspectives—in particular an acute understanding of the value of place in our analytical thinking. To place this argument in perspective, the only truly comprehensible definition of geography with which I am completely comfortable is that offered by A.E. Parkins in 1934, and that is: "Geography is ... what Geographers do."[4]

Lee Schwartz is The Geographer of the Department of State and chairs the USG Human Geography Working Group. He directs geographic research, analysis and fieldwork activities on complex emergencies and other soft/smart power issues. He was most recently (2012) honored with the AAG's Anderson Medal of Honor in Applied Geography.

4.   Whitaker, J. Russell. 1941. "Almon Ernest Parkins." Annals of the Association of American Geographers 31 (1): 46-50.

A Fresh Approach to an Old Challenge

Patrick O'Neill

One of the enduring challenges facing intelligence analysts is the ability to understand the perspectives of foreign audiences. Adopting a foreign audience perspective is crucial to understanding how U.S. words and deeds will be perceived, how U.S. communicators can tailor their messages for maximum impact, how to avoid messages that will have unintended and undesirable consequences, how key influencers in other countries are reaching audiences and how U.S. officials can advance the messaging efforts of allies or counter the efforts of adversaries.

A review of the intelligence lapses that we are all familiar with demonstrates the importance of understanding foreign perspectives:

- Analysts failed to appreciate how Japan, cut off from vital resources by U.S. blockades in 1941, would see the Pearl Harbor attack against the more powerful United States as a rational option.
- Analysts failed to give enough weight to the religious dimension of the opposition in Iran and the shifting views of the country's youth and middle class and thus did not anticipate the depth and impact of the Revolution in 1979.
- Analysts failed to pay sufficient attention to the perspectives of Indian politicians and were surprised when the country tested a nuclear weapon.
- Analysts assumed, given the risk of war with the United States, that Saddam Hussein must have had something to hide when he thwarted Weapons of Mass Destruction (WMD) inspectors.

Understanding foreign perspectives may not prevent all intelligence failures or miscues, but is nonetheless critical to improving the quality and effectiveness of intelligence. A necessary first step toward better understanding of foreign perspectives is more rigorous and sustained understanding of the human geography, especially social, cultural, attitudinal and psychological factors that underpin sentiments, motivations and behaviors.

The role of master narratives

Human nature leads us to assume others must see things from our own seemingly wise and reasoned perspectives. Even when analysts overcome that bias, they often lack a systematic, sophisticated and repeatable means for seeing the world from an alien perspective. Analysts typically compensate by learning the language, immersing themselves in the relevant current events, familiarizing themselves with history and engrossing themselves in the culture of a specific country. These efforts are commendable, but they often fall short because outside analysts lack perspective on how events truly resonate with local groups—they may be looking at the "right" issues, but they are still looking at them through their own pair of glasses. In particular, outside observers do not know firsthand how local groups *feel* about an issue, how it might *stir them*, why it may *anger* them or why it *threatens* them on an instinctive level. Often the local groups themselves may not understand the underlying factors driving their responses—they may be ingrained, subconscious and a core element of their cultural DNA.

Many of the factors that influence how foreign groups view the world are deeply seated and developed over generations, passed on from one generation to the next in the form of stories, values, behavior and convictions. Knowledge of these factors cannot typically be gleaned from monitoring media or intelligence reporting. Instead, one must dig deep to uncover and understand the entrenched themes, stories, history and culture of a given population cohort. And analysts must engage those who "live" these perspectives. These factors and perspectives coalesce over time to define a set of *master narratives*, which are specific to a given group.

The master narratives define a group's view of the world, how it relates to other people and how it makes sense of events unfolding around it. These narratives reflect a group's identity and experiences; explain its hopes, aspirations and concerns; and help people understand who they are and where they come from. This knowledge allows an analyst to anticipate how a specific audience segment will respond to U.S. actions or statements, how key influencers are exploiting master narratives to influence groups, and how the same message can resonate quite differently from one group to the next in the same country.

Relying on narratives to provide insight into the perceptions of foreign audiences is not a new concept. Anthropologists and other social scientists have long focused on the importance of culture, history and stories. Recent work on narratives as they relate to extremism and religion has been conducted by Arizona State University's Consortium for Strategic Communications and ASU's Center for the Study of Religion and Conflict, among others. What makes the master narrative work by Open Source Center (OSC) unique is the underlying methodology and the systematic way in

which narratives are presented to advance U.S. strategic communications and analytic insights.

Much of the up-front work in developing master narratives involves identifying a group of subject matter experts with native understanding of key audience segments and deep insights into the country's history, culture, religions, politics, and even myths and legends. Experts are drawn from such diverse sources as academia, business, government, marketing, religion and entertainment. This input is married with analysts' understanding of U.S. policy objectives and priorities to produce sophisticated and actionable strategic communications support.

Effective influencers and communicators consciously and subconsciously employ content and themes that invoke or align with these master narratives to gain or sustain the attention of a particular audience. These narratives tap into common experiences and deeply socialized belief systems that unite people and shape their view of the world. Influencers repeatedly return to these narratives precisely because they resonate with and generate the desired effects from a specific audience.

- In the United States, for example, an important master narrative is the "American Dream." This nationally held conviction conveys American aspirations in the form of a "dream" about individualistic independence in a land of opportunity. The narrative emphasizes being unconstrained by the past or by rigid ties to conventions. It is conveyed through familiar allusions to the Pilgrims,

the Founding Fathers, the pioneer spirit in the Old West, and the influx and success of immigrants to the United States.
- Another example of an American master narrative is the "Spread of Freedom." This powerful narrative, grounded in U.S. history, holds that American ideals of personal, intellectual, religious, political and economic freedom reflect innate human rights and aspirations. The narrative advances the notion that ultimately the ideal of freedom will spread and triumph throughout the world. While rooted in American history, both narratives are alive and invoked today. They are powerful tools employed by politicians and advertisers to influence public perceptions and move audiences in desired directions.

Foreign leaders and influencers regularly return to themes and images that they know will induce a desired reaction. And they know which themes or images to shun in order to avoid unintended reactions. These communications strategies serve to reinforce established master narratives. Many foreign leaders and influencers also know how to portray the United States and other outside groups in ways that most effectively prompt a desired reaction. Because these master narratives are so ingrained, so core to how an individual or group views the world, target audiences seldom recognize they are being manipulated or that their response is the result of careful programming from master narratives.

Powerful analytic tool

As part of its strategic communications support

mission, the OSC and a contractor partner have developed a methodology to surface and exploit these master narratives. The master narrative methodology offers analysts greater depth by helping to explain the "why" behind public reaction to events and leaders' statements. Effective influencers rely on a native familiarity with local master narratives that U.S. communicators may lack, resulting in a risk of communication failures and messaging gaffes by U.S. officials and the risk of miscalculation and surprise for analysts. Thus, identifying, understanding and employing master narratives is a vital step in helping U.S. communicators and analysts understand the human terrain of foreign audiences, especially those most dissimilar to the United States. Master narratives offer greater contextual understanding of events, surface key assumptions, lower biases, and yield more accurate analysis and more effective communications. Given its place in the world, this capability is even more critical for the United States given the proclivity of many foreign audiences to view the country with suspicion, to see conspiracies where they do not exist, and to accept stories that Americans recognize as outlandish.

The master narrative methodology enables analysts to learn more about key groups and group dynamics through audience segmentation exercises and sheds light on how beliefs, outlooks, values and mindsets vary in a given country.

A specific set of master narratives is not universal for a given country; rather, groups within a country adhere to specific master narratives to varying degrees. Assessing these differences can provide analysts with greater clarity on how beliefs, outlooks and mindsets vary within a given country. Variations in how master narratives play across different groups can reveal common ground between specific cohorts as well as fault lines that could augur conflict. Comparing and contrasting a set of master narratives in a given country can shed light on internal struggles, such as conflict between the "haves" and the "have-nots." Understanding this dynamic also can provide analytic insight to highlight the tradeoffs U.S. communicators face. A message about freedom in the Arab world, for example, will play differently for a group of 18 to 25-year-old college-educated urbanites than for a rural cohort of 45 to 60-year-old men because of the different narratives that resonate with each group.

At times, the same message from Washington may draw in a given audience while pushing away another. This tradeoff and its relation to broader U.S. objectives for a given country is a vital piece of information for analysts to provide policy makers.

In addition to providing key insights, the master narratives methodology can fuel opportunity analysis by enabling analysts to devise communications strategies for U.S. policy makers that counter the narrative-based messaging of U.S. adversaries or support the communications efforts of Washington's allies. Knowledge of how al-Qaida exploits master narratives in a given country or region can be applied to a counter-messaging strategy to discredit the terrorist messages or, for example, to point out contradictions with the tenets of Islam. Conversely, the methodology can be used to construct powerful U.S. statements that resonate and reinforce the narrative-based public messaging of, for example, pro-democracy leaders in Africa.

Audience segmentation

Defining relevant audience segments is a critical step in the master narrative methodology as well as a valuable stand-alone analytic tool. Although some master narratives are so ingrained that they resonate on a national level with nearly all of the population, in most countries different groups tend to respond in varying degrees to different narratives. Influencers in the marketing, advertising and geopolitical realms derive a substantial portion of their success from segmenting audiences into meaningful and actionable groups.

In the analytic context, when asked, "What does Country A think of the role of Islam in governance?" for example, or "How do citizens of Country B feel about the United States?" the correct answers would be, "It depends." Countries are not monolithic, and an entire country is not the correct unit of analysis for these questions given the diverse backgrounds, experiences, levels of well-being, outlook and location of the people who live there.

A more illuminating response to these questions is derived from breaking each country down into audience segments to enable an understanding of, for example, how different groups within Country A view the fault lines between religion and secularism or how various groups in Country B are affected by U.S. engagement with the country. Breaking countries down into audience segments that hold distinct worldviews yields a richer, more precise understanding of complex issues. As a stand-alone tool, audience segmentation helps analysts understand how beliefs, outlooks and mindsets vary within a given country. It clarifies actual and potential fault lines and helps highlight which segments are most important to U.S. interests. While the standard approach to the master narrative is from a country perspective, the nature of the analytic question can make broad segments (for example, a region or diaspora) as well as more narrowly defined segments (subgroups like tribal units, geographic regions, or education levels) the most relevant and effective.

Identifying Audience Segments

Identifying the more obvious, generic audience segments that historically have proven useful in commercial, academic and political settings is the first step in determining appropriate audience segments. Initial audience segmentation can be structured around demographics, affiliations, core beliefs, world views or other broad pointers.

More nuanced country-specific segmentation lenses then can be applied to the initial generic break down to develop a set of competing segmentation paradigms that define specific options. Developing and validating these paradigms requires extensive and deep country knowledge.

Once a set of competing segmentation paradigms has been developed, it must be evaluated using a consistent set of criteria relevant to the analytic objective. Typical criteria include:

- Correlation with local belief and world views. *Do the segments in this hypothesis display meaningful competing interests or viewpoints? Do they facilitate surfacing important master narratives?*
- Usefulness for strategic communicators. *Are the audience segments of interest to the USG? Are they important players in local socio-political dynamics? Do they have the potential to impact U.S. interests?*
- Usefulness for analysis. *Would understanding the identified segments advance U.S. situational awareness and analytic insights? Are they relevant for U.S. interests and national security?*
- Segment endurance. *Are the identified segments durable? Will they be useful in future analysis?*
- Subject matter expert validation. *Do experts believe that the segmentation hypotheses are insightful?*

The answers to these questions help analysts determine which segmentation paradigm is most effective in revealing audience segments with distinct master narratives.

Analyzing key influencers

Having selected optimal audience segments, another phase of the master narratives methodology highlights how key influencers invoke and exploit the narratives. This knowledge helps analysts interpret key influencers' behaviors by shedding light on the persuasion strategies, intentions, themes and messages. Savvy influencers understand the power that master narratives have to shift attitudes and alter behavior among targeted audiences. For example, an influencer may leverage a master narrative to rally supporters to a cause while another may use a different narrative to discredit a political opponent or undermine U.S. objectives.

Key Influencer Assessment

A set of analyst questions can be used to understand the tools and objectives of key influencers. Some typical questions include:

- What are the persuasion strategies or intentions of key influencers who play leadership roles in governments, the military, civil society, religion or other institutions?
- What are the themes and messages promoted by influencers on key issues of concern to the United States? How do these messages translate into public discourse?
- What are key influencers' attitudes toward the United States and other foreign governments? Is that attitude changing?
- Who is the intended audience of the key influencer? Is the influencer calibrating and modulating his message to target it to different audiences?

Understanding the precise nature, utility and potency of relevant master narratives can help explain the objective of the influencer and what their message reveals about underlying intentions and strategies. Master narratives often contain appeals, both implicit and explicit, which may be attitudinal and prompt fear, suspicion, respect or trust, for example; or behavioral and prompt support, rebellion or violence. A key influencer may invoke a master narrative that instills fear about outsiders to attack a political opponent advocating a more expansive foreign policy or closer ties to the U.S. Analysts also can track the ascendency of up-and-coming political leaders by noting the narratives they employ. For example, a rising political figure might draw on narratives that appeal to a more concentrated audience segment to build a core base of support, and then shift to narratives that have broader, national resonance to build and diversify their base of power. *This is a critical component to or layer within the larger human geography that national security decision makers must possess in the coming decades.*

"I hear you, I'm just not listening to you"

The master narrative methodology was developed primarily to support strategic communications. Analysts can help U.S. communicators craft more effective messages by surfacing themes, terminology, and messages that align with master narratives and therefore raise the likelihood that they will resonate favorably. Armed with this information, communicators may invoke narratives explicitly

to achieve desired objectives; use a narrative indirectly by drawing on associated themes, symbols and emotions; challenge a narrative that disparages the United States; or carefully steer clear of a narrative all together to avoid undesired responses. For example, a U.S. policy maker may want to voice support for a nascent democratic movement by drawing on a master narrative that emphasizes themes such as liberty, freedom or pluralism. Such an approach may boost the democratic movement, but the master narrative methodology may reveal that the same narrative could alienate, for example, religion-based groups that perceive freedom as a threat to piety. Alternatively, a U.S. policy maker may want to avoid a master narrative that portrays "outside" voices as unwelcome.

Master Narrative-Based Analytic Questions

- What are the specific messages or themes U.S. strategic communicators can use to connect with audiences in a specific country?
- How should messaging change when addressing specific audience segments in contrast to a range of audience segments? In public compared to private communications?
- What are the themes, messages, topics or symbols that U.S. strategic communicators should avoid?
- What local master narratives are aligned with existing U.S. messaging and strategic objectives? Which master narratives are in opposition to those objectives?

- How are other communicators, both domestic and foreign, employing master narratives in the country to advance their strategic communications efforts? What might U.S. policy makers do to support or counter those efforts?

Analysts can help U.S. communicators achieve desired results and navigate around potential conflicts by identifying "red lines" defined by master narratives, explaining the similarities and differences between master narratives, and assessing them in a broad, systems context. For example, some narratives praise or even deify a country's founder, making any criticism of that founder or the ideals associated with the founder objectionable to those who ascribe to the narrative. Other narratives make certain subjects or themes morally taboo.

At the same time, identifying which themes or concepts cut across multiple narratives will help communicators determine how to calibrate their message. In a country with diverse populations and sophisticated media environments, for example, communicators drawing on a narrative appealing to a narrow audience may invite unintended reactions as the message is conveyed to other groups for which the narrative conveys a different meaning.

It also is important for analysts to explain how master narratives interact—whether two master narratives are in direct opposition, whether they reinforce each other or whether they are independent. A notable historic figure, for example, may be characterized as a war hero in one narrative and a villain in another. In this situation, mention of this historic figure can have opposite effects on different audience segments.

Anticipating strategic change

The master narrative methodology also can be applied to anticipate strategic change. The methodology provides insight into how influencers exploit their constituents and can reveal a leader's ultimate plans and intentions. Understanding how a foreign leader is exploiting narratives can shed light on goals, motives and persuasion strategies and can identify those constituencies of greatest concern to the leadership. Heightened activity around a particular master narrative or set of narratives often coincides with trends or disruptions in social, political or security conditions. When employed to validate beliefs or as powerful persuasion tools, master narratives often serve as precursors to important events such as shifts in allegiances, intergroup tensions or major policy decisions.

Because master narratives often involve foreign actors, they can be used to anticipate change in foreign policy. Armed with an understanding of the narratives operating in a given country, analysts can track which of them are gaining traction at the expense of others and assess how the public mood is evolving. Similarly, analysts can be sensitive to the use of master narratives in new areas or on new issues to shed light on influencers' efforts to bring about change. Master narratives also can serve as indicators of intergroup tensions that could lead to upheaval.

Master narratives can be used to test key assumptions, an important exercise to limit the possibility of surprise. Analysts can articulate their key assumptions for a given country, institution or actor and then hold those assumptions up to scrutiny under a narratives microscope—are the assumptions consistent with relevant narratives? And, based on narratives, which assumptions could become invalid under given circumstances? For example, during a constitutional crisis a long-held assumption that a country's military will support the government could come into conflict with a narrative held by the military that it is the defender of the constitution.

Competing vs. complementing and transnational narrative analysis

As analysts grow a master narrative "library," they are able to help policy makers see variations in how actions or messages play across various countries. A matrix arraying countries and their predominant master narratives can enable policy makers to quickly see how U.S. actions or statements appeal to audiences in one country while alienating audiences in another. For example, analysts can raise red flags when "success" in reaching the public in one country may be offset by "failure" in another and provide policy makers with a basis for weighing the associated costs and benefits. This capability is especially important given ongoing globalization, rapid media diffusion, and the proliferation of social media, all of which make it very difficult to limit messaging to intended target audiences. What plays in Peoria also plays in Paris, Prague and Pretoria (if not Pyongyang), but the message may have a unique meaning in each city.

In addition to its application for a specific country, the master narrative methodology can be a powerful analytic tool for transnational audiences as well. Narratives can be "exported" as populations migrate, and it is important for communicators to understand the perceptions of homogenous audience segments scattered across borders. OSC is developing an analytic framework to determine, for example, how master narratives held by segments of diaspora populations in Europe impact assimilation dynamics. This case study application will provide an initial framework for other transnational work.

Concluding thoughts

Even though master narratives tend to endure by their very nature, they must be validated periodically. The narratives typically take years to develop, are strongly held, and are frequently reinforced. Nevertheless, they can evolve over time and regular validation is required to ensure that analysts maintain an accurate understanding of this evolution. A post mortem of how a narrative actually played out following a major U.S. action or speech is an essential element of narrative validation—did the audience segment respond as predicted by the narrative?

Assessing changes in the strength of a given narrative through media content analysis and a review of leadership actions and statements also provides important analytic insights. Analysts should reflect on why a given narrative may not have played out as expected and attempt to determine whether the reason is transitory—perhaps another event affected audience response—or more lasting, thus requiring an adjustment to the narrative. The explosion of social media and availability of quantitative tools to analyze bulk data also provide a means of validating narratives—are the key components of a narrative present among the crowd discourse playing out in social media? Are the sentiments that define specific narratives also the sentiments that dominate social media discourse? This validation technique is limited, of course, by the scope of the audience

segment's social media use—social media analysis is unlikely to be helpful, for example, in validating the narratives that resonate with North Koreans.

In sum, the master narrative methodology developed by OSC offers a systematic way for analysts to support U.S. strategic communicators and gain fresh insights. The approach provides an organized way of thinking about factors influencing public opinion and sentiment and the dynamics motivating and shaping local leaders' public statements. An understanding of master narratives can help policy makers support the messaging efforts of allies and counter the efforts of adversaries. Finally, the use and interplay of narratives can shed light on inter-group conflict and help analysts anticipate strategic change.

A library of master narratives for countries of strategic interest and for important demographics existing within and across states will provide a baseline for understanding to the United States and enables policy makers and analysts to forecast how the same U.S. action or message can play differently across different countries and regions. The near real-time dissemination of information on a global basis today places a premium on all of these capabilities. Understanding how actions and statements will be perceived maximizes the prospects of getting the message "right" the first time. Today there is little time for "catch-up" and communications gaffes are difficult to fix.

Patrick O'Neill is Director for Analysis, DNI Open Source Center. Member: DNI's National Intelligence Board, National Intelligence Analysis and Production Board. Leadership positions at CIA on East Asia, Latin America, global economics; Deputy National Intelligence Officer for Economics; and CIA Director's staff. MS Economics, Michigan State University, BA International Relations (MSU).

Section 2

Administratively Derived Socio-Cultural Data in Human Geography and GEOINT

WARRING AND ADMINISTRATIVELY DERIVED SOCIO-CULTURAL DATA

Geoffrey Demarest

It is advanced practice for the intelligence professional to recognize and react to the opportunities and challenges of data collected by governmental and non-governmental administrative processes. Perhaps the apex of that practitioner's art, however, is in growing and shaping those processes so that they freely and voluntarily yield relevant knowledge. This chapter offers descriptions of advanced and not-so-advanced public administrative environments, along with the consequences of that development for knowledge creation and for being able to influence events and conditions. Other articles focus on real estate property records. This is fitting, given the importance of the control of land in conflict situations, both in terms of combat advantages, and as the fundamental means of economic production. Real estate information may indeed be the center of mass. There are other types of administrative data, although these fairly could be considered within a broader notion of property.

By "administratively derived data" we refer generally to data acquired, processed and stored for reasons other than finding, suppressing or repressing lawbreakers or other enemies of the state. In other words, administrative data is rarely developed in response to "requirements" as determined within some competitive intelligence function or "cycle." Rather, it is created for its own civil purposes unrelated or only indirectly related to law enforcement. Nevertheless, when combined with traditionally developed, often classified intelligence, this administratively derived knowledge can greatly enhance understanding of local conditions, patterns of human behavior, and the distribution of power. Census, personal identification, cadastral, environmental, matrimonial and polling data are among the most familiar forms, but there are many other useful types as well. Almost all of the data present opportunities, challenges and surprises in the context of armed conflict.

For ease of consideration, administrative data can be placed in the following non-exclusive categories:

- developed and maintaining by voluntary contribution, versus those that are mandated;
- subject to access by other agencies of the government, versus those that are exclusive;
- caveated in ways that impinge on use by the government itself as to evidentiary or investigative use, versus those that can be readily used as criminal and civil evidence;
- caveated in ways that limit distribution and acquisition for proprietary commercial reasons versus those that are considered subject to free use;
- already found in relational datasets versus those that would require format and input labor;
- protected physically such that their collection would require covert invasive methods versus those that can be easily if not overtly obtained;
- can be economically purchased versus prohibitively expensive.

Beyond the contents of administrative data, the intelligence officer should be conscious of legal jurisdictions associated with each type of record and the inter-relationship of various units of territorial measure—which is fundamentally a geographic concern. More than a question of which records to use or how to use them, intelligence professionals should look to the question of which administrative efforts should be encouraged or introduced because they could be or should be self-managing engines of useful data. *Administration* is inevitably tied to administrators and so these administrators (who they are, where they sit, etc.) will likely constitute their own significant, identifiable category of human geographic knowledge.

Administrative records are always tied to legal requirements and limitations, and so it is ultimately impossible for the intelligence officer to be fully engaged with the idea of knowledge-from-administrative-data until he or she is immersed in the question of legal requirements and liberties. In this regard, it is to be kept in mind while reading the chapters in this section that U.S. interests may not always lie with the "counterinsurgent," but are likely in the future to fall into a category more akin to insurgency. Some of what is useful to the counterinsurgent may be anathema to the insurgent. As well, the processes of building actionable intelligence, including the competitive use of administratively derived, unclassified knowledge, can itself be deleterious to other goals of the intelligence officers' command. For instance, transparent administrative data often constitutes the evidence of a healthy social contract; therefore uses that compromise, redirect, or

secretize that public knowledge could be so harmful to sustained peace as to outweigh the immediate military tactical advantages of its use.

Detective possibilities increase with each new area of knowledge about a place that is geo-coded, so that when voting data, environmental data, land use plans, appraisals, political opinion and fealty polls, or licensing data of various kinds are made commonly correlateable, then relevant anomalies and patterns more easily appear. One of the connotations of property is its implication regarding *where*, an implication that our analyses must limit not to where things are located, but to where ownership rights reside.

To one soldier's question regarding how a property records mindset might be applied to better understand a village in Afghanistan, the advice given was to have the command try to buy a house in that village. The right to dispossess oneself of rights is one of the most revealing rights. A counter-question from the soldier included the troubling detail that the people living in the hypothetical house probably paid rent to someone living in another country. "Ownership" of a residence generally includes the right to receive rents, the receiver of rents usually having some influence over the mechanisms by which that right is enforced—over who might be hired to evict non-paying tenants, or over whoever pays the force doing the evicting. Without testing the question of how to buy, occupy, lease,

sell and evict, it is hard to see how the true relationships of power could be well known in any given place. Meanwhile, it is hard to imagine how distant owners could accumulate much power without some form of record keeping. Allowing the key controllers of the social contract to be located in another country, and their records anonymous, could relegate a military occupier to being the unwitting servant of the wrong landlords.

It could be that the "locals" are not even part of an owners' social contract at all, but merely human elements of the physical geography—accoutrements for the real owners to buy and sell as part of the real estate—as chattel. These facts of social life are hardly new or strange, as hard as they are for Americans to digest. They are, nevertheless, easier to grasp when significant administrative records are finally unearthed or created. Comparing Karol Boudreaux's description of African property regimes with Richard Grovers' outline of the complexities of the property regime in the United Kingdom provides us with a marvelous pair of bookends.[1] The conclusion might not be altogether sanguine, seeming as it does that the conditions of transparency, comprehensiveness and precision, which might constitute a useful formality, seem to take ages to achieve.

Why private detectives find their mark

Probably every plaintiff's law firm in the United States has on staff or contracts a private

---

1.   See Sections 2.3 (Grover) and 2.4 (Boudreaux).

investigator (PI), or "Sam Spade." That's because in America, if a person wants to evict, sue, or make some other demand against someone else using the legal system, a lawyer or his PI has to find the opponent and give him or her a piece of paper. That is what Sam Spade is paid to do: find that opponent and give him an unfriendly piece of paper that puts him on notice or calls him to court. "You've been served." It is called *service of process*; fair processes being considered an indispensable element of justice and the touted "rule of law." The plaintiff's lawyer also wants the PI to find the nemesis' things—a car, boat, house or bank account— because lawyers want to be paid. Sam Spade does, too, and to keep putting food on the table he has to find his mark, and he almost always succeeds in spite of not having satellites, phone taps or even a very good camera. There are two main reasons why Sam Spade succeeds. The first is because he knows local culture. He knows what's going on in his town or county. For him, every bit of knowledge about the local culture helps him with the whereabouts. He knows which bumper sticker goes with what congregation, what kinds of vehicles will show up in the parade, who organizes the service club charities, etc. He follows all the sports teams and every public event. He knows the favorite cigarette brands.

The other big reason Sam always finds his prey is that he is familiar and competent with public records. He can get hold of school registration lists, team rosters, tithing reports, street signs, water taps or road easements, and can decode the license plates and tombstones. He recognizes

that the high school football schedule is a transparent, accurate property record because it evidences a specific right that a specific group of persons has to be doing a particular thing in a single place at a precise time. It is at one of those times and places that Sam Spade will go into the north bleachers to serve a summons to the starting right tackle's dad.

Sam might not contemplate the role public records have as evidence of the social contract, or worry that for a liberal society to thrive, its public records must be transparent and stable. Nor will he worry that the perfection of administration and administrative records may be tantamount to construction of a pernicious Big Brother. For him, public records are simply part of what makes it possible to find people and their property so that he can get paid. If the public records are shoddy and inaccurate, if they are hidden from inspection, are not comprehensive or are subject to manipulation and fraud, it is harder for Sam to succeed— and, meanwhile but related to Sam's failure, the social contract is at risk. It would be at risk partly because of Sam's failure itself. The administrative records are a lubricant to peaceful conflict resolution. If the Sam Spades cannot serve paper, others will likely serve lead.

How to

The sophistication, comprehensiveness, precision and transparency of administrative data vary from society to society, locale to locale. To say how, on a global or broadly theoretical level, to develop the best data is to presume too much. In some places, however, where the most revealing data (usually

related to rights in land) seem to be lacking, some form of participatory research is perhaps possible. To be successful, "participatory" research (in which elements of the public voluntarily join in the compilation of social administrative data) focuses on information people will own and which empowers their control over their own well being as they perceive it. When the knowledge sought is knowledge everyone needs and wants, the costs of data collection and input go down precipitously. In other words, if you design an inventorying method that is clearly advantageous to the flourishing of peoples' lives as they see it, the inventory will be much more realizable. Some obvious examples are inventories of water and water pollution sources, home titles and appraisals, and insect infestation or communicable disease data. Participatory research examples could also include entertainment, tourism and recreational data, or broader market information. The phone book with its "yellow pages" is an example; likewise the social information sites on the Internet.

This may be a good place for a cautionary note. Administrators, governments that administer, legal systems that guide administration, even the populations administered, are not necessarily just or righteous. Disqualifications, that is, formalized negative administrative discriminations, often start in the realm of property rights, and can, in later stages, reach the thresholds of war. If a clearly contrasted collective human identity exists within a polity, then the occurrence of *newly* prejudicial legal and administrative impositions can mean impending trouble. The following list of impairments is adapted from Raul Hilberg's *The Destruction of the European Jews*:

- Restrictions on professions
- Restrictions on divestment and purchase of real estate
- Special physical or clothing markings
- Special naming conventions
- Marriage and intercourse restrictions
- Off-limits locations or concentrations
- Any form of mandatory migration
- Marking of transactions
- Special taxes

Restrictions on intermarriage and sexual relations are especially significant as in-group/out-group separators. Such restrictions are easily detectable as either a social norm or formal restriction, and may be a condition imposed from within the potential victim identity or by the potential perpetrator. This classic phenomenon is an inspiration for literature, art, and feud, and is also one of the clearest markers of group cohesion and inter-group friction. These disqualifications, these impairments, are often readily apparent in administrative data. It is easy to overlook them, even become complicit in their construction, partly due to the banal nature of their construction.

Scale

Proper selection and matching of scale bears on the acceptability of a human geographic inventorying. If people involved believe information will be made public at a scale controllable by them, they are far more likely to participate in an inventory. The *county* (not *country*) may

or may not be the right scale of formal territory, but, as a beginning assumption, the county is a better territorial scale for understanding, planning, and prosecuting military, police, or development operations than is the country.

Almost every country in the world has an administrative or formal territorial unit approximately equivalent to what in the United States is known as a county. In Iran they are called *rayons* and in Colombia *municipios*, etc., and they generally have a great deal in common as a geographic unit. They are often the objects of considerable local geographic data-collection. Most Mexican counties (also called *municipios*), for instance, have their own website, which is usually very informative. In Colombia, every *municipio* government is required by national law to prepare a land-use plan (*Plan de Ordenamiento Territorial* or POT). Even rural, under-populated and poor *municipios* often produce a sophisticated POT. For instance, Toribío (a conflictive *municipio* in southern Colombia through or by which FARC smuggling routes pass) received an international grant and the help of foreign specialists to prepare its plan. It is exquisitely detailed, and includes numerous GIS-generated maps that represent both physical and non-physical cultural phenomena. Included are the lines of privately owned plats, along with tribal boundary lines, township lines and environmental risk areas.

The Canadians have managed to confuse the county level of governance, but within most of their provinces they have something akin to the county. A few of the smaller

U.S. states have eliminated the county. Counties today are one of the greatest employers of practical geographers, who earn their livelihoods on the basis of expertise in geographic representation and analysis. For them, GIS has almost become the universal epistemology for land-use planning. Precise geographic predictions regarding traffic, floodplains or development costs have become an administrative expectation at the county level. County governments do almost nothing in the absence of knowledge about land ownership.

Not only does most knowledge about real property ownership reside at the county level, the size and shape of the county is often intimately associated with familial histories and shared ownerships, physical compartmentalization of terrain, peculiar economic phenomena such as watersheds, mines or a popular beach, or other fairly obvious factors that guide decisions, affiliations and identities.

For internal or irregular armed conflicts, the county is probably a good choice of scale for analysis and operational design—or at least a good place to begin. The county can be a useful tag upon which to build an understanding of the relationship of residents with their surrounding environment, and of the local fit in the greater world. In many countries, including most in the Western Hemisphere, the county is a focus for tax collection and redistribution, developmental programs, land-use planning and reform programs, quality of life statistics, distribution of government services, voting representation, marriages, notaries, cadastres, school planning, etc.

To not have a collection of county-level data and a grasp of problems at the county scale might equate to being out of touch with the most revealing administrative events and social performance facts. Rural insurgents especially know counties; understand differences among counties; and deal with county governments. Innumerable popular seasonal events ranging from religious celebrations to concerts, fairs and contests are planned and organized at the county level. Many profitable extortions occur at the county level as a result. In Colombia, for instance, the central government redistributes a percentage of the national oil, gas and coal production profits to county governments, with those counties that produce hydrocarbons receiving a larger percentage. From some rural counties the FARC would threaten away large portions of those hydrocarbon royalties.

Mexico has about 1,500 counties and Colombia about 1,100. China has about 2,000. Iran has over 300 and Liberia about 15 (which have senators). The point is that while the country, national or federal level is impressive, the right knowledge or operational starting scale for your approach to an internal war might be the next level down (state, province, department), and more probably the next one down from that. It is advantageous to dominate land and property knowledge, details of which are often only available or understandable at the county scale; but if there is a rule regarding scale, it is probably that we should not bite off more territory than our resources can cover.

Anonymity and personal identity

Anonymity and personal identity are inseparable. Anonymity means one cannot be identified as themselves; nor can their things, relationships or locations be identified as theirs. Personal identity, beyond simply being the most particular of ownerships, often rests on relationships, possessions, memories and aspirations—these things and personal identity might be considered co-constitutive. If one were to gain perfect anonymity, he or she would run the risk of losing personal identity, or maybe the ability to express that identity. The spy sometimes suffers this crisis of identity, but not so much the insurgent, who at some point generally has to express his or her identity if he or she is ever to translate identity into power. Anonymity is, as such, a dilemma for the insurgent. Criminals, who want to enjoy their ill-gotten lucre, are often in the same boat as the insurgent—needing to keep some anonymity in order to survive, but remembering that ostentatious enjoyment of material luxury was an elemental goal of their behavior. Finding the right balance of anonymity and profile is of central importance in every thoughtful, organized challenge to the structure of things, and so the destruction or preservation of personal identity is concomitantly important.

Careful ID carding of populations and centralized ID inventories can serve either to protect or to endanger personal identity. Creating firm evidence of identity is a practical step against theft or fraudulent use of personal identity. It is also matched to the quality and usefulness of property records, given that a central test of the quality of those records is precision and transparency regarding *who* is associated with *what*. There cannot exist, in other words, perfect property records without perfect personal identity records. On the other hand, identity and marking systems have been implicated in assisting the perpetration of genocides, so ID cards are not necessarily or always a positive tool of peace or moral behavior. Nevertheless, no property system that orders rights and duties related to land, professional licenses, bandwidth, etc., can be fully functional as a tool of a peaceful social contract unless there is a parallel, transparent method of ensuring correct personal identification. Owner and owned are absolutely co-constitutive. Accuracy and transparency of the things owned is almost meaningless without accuracy and transparency of the identity of owners. This creates a practical and philosophical clash between identity and privacy values, but it is not necessarily unmanageable.

Moderation and reasonableness in transparency as to types of wealth, location, timing, etc. can be built into identification systems. For instance, while real property might be subject to the transparency of public knowledge, purchases of personal items should not be. And although records pertaining to real property might be available for public inspection, the property itself (at least from the ground up) should not be. While there might be a requirement to carry an ID card, a requirement or the right of the government to inspect the cards can be limited to specific places and times. In this regard there are common and varying practices in jurisdictions around the world, which should suggest considerable room for creativity in balancing the needs of anonymity and privacy against the needs for transparency and forensic power.

Sense of place

"Where you from, son?" must be the number one cliché question that the General asks the Private. Trite, expected and unimaginative, everyone likes it and is almost always happy to answer. The General can't go wrong because it is an essential question for most people. It is almost like asking "Who are you, really?" Personal identity, who we are, is often tied to physical geography, and even to some imagined and remembered physical geographies. We might be Southerners, Yankees, Paisas, Texans or whatever, and we can be more than one thing at a time and feel ourselves more from one place than another depending on a whole rafter of other situational factors, including not only where those making up the rest of the "we" are from, but where "they" are from. Some say it is harder to get people to fight for the revolution than it is for them to fight for Mother Russia. Strangely, we often can be *we* and keep them *they* for only the duration of a basketball game, or for generations. Knowing where people are from, and where they think they are from, is therefore a significant administrative question. Where persons *are*, on the other hand, is a matter of human rights and an American social jurisprudential inheritance.

The historical appearance

of prerogative writ of Habeas Corpus was a major step in Western liberal governance. Conspicuous in the Constitution of the United States, the writ of *habeas corpus*, which means something like "produce the body" or "show the body," is commonly associated with imprisonment—meaning that a government custodian of a captive person must show that he has detained someone, why and where. The notion is that a person cannot be held "*incommunicado*"— that whatever the offense or crime, a person has a right to communicate his or her existence to the outside world. The American constitutionalists of the 18th century, to achieve a practical manifestation of the right to life, determined that a right to be meant a right to be someplace, and that a right to life meant—as a practical concern for good governance—that a person's creditors and loved ones had a concomitant right to know where a person was. It was a matter of emotional value tied to scientific proof. Clandestine imprisonment, disappearance, kidnapping and murder (which all draw close to one another as a practical matter) were seen as the dark side of anonymity. The writ of Habeas Corpus expressed preoccupation about the right to personal identity, to proof of life, and to proof of death.

In an age of DNA and GIS, it is harder to escape the forensic unraveling of a mortal crime. Not only is it harder to get away with murder in a world of genetic mapping, it is harder to get away with false accusations of human rights abuses, not only because of new technologies, but because researchers, journalists and

even common citizens are equipped and increasingly expected to give plausibly accurate location data with their denunciations. Rule-of-law is about people knowing and believing in certain rights. It is also about things written down. The American legacy, as reflected in our most basic laws, is one that ties theoretical values to worldly proof. Because human identity, dignity, place and liberty so overlap, it behooves us to be respectfully scrupulous regarding both human identity and location, even after death. The writ of *habeas corpus* was invented with the understanding that human rights have a geographical reference. *Where* people are is part of *what* they are. The right to life becomes an administrative question.

Balance

Administrative data comes in all shapes, with the most revealing data probably being that which directs itself to the ownership of land. In the process of describing one of the world's most advanced land ownership regimes, Richard Grover gets right to the central point of asking how accessible the data should be. The question of accessibility relates to the frictions between the protection of rights and their abuse, and between advantage in armed conflict and the construction of a peaceful social contract. The cross-examination of public records can provide insight into the essential matter of who has what power, if power is abused, and where power-holders are physically located. Beyond cross-examination of files lies the purposeful development of effective and disciplined administrative files, along with righteous administrating institutions.

If we were to measure the condition or progress of an ongoing "pacification" campaign, and were given to know only that the public records were inaccurate, incomplete, and hidden, then on that knowledge alone we could be all but sure that the pacification program was not sustainable and was probably not going well. No social contract will be sustainable without solid evidence. It is like a complex contract with no writing. Few of us would buy a house or a car without a written document of the transaction. Likewise, a society without solid, accurate, comprehensive public records is a society that will eventually be in conflict. The worlds of peaceful social development and of competitive forensics do not collide; rather, they greatly overlap. They overlap in administrative files.

Geoffrey Demarest is a Senior Researcher of the Foreign Military Studies Office at Fort Leavenworth, Kansas. He holds a PhD in International Studies from Denver University and a Masters in Strategy from the Army War College. He also has practiced law and is currently pursuing a degree in Geography.

Napoleonic Know-How in an Era of Persistent Engagement

Douglas Batson
Al Di Leonardo
Christopher K. Tucker

A bevy of prominent national security thinkers have suggested that the U.S. has entered an era of persistent engagement with troubled regions of the world. From this perspective, failing or failed states are likely to lure the U.S. into counter-insurgency (COIN) operations, foreign internal defense and other modes of irregular warfare for decades to come. The sources of these difficult situations will inevitably vary greatly, from ethnic conflicts to natural-resource grabs; predatory kleptocracies to narco-terrorist regimes; proxy wars to religious extremism; and more. Yet all of these situations owe their origins in large part to the absence of the same governance infrastructures that have enabled successful modern states since the days of Napoleon.

Kinetic operations will almost always play a role in achieving conflict termination and establishing some measure of stability. But, too often, field commanders and national security policymakers fail to understand the administrative underpinnings needed to find and fix an elusive enemy, to achieve post conflict "stability, development, peace, and effective local sovereignty," and to keep insurgencies and the like from forming in the first place.[1]

This article asserts that a suite of administrative capabilities first mastered by Napoleon, what we call "Napoleonic know-how," should be elevated in the considerations of commanders and national security policymakers as they wrestle with courses of action in the engagement of nations and regions of special interest. Only when the U.S. prioritizes the pre-emptive establishment of such administrative capabilities over post-crisis kinetic action will we know that the U.S. foreign policy community is truly interested in conflict prevention and long-term stability during this era of persistent engagement.

An introduction to Napoleonic know-how

In a classic 1975 biography of Napoleon Bonaparte, Will and Ariel Durant state that the Emperor "became almost as brilliant in government as in battle. He predicted that his achievements in administration would outshine his martial victories in human memory, and that his legal codes were a monument more lasting than his strategy and tactics. He longed to be the Justinian as well as the Caesar Augustus of his age."[2]

But Napoleon was no benevolent emperor. His art of government was to keep people reasonably happy by giving them what they wanted and to take everything from them that could be taken. Despite their clamor for it, liberty was not viewed among peoples' basic

1. Demarest, Geoffrey. 2011. *Winning Insurgent War: Back to Basics.* Ft. Leavenworth, KS. The Foreign Military Studies Office. p. 352.; Manwaring, M.G. 2006. *Defense, Development, and Diplomacy (3D): Canadian and U.S. Military Perspectives.* Strategic Studies Institute, Carlisle, PA: U.S. Army War College Press. http://www.strategicstudiesinstitute.army.mil/pubs/display.cfm?pubID=732.
2. Durant, Will and Ariel. 1975. *The Age of Napoleon.* Simon and Shuster, New York. PT II, p. 250.

wants. And if certain conditions were met, Napoleon could easily repress liberty with impunity. Concerning liberty he quipped, "they would gladly renounce it if everyone could entertain the hope of rising to the top ... What must be done then is to give everybody the hope of being able to rise." And this Napoleon genuinely did. His is no empty boast, "I have closed the gaping abyss of anarchy, and I have unscrambled chaos ... Liberty means a good civil code. The only thing modern nations care for is property."[3]

Even a Napoleonic ego is woefully insufficient to adduce what an understatement those last words are for the 21st century. If he were alive today Napoleon would certainly gloat at how modern nations, a.k.a. the International Community, have failed to heed his example and instead pour billions of dollars, and millions of military and civilian personnel, into foreign aid and counterinsurgency operations that achieve far too little of the desired aims of peace and stability. He would berate with scorn the G8 leaders who are vexed, not by competing nation states but by non-state actors, who should have been marginalized long ago by three of the Emperor's methods: the census, the cadastre, and the national identity (ID) card. The following will examine these three ingredients of "Napoleonic know-how."

1. The census
The increasing sophistication of the Napoleonic state led to the development of historical statistics. Therefore, while it was the nascent United States of America that conducted the first modern, recurring census in 1790, Napoleon had more extensive uses for his census than mere congressional districting. With the manpower that he did not conscript into his Grande Armee' via the census, Napoleon created a legion of civil officials. He dispatched these bureaucrats into every village, town and city in order to link first the entire French nation, and later an Empire that encompassed half of Europe, to a rational, strong, centralized civil administration that registered births, deaths and marriages among other public records.[4] Indeed, the compilation of public data under Napoleon led to the formation of government investigative and regulatory commissions, even outside of France.

In fact, "the country where the French revolution had most immediate and permanent effect was the Netherlands."[5] The "French period" of the early 19th century changed social structures and politics in Holland and revived Dutch national mercantilism. And, it profoundly impacted the identities of individual Dutchmen. Napoleon's administrators forced them to have surnames, which was not a common practice in all the Low Countries. The Dutch were wise to the Emperor's designs on taxes and soldiers and, thinking this would be a temporary measure, offered comical names as a practical joke on their French occupiers. But, ultimately, the joke was on the descendants of those Dutchmen of yesteryear, some of whom are stuck with ridiculous last names such as Suikerbuik (Sugarbelly), Naaktgeboren (Born Naked) and Zondervan (Without a Surname).

Under Napoleon's system, each person was tied to a physical address that fell within an administrative district. The milestones of these individuals' lives were recorded as official government statistics, which in the aggregate allowed civil authorities to promulgate regulations and administrative actions based on concrete data, and to monitor the effect of these measures. The effect? Little breathing room remained for scofflaws and illicit activity. With Napoleon's Census, everyone and everything was accounted for.

2. The cadastre
As Napoleon's continental administration expanded, it became increasingly reliant upon the cadastre (land and property registry). This extension of the government's role was based on three assumptions. First, private land ownership was intrinsic to the territorial economy. Second, the cost of governing the territory was generated mostly from taxation of the privately owned parcels. And third, a record system, uniformly organized, would serve to protect property rights and facilitate the collection of taxes.[6]

3.   Herold, J. Christopher. 1963. *The Age of Napoleon*. American Heritage Publishing, New York. pp. 97-99.
4.   Kreis, Steven. 2000. *The History Guide: Lecture 15 on Modern European Intellectual History*. A World Wide Web Project at www.historyguide.org/intellect/lecture15a.html.
5.   Johnson, Paul. 1991. *The Birth of the Modern, World Society 1815-1830*. HarperCollins Publishers, New York, NY.
6.   Mitchel, W.H. 1976. "Information Technologies and Government Process." Pan American Meeting of Integrated Surveys and the Development of Countries. Bogota, Colombia: 26.

Professor Robert Burtch explains that the Napoleonic cadastre did not just develop from the whim of the Emperor, but rather evolved due to the expansion of the French Empire into areas of Europe that had retained feudal land tenures that poorly defined peoples' rights and interests in land.

"Half-measures always result in loss of time and money. The only way to sort out the confusion in the field of general land records is to proceed with the surveying and evaluation of each individual land parcel in all the communities of the Empire. A good cadastre will constitute a complement of my [Civil] Code as far as land possession is concerned. The map must be sufficiently precise and complete so that they could determine the boundaries between individual properties and prevent litigations" (Napoleon Bonaparte).[7]

But Napolean's rationale went beyond an economy-stimulating land market and ease of administration. Napoleon's statement, "The only thing modern nations care for is property" underscores how well he understood that to imbue his subjects with a sense of their rising to the top, they first had to be somebody; somebody with his name recorded with rights and interests in a land parcel. In other words, equality, liberty and fraternity were made manifest to millions by their obtaining a postal address— another Napoleonic civil

administration reform. A key to the Napoleonic cadastral effort was a record system designed to meet several purposes. Three of the more important are:
1. The record would consist of a complete history of all the transactions that occurred within the parcel.
2. The record was expandable and capable of including other types of informational needs that became obvious through government and private industry operation.
3. The record formed a basic management information system in that the government's managers could generate summaries of selected jurisdictions (Mitchel, 1976).

Under this system, criminal actors (as Napoleon would have characterized any citizen generating wealth off of untaxed property transactions) were pinched. This had the side benefit of minimizing the extent to which bad actors could engage in predatory behavior and organized illicit activity. Sanctuary was largely eliminated through these public administration advances.

3. The national ID card
Napoleon's 1803 implementation of national ID cards, the ancestor of all modern ID cards, transformed the free society of the earlier French Republic into a tightly controlled police state.

"The Republic had created a degree of freedom unheard of in Europe, allowing free speech and giving workers the right to change their job or go somewhere else.

By contrast, in most of Europe at this time…the majority of the population lived in various forms of bondage, such as indenture. Unfortunately, in France, a free market and mobility of labour were driving up wages. In response, the French authorities criminalized industrial action and introduced an ID card for workers, which aimed to …make it impossible to change jobs [in search of better wages] without an employer's permission and [to] restrict movement, by requiring workers to get an impossible string of visas to move legally."[8]

Allonby notes that after the demise "of the French Empire, the liberated countries often retained the systems of census and control [that] Napoleon had introduced— they were too useful and efficient to abolish."[9]

Allonby sums up the matter from Napoleonic history. "Identity systems require dependency to provide control. They have to be inescapable to work. Napoleon … felt [his] authority undermined by workers' self-help and welfare groups, where people helped each other out and disseminated information on how to get around the system."[10] Napoleon's national ID cards came about to control labor costs and ultimately repressed civil liberties. However, such identification systems have also become the basis for the provisioning of both public and private services in civilized societies.

7. Blachut, T., 1975. "What Constitutes a Land Records System—A Cadastre?" Proceedings of the North American Conference on the Modernization of Land Data Records, Washington, D.C., April, pp 5-13.
8. Allonby, Nathan. 2009. "ID Cards – an Historical View." 16 September, www.globalresearch.ca/index.php?context=va&aid=15231.
9. Ibid.
10. Ibid.

Napoleonic know-how in the context of population-centric operations

Attorney and former U.S. Defense Attache' Officer Geoffrey Demarest recognizes the same civil-military-legal quandary COIN operators share with Napoleon: there is a significant "overlap of the concepts of public intelligence that underpin a peaceful society and the Big Brother intelligence that allows the State to repress resistance and opposition."[11]

Nevertheless, Demarest underscores precisely how and why elusive non-state actors remain beyond the reach of law enforcement and COIN operators. They resist cadastral surveys in their ungoverned sanctuaries just as they resist any public administration advances that threaten their anonymity and impunity. Unlike the European serfs and indentured peasants of 200 years ago, modern insurgents don't want to be somebody. They don't want a fixed address. When dealing with bad actors in the context of population-centric operations, the more administrative systems in place that tie identity to property parcels, the more civil/law enforcement authorities can limit the mayhem they can cause.

Particularly at Phase 0 (e.g., at the pre-conflict "shaping" phase of involvement), military commanders and civil authorities must be involved in achieving comprehensive, transparent and available public records, (i.e., census, cadastre and national ID cards), or else they are needlessly aiding and abetting havens for the insurgent. Such neglect also means a failure to build the administrative infrastructure necessary to achieve and sustain peace, prosperity and security. However, the positive identification that such Napoleonic know-how can enable can be just as important during Phase 3 or 4 kinetic operations, in support of more traditional ISR assets. In the end, as ADM Eric T. Olsen points out:

> "DoD defines irregular warfare as a 'violent struggle among state and non-state actors for legitimacy and influence over the relevant population(s).' IW is then inherently both political in purpose and local in character. The focus is on populations and effective governance rather than on territories and material dominance. This has distinct implications for the way irregular wars must be fought and for the forces that fight them."[12]

In post-conflict Afghanistan and Iraq, competing land claims have impaired stability operations (SO) and thwarted hopes of a lasting peace. This situation will occur more frequently until commanders and civil authorities appreciate the relationship between people and their land, information typically registered in a cadastre (land and property registry). An enlightened commander engaged in a population-centric operation is interested in the demographics and behavioral characteristics of the population, the center of gravity, within his footprint; namely, identifying the power brokers on the ground whose support or obstruction may determine mission success. By tying a name to a place, cadastral data can answer the difficult "who" question, i.e., who is impeding road construction or restricting access of a minority group to a health clinic? The intelligence analyst is interested in psychological characteristics of a people group, and cadastral data can identify a group's ideologies and economic pillars.[13]

Two centuries ago Napoleon Bonaparte, renowned for his military genius, moved decisively to improve post-conflict governance and called his cadastre the greatest achievement of his civil code. Perhaps his only oversight in that statement is the powerful impact that the cadastre has in combination with his other administrative feats, the census and national identification.

Napoleonic know-how in action (and inaction)

Such administrative capabilities, and the data they accrete over time, can be useful in enabling effective population-centric operations at all phases of operational engagement, and are key to reconstructing a shattered nation. Operational examples of their importance abound. In fact, "stability, development, peace, and effective local sovereignty" cannot be realized without them.[14]

11. Demarest, Geoffrey. 2011. *Winning Insurgent War: Back to Basics.* Ft. Leavenworth, KS. The Foreign Military Studies Office.

12. Olsen, ADM Eric T. 2010. "Context and Capabilities in Irregular Warfare." Joint Forces Quarterly. January.

13. Batson, Douglas E. "Napoleonic Know-how for Stability Operations." p. 330 in *Modern Military Geography*, Galgano and Palka, Editors. Routledge 2010.

14. Manwaring, M.G. 2006. *Defense, Development, and Diplomacy (3D): Canadian and U.S. Military Perspectives.* Strategic Studies Institute, Carlisle, PA: U.S. Army War College Press. http://www.strategicstudiesinstitute.army.mil/pubs/display.cfm?pubID=732.

Afghanistan: In the current counter-insurgency campaign in Afghanistan, the complete lack of land ownership records and postal addresses (outside the major cities) creates major impediments for ISAF military forces. Analysts have been forced to create geospatial databases based purely on location descriptions and historical activity of civilian and insurgent-related compounds and buildings. This painstaking task is done to aid in the characterization of the insurgent landscape and to decrease the likelihood of civilian casualties. Yet, the fact that the data is sometimes the result of misinformation or disinformation rather than validated civilian, administrative data means that unfortunate military accidents occur more frequently in the population of noncombatants. A comprehensive set of land ownership records and corresponding postal addresses would serve to eliminate many of these events, helping the Government of Afghanistan and ISAF win the hearts and minds of the Afghan populace by reducing civilian casualties. The lack of a national identification scheme only magnifies this problem, making it difficult to irrefutably tie individuals to locations. And, in a country where the lack of a census means a chronic misestimation of the population on the scale of several million, it can even be difficult to determine who is and is not Afghan.

Iraq: Not only does cadastral data enable population-centric operations, but understanding the differences in cadastral data allows irregular warfare forces to swiftly adapt to the areas in which they operate. For example, the parcels of Iraq's urban areas are based on a rigidly structured and well-designed address system where streets and houses are assigned numbers. The Iraqi people may indicate the precise location of a nefarious actor using this system, as it is one they use themselves every day to travel the city. While military operations are often run using geographic coordinates, the existence of an address system and parcel database can determine the accuracy, speed and footprint required to undertake a successful security operation with minimal impact on the population.

Major Dan E. Stigall, a U.S. Army Judge Advocate (JAG), trained in continental civil law at Louisiana State University, deployed to Iraq in 2003, and has published widely on Iraqi civil law since that time. Stigall notes that Iraqi property law is derived primarily from Continental (Napoleonic) civil law but also contains elements of Ottoman and Islamic land law. Though there is still a great need to increase the administrative capacity of the judiciary, Iraq has been and remains capable of sound land administration.[15] Even within Iraq, land administration systems differ but still offer the advantages of Napoleonic know-how. While addresses in urban areas are based on street and house numbers, the rural areas of Iraq are based on an agricultural and irrigational parcel system. For example, land plots in areas of Sulaymaniyah Province are defined by a canal system that derives an address based on canal segment-branch-parcel. A rural location can be found at stunning accuracy based on this system. Similar to the urban example, the accuracy and footprint required are inherently linked to the success, scale, and impact of the operation. Of course, a rigorous addressing scheme does not always imply an orderly administrative infrastructure for maintaining land parcel ownership information. And, this can undermine their value in achieving positive identification and legal occupancy, and winnowing on illicit activity.

Regardless, respecting and understanding the systems that already exist increases the degree to which irregular warfare forces can work with the local population to find what they are looking for, regardless of the operating environment. Further investment can help a nation (or region) mature its cadastral system, build a personal identification system that ties legitimate individuals to property, and track the dynamics over time through an ongoing census. Aiding developing nations in the establishment of or improvement to their Napoleonic administrative systems benefits both the irregular forces and the host nation in many ways.

Sudan: There are also cases in which systems that vaguely resemble those of Napoleon are abused to empower certain factions of a society over others. Yet, these are also the same administrative

---

15. Stigall, Daniel E. 2008. "Refugees and Legal Reform in Iraq: The Iraqi Civil Code, International Standards for the Treatment of Displaced Persons, and the Art of Attainable Solutions," pp. 20-21. Social Science Research Network. http://papers.ssrn.com/sol3/papers.cfm?abstract_id=115744.

systems that an irregular expeditionary force should pay the most attention to in the future. In the currently unfolding crisis in Sudan, the Khartoum government has manipulated its census so that the southern population (where the oil fields predominantly are) cannot demonstrate its majority status and carry out a legitimate secession. In the face of the January 2011 referendum, the Sudanese Government conducted a National Census in April of 2009 in which they intentionally left off questions on tribe or clan affiliation. The government felt that if the Ethnic Dinka in the South realized they now outnumber the Northern tribes, then they would most certainly vote for succession.

In such a context, establishing a census system (or overhauling an existing one) and making it rigorous by tying identity to individual land parcel records, can be powerful tools in bringing about sustainable governance. As such, before falling into an abyss of kinetic action, military commanders and the larger community of national security decision-makers should seek to institute Napoleonic systems in the target country.

Somalia: While Somalia represents a failed state in many respects, the northern parts of Somalia, Somaliland and Puntland, are far more stable than Southern Somalia. This is in part because the basic concepts of Napoleonic know-how were put in place with local government. Disparate clans control the South much more than in the Northern

parts of Somalia, with no real land administration/cadastral property rights scheme to temper the competing claims to legitimacy. The result is an absence of stability and with concomitant local and global terrorist activity from elements like Al-Shababb in Southern Somalia.

Senegal: Senegal has for many years taken a strong stance against terrorism and in addition to signing on to regional (Trans-Sahel) counter-terrorism efforts, has worked hard to invest in both the physical and the administrative infrastructure that highly constrains nefarious activity. In September 2009, the Millennium Challenge Corporation (MCC) signed a five-year, $540 million compact with the Republic of Senegal designed to reduce poverty and invest in economic growth by unlocking the country's agricultural productivity and expanding access to markets and services. This goal will be achieved through the rehabilitation of major national roads and strategic investments in irrigation and water resource management infrastructure. The government of Senegal (the Government) has identified two national-level strategies—to reduce poverty in Senegal through economic growth and to increase the country's food security. Both of these priorities will be facilitated through MCC's $540 million compact with the Republic of Senegal.

In order to succeed at development, Senegal recognized that it would need a sound infrastructure for identity.

As a result, Senegal has taken impressive steps.

"The new national identity and voter's card system interfaces with the government's own central database. In addition to personal data, a digital facial image, signature and four fingerprints are collected from applicants at one of the permanent or mobile registration sites. The data is then transferred to a central Dakar site for eligibility checks, including fingerprint comparison. Upon approval the data is transferred to a central production system where an automated, high-speed system personalizes, quality assures and produces up to 80,000 cards per day. The National Identity and the Voter's Card are produced from a single system. Both card types are laminated Teslin, incorporating multi-layered security features and a 2D barcode to store the biometrics. Senegal's National Identity and Voter's Card system was implemented within 10 months and included the training of 1,800 personnel. Once launched, the system issued 9 million cards within a 12-month period."[16]

Yet, Senegal comes up short on the land administration front, as demonstrated in this quote from a USAID publication:

"Despite the efforts to control land tenure in Senegal through a framework of formal law, customary law continues to govern land rights and the transfer of land in much of the country. In Senegal's

---

16. www.delarue.com/Download.aspx?ResourceId=9199.

highly stratified society, customary practices tend to favor elites (i.e. elders, and religious and political figures) at the expense of lower-caste farmers. The outcome of purportedly democratic elections of rural council members is strongly influenced by candidates' social status and political party. The council members, who wield the power to manage territorial lands, may themselves serve as elite landholders and village chiefs, and it is common for them to approve tacit land sales and leases, circumvent legislation, and engage in other corrupt and self-serving tactics in many areas" (USAID Country Profile, Property Rights and Resource Governance).[17]

The lack of formality in land administration, and the gross infrequency of a census (the first took place in 1976 and the most recent in 1988), has led to far too much breathing room for nefarious actors. Yet, the progress Senegal has made on identity offers great promise for the future of Napoleonic know-how in diminishing the threat of terrorism in Senegal.

Mali: Mali is an example of a place where the lack of a rigorous identity infrastructure allows nefarious actors—i.e. Al-Qa'ida in the Lands of the Islamic Maghreb (AQIM)—too many degrees of freedom. All data in Mali is stored on paper and is physically filed away in

one of the many decentralized government buildings in Bamako. Passports, while controlled, do not contain biometrics and are not held by everyone. Driving a vehicle requires a license made of paper, and the license plates in most cases are numbers painted on the back side of the truck or car. Most Malians drive mopeds, which require no license and are completely unregulated. As such, policing nefarious actors is highly problematic.

Refugee camps—Pakistan/ Kenya/Somalia/etc.: Terrorists recruit many of their ranks from refugee camps in which people have little identity, property or representation in a census that might even use statistics to articulate their struggle. The means for unwinding this complicated and nefarious situation is the subject of long debates. Beyond a focus on aid that alleviates the most acute suffering, national security decision-makers should look to the establishment of Napoleonic administrative systems as a way slowly to untie these Gordian Knots and instill order. Establishing individual identity, determining a population's needs through a census, and, as land administration capacity allows, recording refugees' claims to physical land parcels is key.

The new Napoleonic complex

Sophisticated military commanders, civilian authorities and national security policymakers understand that they must

develop an understanding of the socio-cultural dynamics at play over their geography of strategic concern. LTG Michael Flynn's bold 2010 report "Fixing Intel: A Blueprint for Making Intelligence Relevant in Afghanistan" had this imperative at its core.

The census, the cadastre, and national identification silently underpin peace and stability in developed societies. Unfortunately, policymakers have not made socio-cultural information collection a priority in countries or regions of interest. Nor have they set the establishment of administrative infrastructures as reconstruction and stability goals, despite the many lessons learned from counter-insurgency.[18] Instead, policymakers leave the collection and analysis of critical socio-cultural information to either an intelligence community ill-equipped to collect and analyze open source data from public records, or they expect practitioners with other duties (for instance, Provincial Reconstruction Teams or NGOs) to "gather as they go." The work of the Human Terrain Teams (HTTs), while admirable, were never meant to and cannot meet the standards set by Napoleon's administrative infrastructure.

These realities virtually guarantee that the necessary socio-cultural data will remain unavailable to support foreign aid and investment, development activities, stability operations, law enforcement or even the more coercive

17. Faye, Jacques. 2008. "Land and Decentralisation in Senegal: Increasing popular participation to enhance the efficiency of Senegalese land and decentralisation policies," Issue Paper No. 149, IIED. http://www.eldis.org/go/country-profiles&id=39514&type=Document (accessed 2 June 2010).; Cotula, Lorenzo, ed. 2006. "Land and Water Rights in the Sahel: Tenure Challenges of Improving Access to Water for Agriculture." LSP Working Paper 25, Access to Natural Resources Sub-Programme. Rome: FAO.

18. Galula, David. 1964. *Counterinsurgency Warfare: Theory and Practice.* Praeger Security International. Westport, Connecticut.; Sepp, Kalev I. 2005. "Best Practices in Counterinsurgency." *Military Review.* May-June.

actions usually associated with the military. When a nation lacks systems for positively identifying individuals, for keeping demographic records and for rigorously tying individuals to precisely defined land parcels, it lacks the capacity to govern properly, to thwart non-state actors, to curb corruption, organized crime, and illicit transactions, or to defend legal freedoms. A government must invest in its citizenry so that the voluntary institutions of civil society emerge to reinforce democratic gains, invigorate commerce and promote peace and stability.

There is a need for a radical doctrinal shift in the way the U.S. national security community thinks and behaves; it must prioritize the rapid establishment of administrative processes that accrete Napoleonic know-how in regions of the world predisposed to persistent conflict. Such steps would constitute a major but necessary departure from the way the U.S. national security community has expended its resources to counter instability in the post-Cold War era. In an era of diminishing budgets to conduct 21st century military operations abroad, now, more than ever, an ounce of prevention is worth a pound of cure.

Douglas Batson joined the National Geospatial-Intelligence Agency (NGA) as a toponymist in 2004. He earned the Deutsches Sprachdiplom des Goethe-Instituts and a diploma with honors in Turkish from the Defense Language Institute. He has been twice selected an Office of the Director of National Intelligence Exceptional Analyst Research Fellow.

Al Di Leonardo is Co-Founder and CEO of HumanGeo. He is a retired U.S. Special Operations Innovation Officer turned entrepreneur. He currently works at the intersection of geospatial analytics, technology and social media in commercial and government sectors. Di Leonardo was awarded the Bronze Star for work with U.S. Special Operations.

Dr. Christopher K. Tucker thinks and works at the intersection of technology, strategy, geography and national security. Tucker manages a portfolio of social ventures and technology companies across the domains of international affairs, defense/intelligence and academe. He serves on a variety of government, private sector and non-profit boards.

OPENNESS AND PRIVACY IN PUBLIC SPATIAL DATA

Richard Grover

Modern governments produce a vast array of data as a product of their aims of managing the economy and society. For example, periodic censuses provide a wealth of socio-economic and demographic data about the population, including information about housing conditions, educational qualifications, employment, migration and travel to work.

Governments collect data about production from all parts of the economy, including agriculture, manufacturing, services, tourism and banking, in order to measure the national income and inform economic policy. Other parts of the public sector such as regional and local administrations, agencies and trading bodies also collect data. Sometimes the data is a by-product of another government activity, such as taxation. For example, statistics on wealth may be produced from inheritance taxes or information about housing transactions from stamp duties or similar taxes on property transactions. In addition to the regular collection of statistics, data is also produced on a one-off basis, such as for a government or parliamentary inquiry, or sporadically, such as surveys undertaken by a local authority when periodically updating town plans.

The availability of data has increased greatly in recent years as a result of access via the Internet. Not only are data that would have previously only been available in specialist libraries and archives now published online, but also databases from which researchers can undertake their own searches. This does not just apply to new data but also to historical material. For example, in the U.K. the 1901 census was released online after its statutory period of closure rather than through opening it up to National Archives researchers. The 1901 census data thus became available to many more interested persons than was previously possible.

Whilst much government data is available at the national level, a significant amount is also either geo-referenced to local areas or also produced for smaller, sub-national areas. The locations where crimes are committed or the price paid by the purchaser when a specific house is registered after being sold are examples of geo-referenced data. For reasons of confidentiality, census information about households, which is capable of being geo-referenced by where a person lives, is not released for a period of time—in the U.K. for 100 years—but small area statistics are produced. The smallest area for which such data is available in the U.K. is the census enumeration district, an area of approximately 200 dwellings for which a single census enumerator was responsible for the collection of the data.

Data can be organised in a number of different ways for analysis and interpretation, but using a geo-referencing system is a particularly useful means of bringing together information from a variety of sources. For example, if I am considering buying a new house, the ability to access house price data for comparable properties, the socio-economic characteristics of the area, local crime statistics, in which local government and electoral districts the property is located, its property tax band, its town planning history, the property rights and obligations, charges on the property, and information about the quality of local schools and health services using a geo-referencing system for searching by addresses or postcodes is extremely useful, particularly if such data can be downloaded from the Internet. Better still if much of this data is available through a single portal that can be accessed through a geo-reference system.

There can also be important implications for policy makers from the spatial organisation of data. For example, knowing where families with children whose income is below the poverty line live can help frame appropriate intervention policies. If the majority tend to live in clusters, then policies aimed at improving housing, schools, and the provision of pre- and after-school clubs and child care may be effective. However if such families are widely scattered geographically, then localised interventions may fail to reach the intended targets. Income-orientated interventions, such as the provision of means-tested benefits, may be more effective. Policy makers are frequently faced with questions about where to place services; for example, where to locate a new primary school, which secondary school to close because of falling pupil numbers, or where to locate an emergency response facility. Such questions require geographical information, such as where potential users are located and travel times between them and the location of the public service, to produce optimal solutions.

Whilst government officials can access official sources of data, their use by independent researchers, households, private businesses, or journalists raises a number of issues.

Although this paper is written from the perspective of the U.K., these questions are of general applicability. They include what governments should publish and the terms and conditions on which others should be able to access public information. Whilst transparency on the part of government is highly desirable, individuals and businesses have rights to privacy that the publication of confidential data about them by public bodies can undermine. Governments may resist openness for political reasons. They are unlikely to welcome the publication of data that shows them failing to meet pledges to the electorate. They may prefer to "bury" bad news—for example, that child poverty reduction targets have not been met—by publishing it on a day when the eyes of the media are on, say, a natural disaster or major accident or a royal wedding, rather than having regular and publicised publication schedules.

In the U.K. there are several drivers towards greater openness on the part of government. Government has embraced a freedom of information policy. In one important area—information about the environment—greater openness is being driven by European Union policies. Greater availability of data about public services and their performance is also being driven by the restructuring of many of these services under a group of policies that are generally collectively known as the New Public Management.

The New Public Management

The New Public Management is a term that has been applied to a series of policies aimed at increasing the efficiency with which public services are delivered. They aim to improve efficiency by reducing top-down controls over their delivery in favour of greater freedom for front-line staff, for example, head teachers rather than the local authority or Ministry of Education. Front-line managers operate within the policy framework set by the elected government.

Professor Christopher Hood, Gladstone Professor of Government at Oxford University and one of the first to use the term New Public Management and to identify its principal features, has argued that it is a fusion between the new institutional economics, with its emphasis on public choice, transactions costs and the relationship between principals and agents, and managerialism in the public sector.[1] The term was particularly associated with the governments of Margaret Thatcher during the 1980s, though subsequent governments in the U.K. have followed similar policies. The New Public Management has been a feature of public sector reform in a number of the richer OECD countries, including Australia, Canada, New Zealand, U.K., the Netherlands, Sweden, and the U.S. Yet the emphasis in the approach and the precise policies used do vary between countries.[2]

The adoption of the New Public Management reflects the belief that the public sector is not as efficient as it could be. It is protected from competition and public services may be managed in the interests of producers rather than consumers. The countries that have been at the forefront of its development have very strong controls to prevent the misuse of public

1. Hood, C. (1991) A Public Management for all Seasons, *Public Administration*, 69, pp 3-19.
2. Glor, E.D. (2001) Has Canada adopted the New Public Management? *Public Management Review*, 3 (1), pp 121-130.

assets, the misappropriation of public funds and misconduct in public office. These controls tend to encourage public servants to avoid risk and to follow procedures rather than incentivising them to improve efficiency. Often the driver behind the approach is financial pressure that requires better public services to be provided using fewer resources. The shift in responsibility to front-line staff should mean that those who understand the operational requirements have power to improve efficiency. Front-line staff does not have to be within a government department or local authority but can be part of an arms-length agency, or may work for a private company or a not-for-profit organisation. They may not be public servants and can receive performance-related pay. They may not have the job security that public servants traditionally have enjoyed and can be held accountable for failure to meet targets.

The New Public Management can only work effectively if the centre sets clear targets to be achieved and collects reliable data about whether they have been achieved. In the U.K. an important aspect of the enforcement of standards and the achievement of customer-orientated public services has been to enlist the public to help police the system rather than to rely on auditing alone. This is only viable if the public know what the standards for services are and have effective means of securing what they are entitled to. The U.K. has tended to make use of citizens' charters that specify what users of public services

can expect and the means by which complaints can be made and redress sought. In a number of services, such as education and health care, a competitive environment has been created in which the public can use information published about performance to choose between alternative providers with the services being free at the point of consumption. This policy is also applied in areas like policing where the public has no choice of service provider.[3] No senior manager wants to be labelled as running a failing organisation, so the publication of data acts as a spur to better performance.

Freedom of information

In the U.K. there is a legal presumption that public bodies must publish the data that they hold except in certain limited circumstances. Historically, public bodies have tended to be quite secretive, particularly about their internal workings and deliberations, so this is a radical change of position brought about by a combination of favourable circumstances.

The election of a new left of centre government in 1997 made legislation possible. The left in British politics traditionally interprets the actions of some public bodies as conspiracies against the public and has sought greater transparency in government. The right in British politics favours smaller government. It has embraced greater transparency as a means of exposing inefficiency in the public sector. During the last two decades public bodies

have been making increasing use of the Internet for the publication of information and the legislation has encouraged them to move further in this direction.

The Freedom of Information Act 2000 gives members of the public (including journalists and researchers) the right to request official information held by public bodies. This information must be disclosed unless there are good reasons for keeping it confidential. Strictly the act applies to England, Wales, Northern Ireland and U.K.-wide bodies, as Scotland has its own similar legislation. The act is policed by an Information Commissioner, whose office produces a range of guidance material to help public bodies satisfy its requirements.[4] A public body can appeal against the commissioner's ruling to the Information Tribunal.

The term information is defined very broadly. It includes statistical data, but also research reports, minutes and emails. The Act applies to a wide range of bodies, including central government departments, local authorities, agencies and companies owned by public bodies, the National Health Service (i.e. the hospitals, clinics, dentists, pharmacists and opticians used by the overwhelming majority of the public), the state education system, including schools and universities in receipt of public funding, and police forces. The Act does not give the right to see personal information held by public bodies as individuals can use other legislation to gain access to this, though some,

---

3.   Grover, R. (2009) State and public land management: The drivers of change, *Land Reform, Land Settlement and Cooperatives*, 2009/1, pp 59-68.
4.   These can be accessed via the Information Commissioner's Office website, http://www.ico.gov.uk/.

like criminal records, are not accessible. The Act does not enable access to be gained to personal information about other people.

As public bodies know that the public has the right to access their information, it makes sense to be pro-active and develop a publication policy. Publication then becomes a routine part of a public body's business. This can be through a website. The publication policy can include explaining what the body does, its policies and procedures, how it makes decisions, how it spends its budget and raises revenue, the services it offers, any charges for supplying information such as photocopying charges, and how information can be requested. The Information Commissioner's Office has developed a model publication scheme.[5] The destruction of records outside of a normal policy—for example, when a Freedom of Information request is received—is unlawful.

A public body must respond to a request for information within 20 working days. Information must be disclosed unless there is legal justification for not doing so. The public body must set out its reasons for rejecting a request, which are open to challenge. A public body can delay responding for a period of a further 20 days where it is considering whether the request is legal but, again, must state the reasons why it is considering the legality of the request. The main reasons for refusing a request include: if it would prejudice national security or international relations, breach the duty of confidentiality to

other individuals, interfere with the course of justice, damage commercial interests, the cost of supplying the information is excessive, and if the balance of public interest in withholding the information outweighs the public interest in its publication. If the person requesting the information is dissatisfied with the refusal, it is possible to seek an internal review of the decision. Once the internal procedures have been exhausted, a complainant can appeal to the Information Commissioner.

The act helps to create a culture of openness and accountability by public bodies and encourages systematic publication of data. Whilst not all the data released is geo-referenced, a significant part is. Some of the public bodies, such as local authorities, National Health Service Trusts and police authorities, have defined jurisdictions so that their data relates to specific locations. Other data comes from bodies that serve particular communities, such as schools.

Environmental information

The lead in developing greater openness about environmental data for the 28 nations that make up the European Union has been the EU, which adopted a directive giving the public access to environmental information in 2003.[6] The directive brought into effect the EU's 1998 Aarhus Convention on Access to Information, Public Participation in Decision-Making and Access to Justice in Environmental Matters. Once the EU adopts a directive, member states must harmonise

their laws with that of the European Union. Although each country is a sovereign state, there has been a significant pooling of sovereignty in the areas of the Single Market in which goods, services and factors of production can be traded freely. As will be discussed later, the EU has also taken steps to ensure that there is access to geo-referenced environmental data and this is having the effect of opening up the geo-referencing systems of the national mapping agencies. The measures taken in this area are much more far-reaching in their effect than just to make environmental data more accessible.

The U.K. brought the environmental information directive into effect through the Environmental Information Regulations 2004. These regulations apply to most of the public bodies affected by the Freedom of Information Act and are based upon this act. They could also apply to other bodies carrying out a public administration function. Thus, they could be extended to include a number of private bodies and companies. The privatisation of the utilities industries has meant that a number of private companies have the role of statutory undertakers and have powers such as compulsory purchase that can be used in this context. There are also public works concessions in which private companies provide infrastructure, such as roads, in return for the right to collect fees and tolls.

Environmental information can be in written, visual, aural,

---

5.   Commissioner's Office (2008) *Model Publication Scheme*, version 1, April 2008.
6.   Directive 2003/4/CE.

electronic or other material form. It includes information about the state of elements of the environment, such as air, water, soil, land, landscape and natural sites, biological diversity and genetically modified organisms; emissions and discharges likely to affect the environment, such as energy, noise and radiation; environmental measures, such as policies, legislation, plans and programmes; reports on the implementation of environmental legislation; cost-benefit and other economic analyses and assumptions used in environmental measures; and the state of human health and safety, including contamination of the food chain and the impact on human life, cultural sites and the built environment. The use of the term *likely* to affect the environment sets a relatively low threshold for possible causation and serves to draw in a wider range of emissions and discharges than if proof of the effect had to be furnished. Similarly, the use of *such as* in the regulations means that the list is not exhaustive.

Although there is no obligation on a body to manipulate data to create new information, it must extract the information it has.[7] Requests for information can be refused if the cost of supplying it is disproportionate in the sense that it is manifestly unreasonable. A fee can be charged for the information, though this must be a "reasonable amount". Requests for information must be responded to within 20 working days. Like the Freedom of Information Act, the Environmental Information Regulations are overseen by the Information Commissioner.

Threats to the availability of small area statistics

The publication of small area statistics serves to provide much needed data about small communities for the use of policy makers, business and researchers whilst preserving the anonymity of individuals and their rights of privacy. However, the continued collection of small area statistics is under threat. They are costly to collect. In the U.K. each time the legislation for the collection of a census is debated, the need for intrusion into people's privacy has been questioned. Perhaps more significantly the need for this type of information has been questioned within governments. This is because governments need real time data that devices to collect small area statistics, like censuses, cannot satisfy. They are held too infrequently and take too long to process so that the data from these is substantially out of date during much of its period of use. The response has been to make greater use of sampling, not just in censuses but also in other areas that produce small area statistics, such as agricultural censuses and the revaluation of property tax assessments. Sampling reduces the cost of collection and can provide data at more frequent intervals. However, this has the effect of reducing the integrity of local data.

Public access to mapping systems

If the vast array of public data is to be used for spatial analysis, there must be a comprehensive geo-referencing system to which it can be related. However different public bodies hold their data in different ways. Location data can be held, for example, as postcodes, addresses, place names, or through a geographical information reference system. Databases created by different public bodies may not have compatible geo-referencing systems, making it difficult to link them together for purposes of analysis. A study by the British government suggested that users of geographical information spend 80 percent of their time collating and managing the information and only 20 percent analysing it.[8] The analysis requires a base map to which all the various ways in which locations can be described can be related. It is then possible for data from different sources using alternative means of describing location to be added as layers.

There are different approaches to the creation of a base map. In much of continental Europe there is a cadastre. In the case of countries like France or the Netherlands, it is a product of the Napoleonic system. In others, such as Romania, the cadastre has been created with the support of loans from the World Bank as land registration and cadastres are seen as being necessary for the efficient functioning of land

7. See the examples in Information Commissioner's Office (2009) *ICO Guidance – environmental information regulations: What is Environmental Information?* version 3, 16 March 2009.
8. U.K. Department of Communities and Local Government (2008) *Place Matters: The Location Strategy for the United Kingdom*, November, available from www.communities.gov.uk.

markets and these, in turn, being a necessary condition for economic development. It has been influenced by the ideas of the Peruvian economist, Hernando de Soto, who argued that a key difference between developed and undeveloped economies is the ability of property owners to release capital through loans secured against real estate.[9] A cadastre is defined by the International Federation of Surveyors (Fèdèration Internationale des Géomètres), usually known by its French acronym FIG, as "normally a parcel based and up-to-date land information system containing a record of interests in land (e.g. rights, restrictions and responsibilities)". It usually includes a geometric description of land parcels linked to other records describing the nature of the interests, the ownership or control of those interests, and often the value of the parcel and its improvements.[10]

At the core of a cadastre is an accurate base map on which property boundaries are recorded. The combination of guaranteed property rights and charges from land registration and guaranteed boundaries from the cadastre provides strong protection of property rights. Owners can be obliged to have their properties resurveyed in the event of changes like sub-division or sale. Typically this is done by a licensed surveyor, who is registered with the cadastre as being empowered to make changes to the base map. The base map is typically the responsibility of the national mapping agency. Historically the maps were analogue but digitisation has taken place over the last decade. In many cases this has been through the digitisation of analogue maps rather than resurveying. The use of digital maps allows the creation of different layers so that the various public bodies can link their databases to the base map.

The U.K. has compulsory land registration but no cadastre. As a result the maps in the Land Registry (and its regional equivalents for Scotland and Northern Ireland) are indicative of the location of the property but are not legally definitive. A joint statement between the Land Registry (the land registration body for England and Wales) and the Ordnance Survey (the U.K.'s official mapping agency) makes it clear that the maps in the Land Registry do not contain legal boundaries.[11]

The result is a rather unusual situation in which there is a partial Torrens system in the U.K.—the ownership of rights is proved through entry in the register rather than through deeds—but there is no central or official record of the boundaries of these rights.

Since 1841 the Ordnance Survey has had the power to establish official boundaries, for example, of local government areas. It has no power to determine private boundaries but it does map boundary features and has a right of legal trespass to enable it to enter private property without the consent of the owners to undertake mapping. The U.K. has a "general boundaries" system in which boundary features are mapped but their ownership is not identified in the maps. Mapping does not determine whether a boundary lies on one side of a wall or the other, or at some point within the physical boundary marker. Land registration documents, like title deeds, may provide guidance and common law principles can also be used to determine boundaries. The implication is that parcel boundaries cannot be used as the basis for mapping public data, as no register of parcel boundaries exists.

There have been proposals for the U.K. to establish a cadastre. In 1836 R.K. Dawson, a Royal Engineer officer on secondment to the Tithe Commission to organise the tithe surveys, put forward a well-argued case for a cadastre and how it might be accomplished.[12] Under an act of 1836, tithes in kind were to be replaced by a fluctuating money payment. This required the determination of the boundaries for each parish for which tithes were payable and the apportionment of tithes to be apportioned between landed estates according the value of the produce they produced. Most parishes in England and Wales, other than urban ones, had to be mapped, with legal boundaries recorded, areas measured and the land valued. There was strong political opposition to the proposal for a cadastre so that the legislation was amended to prevent the tithe surveys for being used in this way.

9. de Soto, H. (2000) *The Mystery of Capital: Why Capitalism Triumphs in the West and Fails Everywhere Else*, Black Swan.
10. FIG (no date) *Statement on the Cadastre*, International Federation of Surveyors, Copenhagen, available on FIG website, www.fig.net.
11. Joint Statement by Land Registry and Ordnance Survey, www.landregistry.gov.uk.
12. Kain, R.J.P. and Prince, H.C. (1985) *The Tithe Surveys of England and Wales*, Cambridge University Press, Cambridge, chapter 3.

The fundamental distrust the British people have of the government having access to information over their property has not diminished over time. As recently as 2008, a government initiative for sellers of property to provide potential buyers with a Home Information Pack lapsed as a result of hostility from the public. There are fiscal cadastres for commercial and residential property. These are based upon market value so the usable area of the buildings and their location are the key determinates rather than the footprint of the parcel. The only real cadastre that exists is for agricultural land. In 2005 the European Union changed the basis of the Common Agricultural Policy from a system of guaranteeing prices for farmers for particular commodities to one in which the subsidy was paid according to the land occupied.[13] Member states had to create and maintain a database of agricultural land parcels with their sizes and geo-references, linked to records of farmers and their aid applications. The U.K. therefore had to create the Rural Land Register.

The introduction of the new system resulted in significant problems in England (though not the rest of the U.K.), with serious delays in making payments to farmers.[14] The cost of establishing the Rural Land Register for England was £16.1 million compared with an estimate of £6.8 million, which included £9.8 million being spent on mapping applicants' land.

The absence of a cadastre raises fundamental questions about how a government can organise spatial data. In this respect the U.K. is similar to many countries around the world. However, unlike many of them, it has an extremely sophisticated national mapping system. Digitisation was completed by 1995. In 2001 Ordnance Survey developed OS Master Map, which references more than 440 million man-made and natural landscape features. It has a series of layers including topographical data, addresses and aerial photographs. In effect it offers an alternative to the cadastre approach of surveyed boundaries through using a series of points as the basis for locating data. Countries lacking a land administration infrastructure could copy the U.K.'s approach by harnessing the cloud of individuals with GPS appliances in devices like mobile phones to map physical features. Such initiatives have produced street maps of previously unmapped towns, particularly ones with large quantities of informal housing.

The development of an infrastructure for spatial information is not just a national matter for countries in the European Union as a result of the EU's INSPIRE Directive for establishing an Infrastructure for Spatial Information in the European Community. This became EU law in 2007 and member states had to transpose it into their own laws by 2009.[15] The driver behind this directive was to enable policies and activities that impact on the environment to be presented using spatial data held by public authorities. As was discussed previously, a 2003 EU directive gives the public access to environmental information. The usefulness of such information is greatly improved if it is presented in spatial form. For example, this enables the areas and properties affected by environmental policies and activities to be identified, such as which properties are in areas at high risk of flooding. The directive provides for certain spatial data to be provided to the public free of charge. It is brought into effect by Implementing Rules in the form of legally binding decisions in areas such as metadata, the interoperability of datasets, and data and service sharing.

The data affected by the INSPIRE Directive is listed in three annexes, with member states having to create metadata for the first two annexes by 2011 and for the third by 2014. Metadata is defined by the directive as including conformity of the spatial data sets with the implementing rules; conditions of access to and use of spatial data; the quality and validity of spatial data sets; the public authorities responsible for the establishment, maintenance and distribution of spatial data; and limitations on public access and the reasons for this. Annex I includes coordinate references systems, geographical grid systems, administrative units, addresses,

13. Grover, R. (2006) *European Union accession and land tenure data in Central and Eastern Europe*, Land Tenure Studies 1, Food and Agriculture Organization of the United Nations, Rome.

14. NAO (2006) *Department for Environment, Food and Rural Affairs and Rural Payments Agency: The Delays in Administering the 2005 Single Payment Scheme for England*, U.K. National Audit Office, Report by the Comptroller and Auditor General, House of Commons HC 1631 Session 2005-2006, 18 October 2006.

15. Directive 2007/2/EC of 14 March 2007.

and cadastral parcels. Annex II includes elevation, land cover, orthoimagery, and geology. Annex III includes statistical units, soil, land use, human health and safety, utilities and government services, environmental monitoring, demography, agriculture, production, meteorological and oceanographical features, atmosphere conditions, natural risk zones, habitats, biotopes and species distribution, and energy and mineral distribution. Data necessary for national defense and security or the course of justice, is commercially confidential, or is concerned with personal data can be protected from public access.

A particular point of controversy concerns whether this data should be made available for free. Clearly there are commercial bodies that would wish to use it as the basis for creating proprietary systems for which they would charge users. Similarly, environmental activists and interest groups want access to the data without charge. The directive does allow member states to levy some charges but there are substantial differences between the countries in the EU as to how they fund the maintenance of geospatial databases. In a number of the countries, the national cadastre and the national mapping agency receive public funding for their work. Their argument is that the data generated has been paid for by the public and should therefore be made available free of charge

to the public. Users do pay search fees and those wishing to change the base map, for example, by sub-dividing a property, are faced with the cost of employing a licensed surveyor. In the U.K. bodies like the Ordnance Survey operate as public trading bodies. Their funding mainly comes from the sale of information to users. It raises important questions about the extent to which spatial data should be regarded as a public good and to what extent the public bodies that generate it should be able to profit from their monopoly of this data.[16] It includes deciding how much processing of data public bodies should undertake when releasing data. For example, should a map be made freely available or just the base geo-reference codes? This is particularly pertinent as bodies like Ordnance Survey are potential candidates for privatization.

There is a potential conflict between the U.K. government's policy of openness in data, strongly supported by EU law, and the government's desire to exploit the commercial benefits of intellectual property rights over data created by public bodies to recoup costs from the users of this data rather than the taxpayer. The competition authorities in the U.K. have also been concerned about the monopoly public bodies have over certain types of data, including geo-data, and its potential harmful effects on business.[17] However, reliance on fee income does

tend to make such bodies sensitive to the needs of their customers. The provision of geo-data is also becoming increasingly contestable as private companies like Google develop their spatial information systems. The government is aware of conflicts in its own policy.[18] A consequence has been that Ordnance Survey data has been made more widely available to public and educational bodies and it has been encouraging bodies from the public and voluntary sectors to examine ways of adding value to its data.

Whilst the EU sets a *minimum* set of requirements for a country to comply with European environmental law, an individual country's needs for spatial information are likely to go beyond these requirements, for example to include land registration, traffic management or property valuation. This led the U.K. to adopt a location strategy in 2008.[19] The government's vehicle for achieving this has been the local authorities. Central government is able to exercise a strong influence over local authorities as approximately half of the local authorities' income comes in the form of central government grants, much of which are for specific activities. The logic behind using local authorities is that they are town-planning authorities responsible for granting planning consent for changes of use, for new development, and for alterations to existing buildings. They are responsible for the compilation

16. Coopers & Lybrand (1996) *Economic aspects of the collection, dissemination and integration of government's geospatial information, A report arising from work carried out for Ordnance Survey by Coopers and Lybrand*, May 1996, available from http://www.ordnancesurvey.co.uk/oswebsite/aboutus/reports/coopers/index.html.
17. U.K. Office of Fair Trading (2006) *The commercial use of public information (CUPI)*, OFT861, December 2006.
18. U.K. Department of Communities and Local Government (2009) *Policy options for geographic information from Ordnance Survey Consultation*, December 2009.
19. U.K. Department of Communities and Local Government (2008) *op.cit.*

of and maintenance of the register of electors and for the collection of property taxes. This unique position makes local authorities ideal custodians of the National Land and Property Gazetteer. Local authorities have the statutory responsibility to name streets and to number them. Each property is given a Unique Property Reference Number. The Gazetteer is continually maintained and users receive a daily update. In order to ensure that addresses and the identification of properties is done consistently, the British Standards Institution has developed a standard to which local authorities must conform, BS 7666:2006, *Spatial datasets for geographical referencing*. Part of this is based upon a European and International standard, BS EN ISO 19112, *Geographic information—Spatial referencing by geographic identifiers*, but BS 7666 goes beyond these in setting out the requirements for a national gazetteer.

The government has also supported local authorities in a digital mapping initiative. This has enabled local authorities to provide online access for the public to large scale Ordnance Survey maps in which different types of information can be accessed as a series of layers. This includes the public bodies and electoral areas in which a property is located, where the nearest public services are located, small area statistics from the census, listed buildings and protected trees, and planning histories. These bring together databases from both central and local government bodies, exploiting the potential of the Ordnance Survey's Master Map and the National Land and Property Gazetteer.

Openness versus privacy in public data

The data collected by public bodies includes a great deal of material that most individuals would regard as being confidential. Governments collect information about our incomes, wealth and tax affairs, our health, our finances, family matters, housing, and who we communicate with, amongst other matters. Generally we accept that the collection of such data is necessary in the public interest, for example, for national security or to finance public services, or because we benefit from its use in the provision of public services such as healthcare. That does not mean that we have given informed consent to such data being made public. For some groups in society, children being a prime example, there is a question as to whether they have the capacity to give informed consent about the release of data about them. If public data is to be made generally available, it is important that safeguards are put in place to protect individual privacy.

These issues traditionally have been addressed by the British government in two ways. The first has been to place a time limit on the period before there can be public access to records containing data about individuals. This is set at 100 years. Therefore, for example, 2012 saw the full release of data from the 1911 census, though some elements have been available since the beginning of 2011. Policy and other confidential documents for government, such as cabinet minutes, are generally released after 30 years, though they can be held for longer for reasons of national security or because of their potential impact on living individuals. For small area statistics from census enumeration districts, there is a danger that individuals could be identified; for example, the only person living in the district who is a university graduate. The device that has been adopted has been to randomise data between districts in order to protect the privacy of individuals without compromising the integrity of the dataset.

Many countries have privacy laws that specifically protect data relating to individuals, and the use of public data must clearly respect these. In Europe, the ultimate protection of privacy is the European Convention on Human Rights.[20] Article 8 states that everyone has the right to respect for private and family life, home and correspondence. Ultimately a person can apply to the European Court of Human Rights in Strasbourg for judgement once all national legal remedies have been exhausted. In the U.K. there is further protection of personal data in the form of the Data Protection Act 1998. The act requires organisations which possess personal information to abide by certain principles. These include only processing the information for the limited purposes for which it has been collected, to process it fairly and lawfully, to maintain accuracy, to keep it secure, not to keep it for longer than is necessary and not to

20. Council of Europe (1950) *The European Convention on Human Rights*, Rome 4 November 1950.

transfer it to other countries without adequate protection. These legal provisions also apply to data collected by researchers. It is unlawful to disclose personal information knowingly or recklessly without the consent of the organisation holding the information; in other words, for individuals working for an organisation to pass this information on to third parties. Individuals have the right to access data held about them and to correct errors. There are some restrictions, for example, if the information is subject to a criminal investigation. The act is policed by the Information Commissioner. The Commissioner has recently expressed concern about breaches of privacy by private investigators and the press and about the trade in personal information, and has proposed changing the offences in law and increasing penalties.[21] This, and some recent high profile blunders by public bodies in losing information stored on disks, could well to lead to greater protection of personal data.

Conclusions

Public data contains a wealth of material of great value to individuals, businesses and researchers if it is organized geospatially. This is not an easy task as public bodies organize their databases differently. This includes using different ways of geo-referencing data, such as addresses, postcodes and grid references. The first essential step towards the exploitation of public data is to bring it together within a single geo-reference system. In countries with cadastres, the cadastre can be used for this purpose. In those without cadastres, like the U.K., a point based system can be used in which reference objects are plotted. In both cases the base map needs to be linked to a national gazetteer of place names, addresses and postcodes if it is to be effective. There are important financial issues that need to be resolved, particularly about how national mapping agencies are to be funded. If they are funded through government grant, then the base mapping data can be made available free. If a cost recovery model is used in which users fund the service through charges, then it is difficult to see how the base mapping data can be given away.

Openness and transparency in government are generally regarded as being desirable and this extends to access to public data. Without such access it is difficult to see how governments can be held to account unless there is independent verification of the consequences of their policies. This has tended to be the driver towards freedom of information policies. A further factor has been changes in the way in which public services are delivered, the so-called New Public Management. The greater power that these policies give to front-line staff requires greater openness about the performance of these services. For the 28 countries of the European Union, the development of the internal market has produced a pan-European policy of disclosure of environmental information and the mapping systems needed to interpret it. There is also pressure to reduce the amount of geo-referenced data in the form of the use of sampling to produce data available in real time and at lower cost rather than census-type surveys of an entire population. Whilst greater openness in public data is generally desirable, individuals value their privacy. Safeguards include time limits before individual data is made available to the public and the use of randomization in small area statistics. Some countries have privacy laws that protect individuals from having data relating to them being disclosed. A balance has to be struck between the public and private interests involved.

Richard Grover teaches property economics and valuations at Oxford Brookes University, U.K., where he has worked for 25 years. Before retiring he was assistant dean of the School of Built Environment. He is a chartered surveyor and is particularly interested in property rights and in the development of transition economies.

21. Information Commissioner's Office (2006) *What price privacy? The unlawful trade in confidential personal information*, ordered to be published by the House of Commons 10 May 2006, The Stationery Office, London, HC 1056; Information Commissioner's Office (2006) *What price privacy? The first six months in halting the unlawful trade in confidential personal information*, ordered to be published by the House of Commons 13 December 2006, The Stationery Office, London, HC 36.

The Two-Edged Sword of Administratively Derived Data in Sub-Saharan Africa (SSA)

Karol C. Boudreaux

Much of the social landscape we in the developed world take for granted is built on a foundation of information, and much of this information is administratively derived. This data supports trade and investment and in turn, economic growth and entrepreneurship. It reduces risks and uncertainty and helps reduce the likelihood that conflict escalates to violence. This information also helps to limit degradation associated with conflict over resources/assets.

Administratively derived data is a double-edged sword. Consider information related to real property: while it may provide useful information and dependable evidence of location, value, ownership and subsidiary rights, it provides a basis for taxation and can also be used to support predatory actions by public and private-sector actors. Aggregating data in the hands of a corrupt or predatory centralized authority can make it easier for that authority to use information to harm political, economic or other enemies.

In sub-Saharan Africa (SSA), the sword of administratively derived data (ADD) mostly cuts (or people believe it cuts) in this undesirable direction. The persistence of high levels of legal informality reflects a combination of high transactions costs (resulting from corruption, costly regulatory structures and lack of capacity) and a deep mistrust of government ministries to use information for good. As a result, the scope, the reliability/trustworthiness, and the usefulness of ADD is lower in SSA than in most other regions, which frustrates economic growth and exacerbates a host of conflicts.

Recognizing these constraints, it would be useful to identify effective strategies that capture data in ways that are least harmful/most useful to the citizenry. One recent approach, taken by many SSA officials with strong backing from donor agencies and MFIs, has been to implement policies and legislation designed to improve formal-sector land administration and land-use planning. Results of these efforts are mixed and even in "good" property environments informality remains a significant challenge (i.e., South Africa). *De jure* laws are only as good as enforcement mechanisms permit and enforcement (whether in courts, by officials, or by police) remains a troublesome weak link in most of SSA.

This means that much data, particularly property data, remains in private hands—notably in the hands of traditional or customary authorities who continue to allocate use rights to property in SSA (in some urban and many rural areas). Data held by these authorities is rarely "collected" and it is not broadly dispersed. It may be accessible for community members but is accessible to most outsiders only at high cost. Thus a challenge facing citizens and officials in SSA is how best to integrate the enormous quantities of community-derived data (CDD) held by traditional/customary authorities and community members with public and private-sector formal data systems.

Community mapping efforts, community-led slum upgrading, paralegal surveying and NGO-led dispute resolution mechanisms are among the ways being used to gather and feed CDD to official sources for use in administration and planning. However, in countries where the rule of law is limited and where transaction costs remain high, concerns over the potential harm—intended or unintended—of such efforts remain.

Across SSA, companies, individuals, and investment funds have been on a buying spree.[1] The desired good is not one of the traditional African commodities—minerals, coffee or cocoa—but instead the land that supplies these and other resources. Investors, both foreign and domestic, are acquiring land in Mali, Mozambique, South Sudan, Tanzania, the DRC and Ethiopia, among others. A key driver for these acquisitions is high food prices in 2008 and again in 2010/11. High food prices led to social unrest and rioting in some countries and changes of political leadership in others, but these prices also encourage investors to look for land for commercial agricultural development. Some acquisitions are relatively small; for instance, a former cabinet minister in Tanzania

has been accused of wrongly gaining occupancy rights over 100 hectares.[2] However, other allocations are massive. In Sudan, U.S.-based Nile Trading and Development acquired a 49-year lease for 600,000 hectares for the equivalent of $25,000 with an option to acquire an additional 400,000 hectares.[3] Only recently, following independence from the government of Sudan, have community leaders in South Sudan been able to reject this transaction.[4]

These large-scale land acquisitions are routinely labeled "grabs," and most are painted as unconscionable and implicitly illegal transactions that benefit a few privileged and well-connected individuals and threaten many less powerful and poor communities.

The problem of land grabbing is just one manifestation of a troubled land environment. In Eastern DRC, militia fight over access to mineral-rich lands, which pushes villagers (often already displaced by long years of fighting) off lands. In the Sahel, farmers kill pastoralists in spasms of cyclical violence based in part on ethnic and/ or religious antagonism and in part on fierce competition over access to fertile lands, pastures and water sources. Across Africa, even in countries that have formal laws to protect women's property rights, widows and divorced women face a different kind

of land grabbing as families of deceased or divorced husbands throw them off the land they depend upon to support themselves and their children. And in rapidly urbanizing African cities, people looking for economic opportunity crowd into informal settlements that offer few public goods or services and little in the way of security.

These are not isolated phenomena; instead, they represent the fractured, troubled state of land and property relations in much of SSA. Rampant insecurity drives violent conflict across SSA; it limits economic growth and efforts to improve food security by creating disincentives for some investments and by destroying existing infrastructure; it frustrates the development of a rule of law because burdensome regulations and confusions provide myriad opportunities for corrupt officials (who prefer a status quo where rights are unclear and, hence, exploitable) to seek bribes, curry favor, reward friends and families, and frustrate justice.[5] In these ways and more, the land environment increases human suffering and misery.

In order to overcome these challenges, governments in SSA need to address problems that include: poorly functioning land administration systems, complex and contradictory legal and regulatory frameworks, few trained property

1. Klaus Deininger, "Rising Global Interest in Farmland," *The World Bank*, 2011.
2. Lucas Linganga, "MPs Accuse Ex-Presidents over Land-Grabbing," *The Citizen*, 15 August 2011, available at: http://allafrica.com/stories/201108170003.html.
3. "Understanding Land Investment Deals in Africa: Nile Trading and Development Inc. in South Sudan," *Oakland Institute*, Land Deal Brief (June, 2011), available at: http://media.oaklandinstitute.org/sites/oaklandinstitute.org/files/OI_Nile_Brief_0.pdf.
4. Waakhe Simon Wudu, "Mokaya-Payam Leaders Reject 600,000 Ha Land Lease," *Gurtong*, 15 August, 2011, Available at: http://www.gurtong.net/ECM/Editorial/tabid/124/ctl/ArticleView/mid/519/articleId/5582/Mokaya-Payam-Leaders-Reject-600000Ha-Land-Lease.aspx.
5. Jina Moore, "Africa's Continental Divide: Land Disputes," Christian Science Monitor, 30 January, 2010, available at: http://www.csmonitor.com/World/Africa/2010/0130/Africa-s-continental-divide-land-disputes.

professionals, vested interests opposed to change, ineffective and overwhelmed dispute resolution mechanisms, and a lack of functioning interface between the customary property institutions that serves most Africans and the formal *de jure* system.

The traditional approach to dealing with these problems has been to focus on modernizing that *de jure* land administration system. Over the past decade numerous donors including, but not limited to, the World Bank, USAID, UN-HABITAT, the FAO, the Inter-American Development Bank, DFID and SIDA (the Swedish aid agency) have spent hundreds of millions of dollars to help African countries build land administration institutions, train officials, provide equipment to map and survey lands, craft land policies, and revise land laws and implementing regulations. Less attention has been paid to supporting or strengthening customary land institutions as it was thought that these institutions needed to be replaced by more modern formal systems designed to identify, value and record land rights and resolve land disputes. However, building formal land administration systems has proved to be a contentious, time consuming and costly process. It is fair to say that no country in SSA, not even South Africa, has a fully effective land administration system.[6]

Donors and development experts underestimated the difficulties involved in either merging two disparate systems or in replacing the older, traditional system with a foreign modern system.

If the idea was to promote development, the strategy was to provide the institutions poorer countries needed to become wealthier. A bit of humility and a better sense of history might have alerted people to the fact that in Europe very similar social engineering projects proved extremely difficult to manage. James C. Scott writes of the European process of attaching every parcel of taxable property to an individual or institution responsible for paying for it:

"As straightforward as this procedure seems in the context of the modern state, its achievement was enormously difficult for at least two reasons. First, the actual practices of customary land tenure were frequently so varied and intricate as to defy any one-to-one equation of taxpayer and taxable property. And second, as was the case with standardizing measurement, there were social forces whose interests could be damaged by the unified and transparent set of property relations desired by the state's fiscal agents."[7]

This description of early modern Europe is a surprisingly apt description of the contemporary land tenure and property rights environment in SSA. Only recently has it become more common for donors to support efforts to bridge the knowledge and enforcement gaps that exist between the formal and the informal systems. Building these bridges, while admittedly arduous, is important

for several reasons. First, customary systems provide the rules, norms and enforcement apparatus for property relations for most people living in SSA. Dismantling these institutions would be hugely disruptive without a) an effective, respected replacement—which does not currently exist in most countries—and b) capturing the deep knowledge they represent. Second, despite their shortcomings, these customary systems provide accessible and efficient access to justice. And third, again despite their shortcomings, these systems are recognized as legitimate authority by most people living in SSA. The state, too, often predatory in much of SSA, is often not viewed as legitimate and hence is less capable of directing positive social outcomes.

Rather than rejecting customary systems and institutions out of hand in favor of western-style formal land systems and institutions, it will be more appropriate in Africa (and elsewhere) to work to capture local knowledge and build on the efficient elements of these institutions in order to increase stability and security—particularly for rural citizens. This is an essential (though certainly not sufficient) step in the direction of improving administratively derived data collection in Africa because without such bridges the vast quantities of community-derived, community-controlled data that exist in SSA will not be captured, except perhaps notionally, by the formal sector. The goal should be to create a

---

6. Karol C. Boudreaux, "The Legal Empowerment of the Poor: Titling and Poverty Alleviation in Post-Apartheid South Africa," *Hasting Race and Poverty Law Journal* (Spring/Summer, 2008).

7. James C. Scott, *Seeing Like a State: How Certain Schemes to Improve the Human Condition Have Failed*, (1998): 33.

marriage between formal and customary, a union greater than the sum of its parts that builds on the best elements of each. How to arrange the marriage, and how to help the spouses learn each other's language, will vary from country to country.

Complexities and confusions in the African land environment

Before colonial powers arrived in Africa, land relations were governed by customary laws and norms. These rules governed how land was allocated, to whom it was allocated, which kinds of transfers (if any) were permissible, and how infractions of rules should be dealt with.

In general terms, lands were acquired by conquest or by clearing virgin lands and turning them into fields, pastures and/or homestead areas. Chiefs and other traditional authorities had and to this day still have the responsibility to allocate lands to members of the clan or group over which they preside. Families would be given lands according to recognized needs. Some lands would be set aside as communal grazing lands or other community purposes (sacred groves, forested areas). Some lands would be given by husbands to wives as their "property" which they could use to support themselves and their children.

On a single piece of land different resources might well have different owners. For example, on a family plot, the husband might have rights to plow and plant a staple crop and to lend the land (for this purpose) to others. The wife might have rights to collect any branches

or dung on the land for use as household fuel. Migratory pastoralists might have negotiated temporary use rights to graze their animals on the stubble left after harvest. Other members of the community might have rights to collect any fruit growing on fruit trees on the plot, and the chief might have retained rights to reallocate the plot if the family was perceived to be neglecting or otherwise not making good use of the land. This customary system provided for a variety of primary, secondary and tertiary rights, some of which were tradable to others.

The distinguishing feature of this system is that lands were typically not individualized into private property along the lines of fee simple or freehold tenure systems. Instead, communities/clans controlled lands jointly; they jointly managed common resources such as pasture lands, water and forests. And they allowed for leasing of lands, lending of lands, mortgaging in some cases and transfers through inheritance. In areas where lands became scarce, and hence more valuable, some communities did move to create more individualized rights to land: 19th century Lagos is one example today, where informal privatization occurs when farmers or herders fence "their" lands to keep others out. These customary systems were flexible and evolved to meet the changing needs of community members.

Africa is a land abundant continent and given the ready supply of land in most areas—at least until relatively recently—it is understandable that a communal land system developed and persists. When

colonial powers arrived in the 19th century they responded to this system either by attempting to replace it with European-style formal civil code to address land relations or by creating a bifurcated system that created new legislation, rules and court systems for white settlers (typically white settlers could acquire freehold rights) but that recognized that customary rules and institutions applied to land relations among black Africans. Local chiefs or headmen were allowed to continue allocating lands and resolving disputes.

This broadly describes the indirect rule system imposed in British colonies, while the French tended to adopt a direct rule strategy. In neither case were the colonial powers successful at modernizing or eliminating the customary system so that after the wave of independence in the 1950s and '60s African countries typically had two distinct sets of laws for dealing with land: a colonial-era set of statutes, regulations and institutions (including registries, courts and land administration ministries) and a diverse set of customary, "informal" institutions for most black citizens. As Scott notes (describing Europe):

> "Administratively, of course, such a cacophony of local property regulations would be a nightmare. The nightmare is experienced not by those whose particular practices are being represented but by those state officials who aspire to a uniform, homogenous, national administrative code … Accommodating the luxuriant variety of customary land tenure was simply inconceivable."[8]

---

8. Ibid., 35-36.

The European solution, Scott argues, was the "heroic simplification" of freehold tenure. This simplification was carried by the Europeans to Africa; however, it takes a strong centralized state with a will to act to impose the simplification, and in general terms, African countries have lacked the capacity, the resources, and the will to act.

Indeed, after independence the bifurcated property environment continued: the new political elites often found it convenient to limit access to freehold lands (which they could control) and powerful rural elites benefited from retaining control over land allocations. Complicating matters, in the 1970s and '80s a large number of SSA countries nationalized land, making the government or president the radical title holder of all lands in trust for the citizenry.[9] This arrangement continues to this day in many countries, which means that in most SSA countries there are now layers of laws, some contradictory, that apply to land relations. There are still colonial-era laws on the books, customary law applies in many areas, in some countries shari'a law applies to some property transactions, newer post-colonial laws revise and modify older rules, and international and regional commitments (such as the Convention on the Elimination of all Forms of Discrimination against Women/CEDAW) create other obligations.

In all countries formal land administration systems are challenged. Given the rampant poverty of most countries few domestic resources are available to build and maintain land registries or cadastres, record keeping is poor, there are few trained professionals, corruption is rampant, and formal transactions are costly, time consuming and often inaccessible to the poor. Land use planning is minimal to non-existent. Building regulation can be excessively burdensome. Little in the way of formal land markets exist. This contributes to a situation in which claims over land can be difficult to verify or enforce. Lack of clarity means that land relations are often the source of insecurity, confusion and conflict that ravages the African landscapes and Africa's communities.

The double-edged sword and informality

People living in developed nations experience an almost magical world of instantaneous communication, of vast and efficient trade with neighbors and strangers, of relative peace and stability, of cultural exchange that exposes us to the products and artifacts of lands near and distant, and of routine interaction with public sector projects designed to promote health, education, safety and a host of other activities.

A part of the magic that we tend to take for granted is the system of land administration that makes it possible for us to identify, with a strong degree of certainty, who owns which pieces of land, where the boundaries to the land are, who has which rights over that land (mortgagors, easement holders, lien holders, etc.) and the approximate market value of land. The administratively derived data generated by this system is of inestimable value. This system, developed over the course of centuries, allows us to buy, sell or lease land with a large degree of confidence that what we transfer is lawfully transferred. This security encourages us to develop the land in ways that we find most appealing/profitable (putting regulatory considerations to one side) because secure property owners are able to reap the benefits of investments. It allows us to leverage our ownership rights to access credit and it allows us to bequeath land to family, conservation trusts, or to others whom we favor. Because of this nearly invisible infrastructure we avoid the kinds of violent conflict, environmental degradation and lack of investment that so frustrates and limits development in SSA.

Administratively derived data is a double-edged sword. The kinds of data produced and managed by a land administration system is extremely useful for buyers, sellers, creditors and for various levels of government for a variety of purposes (taxation, land use planning, extending or providing services, etc.). It provides dependable evidence of location, value, ownership and subsidiary rights, all of which supports a well-functioning land market, helps reduce conflict over land, and helps direct investments in productive ways. However, this data also supplies a basis for a number of centralized government activities, and this presents a problem in many developing countries.

For several reasons people in SSA tend not to use the formal

---

9. Karol C. Boudreaux, "Urbanisation and Informality and in Africa's Housing Markets," *Economic Affairs* 28, no. 2, (2008): 20.

land administration systems that create administratively derived data. Why? First, formal land administration systems are costly to use and do not provide sufficient benefits to justify incurring these costs.[10] Particularly for the poor, these costs are prohibitive and so they typically opt to transfer urban property informally. In rural areas, unless decentralized and low-cost options for registering land tenure rights exist, few rural people register.[11]

As the World Bank reports in its 2011 *Doing Business* study, the costs of formally registering property in SSA are substantial. To sum up the most recent findings, formal transfers require applicants, on average, to follow seven steps (compared to five steps in OECD countries); to complete these steps it takes on average 68 days (compared to 33 days in OECD countries); and the cost of the transfer is, on average 9.6 percent of the value of the property (the highest of any region). Formal regulatory requirements make the cost of transferring property through government channels high as do "[h]igh transfer taxes (averaging 7 percent of the property value) and high professional fees, such as for lawyers and notaries."[12] And of course, once property is formally registered the government then has a basis for taxing the owner. Many people avoid formalizing property in order to avoid the tax liabilities associated with formalization.

The *Doing Business* study further notes that:

"[a] cumbersome system can create opportunities for corruption. In Kenya in 2010 a raid uncovered thousands of land files locked in the drawers of public officials hoping to collect bribes."[13] The costs associated with bribery are not captured by the study, but obviously, they would add to the costs of an already costly system. Other costs include the need to travel to complete the various steps and obstacles associated with dealing with official forms that may need to be completed in a language that some citizens do not speak (and so require finding or hiring someone to complete).

In many cases, the benefits of formalization that exist in the developed world do not exist in SSA. It might be worthwhile to formalize rights if formalization provided you with increased access to credit, but for the poor and for rural citizens this is simply not the case. Likewise, it might be worth the expense and trouble of formalizing property if by doing so your property was then linked to the provision of services such as electricity, water or sanitation. Again, this is rarely the case. Formalizing rights may create tax liabilities but it does not guarantee service provision in countries where infrastructure and resources are lacking. For less powerful and less educated citizens, formalization may create additional risks of losing lands if educated elites are better positioned to challenge land claims (a common criticism of Kenya's

efforts to formalize land rights). Formalization might actually harm secondary and tertiary rights holders, such as women and pastoralists for whom formalization might lead to an outright loss of traditional use rights. And finally, even if the costs of formally registering property are low enough that people act, it is not necessarily the case that they will record subsequent transfers. Taken together, these concerns limit the use of the systems and so limit the quality and quantity of administratively derived land data.

Furthermore, in the wrong hands, this kind of data can be used for predatory purposes. Aggregating data in the hands of a corrupt or predatory centralized authority can make it easier for that authority to use information to harm political, economic or other enemies. When governments know where people live, governments can find people and inflict a host of harms. Such concerns rise in environments where the rule of law and good governance are in short supply.

This is not to say that the situation is entirely bleak. Since at least the 1990s, more than 20 African countries have recognized the limitations of their land administration systems and have been working with donors to improve this important sector. Key reforms have focused on decentralizing formal land administration and land management services to

---

10. These costs ARE coming down but they still remain high compared to more developed regions of the world. *Doing Business 2011: Making a Difference for Entrepreneurs*, World Bank/IFC (2010): 33-34.
11. Because most rural land remains under customary tenure rural residents would be likely to register (assuming legislation exists that permits this) rights to occupy and use land. A number of countries now have projects to register these kinds of customary land rights (Ethiopia, Uganda, Tanzania, among others).
12. *Doing Business*, 34.
13. Ibid, 34.

the regional and, in some cases, local level and on creating new land policies and laws.[14] The movement to decentralize land administration and management services represents an attempt to bring the services to rural Africans in hopes of increasing the degree of formalization of property relations. Decentralization may lower costs for service users but countries need resources to staff and operate decentralized facilities. If officials in decentralized offices are incompetent or corrupt, and if costs of formalization remain high, the benefits of decentralization are limited.

An example of a successful decentralized system comes from Botswana where, starting in 1970, the government created and has iteratively modified Land Boards. These boards (there are Main Boards and Local Boards) are comprised of elected community members and government appointees who are empowered to make decisions related to customary and non-customary land rights and to resolve land disputes. Board members have age and education/training requirements to better ensure appropriate service.[15] As over 70 percent of the land area of Botswana is held under customary tenure rules, Land Boards play an extremely important role in allocating

lands, registering claims and rights, and capturing local-level data about control of lands and availability of land-based resources.[16] Although it has taken decades for these boards to mature, and although resource constraints continue to create challenges for effective management, Botswana's Land Boards have been called the most "judiciously administered" in Africa and an important source of good governance.[17]

Unfortunately, the Botswana experience of developing effective Land Boards has not been widely replicated, nor have urban informal settlements been effectively demarcated and rights registered. Though figures are difficult to find for SSA, experts suggest that "only about thirty percent of land (in the developing world) is covered by some form of land registration system. It will take centuries to get full coverage in a large number of countries."[18] Slum upgrading is proving to be a painfully slow process. And so it remains the case that much of the information concerning land relations in SSA remains in the hands of private actors, chiefs, housing lords and others who speak a customary or informal language of rights allocations and conflict resolution. Finding ways to translate this customary language so that

people within the formal sector can develop a stronger and deeper understanding remains a challenge.

Community-derived data in Africa

What options exist to begin the translation process? As noted previously, over the past decade donors have spent more time considering how to work with, rather than against, customary land systems.[19] Two interesting options include participatory community mapping efforts (sometimes used in conjunction with paralegal services to register rights) and the Social Tenure Domain Model, designed to capture the complex relationships that exist in customary systems between people and resources. These approaches provide methods for capturing and retaining valuable community-level, community-derived data. Once captured, this data can subsequently be transferred into a formal system to formalize rights and to create a more accurate sense of on-the-ground realities in land relations.

Community (or participatory) mapping can be high tech or low tech. Low-tech approaches may involve community members coming together with a facilitator or on their own, to produce a map of land boundaries and land relations

14. Liz Alden Wily, "A Review of Decentralisation of Land Administration and Management in Africa," *International Institute for Environment and Development*, (2003), available at: http://pubs.iied.org/pdfs/9304IIED.pdf.
15. Martin Adams, Faustin Kalabamu and Richard White, "Land Tenure Policy and Practice in Botswana: Governance lessons for Southern Africa," Austrian Journal of Development Studies, XIX, no. 1 (2003): 59, available at: http://www.scribd.com/doc/9162130/Land-Tenure-Policy-and-Practice-in-Botswana.
16. Emmanuel Tembo and Julian V. Semela, "Improving Land Information Management in tribal lands of Botswana," Paper presented at the Expert Group Meeting on secure land tenure: `new legal frameworks and tools,' UN-GIRIRI Nairobi 10-12 November, 2004: 3, available at: http://www.fig.net/commission7/nairobi_2004/papers/ts_07_3_tembo_simela.pdf.
17. Adams, Kalabamu, and White, 66.
18. Jaap Zevenbergen, "A Pro-Poor Land Recordation System; Towards a Design," (April 25, 2011): 5, available at: http://www.gltn.net/en/home/land-information-management/towards-a-design-for-a-pro-poor-land-recordation-system/details.html.
19. For example, USAID currently has several projects in SSA that adopt this approach (Kenya, South Sudan and Liberia).

based on the consensus of participants. In the past maps have been hand-drawn but today, as the costs of using technology fall, more communities mark maps produced using Google Earth or other accessible printed or digital maps. As noted in a recent International Lands Coalition report:

"Community mapping methods are applications driven. They are pragmatic and opportunistic combinations of traditional and Western technology and practices, guided by considerations of what works, what is available, and what can be afforded … community mapping may perversely entail the deliberate scaling down of mapping technologies localizing and simplifying them as to make them accessible to community mapping groups."[20]

Increasingly, however, and in some cases with the support of non-governmental organizations, civil society organizations and/or donors, communities are supplementing this low-tech mapping approach with Global Positioning Systems (GPS) devices and compass binoculars.[21] Although not ideal, GPS devices are low cost and allow communities to identify boundaries quickly and with some degree of reliability. And some communities are able to adopt computer mapping which allows for greater

precision in terms of boundary demarcation, but at higher cost and requiring more investments in training and skills building (though costs and accessibility of these technologies continue to fall).

Once these maps are produced, communities in some countries (Bolivia, Nicaragua, Ethiopia and Madagascar, among others) have been able to use the information to secure land tenure rights. The process of coming to consensus around boundary issues and making such agreements public can also help to decrease local conflict. And finally, community-mapping efforts allow governments to gain access to previously opaque data. Although the data may quickly become outdated (if subsequent allocations/transfers are not recorded) the benefit of having at worst a one-time snap-shot of an area and at best new, useful information may help to support some economic growth by increasing security and reducing conflict.

Alternately, the Social Tenure Domain Model (STDM) is a relatively new tool that captures community-level data but would be managed by formal land administration offices/ministries *in collaboration with* local communities. As described by Christiaan Lemmen, the STDM:

"Allows for the recordation of all possible types of tenure; STDM enables to show what can be observed on the ground in terms of

tenure as agreed within local communities [*sic*]. This agreement counts as evidence from the field."[22]

STDM is a variation on a theme: it provides a harmonized/standardized methodology to capture the continuum of customary land rights that are recognized by community-derived data. Because the data that is collected in the field is in a standard form, it can more easily be integrated by the formal land administration system.[23] The system, developed by UN-HABITAT, is flexible and can be modified to meet the needs of particular countries or even sub-units.

The process begins when a community works with a facilitator to identify, on a high-resolution satellite image, a parcel index map by drawing parcel boundaries onto the image. This data is verified in the field by rights' claimants and local officials. The modified image is scanned and vectorized to produce identifiers after which personal data, such as fingerprints or photographs, can be linked to the maps. This information is then brought before the community for public review and approval. This process creates "an inventory of informal rights" and may point the way to help policy makers identify best "next steps" for improving the formal system to better serve the needs of customary rights holders.[24] As exciting as this

---

20. Stefano di Gessa, "Participatory Mapping as a Tool for Empowerment: Experiences and Lessons learned from the ILC Network," *International Land Coalition* (2008): 5.
21. Ibid, 5.
22. Christiaan Lemmen, "The Social Tenure Domain Model: A Pro-Poor Land Took," *International Federation of Surveyors, Global Land Tool Network & UN-HABITAT*, (2010): 5.
23. Ibid, 7.
24. Ibid, 15.

development is, there is an obvious constraint: the process is only as good and as trustworthy as the information that is poured into it and in some cases, creating greater transparency around land relations will be an unwelcome change. For example, in Ghana, chiefs and other traditional authorities benefit from insecurity in the customary system. As Sandra Joireman reports:

"Customary leaders can play a role in resolving land disputes that arise, but they can also be the cause of disputes. A lack of clarity regarding both boundaries and responsibilities within the customary system makes it possible for chiefs and sub-chiefs to sell the same plot. When land becomes valuable, these chiefs are all interested in exercising their rights of sale, which sometimes conflict."[25]

While most people living under customary land tenure regimes want security to promote stability, peace and economic growth, some prefer insecurity because it provides opportunities for personal enrichment. Similarly, while most citizens have a strong preference for an efficient and low-cost formal land administration system, unwieldy and opaque systems, whose mysteries must be mediated by the intercessions of lawyers, notaries and bureaucrats, benefit those particular high priests and so they resist change.

Conclusion

Where does this leave us? Traditional Western-style systematic surveying and registration managed by centralized land administration authorities in partnership with the private sector will remain, for the foreseeable future, an unrealistic model in most of SSA. However, without the data that such systems produce, SSA countries, and therefore their citizens, will face real constraints growing their economies and increasing investments in sectors such as agriculture. Conflicts related to land and land-based resources are likely to continue as is the resource degradation that follows from such conflicts.

A workaround is clearly needed. This may entail identifying and making much broader use of lower-cost, accessible alternatives that recognize the complex nature of land relations in SSA. Happily, as the cost of technology falls and as new, innovative models such as the STDM come off the shelves, this strategy becomes more of a reality. And this reality, one in which community-derived data is captured so that it can be recognized by national governments in the form of land tenure and property rights that are respected and enforced is an important step in the direction of a more peaceful and prosperous Africa.

Karol C. Boudreaux is currently Director, Investments in Property Rights at the Omidyar Network. Most recently, she was Africa Land Tenure Specialist at USAID. Previously, she was Lead Researcher for Enterprise Africa! and an Instructor at the George Mason University School of Law. Her Juris Doctor is from the University of Virginia.

25. Sandra Joireman, *Where There is No Government: Enforcing Property Rights in Common Law Africa* (2011): 114.

Section 3
Natural Resources, Human Dynamics and Security

WATER INSECURITY, HUMAN DYNAMICS AND COIN IN THE SISTAN BASIN[1]

L.J. Palmer-Moloney
K.U. Duckenfield

"People pursue essential needs until they are met, at any cost and from any source. People support the source that meets their needs."

—*Field Manual 3-24, Paragraph 3-68*

Counterinsurgency (COIN) operations depend upon establishing security among the local populations to ensure stability. Security is most often tied to protection and freedom from danger; however security also includes water security. The focus of coalition efforts has been directed to water availability and infrastructure, yet water security is not only an adequate supply of clean water, but also accessibility so that everyone who needs clean water can obtain enough of it when—and where—they need it. This chapter provides a detailed example of what severe, long-term water insecurity can look like, how people interact with their environment to affect water security, and how closely water insecurity and population instability are linked. Finally, it lays out the role of ensuring water security and population stability in COIN success.

In the Sistan Basin, at the border between Afghanistan (Nimruz Province) and Iran (Sistan and Baluchestan Province), people have struggled to live for the last several hundred years in the face of profound water insecurity. They have responded with many strategies and tried many ways to plan for the challenges this water insecurity brings. But typically, when water becomes scarce, stability is lost. Likewise, when the perception that others are threatening water security arises, conflict follows.

Iran sees current Afghan stabilization and reconstruction efforts—agricultural development and water withdrawal, diversion, and containment projects—in the middle and lower Helmand River watershed as undermining water security in southeastern Iran. The concern is particularly relevant in Sistan and Baluchestan, the most desolate, marginalized and least stable of Iran's provinces. This region's instability is Iran's Achilles' heel, and Iran is sensitive to actions that may undermine its tenuous grasp over it.[2]

Though population dynamics and consumption patterns are at the root of near-term water challenges in both Iran and Afghanistan, changes in climate are expected to exacerbate the situation. Accordingly, U.S. and Afghan efforts to harness or divert water from the Helmand watershed without resolution of the water dispute between Afghanistan and Iran—one that has festered intermittently since 1870—have encouraged Iran to adopt a paradoxical mixed strategy of destabilization and cooperation in Afghanistan. Failure to address water concerns has the potential to

---

1. Public release, distribution unlimited.
2. Dehgan, A.O., L.J. Palmer-Moloney, and M. Mirzaee, "Water Security and Scarcity: Destabilization in Western Afghanistan due to Interstate Water Conflicts", in *Water and Post-Conflict Peacebuilding*, eds. Erika Weinthal, Jessica Troell, and Mikiyasu Nakayama (Earthscan Books: London, in press).

increase tensions between both countries and to slow or prevent stability gains in Afghanistan's southwestern provinces. However, handling water concerns adroitly could encourage closer cooperation on stability and development in Afghanistan, turning challenge into opportunity.

The first section of this chapter lays out the environmental setting and history of water insecurity in the Sistan Basin. This region's environmental history has been dominated by typical inland deltaic processes in an arid to hyperarid climate: the surface water shifts frequently, the soil is very dry and the water supply is highly variable, with both droughts and floods regularly bringing misery. The rural society in this area has changed little in the past several centuries. There is little resilience to cope with hardships: when disaster arrives, crops are lost and animals and people die, or move. Over the centuries, hundreds of villages—even capital cities—and systems of irrigation canals have been abandoned.

The second section discusses human responses to water insecurity in this region, focusing on detailed records covering the period between 1850 and the present. People from both Afghanistan and Iran have organized and worked cooperatively across the border. Customary and governmental systems of behavior have been developed. In bad times, whole cities—on both sides of the border—have

been moved. People have tried time and again to find diplomatic solutions, and they have each used civil and social engineering to try to solve their problems alone. They have squabbled and cheated, burned each other's property, and even attacked each other. A review of the timelines of environmental processes and social dynamics shows that episodes of acute water insecurity reliably precede incidents of unrest, instability and even violence. This trend continues into the present day, with examples as recently as September of this year.

The third section highlights water's role in the COIN environment of Regional Command Southwest (RC-SW—Helmand and Nimruz Provinces). Ten years into operations in Afghanistan, the International Security Assistance Force (ISAF) faces a lack of actionable data that can be used for planning purposes or to guide policy responses to measure the success of counterinsurgency operations. This section spells out how water fits into COIN and describes how water data can serve as "proxy observables" to measure security and stability results of population-centric initiatives in RC-SW.

The fourth and final section highlights ISAF and Government of the Islamic Republic of Afghanistan (GIRoA) water projects on the middle and lower Helmand and their effects on physical and human geographies of the Sistan Basin. Geospatial

support in this data-sparse region is playing a critical role. The historical record suggests that people in the Sistan Basin can make a living, and live amicably with their neighbors across the border, in the absence of an acute water crisis. COIN should therefore pursue increased resilience to water insecurity in this area of Afghanistan.

Part 1: Environmental setting and history of water insecurity

For the past several thousand years people have cultivated land in the Sistan Basin, an arid inland delta region straddling the Iran-Afghanistan border fed by the Helmand River. Evidence of irrigation canals dates back to at least 1300 B.C.[3] Animal husbandry of cattle, sheep, goats, donkeys and camels has also historically been practiced.[4]

This region's environmental history has been dominated by typical deltaic processes in an arid to hyperarid climate (see Figure 1). The channel of the Helmand and its tributaries shift periodically, driven by changes in the upstream water supply, and deposit riverine sediment throughout the basin (see Figure 2). As a result, the surface soil is predominantly fine, and regions of dunes surround the cultivated areas. Water supply is highly variable from year to year, with periods of drought bracketed by flooding events. The Helmand drains into a basin (the Sistan) that in drier years separates into three shallow lakes

3. Whitney, J., *Geology, water, and wind in the Lower Helmand Basin*, Southern Afghanistan. USGS Scientific Investigations Report 2006–5182 (Reston, VA: US Geological Survey, 2006).

4. Whitney, 2006; Tate, G.P., *The Frontiers of Baluchistan* (1909), London; McMahon, A.H., Perso-Afghan Arbitration Commission Irrigation and Revenues Report and Notes 1902-5, 3 volumes (Simla: 1906); International Engineering Company Incorporated (IECI), Precis of Report of Program for the Development of Iran (1947); and Bolster, H.G., Report of the U.S. Agricultural Attaché to the U.S. Embassy in Tehran (1947).

Figure 1   Map of the Sistan Basin

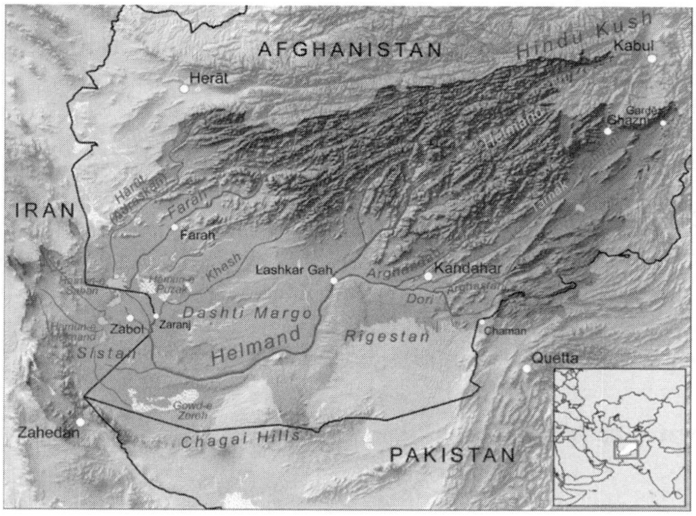

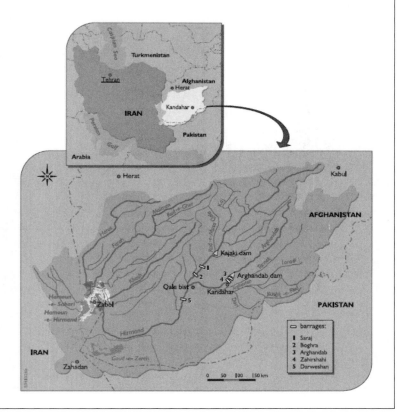

Figure 2   Rivers of Afghanistan and Iran feeding into the Sistan Basin
Source: van Beek and Meijer 2006

(known as hamuns) or dries up altogether. In times of major flooding, the basin overflows to the south where a saline lake (the "Gaud-i-Zirrah") has sometimes formed in response.[5]

The Sistan Basin depends predominantly on the Helmand River for its surface water supply. The variability of this supply is substantial on many scales. It has been estimated that the discharge of the Helmand River ranges over three orders of magnitude depending on flood conditions, from 57 to over 2,000 cfs (cubic feet per second).[6] Water supply is highly variable from year to year, and rarely are similar conditions experienced for more than a couple of years in a row (see Figures 3a and 3b). "Wet" and "dry" annual seasons control both local precipitation and water supply from the river, making water resource management still more challenging (see Figure 4). The difficult living conditions are also exacerbated by the extreme seasonal wind regime—this region is famous for the "wind of 120 days"— that drives extensive erosion and regular dust storms, and by the relatively large annual temperature range, with both very hot summers and freezing winters.[7]

Figure 3   Interannual variability of river water supply in the Sistan Basin

3a. The joint Perso-Afghan arbitration commission classified each water year (October-September) between 1872 and 1900 using a five-point scale: 1 = dry, 2 = normal, 3 = moderate, 4 = great, and 5 = extraordinary.[8] Rarely are similar conditions seen for more than two years in a row, and no general trends in water supply appear on a longer time scale.

3b. Annual discharge of the Helmand River measured at Chahar Burjak (roughly 50 km upstream of Kohak and the Band-i-Seistan) from 1949 to 1978.[9] (Note that data are missing for 1948 and 1973). The mean discharge for this period is 185 m^3 sec^{-1} (shown by the dashed line), the median is 195 m^3 sec^{-1}, and one standard deviation is 91 m^3 sec^{-1} (the arrow shows two standard deviations from the mean). Again, variability is substantial from year to year, with periods of similar conditions rarely lasting more than a few years, and no decadal trend is apparent.

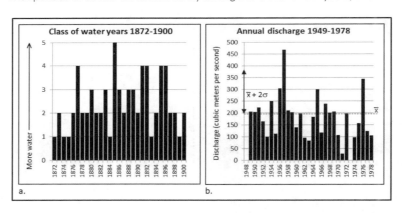

5. Whitney, 2006.
6. Bolster, 1947.
7. Whitney, 2006.
8. McMahon, 1906.
9. Williams-Sether, Tara, *Streamflow characteristics of streams in the Helmand Basin, Afghanistan.* U.S. Geological Survey Data Series 333 (Reston, VA: U.S. Geological Survey, 2008, 341 p).

Figure 4

Seasonality of water supply in the Sistan Basin. The narrow bars show average monthly discharge of the Helmand River at Kohak or Kwabgah (about 5 km upstream) in cubic feet per second for three time periods: 1872–1902,[10] 1903-1905[11] and 1948-1979.[12] The wide bars show average monthly precipitation at Zabol, Iran, from 1990–2004.[13] (Again, the supply of water from precipitation in the Sistan is almost negligible relative to the supply from the Helmand; note that the left-hand axis shows river flow in cubic feet per second, while the right axis gives precipitation in centimeters per month.) Earlier estimates of seasonal precipitation agree with these data; for example, in the 1906 report of the Joint Perso-Afghan Commission, average monthly precipitation at Zabol for October-May is given as 2.49 inches, or 6.30 cm (the average of the data shown here is 7.44 cm), and for June-September, 0.01 inches, or 0.03 cm.[14] Note that the total annual precipitation is consistently well below 15 cm (or 150 mm), the point at which a region's climate is traditionally classified as desert. These low precipitation levels combine with low humidity, high evapotranspiration, seasonal timing of precipitation and other factors to render the Sistan Basin climate arid to hyperarid.[15]

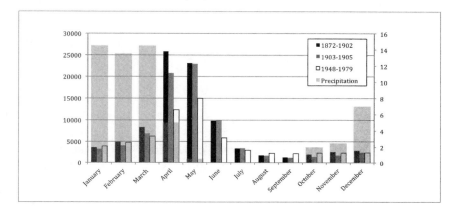

The population of the Sistan Basin has never had much resilience against the sharp interannual swings between drought and flooding, and this can be seen from the earliest archaeological records up to at least 2001.[16] Extensive irrigation canal systems were built and maintained to support clusters of villages with free-grazing populations of domestic animals (supported in part by the wetlands). When a channel shift left a populated area without water, or when a flood drowned a settlement, cattle and crops were lost and the inhabitants moved elsewhere. Even capital cities were periodically abandoned. In cases of a major channel shift or extreme periods of drought, tens to hundreds of villages might be left to the sands.[17] As a result, the area is peppered with ruins and the traces of ancient irrigation canals (see Figure 5).[18]

10. McMahon, 1906.

11. McMahon, 1906.

12. Williams-Sether, 2008.

13. Miri, Abbas, Hassan Ahmadi, Ahmad Ghanbari, and Alireza Moghaddamnia, "Dust storms impacts on air pollution and public health under hot and dry climate," Intl. J. Energy Environ. 2 (1) (2007), 101-105.

14. McMahon, 1906.

15. Whitney, 2006.

16. Whitney, 2006; United Nations Environment Programme, "History of environmental change in the Sistan Basin based on satellite image analysis, 1976–2005" (Geneva, Switzerland: United Nations Environment Programme, 2006, 56 p); Breshna, Abdullah, "Shelter for the homeless after a flood disaster: Practical experience in southwestern Afghanistan," Disasters 12 (3) (1988), 203-208; and LeStrange, Guy, The lands of the eastern caliphate: Mesopotamia, Persia, and Central Asia (Cambridge, U.K.: Cambridge geographical series, General editor, F. H. H., 1905).

17. Whitney, 2006; Breshna, 1998; and LeStrange, 1905.

18. Tate, 1909; McMahon, 1906; and Stein, Sir M.A., Innermost Asia—Detailed Report of Explorations in Central Asia, Kan su, and Eastern Iran (Oxford, U.K.: Oxford University Press, 1928, 3 volumes).

Figure 5 A timeline sketch of habitation of the Sistan basin over the past 5,000 years.[19]

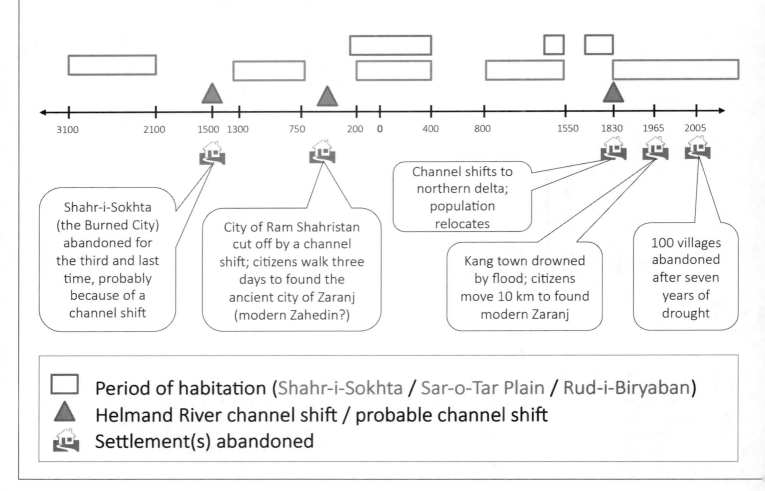

HABITATION OF THE SISTAN BASIN
3000 B.C. – A.D. 2005

3100 2100 1500 1300 750 200 0 400 800 1550 1830 1965 2005

Shahr-i-Sokhta (the Burned City) abandoned for the third and last time, probably because of a channel shift

City of Ram Shahristan cut off by a channel shift; citizens walk three days to found the ancient city of Zaranj (modern Zahedin?)

Channel shifts to northern delta; population relocates

Kang town drowned by flood; citizens move 10 km to found modern Zaranj

100 villages abandoned after seven years of drought

☐ Period of habitation (Shahr-i-Sokhta / Sar-o-Tar Plain / Rud-i-Biryaban)
▲ Helmand River channel shift / probable channel shift
🏠 Settlement(s) abandoned

19. Tate, 1909 (see note 3); McMahon, 1906 (see note 3); LeStrange, 1905 (see note 15); Marchand, *Note on Geography and Place-Names of Seistan*, 1950; and United Nations, "Afghanistan" (map, revision 279, number 3), March 1962.

Part 2: Human responses to water insecurity in this region, focusing on detailed records covering the period between 1850 and the present.

An examination of historical accounts of farming practices in the Sistan Basin between the mid-19th and mid-20th centuries suggests little change during this time. The main sources for this assessment are technical reports prepared in order to inform periodic water-rights disputes between Iran and Afghanistan, along with drafts of water-sharing agreements and some correspondence on the subject. Historical and modern maps were also consulted.

Agriculture and water management

The local climate requires that crops be irrigated. Farmers used flood irrigation with hand-dug, unlined, ramified systems of canals, with subcanals typically ending at a village.[20] Between 35 and 78 percent of the water was lost on the way to the fields.[21] The 1947 International Engineering Company, Incorporated (IECI) report describes the irrigation in this area as "more crude and inefficient than anywhere else in Iran."[22]

Dams, weirs and barrages, collectively called bands, were used to divert and control water flow in the canals. By far the most important of these was the Band-i-Seistan, which crossed the river at Kohak and at which the water supply was traditionally divided between the Iranian and Afghan sides.[23]

Farming and water management were governed by systems of community and cross-border cooperation. A set of common rules dictated the building, maintenance and use of the canal systems.[24] Villages on both sides of the river cooperated to rebuild the Band-i-Seistan every summer.[25] The planting system involved annual assignments of land parcels by officials; the amount of land planted determined the amount of water to be allocated to each village's canal.[26]

Based on the written and archaeological record of human and environmental history in the Sistan Basin, it is hard to understand how perceptions of this area as the breadbasket of Iran persisted for so long.[27] Whatever the conditions may have been in ancient times, the archaeological record indicates that the area has not prospered agriculturally since the early 16th century.[28] Despite recurring praise for the crops, soil and water quality in reports prepared between 1872 and 1950, by the middle of the 20th century assessments had taken on a markedly negative tone.[29] The IECI and Tudor reports describe saline, alkaline and infertile soils and a high water table, and criticize the farming practices as primitive and inefficient.[30] Life in the Sistan Basin appears to have remained tenuous up until the present: a period of severe meteorological drought from 1998 to 2005 resulted in the loss of crops, millions of fish, and untold livestock; by 2003, half the 1997 population had left, abandoning over 100 villages to the sands.[31]

Human dynamics and conflict

Human habitation in the Sistan depended on cooperative practices as observed in the mid-19th to mid-20th centuries.

---

20. McMahon, 1906.
21. Helmand River Delta Commission, Report of the Helmand River Delta Commission, 1951; Jones, technical report delivered in Tehran to "Jones," March 1950; Afghan Delegation, memorandum from the Afghan delegation to the Iranian delegation, 12 July 1956; and Afghanistan, Afghan response to Department of State questionnaire, 1947.
22. IECI, 1947.
23. See, for example, Goldsmid, Sir F., *Eastern Persia: An Account of the Journeys of the Persian Boundary Commission*, 1870-1871-1872 (London: Mac-Millan, 1876), Volume I: The Geography.
24. McMahon, 1906.
25. Tate, 1909; and Stein, 1928.
26. Tate, 1909; and McMahon, 1906.
27. See, for example, Goldsmid, 1876.
28. Whitney, 2006.
29. See, for example, Tate, 1909; and McMahon, 1906.
30. IECI, 1947; and Tudor Engineering Company, *Report on Development of Helmand Valley Afghanistan*, 1956.
31. Although the meteorological drought ended in 2005, intensely dry conditions have persisted to the present; some water has returned to the Sistan Basin, but the wetlands have not recovered, and life and livelihoods have not returned to pre-drought circumstances. Although in the past the area has rebounded from such traumas, there is some suspicion that this time a tipping point may have been reached. Between severe periods of drought in the last decades of the twentieth century; an ever-increasing fraction of water siphoned off; and the disruption of 30 years of conflict, the Sistan Basin may have been desiccated beyond the point of return. (See, for example, Meier, John, "From Wetland to Wasteland: the Destruction of the Hamoun Oasis" (online publication: NASA Earth Observatory, 13 December, 2002; link: earthobservatory.gov/Features/hamoun; accessed 22 August, 2011)).;Whitney, 2006; and Miri et al., 2007.

But cooperation broke down in times of water scarcity, leading to local and diplomatic tensions, and on occasion even destructive incidents. In 1902 the Helmand River nearly ran dry; in 1904 the new Band-i Pariun was built, channeling water into the Nad-i-Ali canal, and in 1905 Iranians burned the Afghan weir at Nad-i-Ali.[32] In the 1930s Iran expressed her anger and concern as Afghanistan planned major civil engineering projects such as the Seraj and Boghra canals.[33] In 1947, as the Helmand and the hamuns (lakes) dried out, a harsh demand for water went from Tehran to Kabul.[34] In April 2011, news reports described an outbreak of violence in which, after an alleged attempt by Iranians to redirect water inside Afghanistan was stopped by Afghan border police, Iranian border police shelled an Afghan security post.[35] Iran has long been concerned about the prospect, recently revived, of a dam at Band-i Kamal Khan, just upstream of the outtake to their Chanimeh reservoir system.[36] And as recently as September 2011, fire was exchanged across the border at Zaranj. This clash began when Iranian border guards attempted to establish a canal in the disputed Helmand River region.[37]

Though diplomatic solutions have been pursued repeatedly over the last 150 years, rarely have the parties reached formal agreement. A sharp drop in water supply preceded an 1870 dispute that led to the Goldsmid Award in 1873.[38] Amidst repeated Helmand River channel shifts at the end of the 19th century, disagreement arose again, to be addressed by the McMahon Study and ruling in 1905; but Iran never accepted this ruling.[39] A 1936 temporary water-sharing agreement failed to be ratified in 1938; negotiations failed in 1956, 1959, and 1968; and a 1972 agreement also went unratified (see Figure 6).[40]

32. McMahon, 1906.

33. See, for example, Tashikkori, Engineer, Report to Iran, 1948, in which the engineer attributes the ongoing drought partly to the Seraj Canal and Afghan focus on improving agriculture; and Governor General of Baluchistan, letter to the Iran Minister of War, 22 March 1949, in which the governor states that in 1948 Afghanistan caused loss of life in Sistan by stopping the flow of Helmand River water and that the Sistan people had to be dissuaded from taking action.

34. Leigh, Monroe, notes on a legal brief in the Hirmand River dispute recorded 1 February, 1950. The notes cite a note dated 3 August 1947 from Iran's ambassador to Afghanistan that "...demanded that water be delivered within fifteen days or Iran would be forced to take action and hold Afghanistan responsible for the damage." On 22 August 1947 the ambassador "reported a negative response."

35. Ramin, "4 Injured as Iranian forces shell Afghan post" (online publication: Pajhwok Afghan News: 11 April 2011, http://www.pajhwok.com/en/2011/04/11/4-injured-iranian-forces-shell-afghan-post, accessed 2 August 2011). According to the report, the canal the Iranians were attempting to tap was built in 2010 and funded by USAID.

36. See, for example, Daily Outlook, Afghanistan, "Iran Concerned About Dam Construction on Helmand River" (online publication: http://outlookafghanistan.net/newspost_id=1872, Editor in Chief, Dr. Hussain Yasa, 8 September, 2011, accessed 30 September 2011).

37. Frontier Post, "Afghan, Iran border guards exchange fire" (online publication: The Frontier Post, http://www.thefrontierpost.com/?p=55856, 15 September 2011, accessed 30 September 2011).

38. Goldsmid, 1872.

39. Whitney, 2006.

40. Laylin, B., memo on being retained to represent Iran, 1968.

Figure 6 Selected climatic and sociopolitical events in the Sistan Basin, 1870–2011.[41]

Over the past century and a half, water-driven hardship has been linked with several types of social responses, especially negotiations, tensions and conflicts, and civil works projects. It is also noteworthy that the completion of the Arghandab and Kajaki impound dams co-occurs with the cessation of channel shifts in the delta region.

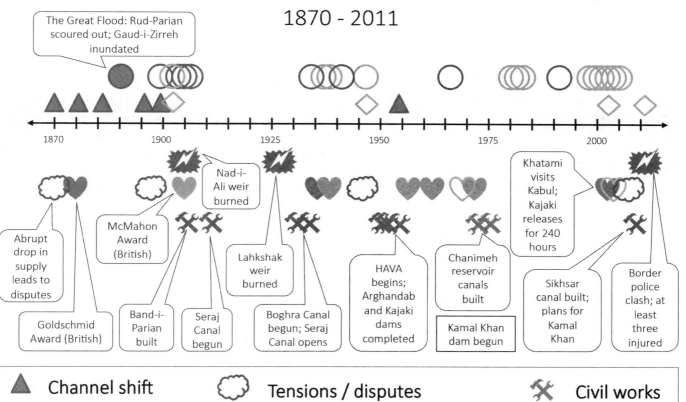

RECENT HISTORY OF THE SISTAN BASIN
1870 - 2011

41. Goldsmid, 1872; LeStrange, 1905; McMahon, 1906; Tate, 1909; Stein, 1928; Stamp, Lawrence Dudley, 1944; Bolster, 1947; Tashikkori, 1948; Leigh, 1950; Laylin, 1968; Whitney, 2006; Ramin, 2011; Daily Outlook, Afghanistan, 2011; and Frontier Post, 2011.

Part 3: The role of water in security and stability operations.

Environmental stress, such as that caused by flooding or drought, can intensify latent ethnic and political fissures, particularly in countries with weak governance.[42] In these instances, second and third order effects on economic and social well-being can increase the likelihood of instability. Environmental stresses involving water are relevant to COIN operations in Afghanistan because water supply, quality, availability and accessibility—collectively referred to as "water complexities"—link to population-centric issues that win or lose support for the legitimate government.[43] Hence information about an area's water complexities could be used to generate "proxy observables" for measuring a population's security and confidence in its government.[44] During ISAF engagements in

Figure 7   ISAF Regional Commands, Afghanistan. [45]

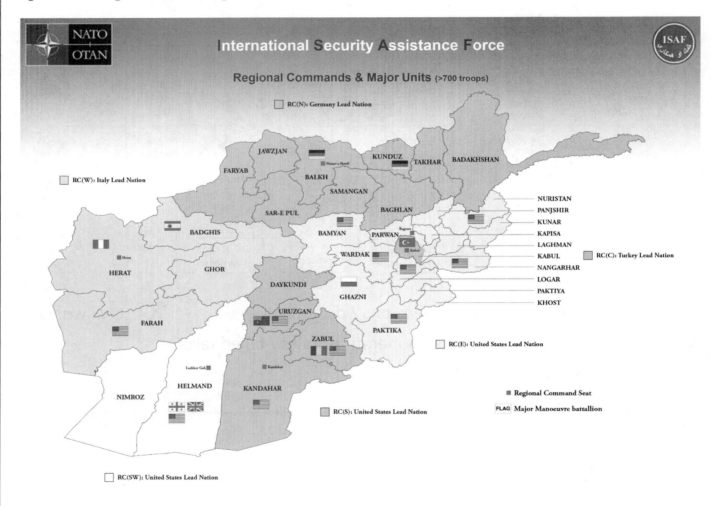

42. Krakowka, A.R., "The environment and regional security: A framework for analysis," in *Modern Military Geography*, eds. F. A. Galgano and E. J. Palka (New York: Routledge, 2011).

43. Though many question the legitimacy of the President Karzai's election, for purposes of this chapter, his government and the current Government of the Islamic Republic of Afghanistan are considered legitimate government.; Palmer-Moloney, L.J., "COIN ties to water: examples of water complexity indicators to support development metrics" (briefing presented to the Development Syndicate, NATO System Analysis and Studies workshop, NATO Consultation, Command, and Control Agency (NC3A). The Hague, Netherlands: 8 December 2010).

44. Palmer-Moloney, L.J., "Water's role in measuring security and stability in Helmand Province, Afghanistan," *Water International*, 36 (3), 2011:207-221.

45. International Security Assistance Force, "NATO-ISAF Placemat" (online publication: Troop numbers and contributions, http://www.isaf.nato.int/troop-numbers-and-contributions/index.php, accessed 30 September 2011), September 2011.

Afghanistan (Operation Enduring Freedom and Operation New Dawn), water's significance in the socio-economic development of the middle and lower Helmand watershed in RC-South and RC-Southwest (see Figure 7) was linked clearly to quantifiable development outcomes, but the potential for water to play a lead role for determining security and stability impacts in COIN operations was underappreciated, if it was considered at all. Yet ISAF bemoaned a lack of actionable data that could be used to gauge "COIN effect."

On 2 July 2009, U.S. Marines launched Operation Khanjar in Helmand Province, and one month later the U.S. Department of Defense initiated the "Helmand Deep Dive" research project. The goal of the project was to develop a "rich contextual understanding" of Helmand Province that could be used to strengthen and support counterinsurgency operations. Originally, the research plan focused on human factors—the behavioral psychology, sociology, cultural anthropology, history, economics and political science—with no regard to human geography, water, or to human-environment interactions. By the end of the research and reporting period, however, the briefings presented to the civilian and military decision makers laid out the significance of water to the security and stability of the region. The interagency research team, composed of members from USACE, USGS, and DOS, reviewed and analyzed archival records (written documents and aerial photography, circa 1950–1978), intelligence and open source reports from 2002–2009, satellite images (1975–2009), geospatial information from ISAF forces, and open source maps of the Helmand River watershed and reached the following conclusions:

1. ISAF efforts to stabilize Afghanistan must balance near-term gains in agricultural production with: (a) the potential of increased transboundary conflicts over water; and (b) the potential to exhaust Afghanistan's water resources. Actions must focus on improving resource policy/water resource management capacity and effectiveness, with special focus on increasing efficiency of water quantity and quality monitoring and assessment.

2. There is sparse, uncoordinated data collection on the depth of groundwater. In unconfined and confined aquifers, the water level is dropping as a result of drought and groundwater overdraft. Augmenting reduced surface-water flow by tapping the unconfined water-table aquifer and withdrawing from the deeper, confined fossil groundwater sources is not a sustainable alternative if the amount of withdrawal is greater than the rate of groundwater recharge.

3. There is no coordinated, cross-ministry, ongoing watershed-scale water-quality data collection/dissemination/analysis. Data about water quality are more difficult to come by than surface-water and groundwater supply data. Little information is found in the literature; most reporting is anecdotal.[46]

---

46. Palmer-Moloney, 2011.

Part 4: Dealing with the two sides of COIN effect in stability operations.[47]

"Helmand Kajaki Dam is very irreplaceable and valuable asset for both saturation and incalculable farming purposes…Snow and precipitation play a paramount role in swelling the Kajaki Dam and keeping its water level steady and lasting. When compared with previous years amount of water Kajaki Dam held, this year's is much more lesser that we could have anticipated … Nimruz Province deserves as much (of Helmand River water) as Helmand does … Today I telephoned Kajaki District. We discussed water issue and finally we arrived at an agreement aimed at prioritizing and saving some amount of already still water in Kajaki Dam."
—*From radio Interview with Deputy Director of HAVA, 24 September 2011*

It was 10 years into the fight before the intelligence and research communities sent out their "requests for information" on the water situation in the lower watershed. From 2002-2011, the lion's share of money and attention from the international coalition went to Kandahar Province and to the districts in central Helmand Province rather than to districts in southwestern Helmand or to Nimruz Province. Located in the extreme southwestern reaches of Regional Command Southwest (RC-SW), Nimruz

did not show up on Coalition Force radar until fall of 2010, when the II Marine Expeditionary Force (MEF) C-9 (Stability Operations) at Camp Leatherneck began engagement with government officials to discuss illicit trade and border security.

Summer of 2011 found Nimruz Province in dire straits. Daytime temperatures had averaged well over 100°F for weeks, and water in the Helmand River and in all of the region's irrigation canals had run dry (see Photograph 1). At the behest of Nimruz's Provincial Governor, the Minister of Energy and Water in Kabul directed the Helmand Arghandab Valley Authority (HAVA) to close central Helmand Province's primary irrigation canals for 24 hours so that water from the Kajaki Dam would flow downstream to the stressed lower watershed.

Shortly after the release of water for Nimruz, HAVA announced a fall water discharge reduction from the Kajaki Dam. The plan was to close two irrigation valves, reducing discharge by approximately 15–20 percent.[48] No one questioned that water level in the Kajaki reservoir was critically low (see Photograph 2). Few challenged HAVA's decision to try to replenish the reservoir because they were told that water captured and held now would provide water for crops in the next growing season. And no one in HAVA acknowledged that the planned

irrigation water shutdown would impact water availability below the confluence of the Helmand and Arghandab Rivers. From a geopolitical perspective, the reduced water flow in the lower Helmand River watershed was destined to sharpen rising tensions (tribal, district, provincial and international) over competition for diminishing water resources.

In 2010, irrigation water coming from the Kajaki Dam had been shut off for 21 days. In fall 2011, irrigation water shutdown was scheduled to last an additional 11 days (from 7 October to 6 November) to store water to support the growth of crops other than poppy.[49] There was little doubt that the planned Kajaki irrigation valve closure would exacerbate the already severe water shortages in southern Helmand Province and in Nimruz Province, or that people who depended on the river's surface water for consumption could be at risk.

With the lack of data on the effects of water reduction in the past, specifically the stream discharge during this time of year, and no knowledge of the time it takes for the lower Helmand to feel the effects of water discharge reduction at the Kajaki Dam, it was difficult to impossible to determine the exact impact. At the time of this writing, concerns from those in Helmand and Nimruz Provinces were that water in the river and canals was desperately low

---

47. The information provided in this section comes from primary research conducted in the field by Palmer-Moloney, Jul-Sept 2011.

48. This figure is based on unpublished, unclassified 2009 and 2010 Kajaki Dam discharge records provided by the U.S. Army Corps of Engineers.

49. The central Helmand wheat seed distribution program was in full swing during September 2011. If anticipated winter rain failed to fall, water from the reservoir would have to support this agricultural effort. If water for irrigation came neither from rain nor from the reservoir, the fear was that the drive to plant poppy would increase, and it would become the crop of last resort. This would have implications for long-term effects of the Helmand Counter Narcotics Plan, Governor-Led Eradication effort, and continued income for the insurgent forces.

Photograph 1   Helmand River in Zaranj, Nimruz Province,
                25 September 2011

Photograph 2   Kajaki Dam and Reservoir,
                Helmand Province,
                28 September 2011

and the distribution of water among districts and between provinces was inequitable. According to reports from the field, communities in Nimruz believed that water was being held in Helmand and kept from them, while farmers in central Helmand felt threatened when the canals were closed for the flow to continue unabated to Nimruz.

Before a watershed can be managed in a sustainable fashion, there must be an understanding of the water budget (input/out-take that includes extraction, consumptive use of water, and rate of evaporation). Gauging stations with reliable monitoring technology are needed to capture information about a river system's rate of discharge and to develop a water budget. This holds true for the Helmand, yet no monitoring of the Helmand has taken place since 1978.

In late September 2011, in an attempt to address the stream flow data gap, rudimentary stream depth gauging of the lower Helmand began. A joint Stability Operations team from the II MEF C-9 (Regional Command strategy-level) and G-9 (Task Force Leatherneck tactical-level) traveled to Khan Neshin District and installed a stream depth gauge in the river channel (see Figure 8). Measurements began on 23 September 2011 and were continued through at least 16 November 2011. The stream depth gauging will help establish an environmental baseline prior to water reduction caused by the planned closure.

To augment the stream depth gauging in the short-term, RC-SW Space Operations cell ("Space Ops") was asked to collaborate with C-9/G-9 Stability Ops. From September-November 2011, Space Ops provided geospatial analysis that helped all concerned gain a better understanding of the pre- and post-water shutdown situation. The information needed required fusing together factors of human geography and physical geography. Geospatial tools/ analysis provided information for data sparse areas—which are the norm rather than the exception in the RC-SW area of interest.

Space Ops has focused its geospatial tools/analytic skills on the following interrelated issues/problems/concerns:

1. Land use/land cover change over the past five years in the lower Helmand watershed (especially related to population increase, agricultural fields, canals/ reservoirs) at the Iranian border with Afghanistan.

2. Proposed Kamal Khan Dam (Nimruz Province) modeling to see effect of a potential dam's construction.

3. During the Kajaki Dam water release reduction/irrigation canal closures (6 October to 7 November 2011), monitored for indicators of changes in reservoir capacity increase (the purpose for withholding water from the river system) and agricultural activity (particularly in canals in districts of Nawah and

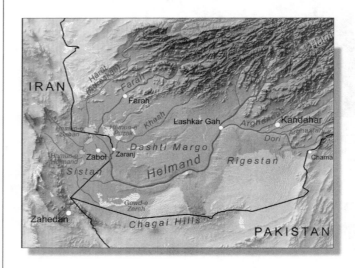

Figure 8   Approximate location of stream depth gauging, Khan Neshin.
(For security reasons, exact coordinates cannot be provided.)

Garm Ser and in historically productive agricultural areas of Nimruz Province from the Helmand Province border up to the Kamal Khan Dam site. Though support from RC-SW Space Operations will help establish an environmental baseline, the fact remains that no functioning monitoring stations are on the lower Helmand River from Dishu district (Helmand Province) into Nimruz Province.

Conclusion

Human security in the Sistan Basin has historically varied with not just the water, but also human perceptions of water—both of supply, and of external control over that supply. This continues to be true today. Threats the Afghan farmers in Nimruz perceive to their water security may include the Afghan government, users in Helmand Province, and neighbors on both sides of the Iran/Afghanistan border. Iran, too, perceives threat in plans to improve Afghan management and use of the Helmand River water resources. In conjunction with actual water scarcity, these perceptions themselves pose a threat to security in the Sistan. Therefore, both the scarcity and the perceptions of threat should be addressed.

Data collected and analyzed will offer geospatial aspects to help craft the water transition plan for the middle and lower Helmand River watershed that has been requested by the RC-SW command. An integrated water resources management (IWRM) program for the Helmand River will require the inclusion of all stakeholders (lower Helmand, in the middle and lower watershed, not just those in central Helmand) whom HAVA considers relevant. By also including the concerns and needs of the Iranian residents of the Sistan Basin, the chances for achieving lasting security in the area will be substantially improved.

Dr. Laura Jean Palmer-Moloney is a senior research geographer at the Engineer Research and Development Center (ERDC), U.S. Army Corps of Engineers; former AF PAK Hands with the Pakistan-Afghanistan Coordination Cell, serving as senior adviser for watershed management on the Stability Operations staff, Regional Command Southwest Camp Leatherneck, Helmand Province, Afghanistan (2011–2012).

Dr. K.U. Duckenfield is a Geospatial Intelligence Analyst for the Economic and Environmental Security Division (PRE) of the National Geospatial-Intelligence Agency. Duckenfield is a former Atmospheric Composition and Climate program associate in the Climate Program Office of the National Oceanic and Atmospheric Administration (NOAA) and Science To Achieve Results (STAR) research fellow of the Environmental Protection Agency (EPA).

RELATIONSHIP BETWEEN FRESHWATER RESOURCES, SOCIO-CULTURAL DYNAMICS AND GEOPOLITICAL STABILITY

Jennifer C. Veilleux
Matthew Zentner
Aaron T. Wolf

Introduction

Water security is the availability of the right quality and right quantity of freshwater resources at the right times. The availability is dependent on both physical and human geography. Water security is a prerequisite for human, national and environmental security, as well as economic growth. Use of global freshwater resources can compete between basic needs of individual consumption, subsistence agriculture and ecosystem services, and the economically driven sectors of agriculture, energy, industry and transportation. Due to this complexity, effective and harmonized geospatially relevant policy and management of global freshwater resources is vital for national and international security and instability concerns, now and into the foreseeable future.

Relationships between political and social instability and changes to the physical environment have been postulated by numerous scholars, with shifts in freshwater resource access, quality and quantity often noted as a key influence on societal and political stability.[1] Because water accessibility interacts with broader security concerns and drives global economics, it can contribute to state instability and social disruptions. Changes in water resources can alter the relative wealth of countries and cause shifts in relative power. Inadequate water supply tempers economic growth in many countries, particularly in developing countries where hydropower serves as a main power source. Unavailability of water during key agriculture seasons poses risks to both local and global food markets. In many ways, freshwater resources hold societies together and when these systems are altered, the myriad connections become evident.

This chapter examines the interaction between environmental stresses, institutional and human system responses at various scales, and state stability (as has been described by scholars through the lens of resilience theory and securitization).[2] Resilience

1. Brown, O., Hammill, A., & McLeman, R. (2007). Climate change as the 'new' security threat: implications for Africa. *International Affairs*, 83(6), 1141-1154.; Eckstein, Yoram, and Gabriel E. Eckstein (2005). Transboundary Aquifers: Conceptual Models for Development of International Law. *GROUND WATER*. Vol. 43, No. 5, September-October 2005. pp. 679-690.; Eckstein, G. (2010). Water Scarcity, Conflict, and Security in a Climate Change World: Challenges and Opportunities for International Law and Policy. *Wisconsin International Law Journal, Vol. 27* (No.3), 411-424.; Swart, R. (1996). Security risks of global environmental changes. *Global Environmental Change-Human and Policy Dimensions*, 6(3), 187-192.
2. Allan, K. (2007). *The social lens: an invitation to social and sociological theory* Thousand Oaks, California: Pine Forge Press.

theory applies to both ecological and social systems, and securitization theory describes the two main areas of stability with which governments are concerned. Finally, this chapter offers four concepts by which to deal with the problems of individual, national and international security concerns with freshwater resources.

Background

Freshwater as a limited resource is influenced by geophysical conditions, geopolitical agendas, and socio-cultural dynamics on several scales.

Geophysical

Availability of freshwater resources is largely dependent upon an array of regional physical geography characteristics, and the relationship of corresponding human population patterns are typically affected by this availability. People commonly live where freshwater is available for basic and community needs. When this is not the case, communities alter freshwater resources to serve their needs. Freshwater resources are under increased pressure from direct and indirect human alterations and use.[3] Direct alterations of freshwater resources include dams, irrigation project development

and contamination, and indirect alterations include changing precipitation and temperature patterns due to global climate change. Global climate change has especially raised concerns that changes to freshwater resources will pose unique challenges to many individual nation and regional security interests.[4] Several studies have examined how vulnerable systems that are already stressed might be driven past a tipping point by shifts in climate.[5] Shifts in climate can impact water availability due to changes in storage in form of snow and ice, and water quality and flow due to changes in rate of melting snow and ice, and other forms of precipitation.

Geopolitical

Little harmony exists in the arena of international water policy, and of those policies there is even less regarding international groundwater resources.[6] Groundwater is the main water resource used by more than 3 billion people for everyday use.[7] As surface water resources become increasingly polluted, contaminated and diverted, dependence on groundwater increases globally.[8] In the absence of international water policy, uncoordinated use of shared freshwater resources

could result in further challenges with quality, quantity and access issues. Though scholars suggest water wars are possible in the near future, there is surprising evidence that international cooperation regarding freshwater resources was more likely than conflict.[9] Where stronger institutional capacity exists in international basins, conflict on all scales is reduced.[10]

International water policy is also influenced by direct foreign investment. These investments may be in the form of development projects, such as building irrigation networks and dams. Recently, these investments have also included land acquisition (the buying or leasing of land in one country by another country) often along surface water resources.[11] The land acquisition phenomena increased subsequent to the world food crisis of 2007-2008 and concerns over 227 million hectares of land, largely in sub-Saharan Africa in countries such as Tanzania, and also in developed nations such as Australia.

Socio-cultural

In the international community, freshwater resources are still debated as to whether they are a human right or a global

3. Brown (2007), *op. cit.*; Eckstein (2005), *op. cit.*; Eckstein (2010), *op. cit.*

4. National Intelligence Council (2012), Intelligence Community Assessment on Water Security, Washington D.C.

5. Barnett, J. (2003). Security and climate change. *Global Environmental Change 13* 7–17.; Dabelko, G. (2008). An Uncommon Peace: Environment, Development, and the Global Security Agenda. *Environment, 50* (3 (May/June)), 33-45.; Mabey, N. (2007). Security Trends and Threat Misperceptions. In P. Cornish (Ed.), *Britain and Security* The Smith Institute.

6. Eckstein (2005), *op. cit.*; Eckstein (2005), *op. cit.*

7. Eckstein (2005), *op. cit.*; Puri, S. and A. Aureli (2005). Transboundary Aquifers: A Global Program to Assess, Evaluate, and Develop Policy. *GROUND WATER.* Vol. 43, No. 5, September-October 2005. Pp. 661-668.

8. Eckstein (2005), *op. cit.*

9. Gleick, Peter H. (1993). Water and Conflict: Fresh Water Resources and International Security *International Security*, Vol. 18, No. 1 (Summer, 1993), pp. 79-112.; Wolf, A. T. (1997). International water conflict resolution: Lessons from comparative analysis. *Water Resources Development*, 13, 333–365.

10. De Stefano, L., P. Edwards, L. de Silva and A.T. Wolf (2010). "Tracking Cooperation and Conflict in International Basins: Historic and Recent Trends." *Water Policy.* Vol 12 No 6 pp 871–884.

11. Jagerskog, A., Cascao, A. Harsmar, M. and Kim, K. (2012). Land Acquisitions: How will they Impact Transboundary Waters? Report Nr 30. SIWI, Stockholm.

commodity.[12] Worldwide, an estimated 1.2 billion people lack access to safe drinking water and more than 2.4 lack access to sanitation.[13] The problem may have technological and economic solutions, but scholars increasingly see the problem nested in the imbalance of power, lack of agency in marginalized populations, and lack of political will in local or national governments. International interests—through efforts such as commitment to the Millennium Development Goals (MDGs) by world leaders in 2000—seek to reduce this number through international development and aid. Accordingly, global dam development has been increasing over the past 12 years despite warnings of consequent social and environmental costs, including an impact on nearly 500 million people dependent on affected rivers.[14]

Given the complicated nature of water resource systems, there exists substantial need for better understanding of these systems, to learn how to more effectively manage them to ensure a sustainable future.

Security and resilience in freshwater

Resilience theory examines complex system dynamics and, by describing how systems react to change by reconfiguring into a different state beyond a tipping point,

addresses the complexity of human and natural systems in the face of change. Securitization examines social construction of the concept of security at different scales in order to better predict how different levels of society will react to real or perceived change.

Resilience theory is best known through C.S. Holling's descriptions of ecological systems as adaptive complex systems. The theory has been used by natural and social scientists to describe the adaptive nature of complex human and natural systems as they absorb non-linear inputs of change, and do so continuously in an ongoing cycle. Change is described as an input into a system. There is a point beyond which a system can no longer absorb the input in its current state, say state A in Figure 1, and transforms to another altered state, state B, in which it can continue until another input pushes it beyond some threshold into yet another state, state C.[15] This alteration between different states changing through inputs and driven past a threshold to another state is thought to be an infinite process and is often visually described by the infinity symbol.

Though social sciences struggle to make use of this theory in practical application, it helps to describe the

changes happening in both the macro system to include environmental, economic and human system variables, as well as nested systems within each of these categories that also include governance and development. The application of resilience theory when approaching international freshwater resources is useful in identifying potential drivers, inputs, and thresholds to help decide where action could be taken to buffer abrupt change or to build a more resilient response for the nested and overall systems.

Buzan considers security from different scales to describe how people or societies construct or "securitize" threats.[16] The three levels used to describe interactions at different scales are individuals, states and international systems.[17] Starting at the individual level, security can be considered as a factor of "life, health, status, wealth, freedom".[18] While defining individual

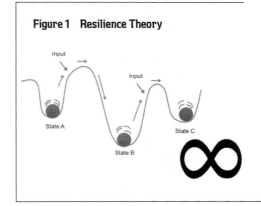

Figure 1   Resilience Theory

12. Glieck, P. (2000). A Look at Twenty-First Century Water Resources Development, *Water International*, 25:1, 127-138.
13. Loftus, Alex. (2009). Rethinking Political Ecologies of Water. Third World Quarterly. Vol. 30, No. 5, pp. 953-968.; Robbins, Peter (2003). Transnational Corporations and the Discourse of Water Privitization. *Journal of International Development*. Dev. 15, 1073–1082 (2003).
14. Richter, B.D.; Postel, S.; Revenga, C.; Scudder, T.; Lehner, B.; Churchill, A. and Chow, M. (2010). Lost in development's shadow: The downstream human consequences of dams. Water Alternatives 3(2): 14-42.
15. Peterson, Garry (2000). Political ecology and ecological resilience: An integration of human ecological dynamics. *Ecological Economics*. Vol. 35, pp. 323-336.
16. Buzan, B. (2000). Security communities. *International Affairs*, 76(1), 154-154.
17. Buzan, B., & Waever, O. (2009). Macrosecuritisation and security constellations: reconsidering scale in securitisation theory. *Review of International Studies*, 35(2), 253-276.
18. Stone, M. (2009). Security Discussion Papers Series 1 Columbia University, School of International and Public Affairs.

security can be complicated by personal differences, Maslow's Hierarchy type-requirements generally hold true (Maslow, 1943).[19] Maslow proposed that physiological needs, such as water access, form the base level of human motivation and, consequently, stability. However, the concept of security at the individual level does not directly translate and apply to national security.[20] For the level of state security, Buzan considers that states are larger, more complicated entities with a constantly shifting hierarchy of requirements in often overlapping sectors of political, military, economic, societal and environmental.[21] Each sector impacts security individually, but these individual sectors are also linked to one another often in intricate and complex ways, making a discussion of individual sectors inadequate to address impacts on security.[22]

Buzan's discussion of security and stability at different scales and for different sectors is especially useful in the context of freshwater resources and climate change.[23] The impacts of water stress is largely of concern for the environmental sector, but it will arguably be as much of a factor and influence on all other sectors, sometimes indirectly, with consequences that are largely unpredictable.

Discussion

The three areas of geophysical, geopolitical and socio-cultural merge together on the platform of freshwater resources. Freshwater can be a component of political and economic stability, as well as influence sustainable development, democracy and equity, but within these sectors its importance fluctuates. Scarcity persists despite the availability of technical knowledge and/or solutions and high profile pledges, such as the MDGs. This is in large part due to politics, power and competing interests rather than technology and/or economics. Specifically, water problems are thought to persist due to the lack of agency in disadvantaged communities, the imbalance of power within and between nation-states, and lack of political will of governments to take action to improve sanitation and freshwater distribution.[24] This may not impact national stability in the short term, but given time, the effects may reverberate through the entire system.

It is only when freshwater issues impact sectors of primary importance to governmental stability and power, such as political stability and economic growth, that nations begin to view freshwater itself as a resource worth political action. Improved freshwater access becomes important in nation-states that are developing and use hydropower to satisfy their energy security such as China, Turkey, India, Tajikistan and Ethiopia.[25] Dams are traditionally thought of as a tangible symbol of modernization and development.[26] Pakistan and Egypt consider freshwater essential to their agricultural production to provide jobs for the majority of their populations, which in turn provides pacification of the population and stability for the government.[27] The uses of freshwater that many consider most vital—potable freshwater for individual consumption and proper sanitation—are not what drive action for some, if not most, governments. Many nations are generally not interested in freshwater components that make up the UN's Human Development Index unless it impacts the stability of a populace and in turn the stability of the government. For

19. Maslow, A. (1943). A Theory of Human Motivation. *Psychological Review*, 50, 370-396.
20. Stone (2009), *op. cit.*
21. Buzan & Waever (2009), *op. cit.*
22. Stone (2009), *op. cit.*
23. Buzan (2000), *op. cit.*; Buzan, B. (2001). Losing control: global security in the twenty-first century. *International Affairs*, 77(3), 696-696.
24. Loftus (2009), *op. cit.*; Molle, Francois (2005). Elements for a political ecology of river basins development: The case of the Chao Phraya river basin, Thailand. Conference paper presented to the 4th Conference of the International Water History Association. December 2005, Paris.; Robbins, Paul (2004). Political Ecology. Blackwell Publishing, Malden, MA.
25. Zentner, M., Stahl, K., Basist, A., Blankespoor, B., Wolf, A.T., & De Stefano, L. (2008). Estimating Flow Probabilities to Meet Water Treaties Allocation Requirements. *Draft paper to the World Bank*.; Zentner, M. (2012). Design and Impact of Water Treaties: Managing Climate Change, Springer Theses Series.; FAO. (2009). *National Investment Brief Sector: Water for agriculture and energy. The Republic of Turkey*. http://www.fao.org.
26. Whittlesey, Denvent S. (1935). "The Impress of Effective Central Authority upon the Landscape." *Annals of the Association of American Geographers* Vol. 25 p. 13.; Wittfogel, Karl A. (1956). "Hydraulic Civilizations." In *The Structure of Political Geography*, Kasperson and Minghi (eds.), 1969 p.442-449, Aldine Publishing Company, Chicago.
27. FAO Water (2010). AQUASTAT. Retrieved 18 September 2010, from http://www.fao.org/nr/water/.; McCaffrey, S. C. (2007). *The Law of International Watercourses* (2nd ed.). Oxford: Oxford University Press.; Whittington, D., Wu, X., & Sadoff, C. (2005). Water resources management in the Nile basin: the economic value of cooperation. *Water Policy*, 7, 227-252.

example, Turkey's interest in the development of its freshwater resources and efforts to improve quality likely stem from the practical relationship between freshwater resource's impact on other sectors and GDP, which in turn has the largest impact on its stability.[28]

The specific cases where political stability is impacted by freshwater resources are where conflict at the higher levels of government appears to be most prevalent, in places that have established freshwater-centric economies such as the Nile, Jordan and Indus basins.[29] Water's relationship to agriculture, land and electric power are of particular importance to a nation's economic and overall stability.

Water, food and land acquisition

Food price increases in 2008 led some nations to struggle to meet their food demands. Most current projections indicate that global food production capacity will be increasingly challenged. Perhaps in response to price fluctuations and climate change projections, a number of water-scarce, developed countries are seeking their own freshwater solutions by securing agricultural land in developing countries. These land acquisitions have the potential to change the geopolitical landscape. Most of the land acquisitions are taking place on the African continent, in countries with existing food security issues such as Sudan

and Ethiopia.

During the World Economic Forum Water Initiative of 2009, it was stated that "rapidly industrializing economies across South Asia, the Middle East and North Africa (supporting approximately 2.5 billion people) will need to acquire additional water resources, including in the form of water-rich agricultural land outside their borders".[30] Countries with abundant freshwater resources will become more attractive locations for investments, and instability might be exacerbated in less developed countries willing to mortgage long-term freshwater scarcity for immediate financial.[31] In this way, the projections (and not the documented impacts) of physical scarcity are driving and influencing changes in geopolitical and socio-economic scarcity both between and within nations.

Water, electric power, and large-scale dams

Development of freshwater resources for hydropower generation and issues with water access are often intimately connected, and electricity shortages can also create water shortages. Despite the lessons learned over the last 50 years outlined in the *World Commission on Dams Report*, and subsequent alterations to practices of some lending institutions such as the World Bank, countries are continuing construction of

large-scale dams. Though the immediate economic impacts of large-scale dam development may be beneficial in general (job creation, electricity generation, water storage for increased agricultural production, flood control), the broader effects of new dams on local communities (to water quality and associated environmental resources) have a negative long-term economic impact (loss of livelihoods, loss of species, degradation of water quality and quantity). In countries such as Tajikistan and Ethiopia, large-scale dam development offers economic development opportunities for crippled national economic systems. For this reason, it is not clear if there is a significant relationship between state security improvements and engineered water projects.

Nexus of freshwater and conflict

Recent research indicates freshwater is of relatively low-level importance to national security.[32] Yet, as is seen in many instances, freshwater issues sometimes extend beyond this low level to become part of the larger, national stability scheme. The National Intelligence Council released an unclassified Intelligence Community Assessment on Water Security in 2012 that summarizes how water can impact other associated sectors such as energy and food, which together can be

28. Warner (2008), *op. cit.*; FAO (2009), *op. cit.*
29. Zenter (2012), *op. cit.*
30. World Economic Forum Water Initiative (2009). *World Economic Forum Water Initiative Managing Our Future Water Needs for Agriculture, Industry, Human Health and the Environment.* Paper presented at the World Economic Forum Annual Meeting 2009.
31. *Ibid.*
32. De Stefano (2010), *op. cit.*; Wolf, A. "A Long Term View of Water and International Security." *Journal of Contemporary Water Research & Education.* Issue 142, pp. 67-75, August 2009.; Ali, S. (2008). Water politics in South Asia: Technocratic cooperation and lasting security in the Indus Basin and beyond. *Journal of International Affairs*, 61(2; Spring/Summer), 167-182.

a driver in national security calculations:

"During the next 10 years, many countries important to the United States will experience water problems—shortages, poor water quality, or floods—that will risk instability and state failure, increase regional tensions, and distract them from working with the United States on important U.S. policy objectives. Between now and 2040, freshwater availability will not keep up with demand absent more effective management of water resources. Water problems will hinder the ability of key countries to produce food and generate energy, posing a risk to global food markets and hobbling economic growth. As a result of demographic and economic development pressures, North Africa, the Middle East, and South Asia will face major challenges coping with water problems."[33]

This suggests that the primary cause for conflict is a shift in the way a nation views freshwater. Change in water politics occurs for a multitude of reasons including change in weather patterns (hydrologic stress), altered freshwater requirements, shifts in the overall political relations between the treaty signatories of shared waters, changes in economic goals, or changes in the utilization of freshwater resources (engineering projects). Such changes or shifts prompt political action. All shifts are unique, but have an overarching theme: the shifts impact the stability of one

of the stakeholder groups in some way.

Freshwater issues arguably become more important, and possibly conflictive, when they are tied to other issues with a higher degree of impact on stability. Countries may be more willing to go through the effort of conflict or issuing a formal complaint to the offending party if it has more of an impact on its stability. Hydrologic stress may only temporarily elevate the importance of freshwater to the level of national-security concerns. Freshwater politics are shaped by other issues that are not easily captured by blanket variables applied to all nations. For example, in the Indus and Jordan basins, many of the freshwater and climate complaints are generated by state relations in general, with hydrologic stresses being inextricably related to geopoltical stresses.

Increased emphasis on freshwater by nations where freshwater has reached a higher level of consideration for stability coincides with areas that have exhibited more conflict in the past. Conflict or disagreements seem to occur where freshwater use/scarcity has raised the importance of freshwater in the national calculus to become a part of the security and stability calculations. Especially for areas within the Middle East (Jordan, Nile, Tigris-Euphrates) where demand largely outstrips supply, the strategic implications have brought additional focus on freshwater. In these countries, the securitization and importance of freshwater, due to limited

supplies, is likely based on the domestic uses captured by stability that in turn reaches the level of consideration for stability.

Freshwater resource issues that challenge under-developed nations, such as flood control and contamination or access issues, may be addressed through international development efforts. One method of development includes dam projects, but dam projects have costs as well as benefits for the environment, economy and socio-cultural systems. Dam impacts have further reaching implications than previously understood, and impacts vary according to scale and sector considered. Also, water development projects inevitably impact geopolitical, geophysical and socio-cultural sectors of a region, nation or basin and may have direct impacts to security through changing both types of stability. Better understanding of these complex interrelationships is necessary prior to implementing foreign direct investments, international development projects and development strategies.

There is a complex relationship between change in a system and the institutional capacity to absorb that change, which involves a series of feedback loops and influence from non-freshwater related sectors. This is well-captured in resilience models. Complaints or conflict associated with freshwater stress are not necessarily indicative of instability or weak governments, but in some cases can illustrate that an organization is functioning

---

33. National Intelligence Council (2012), *op. cit.*

properly. Complaints or low-level conflict may not always indicate inability, but rather, in some cases, enhanced ability for stress management. This potential explanation follows the line of Coser regarding the practical utility of conflict and the possibility that conflict (rather than a condemnation or negative indicator) instead shows that a state or organization is functioning as designed. For example, treaties can act to "release pent-up hostilities, create norms regulating conflict, and develop clear lines of authority" and are a means not of avoiding conflict, but provide a way to "facilitate low-level conflict". [34] Through increased, structured interaction in the form of "low-level and more frequent conflict," the intended purpose of the treaty can be achieved "without threatening the overall stability of the relationships". In this way, low-level conflict or disagreement positively impacts stability and prevents the conflict from reaching higher levels of severity. "Far from being necessarily dysfunctional, a certain degree of conflict is an essential element in group formation and the persistence of group life". [35]

Determining where Coser's "certain degree of conflict" stops being positive and enters the realm of negative is difficult to discern. One way to potentially measure this is by determining an elevated increase in severity and the level of government associated with the conflict. However, the severity and level of government are also directly related to the level of national importance and freshwater's impact on different types of stability and stability. The line where conflict becomes a potential hazard to both stability and stability is nebulous, as illustrated by Buzan's discussion on securitization:

> "The bottom line of security is survival, but it also reasonably includes a substantial range of concerns about the conditions of existence. Quite where this range of concerns ceases to merit the urgency of the "security" label (which identifies threats as significant enough to warrant emergency action and exceptional measures including the use of force) and becomes part of everyday uncertainties of life is one of the difficulties of the concept" (Buzan, as quoted by Stone). [36]

A blanket application of complaints or conflict as negative overlooks the potential nuances of conflict origin and utility. Organizations or nations may facilitate interaction that is sometimes construed as low-level conflict, and discerning between positive conflict and conflict spurred by weaknesses may not be possible without in-depth knowledge of the organization.

Conclusions

Changes to global freshwater resources do not determine where threats to security or instability occur. For example, drought, a severe form of freshwater resource alteration, does not occur any more frequently in areas that have reported climate related conflict than it does in other areas: river basins with climate complaints are in absolute and relative drought less often, have a lower overall drought severity, and have less variability than areas that have no conflict. Therefore, drought is not the primary cause or determiner of whether an area is going to have climate related conflict. Instead, freshwater and the natural environment shape and influence the surrounding socio-cultural, political and environmental situation.

Freshwater resource issues that may impact human security related to human consumption needs have to do more with stability (humanitarian concern) than stability (state concern). This then leads policy makers to make decisions on freshwater resources when they are related to some other sectors with an economic or political tie-in, such as agriculture, energy or employment. In some cases, conflict that is thought to be related to freshwater issues may not be oriented toward the specific issue or intended to produce freshwater-related results. Given the four concepts presented, freshwater resources are complicated with factors that include geopolitical, geophysical as well as socio-cultural dynamics, and there is no blanketed answer for how to manage the current situation we are in, nor the future of global freshwater

34. Allan (2007), *op. cit.*
35. Coser, L. (1956). *The Functions of Social Conflict.* New York.
36. Stone (2009), *op. cit.*

management. Projects such as the MDGs still fail to meet the mark of supplying the world's most impoverished and most in need with adequate access to freshwater supplies. Also, while predictions of climate will likely increase in accuracy and resolution, the impacts from climate change and freshwater issues will continue to be extremely difficult to predict since the effects are dependent on a number of issues that extend beyond just climate. Water as the leading cause of global death, outside of heart disease, is a reality that threatens security on individual, state and international levels.

Jennifer C. Veilleux is a geography PhD candidate at Oregon State University (OSU). Her dissertation centers on dam development human security at different scales, primarily transboundary freshwater resources. Veilleux is a database manager for Transboundary Freshwater Dispute Database at OSU. She worked as a DoD environmental and economic security analyst.

Matthew A. Zentner is a hydrologist for the United States DoD. He earned a PhD in geography from Oregon State University. His research interests include water and environmental security, international water law and water resources management. His experience includes hydrogeology and civil and environmental engineering related to water policy.

Aaron T. Wolf is professor of geography in the College of Earth, Ocean, and Atmospheric Sciences at Oregon State University, focused on water science and policy conflict prevention and resolution. A trained mediator/facilitator, he directs the Program in Water Conflict Management and Transformation, offering workshops, facilitations and mediation (www.transboundarywaters.orst.edu).

Conflict Diamonds as an Example of Natural Resource Conflict

Peter Chirico
Katherine Malpeli

Conflict resources

The concept of "conflict resources" emerged during the late 1990s as details of the diamond trade financing civil wars in West Africa gained public and political attention. The term has since come to refer to natural resources, which are sold or traded in order to finance and sustain armed conflicts. Such resources include rubies, minerals, metals, timber, fossil fuels, rubber, cotton, cocoa, and, perhaps the most well-known, diamonds.[1] These resources have been major factors in conflicts throughout Africa, Asia, and South America over the past several decades. In an attempt to address the issue of conflict resources, a series of legislative initiatives have been passed both by the U.S. and the international community. The 2002 Kimberley Process Certification Scheme (KPCS) and the 2003 Clean Diamond Trade Act were two such measures aimed at stemming the flow of conflict diamonds. More recently, Section 1502 of the 2010 Dodd-Frank Wall Street Reform and Consumer Protection Act requires publically traded companies on the U.S. stock exchange to report on the due diligence undertaken to ensure that the gold, tin, tantalum, or tungsten used in their products does not directly or indirectly contribute to armed conflict in the Democratic Republic of the Congo (DRC) or any neighboring country. This act spurred the creation of the Organisation for Economic Co-operation and Development's (OECD) Due Diligence Guidance for Responsible Supply Chains of Minerals from Conflict-Affected and High-Risk Areas in 2011, which makes non-legal binding recommendations for the responsible sourcing of tin, tantalum, tungsten, their derivatives, and gold, to avoid contributing to conflict.[2]

Collier and Hoeffler were among the first to suggest a correlation between natural resource abundance and the risk of civil war, arguing that primary commodities such as oil, gas, minerals, gemstones, narcotics, timber and agricultural products provide a convenient means to fund rebellions.[3] In the case of civil wars in Angola, Sierra Leone, and Liberia, diamonds, timber and crude oil were sold or traded by rebel groups for materials required to perpetuate fighting. In these conflicts, both state and non-state actors spanning Africa, Europe and the Middle East played substantial roles in the clandestine smuggling networks.[4] Natural

1. Holden, W.N. and Jacobson, R.D., 2007, Mining amid armed conflict—Nonferrous metals mining in the Philippines: Canadian Geographer, v. 51, no. 4, 4 p.; Johnston, P., 2004, Timber booms, state busts—The political economy of Liberian timber: Review of African Political Economy, v. 31, no. 101, p. 441-456.; Ndoye, O. and Tieguhong, J.C., 2004, Forest resources and rural livelihoods—The conflict between timber and non-timber forest products in the Congo Basin: Scandinavian Journal of Forest Research, v. 19, p. 36-44.; Woods, D., 2003, The tragedy of the cocoa pod—Rent-seeking, land and ethnic conflict in Ivory Coast: The Journal of Modern African Studies, v. 41, p. 641-655.; Lujala, P., Gleditsch, N.P., and Gilmore, E., 2005, A diamond curse?—Civil war and a lootable resource: Journal of Conflict Resolution, v. 49, no. 4, p. 538-562.; Olsson, Ola, 2007, Conflict diamonds: Journal of Development Economics, v. 82, no. 2, p. 267-286.
2. OECD, 2011, Due diligence guidance for responsible supply chains of minerals from conflict-affected and high-risk areas: OECD Publishing, 65 p.
3. Collier, P. and Hoeffler, A., 2004, Greed and grievance in civil war: Oxford Economic Paper, v. 56, no. 4, p. 563-595.
4. Orogun, P., 2004, "Blood diamonds" and Africa's armed conflicts in the post-Cold War era: World Affairs, v. 166, no. 3, p. 151-161.

resource smuggling networks are often associated with illegal cash, weapons and narcotics trafficking networks, as resources are traded for these commodities. For example, former Liberian President Charles Taylor supported the invasion of Sierra Leone by the Revolutionary United Front (RUF) by trading arms for Sierra Leonean diamonds and allowing rebels to use the Liberian border as a haven from which to launch attacks.[5] Today, resource-fuelled conflicts continue, to a greater or lesser extent, in DRC (gold, tin, tantalum and tungsten), Côte d'Ivoire (diamonds, cocoa), and Burma (rubies, sapphire).

When examining the role of mineral resources in conflicts, it is necessary to understand the geologic form, accessibility, and geographic location of the deposit as these factors can help to determine the "lootability" of the resource, and its potential role in sustaining conflicts.[6] Mineral deposits can be categorized as primary or secondary. A primary deposit is one that was formed at the same time as the rock enclosing it, has remained in the source rock, and has the potential to have high mineral concentration. Typically, primary deposits require sizeable mining infrastructure, equipment and capital investment for exploitation. As a result, primary deposits are often mined by national or multinational corporations operating under a set of regulatory guidelines established by the host country government.

A secondary deposit is one that has formed as a result of alterations to the primary deposit due to weathering and erosion, and has been transported from the source rock, sometimes as much as several hundred kilometers from the source. Secondary deposits are often considered more lootable as they are easily accessed with basic tools, and have the potential to be spread over vast areas. These deposits are also often located outside the legal and regulatory reach of host governments, rendering them more difficult to monitor and more susceptible to the use and control by armed factions and rebel groups. Lujala and others show that secondary alluvial deposits can increase the feasibility of conflict, particularly where fractionalization and weak states already exist.[7] While secondary deposits can be rich, the majority of these deposits are not rich enough to warrant large-scale mining by industrial companies and, as such, many deposits have been declared uneconomical in the middle part of the last century. However, these secondary deposits are an attractive option for poorer populations as entry barriers for the sector are low, prices and demand are increasing, and the potential exists to generate a quick profit. Little capital investment is required when mining outside the regulatory framework, and often only simple tools such as shovels and picks are all that is needed to extract the commodities. Mining of this nature is commonly known as artisanal and small-scale mining (ASM).

The human dynamics of ASM in West Africa

Introduction to artisanal and small-scale mining (ASM)

The International Labour Organization (ILO) estimates that between 10 and 13 million people are directly involved in the ASM sector worldwide, with an additional 80 to 100 million people whose livelihoods are dependent on ASM.[8] The majority of ASM activities occur in Africa, with an estimated 9 million people directly engaged in artisanal mining and an additional 54 million people dependent on the sector.[9] The popularity of artisanal mining as a livelihood strategy continues to trend upwards as the prices for natural resources continue to rise.[10] The world market price of gold, for example, has increased fourfold in the past eight years, leading to a significant increase in the number of people engaged in the ASM sector. Furthermore, in the past several decades, many African nations have revised their national mining codes to include provisions that legalize and regulate artisanal mining. By the mid-1990s,

5. Montague, D., 2002, The business of war and the prospects for peace in Sierra Leone: Journal of World Affairs, v. p. issue 1, p. 229-237.
6. Le Billion, P., 2003, Fuelling war—Natural resources and armed conflicts: Adelphi Paper 357, 97 p.
7. Lujala, P., Gleditsch, N.P., and Gilmore, E., 2005, A diamond curse?—Civil war and a lootable resource: Journal of Conflict Resolution, v. 49, no. 4, p. 538-562.
8. International Labour Office (ILO), 1999, Report for discussion at the tripartite meeting on social and labour issues in small-scale mines: ILO, 109 p.
9. Hayes, K., 2008, Artisanal and small-scale mining and livelihoods in Africa: Paper presented at the Annual Meeting of the Governing Council of the Common Fund for Commodities, Zanzibar, Tanzania.
10. Van Bockstael, S. and Vlassenroot, K., 2008, in Vlassenroot, K. and Van Bockstael, S., eds., Artisanal diamond mining—Perspectives and challenges: Gent, Academia Press, p. 1-19.

more than two-thirds of African nations had reformed their mining legislation.[11] Such actions were aimed at formalizing the artisanal mining sector through legislative support; however, the costs associated with obtaining a mining license are often too high for many prospective miners. Therefore artisanal mining often continues to take place outside national legal frameworks.

Economic implications: ASM is a dynamic economic activity with important social and cultural implications. While income from ASM is inconsistent, it can provide a source of income to vulnerable populations that may otherwise be unemployed or solely dependent on subsistence agriculture.[12] Money for school fees, medical emergencies, marriages and other important events is frequently sought through artisanal mining. Additionally, ASM activities have the potential to support the economies of surrounding localities through the creation of job opportunities and augmenting the demand for goods and services.[13]

While the official transactions associated with artisanally mined minerals, particularly diamonds, generally follows a consistent hierarchical structure, they can be sold outside of the regulatory framework to unknown buyers and dealers at any point along the supply chain. Such illegal transactions are not uncommon due to the difficulties associated with monitoring and tracking these highly lootable resources. The small size and weight of diamonds, in contrast to oil, tin or timber, also contribute to the ease in smuggling. As a result of these illegal transactions, governments are foregoing access to much-needed sources of tax and duties revenue, which could be used for economic and social development.

Social implications: The social implications of artisanal mining are numerous, affecting the gender roles, health, livelihood strategies and security of ASM populations. For example, permanent or temporary communities in close proximity to artisanal mine sites have higher rates of prostitution and sexually transmitted diseases, such as HIV/AIDS, than other communities, due to the influx of migrant workers.[14] There is also an increased spread of mosquito-borne illnesses such as malaria, yellow fever and dengue fever due to the presence of previously mined pits filled with stagnant water, a result of miners neglecting to backfill mined-out pits. Additionally, drinking water is often not protected from ore washing activities, which can pollute the water and result in gastro-intestinal illnesses.[15] Security risks are also an issue at mine sites and take the form of conflicts with large-scale mining companies and local communities over land-use rights and, in some cases, the presence of armed groups in mining areas.[16]

While the roles of women can differ from site to site, generally women are laborers (transporting ore, washing gravel), providers of goods and services (cooking, selling produce), and perform domestic responsibilities. Women play an important role at the mine site, and ASM provides many women, either directly or indirectly, a means of supporting their family, although the conditions in which they work are often unsafe and unsanitary.

Cultural implications: ASM has led to new migratory patterns, as people cross cultural and national borders to access mine sites (see Figure 1). Such cultural and ethnic diversity is particularly evident in new rush areas, where word has spread of the potential richness of the site, and the surrounding area receives a large influx of miners of varying backgrounds.[17] Migration patterns near artisanal mine sites can be the result of both economic opportunity and regional conflict. For example, during the conflict in the Mano River region of West Africa, large numbers of refugees

11. Jønsson, J.B. and Fold, N., 2011, Mining 'from below'—Taking Africa's artisanal miners seriously: Geography Compass, v.5, no. 7, p. 479-493.
12. Van Bockstael, S. and Vlassenroot, K., 2008, in Vlassenroot, K. and Van Bockstael, S., eds., Artisanal diamond mining—Perspectives and challenges: Gent, Academia Press, p. 1-19.
13. Jønsson, J.B. and Fold, N., 2011, Mining 'from below'—Taking Africa's artisanal miners seriously: Geography Compass, v.5, no. 7, p. 479-493.
14. Hentschel, T., Hruschka, F., and Priester, M., 2002, Global report on artisanal and small-scale mining: Mining, Minerals and Sustainable Development, No. 70, 67 p.
15. The World Bank, 2007, Appalling conditions for growing number of artisanal miners, says World Bank's CASM Initiative—Press Release No:2007/059/SDN : The World Bank.
16. Jønsson, J.B. and Fold, N., 2011, Mining 'from below'—Taking Africa's artisanal miners seriously: Geography Compass, v.5, no. 7, p. 479-493.
17. Jønsson, J.B. and Fold, N., 2011, Mining 'from below'—Taking Africa's artisanal miners seriously: Geography Compass, v.5, no. 7, p. 479-493.

Figure 1

Map showing the distribution of diamond occurrences, population and ethnolinguistic groups in West Africa.

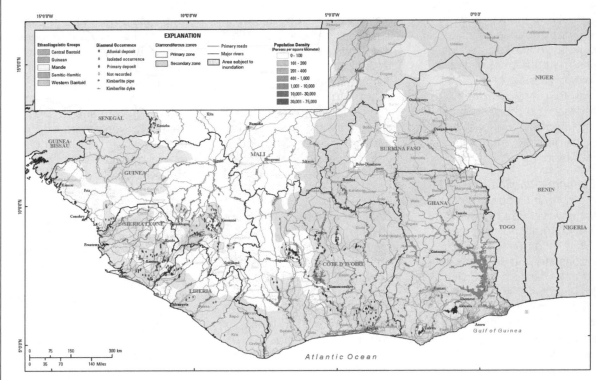

from Sierra Leone settled in neighboring Guinea and began mining Guinean diamond and gold deposits. Today, large communities of Sierra Leonean miners continue to work in Guinea, suggesting a long-term demographic change in these mining areas.

However, while migration and demographic trends may shift with the discovery of new deposits, long-standing ethnolinguistic boundaries tend to have a more significant long-term impact on migration patterns to mine sites than do political boundaries. Historical trade and transportation networks that were often based on ethnic and ethnolinguistic

regions often extend beyond current political boundaries. Malian (Malinke) gold and diamond buyers and collectors, for example, are found throughout West Africa, as part of well-established gold trade networks.[18] The Malinke group, which has historically been involved in artisanal gold mining, spans the border between northern Guinea and southern Mali, rendering the political boundary in this region less relevant. The Kono group is another example. This group originated in Guinea and migrated several hundred years ago to the diamond-rich, eastern portion of Sierra Leone. Part of the Kono,

however, remained in Guinea, and the group was split when the political boundaries of Sierra Leone and Guinea were defined.

Superimposed on traditional African cultural regions is a modern political power structure, with strong ties to regionally based ethnic groups. Knowledge of both the cultural and ethnolinguistic traditions and the modern political environment are critical to understanding the local, national, and regional interactions, as the two are closely interwoven. The political environment can greatly affect the power dynamics amongst the various cultural groups

18. Hilson, G., and Maconachie, R., 2011, Safeguarding livelihoods or exacerbating poverty? Artisanal mining and formalization in West Africa: Natural Resources Forum, v. 35, no. 4, p. 293-303.

within a nation, as prevailing parties may demonstrate preferential or discriminatory treatment towards particular geographic regions, based on their cultural affiliations. Shifting political and cultural influences can therefore affect policies, transportation, trade and exploitation of mineral commodities and activities.

Conclusion

The study of conflict resources in general, and conflict minerals and diamonds in particular, must extend beyond the geologic and economic potential of the deposits. The exploitation, trade, movement and potential for the emergence and perpetuation of conflicts in association with mineral resources is a function of a multi-layered mosaic of environmental, cultural, economic and political landscapes.

In the case of diamonds, the geologic nature of secondary deposits allows for relatively easy extraction by unskilled laborers and with little capital investment. The fact that these deposits are often distributed over such vast areas makes them difficult to monitor, yet accessible to large populations, resulting in informal trading patterns. In the past several decades, West Africa has experienced several civil conflicts that quickly spread to neighboring countries, resulting in the destabilization of the region as a whole. Located within many of these conflict zones are vast deposits of diamonds; it is no surprise therefore that this highly valuable, easily accessible, and widespread resource has in the past become entangled in conflicts. The mere presence of diamonds is not an instigator of conflict; however, easily exploitable deposits can be used to perpetuate and finance conflicts. The present lack of control over the sector in many countries makes it difficult for governments to manage the flow of revenue from artisanal mining activities. The formalization and regularization of the ASM sector by host-country governments are potential solutions to the current gaps in the system that allow for the continued involvement of diamonds in armed conflict.

Peter G. Chirico is the Chief of the USGS Special Geologic Studies Project. He combines field research, geomorphologic mapping and remote sensing techniques in studying conflict resources, hazards, and the physical and human terrain in international areas of interest for agencies within the U.S. government.

Katherine C. Malpeli is a Geographic Research Assistant contracted by Cherokee Nation Businesses to the USGS. She researches the physical and human geographic components of conflict resources and artisanal mining.

Monitoring Growth in Informal Settlements— Anticipating Conflict and Risk for Insecurity

Karen Owen

Introduction

Slums are complex dynamic systems with imprecise boundaries that exist in widely varying historical and cultural contexts. Measuring their growth and change is a perennial challenge due to difficulties in survey reliability, and the lack of safety and security in areas dangerous to traverse. The United Nations Millennium Development Goals (MDG) address the need to improve the lives of slum-dwellers, but enhanced geospatial and imagery-based methods are needed to provide an anticipatory and focused view of where growth is occurring, or where infrastructure improvements may be targeted for greatest benefit.[1] Although the United Nations (UN) now states that progress in slum improvement has been significant, it also acknowledges the original goal is insufficient to counter the continued growth of informal settlements in the developing world.[2] The number of slum dwellers in absolute terms is still expected to grow to 889 million by 2020.[3] This section will address the need for improved monitoring of slums regionally and locally as a major step toward anticipating conflict and risk in urban areas. The foundation upon which slums can be monitored is based on settlement geography and its relationship to urban morphology but also requires an understanding of culture and history. Its premise is that accurate and timely monitoring of settled areas that are now considered slums contributes to better understanding of where populations are most vulnerable to the risks posed by natural and man-made disasters and armed conflict.

Description of the problem— informal settlements and their impact

The United Nations Millennium Development Goal 7D required, "by 2020, to have achieved a significant improvement in the lives of at least 100 million slum dwellers."[4] The UN reported that in 2007 one out of every three city residents resided in slums.[5] Since that time, statistical and

1. Sliuzas, R., Mboup, G. and de Sherbinin, A., "Report of the Expert Group Meeting on Slum Identification and Mapping," International Institute for Geo-Information Science and Earth Observation (ITC), UN-HABITAT Global Urban Observatory, Center for International Earth Science Information Network (CIESIN), Enschede, Netherlands: (2008).; United Nations, *The Millennium Development Goals Report 2010.* New York, NY (2010).
2. UN-HABITAT, "State of the World's Cities," 2010/2011 Bridging the Urban Divide, Earthscan, (2010).
3. Ibid.
4. UN-HABITAT, "Slums of the World: The Face of Urban Poverty in the New Millennium, Monitoring the Millennium Development Goal, Target 11- World-wide Slum Dweller Estimation," Nairobi, Kenya, Global Urban Observatory Program, (2003).
5. UN-HABITAT, "The State of the World's Cities Report 2006/2007: 30 years of shaping the habitat agenda," Nairobi, http://www.unhabitat.org/pmss/listItemDetails.aspx?publicationID=2101, (2006).

data collection methods have improved, and the estimates now anticipate slum growth of 6.1 million per year.[6] Slums, also known as informal settlements, precarious settlements, self-help housing, spontaneous settlements and squatter settlements, are defined as any area where residents *lack* at least one of five principal characteristics: (1) safe drinking water, (2) improved sanitation, (3) security of tenure, (4) sufficient living space, and (5) durable housing.[7] The magnitude of the problem is measured as a percent of the population who are slum dwellers, while its severity is assessed from the sum of concurrent deprivations occurring (Martinez et al. 2008).[8] For example, a settlement suffering from both lack of access to clean drinking water and a lack of access to improved sanitation is considerably worse off than a region that has clean drinking water and public sanitation, but where the residents lack security of tenure.

Informal settlements are primarily an urban phenomenon, often located in close proximity to airports, steep slopes, floodplains, factory effluence and point-source pollution, garbage mountains, superhighways and geologically hazardous zones.[9] The explosive growth of slum populations in the developing world has created living conditions that contribute to poor health, high mortality, excessive crime and economic degradation with inadequate response mechanisms during times of natural disaster.[10] There is a strong positive correlation between the degree of a country's urban population living in slums and its under-five mortality rate, as well as a negative correlation between the degree of urban slum population and socioeconomic status.[11] Martínez et al. (2008) reports a positive correlation between child mortality and poor environmental conditions such as overcrowding, a lack of safe water and inadequate sanitation.[12] Additional security-related problems consistent with conditions in slums include marginalization of unemployed youth, resentment toward governments not providing for basic services, easy recruitment of child soldiers from concentrations of unsupervised youth, and willingness to participate in drug trafficking and other illicit activities in exchange for economic survival.

The demographic shift revealing that more of the world's population lives in urban instead of rural areas occurred in late 2008.[13] Migration trends continue to move from rural to urban, primarily due to the search for employment, and the belief that temporary shelter that is already available can eventually be converted to semi-permanent housing. A study on urban migration in Ivory Coast reported that the top three reasons for in-migration to slums are (1) the availability of land (31 percent), (2) proximity to employment (22 percent) and (3) strong social ties (20 percent).[14] Similar results were reported in a study of informal settlements on the urban fringe of Tehran, where respondents indicated the greatest reason for relocating to slums was access to affordable housing or proximity to their place of work.[15]

Differences in slum structure

6. UN-HABITAT, "State of the World's Cities," 2010/2011 Bridging the Urban Divide, Earthscan, http://www.unhabitat.org/pmss/listItemDetails. aspx?publicationID=2917 (2010). Rapoport, A. Spontaneous Settlements as Vernacular Design. *Spontaneous Shelter: International Perspectives and Prospects* (ed. C. Patton., pp. 51–57). Philadelphia: Temple University Press, (1988).

7. Kostof, S., Tobias, R., *The City Shaped: Urban Patterns and Meanings through History*, Thames and Hudson, London, (1991).; UN-HABITAT, The Challenge of Slums: Global Report on Human Settlements 2003. London: Earthscan (2003).

8. Martinez, J., Mboup, G., Sliuzas, R., Stein, A., "Trends in urban slum indicators across developing world cities," 1990-2003, *Habitat International* 32, (2008):86-108.

9. Kellett, P., and Napier, M., "Squatter Architecture? A Critical Examination of Vernacular Theory and Spontaneous Settlement With Reference to South America and South Africa". *Traditional Dwellings and Settlements Review* 6, No. 11, (1995):7-24.; Kohli, D., Sliuzas, R., Kerle, N., & Stein, A., "An ontology of slums for image-based classification," *Computers, Environment and Urban Systems*, (2012) 36(2):154-163.; Owen, K., & Wong, D. Exploring structural differences between rural and urban informal settlements from imagery: the basureros of Cobán. *Geocarto International* (2013).

10. National Research Council, *Tools and Methods for Estimating Population at Risk from Natural Disasters and Complex Humanitarian Crises.* Committee on 224 (2007).

11. Rice, J., The Urbanization of Poverty and Urban Slum Prevalence: The Impact of the Built Environment on Population-Level Patterns of Social Well-Being in the Less Developed Countries. *Care for Major Health Problems and Population Health Concerns: Impacts on Patients, Providers and Policy,* Research in the Sociology of Health Care (Vol. 26). Bingley, UK: Emerald Group Publishing Limited, (2008).

12. Martinez, J., Mboup, G., Sliuzas, R., Stein, A., "Trends in urban slum indicators across developing world cities," 1990-2003, *Habitat International* 32, (2008):86-108.

13. UN-HABITAT, "The State of the World's Cities Report 2008/2009: Harmonious Cities," http://www.unchs.org/pmss/listItemDetails.aspx?publicationID=2562, (2008).

14. UN High Commission on Refugees, *An Urbanizing World: Global Report on Human Settlements.* New York, New York, (1996).

15. Zebardast, E., "Marginalization of the urban poor and the expansion of the spontaneous settlements on the Tehran metropolitan fringe," *Cities*, 23, No. 6, p.446 (2006).

result from their historical formation process. In some cases, the settlements formed spontaneously as a result of a disaster, a government resettlement program, or a refugee camp that was never relocated.[16] In those cases, the spatial structure may be more regularized or gridded if external (government or United Nations) investment was made in the original build-out. Cultural differences also impact the formation of slums. In Saudi Arabia, the urban poor have taken advantage of Islamic law to legalize certain lands, while in El Dekhila in Alexandria, Egypt, tribal protection offered by Bedouins allowed settlers to occupy certain territories where they are still present today.[17] A different situation exists in Mounira El Gedida in Cairo where informal settlements continue to exist through a strategy of intentional invisibility to government and official channels.[18] The Mounira El Gedida location densified and grew by relying not on government protection or resettlement, but instead on self-contained social structures for help and support in an effort to avoid official government attention.

An important signature of living conditions in slums across world cities is floor area per person.[19] Table 1 displays significant regional difference in measured floorspace per person in cities.[20]

From this table, we can see that the percentage of cities in Africa with less than 10m^2 of floor space per person is 61 percent, compared to Latin America and the Caribbean with 27 percent. These measures relied on demographic and total living space data to explain regional variation. Another signature is roofing materials that vary across cities, from plastic sheeting and wood scraps in Mumbai to corrugated aluminum sheets in Guatemala City to discarded refuse in Kibera, Kenya.

The spatial process by which informal settlements grow can be explained as peripherisation, clustering and densification.[21] Peripherisation and densification occur when eventually the peripheral areas that first became informal settlements are later consumed by urban expansion, remaining as pockets of poverty that continue to pack more densely. This process of structural infill can be observed through imagery as open spaces within settlements previously consumed by greenspace or open area that continue to fill in with buildings over time. Clustering describes when informal areas are grouped

Table 1   Regional Differences in Floor Space Per Person

	Percentage of cities with floor area per person (m^2) in the range					
	≥ 20m^2	15-19 m^2	10-14 m^2	5-9 m^2	< 5 m^2	Total
World	18	18	24	28	13	100
More Developed Regions	56	37	5	2	0	100
Less Developed Regions	7	12	29	35	17	100
Least Developed Countries	4	4	23	37	33	100
Africa	5	1	33	40	21	100
Asia and Oceania	5	15	32	32	17	100
Latin America & Caribbean	15	42	15	23	4	100

16. Pape, J., Deschamps, M., Ford, H., Joseph, P., Johnson, W., Fitzgerald, D, "The GHESKIO Refugee Camp after the Earthquake in Haiti – Dispatch 2 from Port-au-Prince," *The New England Journal of Medicine 362:e27*, (2010).

17. Alsayyad, N., "Squatting and Culture - A Comparative Analysis of Informal Developments in Latin America and the Middle East," *Habitat International* 17, No. 1, (1993):33-44.

18. Ibid.

19. Briggs, D., "Making a Difference: Indicators to Improve Children's Environmental Health," Core Indicators, World Health Organization, (2003):34.

20. United Nations, "Charting the Progress of Populations," Chapter 12, "Floor Area Per Person," http://www.un.org/esa/population/pubsarchive/chart/14.pdf, New York, (2000).

21. Barros, J.X., Urban Growth in Latin American Cities, exploring urban dynamics through agent-based simulation. University College, London, UK, (October 2004).; Sietchiping, R., Proceedings of ICSTM2000. Presented at the International Conference on Systems Thinking in Management, Geelong, Australia, (2000).

together and can be identified within the urban zone separated by non-slum, wealthier, or industrial/trade areas. Focusing on form and shape, or the morphometric qualities of slums, gives insight into their expansion and change. For example, if spread occurs toward a major arterial waterway or urban highway, we expect increased risk of displacement during flood events or increased pedestrian traffic accidents.

Clearly the shape, growth and locational traits of informally settled areas are an integral part of understanding change and anticipating security problems. Decisions to improve infrastructure in such zones can be made by an understanding of form, which can easily be measured remotely through imagery.

In the context of monitoring slums, governments and development agencies seek more accurate population estimates, improved assessment of vulnerability to natural and man-made hazards and a spatial understanding of where a disaster would have greatest consequence within the urban infrastructure. Generally, this means understanding urban zones of highest poverty and population density, two variables that are positively correlated in many urban areas. Metrics on populated areas, their transportation corridors, and their proximity to hazards must be as precise as possible because the demand for humanitarian assistance and disaster response is exerted on increasingly limited resources in a globally depressed economy. Proper monitoring of urban slum populations aids preparedness when armed conflict occurs. It helps to plan evacuation routes when we know where the most vulnerable urban residents are located.

How slums are currently monitored

Slums are currently monitored using both qualitative and quantitative approaches. UN-HABITAT is the primary organization that monitors MDG performance worldwide, an enormous undertaking that uses methodology "structured on collaborative data collection between national, local and metropolitan governments in each country".[22] Related urban monitoring projects have also relied heavily upon expensive field surveys supported by direct observation and limited statistical sampling that is difficult to undertake in areas that are dangerous to navigate.[23] A combination of statistical sources currently used to measure slums are derived from the UN's World Urbanization Prospects; WHO/UNICEF Joint Monitoring Programme on Water Supply and Sanitation (JMP), Demographic and Health Surveys (DHS), Multiple Indicator Cluster Survey (MICS), the UN-HABITAT's Urban Inequities Surveys (UIS) as well as census data when possible.[24] The UN-HABITAT unfortunately aggregates the results to the national and continental level, but methods used and the definition of what is actually collected vary by each country's own national data-gathering strategy.

Consistent with this reporting imperative is an increased recognition that reliance on imagery-derived data sources can reduce cost and improve accuracy of settlement monitoring efforts.[25] Surveys and field work are needed to measure the slum indicators of *access to safe drinking water, access to improved sanitation,* and whether or not residents enjoy *security of tenure* or the legal right to live in their location. These methods risk sampling error and a lack of breadth for any single slum. In addition, the time between surveys, coordination with other statistical collection organizations and changes in the underlying response population prevents such surveys from being longitudinally replicable. This limitation makes current measuring techniques of limited use in monitoring the locations where change is occurring.

22. Hoornweg, D., Ruiz Nunez, F., Freire, M., Palugyai, N., Villaveces, M., & Herrera, E.W. *City Indicators: Now to Nanjing* (Working Paper), World Bank, (2007).

23. Rice, J., The Urbanization of Poverty and Urban Slum Prevalence: The Impact of the Built Environment on Population-Level Patterns of Social Well-Being in the Less Developed Countries. *Care for Major Health Problems and Population Health Concerns: Impacts on Patients, Providers and Policy*, Research in the Sociology of Health Care (Vol. 26). Bingley, UK: Emerald Group Publishing Limited, (2008).; Yeh, Anthony G., "GIS as a Planning Support System for the Planning of Harmonious Cities," *UN-HABITAT Lecture Award Series*, No. 3, UN-HABITAT, Nairobi, (2008).; UN-HABITAT, "Millennium Development Goals Indicators - Method of Computation," http://mdgs.un.org/unsd/mdg/Metadata.aspx?IndicatorId=0&SeriesId=711, retrieved 21 Aug 2011.; Galeon, F., "Estimation of Population in Informal Settlement Communities using High resolution Satellite Image," *International Archives of the Photogrammetry, Remote Sensing and Spatial Information Sciences* 37 (Part B4, Beijing), (2008):1380.

24. Sliuzas, R. *Diversity of global slum conditions - is a universal spatial definition of slums feasible?* Presented at the Expert Group Meeting on Slum Mapping, 21 May 2008, Enschede, Netherlands, (2008).

25. Ibid. Yeh, Anthony G., "GIS as a Planning Support System for the Planning of Harmonious Cities," *UN-HABITAT Lecture Award Series*, No. 3, UN-HABITAT, Nairobi, (2008).

The remaining two slum indicators—*sufficient living space* and *durability of housing* lend themselves to the use of remote sensing image analysis. This is because dwelling size, roofing materials and building heights are measurable from spatial and spectral resolution currently available in commercial very high resolution (VHR) imagery such as Quickbird, Worldview-2, IKONOS and Light Detection and Ranging (LiDAR) sensors. Imagery-based methods are not the only reliable ones, but anchoring current methodologies to physical properties of slums that can be derived from imaging sensors is easily achievable, replicable and suitable for monitoring change in terms of growth directionality, densification or peripherisation.[26]

The UN's Expert Working Group on Slum Metrics concluded that continued research into the use of imagery-based techniques to monitor slums is required.[27] Object-based image analysis, or OBIA, is an approach to feature extraction that uses spatial, spectral and radiometric properties of imagery to derive the boundaries and shape of objects on the ground, with an aim toward replacing manual digitization. The approach is normally scene-dependent, requires a training subset and a validation source from field observation in order to measure accuracy. OBIA relies on such properties as elongation, circularity, texture, color, and the detection of edges to produce boundaries between shapes in the hope of accurately identifying discrete objects. Objects or features such as dwellings and roads and their attributes (length, surface materials, density, proximity) can be used to remotely monitor the human condition, and could be especially useful in measuring the *durability of housing* and *sufficient living space* slum indicators.[28] The OBIA technique was used to classify locations of informal settlements in Kenya with reasonable results.[29] Its primary limitations are the inability to detect discrete structures from continuous rooflines, and improper splitting of singular buildings when a single roof is comprised of multiple materials.

The final report of the Expert Working Group on Slum Identification and Mapping called for a "set of clearly defined indicators related to VHR images," while acknowledging that an initial 20 percent margin of error was acceptable.[30] A clear requirement, then, is for repeatable metrics that can be applied locally and regionally by non-UN organizations as well.

An alternative method of monitoring slums has recently changed the face of spatial information available and is exemplified by the Map Kibera project.[31] Map Kibera is a local effort by volunteers and non-government organizations (NGOs) to publish information about the locations of features in slums. Originally meant to raise awareness of the destitute conditions in one of the world's largest slums in Nairobi, Kenya, the project has grown global through its Internet website. Local residents trained to use GPS report the locations of features they see and use regularly, including medical facilities, water sources, roads and toilets. The features are published using the OpenStreetMap Web mapping model, and also incorporate local news items anchored to a spot that displays on the map.[32] Similar methods have been applied in Sierra Leone to map health risks of residents.[33]

26. Barros, J.X., Urban Growth in Latin American Cities, exploring urban dynamics through agent-based simulation. University College, London, UK, (October 2004).; Barros, J., & Sobreira, F., City of Slums: self-organisation across scales. *Unifying Themes in Complex Systems IV.* Springer Berlin, Heidelberg, (2008).

27. Sliuzas, R., Mboup, G., & de Sherbinin, A., *Report of the Expert Group Meeting on Slum Identification and Mapping* (p. 36). Enschede, Netherlands: International Institute for Geo-Information Science and Earth Observation (ITC), UN-HABITAT Global Urban Observatory, Center for International Earth Science Information Network (CIESIN) p. 11, (2008).

28. Owen, K., Geospatial and Remote Sensing-Based Indicators of Settlement Type – Differentiating Informal and Formal Settlements in Guatemala City, PhD Dissertation published by George Mason University, Fairfax, VA.

29. Hurskainen, P. and Pellikka, P., "Change detection of informal settlements using multi-temporal aerial photographs - the case of Voi, SE-Kenya," *Proceedings of the 5th AARSE conference* (African Association of Remote Sensing of the Environment), Nairobi, Kenya, CD-Publication, no page numbers (18-21 October, 2004).

30. Sliuzas, R., Mboup, G., & de Sherbinin, A., *Report of the Expert Group Meeting on Slum Identification and Mapping* (p. 36). Enschede, Netherlands: International Institute for Geo-Information Science and Earth Observation (ITC), UN-HABITAT Global Urban Observatory, Center for International Earth Science Information Network (CIESIN) p20 (2008).

31. http://www.MapKibera.org 2009, retrieved 11 Oct 2012.

32. http://www.openstreetmap.org, retrieved 11 Oct 2012.

33. Ansumana, R., Malanoski, A., Bockarie, A., Sundufu, A., Jimmy, D., Bangura, U., Jacobsen, K., Lin, B., Stenger, D., "Enabling methods for community health mapping in developing countries," *International Journal of Health Geographics*, (2010) 9:56.

These local efforts have given a voice to the hundreds of thousands of previously anonymous residents. As a new phenomenon with great potential for shared data collection, issues remain that will need to be addressed to use it for systematic worldwide slum monitoring. Such issues include bias by data collectors, common standards for data collection and metadata, and GPS accuracy. The Map Kibera construct strongly espouses the participatory mapping model that will be discussed later.

Anticipating conflict and risk

Planning and anticipating conflict and risk with a focus on urban monitoring requires knowledge of three fundamental properties discernable from imagery: dwellings, roads and the intervening spaces.[34] Built-up areas and dwellings, transportation networks and the composition of parcels, vegetation and soil are useful for understanding spatial arrangement and underlying processes. Settlements occupy multi-dimensional space where the properties of form (morphometric qualities), scale (unit of measurement), and time (historical context) can be used to understand the social forces shaping them.[35] The study of settlement geography can contribute much to a holistic view of slums, especially when enhanced by remotely sensed images of these areas aided by geographic information

systems (GIS) analysis and local participatory mapping. Figure 1 illustrates the process of analyzing slums by focusing on data requirements and extracting settlement primitives to improve spatial understanding of conflict and other risks.

The search for metrics that can be used as proxies for quality of life, livelihoods and relative wealth or poverty is a worthwhile objective in the spatial identification and monitoring of urban areas with greatest risk for conflict. Figure 2 lists some metrics that exhibit significant differences between slums and wealthy areas from prior research, including metrics based on roads, built-up areas, greenspace and soil.[36] Several modeling methods (a discriminant model and a decision tree model) were applied using GIS, remote sensing, and field observation to measure the differences between formal and informal

settlements. Given these differences, one can positively identify those informal settlements in a densely populated urban area for further monitoring where conflict and safety risks may be anticipated.

Analysts wish to identify existing, newly forming and growing slums with minimal field work because of the complications and logistical difficulties in ground-based systematic measurement. Confirming physical observations and measuring change to understand when slum conditions have worsened or size has expanded requires quantitative methods. The added understanding from spatial quantification will improve monitoring outcomes.

Anticipating security and safety problems before they occur in a disaster response or humanitarian assistance scenario means baseline data is already available to plan for requirements such as counting the number of residents,

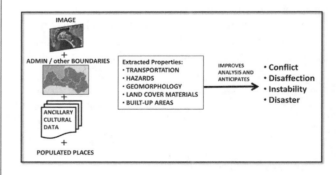

Figure 1 Data and Image Processing Needs to Improve Understanding

34. Pesaresi, M., Gerhardinger, A. and Kayitakire, F., "A Robust Built-Up Area Presence Index by Anisotropic Rotation-Invariant Textural Measure," IEEE *Journal of Selected Topics in Applied Earth Observations and Remote Sensing* 1, No. 3, (2008).

35. Moudon, A., Urban morphology as an emerging interdisciplinary field, Urban Morphology 1, 3-10 (1997).

36. Owen, K. and Wong, D, "An approach to differentiate informal settlements using spectral, texture, geomorphology and road accessibility metrics, Applied Goegraphy, 38,107-118, (2013).

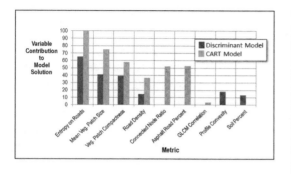

Figure 2   Significant GIS and Remote Sensing Metrics to Quantify Formal and Informal Settlement Differences

estimating building materials to be replaced, logistics for specific quantities of food and shelter, transportation routes for the delivery of goods, or evacuation of residents. Consistent metrics for characteristics of slums in cities can enhance our response to these populations when natural disasters, armed conflict and security problems occur.

Marginalization of populations and limitations of spatial identification

If we understand and can measure densely populated informal settlements, the next assumption is that we can begin to identify likely areas where the marginalization of groups and individuals provides conditions more susceptible to conflict. *Socially disorganized neighborhoods* where residents are marginalized exhibit higher rates of deviant criminal behavior.[37] Informal settlements and slums that suffer a lack of social organization may thereby display conditions that marginalize residents. Other informal settlements display a more self-reliant social structure where such risks may not be as acute.[38] Similar to the concept of social disorganization is the tendency for low *relative political capacity* in slum areas. *Relative political capacity* is a measure of a government's ability to extract resources from the population that is consistent with their level of economic development.[39] Extreme poverty, joblessness and illiteracy are magnified in regions with low relative political capacity, and the result is a government unable to keep conflict in check (Ibid). Governments interested in reducing the underlying conditions that lead to conflict may focus on improving these

areas or targeting development projects to maximize the benefit to the local population. This could include the provision of adequate housing. A number of efforts have focused on slum upgrading projects and most recognize the importance of participatory approaches, where local residents and organized groups contribute to mapping efforts and to the production of geospatial data.[40] Although this process is slow and cumbersome, it can also be more effective in maintaining stability when those involved recognize who stands to gain or lose from the mapping process, and the process is transparent. If we also monitor crowd-sourced slum mapping efforts like Map Kibera, we can now prioritize our quantitative measurement activities by city, and also have a better understanding of locally-known places, including slums.

When analyzing slums, or any urban area, geographical focus is often limited to an administrative boundary. This is because it is easier to limit a study area to regions already used for data collection (census districts, for example) or regions used in prior mapping efforts.

Administrative boundaries have limitations, however. They are politically drawn and the data collected for them can exhibit bias. They change over time and may not be related

37. Pebley and Sastray, Neighborhoods, Poverty and Children's Wellbeing, in Social Inequality, Neckerman, Kathryn, Ed. (2004).

38. Alsayyad, N., "Squatting and Culture—A Comparative Analysis of Informal Developments in Latin America and the Middle East," *Habitat International* 17, No. 1, (1993):33-44.

39. Arbetman-Rabinowitz, M. and Johnson, K., "Relative Political Capacity: Empirical and Theoretical Underpinnings," Presented at the *Annual Meeting of International Studies Association*, San Francisco, CA, (26-29 March, 2008).

40. Barry, M. and Rüther, H., "Data Collection and Management for Informal Settlements Upgrades," International Conference on Spatial Information for Sustainable Development Nairobi, Kenya http://www.fig.net/pub/proceedings/nairobi/barry-ruther-ts13-2.pdf (October 2001).
Lemma, T., Sliuzas, R. and Kuffer, M., "A Participatory Approach to Monitoring Slum Conditions," Paper presented at *Mapping for Change: International conference on participatory spatial information management and communication*, Nairobi, Kenya, (2005).; Martinez, J., Mboup, G., Sliuzas, R., Stein, A., "Trends in urban slum indicators across developing world cities," 1990-2003, *Habitat International* 32, (2008):86-108.; World Bank, "Urban Poverty and Slum Upgrading," http://go.worldbank.org/D7G2Q70170, retrieved 22 Aug 2011.

to how people self-identify. For example, demographic information on women is underreported in certain parts of Pakistan, and permeates the official census that reports an inverse gender ratio (110 men for every 100 women) but this is likely due to systemic gender subordination. Lacking a street address, cadastral map, or physical neighborhood boundaries, the researcher is left to aggregate individual information to a known political boundary where the government has drawn a representative polygon on a map. This is where the use of imagery has shown great benefit. However, singularly relying on imagery to monitor slums also limits our understanding of residents who move across the landscape, travel to distant locations, and sometimes migrate seasonally or have multiple dwelling locations.

Awareness of these limitations is critical when analyzing survey data, determining collection boundaries, or incorporating census demographics to validate slum monitoring methods.

What should be monitored and how

The importance of extracting information about three basic settlement primitives has been suggested: dwellings, roads or transportation corridors, and the in-between spaces. It was also mentioned that informal settlements are often found near natural and man-made hazards.

The next step is to delve more deeply into why these primitives are important, and the linkage between their collection and a better understanding of the conditions in slums. Understanding the physical context of slums helps to establish what should be monitored. The hazards mentioned before include proximity to airports, steep slopes, floodplains, factory effluence and point-source pollution, garbage mountains, superhighways and geologically hazardous zones such as earthquake fault-lines. This does not mean that all informal settlements are precisely adjacent to these hazards, but it does mean that land for housing in such areas is of little value. Devalued land or property for which governments do not record ownership tends to attract squatters and those engaging in insecure forms of tenure. Table 2 provides a summary of hazards impacting slums worldwide, the risk, the type of geospatial, remote sensing, or sample data that could support its measurement, and an example type of analysis that may contribute to improved monitoring.

An understanding of the hazards, risks, supporting data and type of analysis is only part of the guidance researchers need. Population estimates are also needed.[41] Knowing where people inhabit (and their residential density) is the single most important contribution that could be made to monitoring informal settlement growth, and fortunately much research has contributed to solving this problem with imagery-based solutions.[42] This requirement coincides with the needs of development agencies and social science professionals seeking cultural understanding and demographic information prior to engagement in an area.[43]

There are some accuracy limitations when imagery-based methods are used to estimate population that should be mentioned. There are difficulties in counting residents in multi-story apartment houses, and occupancy rate methods do not always consider abandoned or vacant property.[44] There are also variations in diurnal populations, and population estimates must account for such variations.[45] It has also been shown that small area (e.g., village) estimates are often less accurate than large

41. Dobson, J., Bright, E., Coleman, P., and Bhaduri, B., "LandScan: a global population database for estimating populations at risk." *Remotely Sensed Cities* Ed. V. Mesev, London: Taylor & Francis, (2003):267-281.; Bhaduri, B., Bright, E., Coleman, P., and Dobson, J., "LandScan: Locating People is What Matters," Geoinformatics 5, No. 2, (2002):34-37.

42. Checchi *et al.* Validity and feasibility of a satellite imagery-based method for rapid estimation of displaced populations, *International Journal of Health Geographics* (2013) 12:4.; Azar, D., Graesser, J., Engstrom, R., Comenetz, J., Leddy, R., Schechtman, N. and Andrews, T., "Spatial refinement of census population distribution using remotely sensed estimates of impervious surface in Haiti," *International Journal of Remote Sensing* 31, No. 21, (2010):5635-5655.; Yeh, Anthony G., "GIS as a Planning Support System for the Planning of Harmonious Cities," *UN-HABITAT Lecture Award Series*, No. 3, UN-HABITAT, Nairobi, (2008).

43. Foster, D., "The Human Terrain System and Social Science in Iraq," presentation at the *Institute for World Politics*, Washington, DC, (19 Oct 2009).

44. Liu, D., Weng, Q. and Li, G., "Residential population estimation using a remote sensing derived impervious surface approach," *International Journal of Remote Sensing* 27, No. 16, (2006):3553–3570.

45. Kobayashi, T., Medina, R., and Cova, T., "Visualizing Diurnal Population Change in Urban Areas for Emergency Management," *The Professional Geographer* 63, No. 1, (2011):113-130.

Table 2   Hazards, Risks and Supporting Data Needed

Hazard	Risk	Supporting Data	Type of Analysis
Landslides	• Erosion during rainy season • Housing collapse in unstable soils • Structural weakness from poor quality building materials	Hypsographic data Atmospheric data (weather, rainfall) Soils and underlying geology Local building codes	Spatial interpolation Topographic modeling Geomorphology modeling
Flooding/ Drought	• Inundation, dwelling destruction • Crop loss • Grazing conflict in pastoral areas • Road closures, debris flows • Lack of access to health and basic services	Crop production forecasts from imagery Livelihood regions Streams from radar imagery Hurricane, coastal flood history Weather, rainfall	Hydrologic and geomorphic modeling Built-up area proximity to flood risk
Point Source and Industrial Pollution	• Human exposure to toxins • Birth defects • Contaminated drinking water	Water samples Soil samples Locally-produced food samples Drinking water access and collection practices Unsafe labor practices	Longitudinal health surveys Lifestyle impacts from lack of clean water Food insecurity analysis
Landfills	• Human exposure to toxins • Spontaneous combustion	Local knowledge VHR image texture	Micro-economy of garbage dealers & collectors Proximity to settled areas
Highway Proximity	• Exhaust (diesel/lead) pollution • Noise pollution • Traffic fatalities	Mortality records Vehicle repair records Vehicle counts from imagery	Annoyance studies Air quality Transportation and network analysis
Geologic Hazards	• Sinkholes • Earthquakes • Volcanic eruptions	Soil composition Fault zones Volcanic activity and history	Seismic studies Soil/agronomy analysis Geomorphology studies

area estimates.[46] Accuracy also suffers in settlements with continuous rooflines, which obscure the walls that separate one family from another. The Oak Ridge National Labs (ORNL) Landscan population data is the most comprehensive effort to date in estimating population worldwide.[47] However, accuracy varies largely as a function of the corresponding census data collected, and increases non-linearly as the geographic area of estimation increases in size.

For example, one would not use the (~ 1km^2) population pixel values from a Landscan grid cell that intersect a small village in a developing country for planning purposes. In the Landscan dataset, accuracy increases when scaling upward to an administrative boundary for which census data has been collected, but small area estimates of a few pixels are not sufficiently accurate for decision-making where population at the local level must be known.

Similar to the population estimation imperative in monitoring slums, a comparable requirement is to measure the type of growth and the spatial components of directionality and density by estimating "built-up"

areas. Largely derived from the literature on impervious surface mapping that grew from the availability of the mid-infrared spectral band on the Landsat satellite mission, urban estimates of impervious surface continue to contribute to our understanding of land cover and urban classification.[48] Built-up areas, or areas of human-built structures, are used to model impacts on human settlements, impacts on the environment and surrounding natural resources, and to estimate population, and are nearly as important as population counts.[49]

In order to properly evaluate slums, discrete neighborhoods should be identified by local naming conventions and their boundaries should be estimated. These boundaries are often defined by physical barriers to passage (rivers, superhighways, steep slopes), but also from local knowledge. Once neighborhood boundaries have been defined, named and explained, a unit for analysis now exists—whether from imagery, crowd-sourced VGI, or surveys, and change can be measured within that area. To improve the ability to monitor slums, future studies should also attempt to identify ancillary validation

data in advance. These data include surveys, health and demographic compilations such as census, and reports from development and aid agencies. These data provide additional context and help focus the geographic area of study. Evaluations of slum areas should be anchored to identifiable locations on the ground, whether through census-defined locations, administrative boundary names, GEONAMES, or local gazetteer references.[50]

Another form of local place name identification is called *participatory mapping*. This type of mapping involves the residents in the mapping process, who may have varying degrees of literacy, by using their own language and including pictures or drawings of familiar places.[51] Participatory mapping is an effort to map areas previously not mapped by using locally-named streams, hilltops, gathering places or cultural landmarks known to residents relative to their dwelling location. This technique must be applied with caution and a thorough understanding of whether residents or groups might be disenfranchised as a result of map publication.[52] The more recent crowd-sourced

46. Wu, S., Qiu, X. and Wang, L., "Population Estimation methods in GIS and Remote Sensing: A Review". GIScience & Remote Sensing 42, No.1, (2005):80-96.

47. LandScan Global Population Database, Oak Ridge National Laboratory, http://www.ornl.gov/gist/, Oakridge, TN, (2001-2010).

48. Rahman, Atiqur, Aggarwal, Shiv, Netzband, Maik and Fazal, Shahab, "Monitoring Urban Sprawl Using Remote Sensing and GIS Techniques of a Fast Growing Urban Centre, India," IEEE *Journal of Selected Topics in Applied Earth Observations and Remote Sensing*, Vol 4, No. 1, (2011).; Pesaresi, M., Gerhardinger, A. and Kayitakire, F., "A Robust Built-Up Area Presence Index by Anisotropic Rotation-Invariant Textural Measure," IEEE *Journal of Selected Topics in Applied Earth Observations and Remote Sensing* 1, No. 3, (2008).

49. Lo, C.P., "Estimating Population and Census Data, in Remote Sensing of Human Settlements," *Manual of Remote Sensing, Third Edition* 5, Merrill Ridd, James Hipple, eds., American Society of Photogrammetry and Remote Sensing, (2006).; Li, G., Weng, Q., "Using Landsat ETM+ imagery to measure population density in Indianapolis, Indiana, USA," *Photogrammetric Engineering and Remote Sensing* 71, No. 8, (2005):947-958.; Wu, S., Qiu, X. and Wang, L., "Population Estimation methods in GIS and Remote Sensing: A Review". *GIScience & Remote Sensing* 42, No.1, (2005):80-96.

50. http://earth-info.nga.mil/gns/html/.

51. Herlihy, P., Dobson, J., Robledo, M., Smith, D., Kelly, J., Viera, A., "A Digital Geography of Indigenous Mexico: Prototype for the American Geographical Society's Bowman Expeditions," *Geographical Review* 98, No. 3, (2008):395-415.

52. Chambers, R., Participatory Mapping and Geographic Information Systems: Whose Map? Who is Empowered and who Disempowered? Who Gains and Who Loses?, *Electronic Journal on Information Systems in Developing Countries*, 2006, Vol (25), Issue 2, p 1-11.

participatory mapping efforts such as Map Kibera will grow as a source of rich contextual understanding of slum conditions from a local perspective. Survey results should be shared and incorporated with participatory maps so that remote sensing specialists and geographers can validate their findings contextually through these ancillary data.

A multi-stage approach to the classification of informal settlements is recommended, whereby remote sensing and image processing techniques are applied to differentiate slum neighborhoods, and these techniques are enriched by incorporating socioeconomic and statistical data to help interpret results.[53]

Measuring change

Measuring change in informal settlements, at least biennially, is crucial to determine whether conditions are worsening or improving. However, current methods that distinguish good change from bad change need improvement.

Settlement change is most often measured by comparing data from at least two or three different dates, computing the built-up area, then determining directionality or density of change relative to the settlement that is being measured. Making an assessment of the quality

of change can be subjective. "Degree-of-goodness" of urban growth has been proposed as the degree to which observed growth is related to expected growth— measured as consistent growth in all directions— and the magnitude of compactness.[54] This way of measuring degree-of-goodness that only relates to morphological features is missing important socio-economic information about the quality of life of the residents, and whether growth is occurring in areas at higher risk to disaster.

Volunteered geographic information may provide additional context to quality-of-life measures that traditionally relied on survey results and image classification of greenspace. But the validity of using this information for measuring improvements in slum conditions over time is yet to be proven, and prior efforts that only measure the boundary of urban areas don't provide additional characteristics of local change. Measuring greenspace change and transportation network change could be helpful here.

Change at the building-level, another important dimension, has been applied to determine what structures have been removed or added over time and how recently, and for damage assessment.[55] At the village level, Prins detected

burn scars due to civil war in Sudan with Landsat imagery.[56] But village level change, measurable with moderate resolution imagery such as Landsat, doesn't reveal individual small shacks that have either disappeared or emerged between detection dates. Measuring change at the building level requires accurate feature extraction from very high-resolution imagery.

Work performed to monitor informal settlements should focus on whether the kind of change occurring is helpful or harmful to the resident population by taking local social conditions into account, not simply measuring directionality or density.

Conclusion

Governments and agencies with a vested interest in mitigating the impacts of natural disasters, conflict and insecurity need a common approach to monitoring slums in urban areas. Prior approaches are disparate, labor intensive, difficult to replicate and can even generate conflict themselves by exposing (or obscuring) land ownership inequalities when maps are published that have not existed before. However, we should remain cognizant of where crowd-sourced local mapping efforts have taken root, since this provides a unique opportunity to monitor slums from the viewpoint of their residents.

53. Busgeeth, K., Brits, A., and J. Whisken, "Potential Application of Remote Sensing in Monitoring Informal Settlements in Developing Countries where Complementary Data Does Not Exist," *Planning Africa Conference*, Johannesburg, South Africa, (14-16 April 2008).

54. Bhatta, B., Saraswati, S., & Yopadhayay, B. D. (2010). Quantifying the degree-of-freedom, degree-of-sprawl, and degree-of-goodness of urban growth from remote sensing data. *Applied Geography*, 30(1), 96-111.

55. Hurskainen, P. and Pellikka, P., "Change detection of informal settlements using multi-temporal aerial photographs - the case of Voi, SE-Kenya," *Proceedings of the 5th AARSE conference* (African Association of Remote Sensing of the Environment), Nairobi, Kenya, CD-Publication, no page numbers (18-21 October, 2004).

56. Prins, E., "Use of low cost Landsat ETM+ to spot burnt villages in Darfur Sudan," International Journal of Remote Sensing, Vol 29, No. 4, (2008):1207-1214.1. J. Rowland Illick, former Middlebury College professor of geography, as cited by Jerome E. Dobson, 2007, "Bring Back Geography!" *Arc News*, 29 (1): 1-5.

Future research is needed to confirm the accuracy of publicly contributed VGI data while also standardizing its collection. Institutions can and should use remote sensing image analysis with the assistance of GIS to monitor change and morphology of informal settlements, and build more accurate models of residential built-up areas, transportation corridors and their intervening spaces. Quantitative metrics applicable to a variety of slums worldwide should be produced as a baseline product for areas of concern, against which change can be measured biennially without intervention and without threatening the safety of data collectors.

To accomplish this goal, it is necessary to address the extent to which metrics proposed are regionally or culturally bounded. Before meaning can be derived from locating features and objects in imagery related to human habitation, the methods applied must be grounded in a thorough historical understanding of how the settlement initiated and the factors that contributed to its growth. Spatially and temporally measuring physical features and characteristics of informal settlements from imagery using a locally valid baseline classification can therefore be used as a proxy to anticipate zones of potential conflict or instability.

Dr. Karen Owen is a strategist, analyst and scientific researcher of settlement geography. She teaches Urban Geography and Human Geography classes at George Mason University (GMU), and has published in peer-reviewed journals on the topics of neighborhood type differentiation from imagery, image-based morphology of rural vs. urban slums and geographic access to healthcare.

Section 4

The Socio-Technical Dimensions of Culture
and the Modern Geography of Security

SOCIAL MEDIA AND THE EMERGENCE OF OPEN-SOURCE GEOSPATIAL INTELLIGENCE

Anthony Stefanidis, Andrew Crooks,
Arie Croitoru, Jacek Radzikowski
and Matt Rice

1: Introduction

The power of social media to serve as an effective and irrepressible information dissemination mechanism was demonstrated quite vividly during the Arab Spring events across North Africa and the Middle East in early 2011. Platforms like Twitter, Facebook, and YouTube were instrumental not only in reporting news from these events, but also in supporting the organization and coordination of activities that were part of these events.[1]

While this is widely considered to be a watershed moment for the use of social media in geopolitical events, it was not the first time that this happened. Twenty months before Arab Spring, in June 2009, social media platforms were used to broadcast to the world real-time information from the clashes in the streets of Tehran following the rigged Iranian presidential election, bypassing the state-imposed crackdown on crisis coverage.[2]

The Tehran unrest eventually fizzled out, but this experience served notice to the general public in the Arab world. It made them fully aware of the power of social media to bypass state-controlled news channels in order to bring their message to the attention of the rest of their countrymen, and to engage the world community, leading to the organized and purposeful use of social media during Arab Spring. The user-generated and Web-delivered content of social media is complementing established information sources to support open-source intelligence analysis.

The emergence of social media feeds as an intelligence source is presenting interesting challenges and opportunities to the geospatial intelligence community in particular. These feeds more often than not have some sort of geographic content, for example communicating the location from which a particular report is contributed, the geolocation of an image, or making a reference to a specific sociocultural hotspot. It is very interesting to observe for example that Fukushima and Cairo were among the top 10 trending topics of discussion in Twitter during the first six months of 2011, while events were unfolding at the Japanese nuclear plant and the Egyptian uprising.[3]

The geographic content of social media feeds represents a new type of geographic information. It does not fall under the established geospatial community definitions of crowdsourcing

---

1. New York Times (2011), Spotlight Again Falls on Web tools and Change, *New York Times*. Available at http://www.nytimes.com/2011/01/30/weekinreview/30shane.html?_r=1&hp [Accessed on September 1, 2011].; Pollock, J. (2011), "Streetbook: How Egyptian and Tunisian Youth Hacked the Arab Spring," *Technology Review*, September/October 2011. Available at http://www.technologyreview.com/web/38379/ [Accessed on October 15, 2011].

2. Newsweek (2009), A Twitter Timeline of the Iran Election, *Newsweek*. Available at http://www.newsweek.com/2009/06/25/a-Twitter-timeline-of-the-iran-election.html [Accessed on April 27th, 2011].

3. http://blog.twitter.com/2011/06/200-million-tweets-per-day.html .

or volunteered geographic information, as it is not the product of a process through which citizens explicitly and purposefully contribute geographic information to update or expand geographic databases.[4] Instead, the type of geographic information that can be harvested from social media feeds can be referred to as Ambient Geographic Information: it is *embedded* in the content of these feeds, often across the content of numerous entries rather than within a single one, and has to be somehow extracted.[5] Nevertheless, it is of great importance as it communicates in real time information about emerging issues, and also provides an unparalleled view of the complex social networking and cultural dynamics within a society, capturing the temporal evolution of the human landscape. In this paper we present emerging analysis techniques to harvest geospatial intelligence from social media feeds, focusing particularly on Twitter, as a representative data source.

The article is organized as follows. In Section 2 we trace the emergence of social media, followed in Section 3 by a discussion on their geolocation content, and discuss harvesting social media feeds in Section 4. We follow with a discussion of case studies in Section 5, showcasing novel types of geospatial analysis that can be performed using ambient geospatial information. Finally, in Section 6 we offer our outlook assessment.

2: The emergence of social media

During the last few years and aided by the growth and evolution of Web 2.0 technologies, social media applications have emerged to facilitate interactive information sharing, interoperability, user-centered design, and collaboration on the World Wide Web.[6] The term *social media* is typically used to refer to services like Facebook, Twitter, Flickr and YouTube, which enable the general public to communicate with their peers, sharing information with them instantly and constantly in an effortless and intuitive way. By bypassing the need for advanced computing skills to participate, and by enabling practically everybody to contribute, social media has revolutionized information contribution and dissemination through the Internet. This allowed the public at large, who were primarily information consumers in the Web 1.0 world, to become active contributors and disseminators of information, thus bypassing traditional media outlets (such as news organizations).

Today, social media applications thrive. In the spring of 2011, just five years after its 2006 launch, Twitter announced that it had over 200 million accounts, distributed all over the world. Among these accounts, it was estimated that Twitter has at least 100 million active users, logging in at least once a month, and 50 million users who do so daily. A year later, in October 2012, Twitter CEO Dick Costolo announced that these numbers had doubled, with the number of accounts reaching 400-500 millions, with 200 million among them considered regular users.[7] As a measure of reference, if the online Twitter community were to be viewed as a country, a population of 200 million would make it the 5th most populous country in the world, on par with Brazil. However, it is not just Twitter that has a large user community: Facebook had reached 1.1 billion users in 2013, with 665 million of them using it daily.[8] A population of 1.1 billion would have Facebook in a close race with China and India to be the world's most populous community. Extending beyond the English speaking word, QQ is a Chinese service for instant messaging, with over 800 million accounts, while Sina Weibo (a Chinese micro-blogging service) reported over 500 million users in 2012.[9]

In addition to constantly increasing user communities, the amount of data released through social media applications is also increasing at very impressive rates.

4. Goodchild, M.F. (2007a), 'Citizens as Sensors: The World of Volunteered Geography', *GeoJournal*, 69(4): 211-221.; Fritz, S., MacCallum, I., Schill, C., Perger, C., Grillmayer, R., Achard, F., Kraxner, F. and Obersteiner, M. (2009), Geo-Wiki.Org: The Use of Crowdsourcing to Improve Global Land Cover, *Remote Sensing*, 1 (3): 345-354.
5. Stefanidis, A., Crooks, A. and Radzikowski, J. (2013a), Harvesting Ambient Geospatial Information from Social Media Feeds, *Geojournal*, 78(2): 319-338.
6. O'Reilly, T. (2005), What Is Web 2.0: Design Patterns and Business Models for the Next Generation of Software. Available at http://www.oreillynet.com/lpt/a/6228 [Accessed on February 20, 2009].
7. http://www.telegraph.co.uk/technology/twitter/9945505/twitter-in-numbers.html .
8. http://investor.fb.com/releasedetail.cfm?ReleaseID=761090 .
9. http://blogs.wsj.com/chinarealtime/2013/03/12/how-many-people-really-use-sina-weibo/ .

Seven years after its 2004 launch, Flickr was hosting 6 billion photos uploaded by its user community in 2011, with over 3,000 photos uploaded to Flickr every minute and a 20 percent annual rate increase over the past few years.[10] And while 6 billion photos is a very impressive number, it only reflects the estimated number of photos uploaded *monthly* to Facebook by its user community, bringing the total number of photos hosted by Facebook to nearly 100 billion.[11] At the same time, 100 million active users are uploading daily an estimated 40 million images in Instagram, while every minute, Flickr users upload in excess of 3,000 images, and YouTube users upload approximately 72 hours of video.[12]

While their content ranges in format from SMS-like messages limited to 140 characters (Twitter) to images (Flickr) and video (YouTube), these social media feeds share a common nature: they are real-time published expressions of a society's cultural and societal interests. Thus harvesting and analyzing their content can offer unparalleled insight on sociocultural dynamics. For example, they allow us to:

■ map the manner in which ideas and information propagate in a society—information that can be used, for example, to identify appropriate strategies for information dissemination in crisis response;

■ map people's opinions and reaction on specific topics and current events, thus improving our ability to collect precise cultural, political, economic and health data, and to do so at near real-time rates; and

■ identify emerging sociocultural hotspots.

This represents an evolution of the manner in which human landscape data can be collected and analyzed. While traditional human geography approaches are rather static (primarily due to the cumbersome strategies used to collect the necessary data, for example censuses), this emerging opportunity allows us to treat the human landscape as the living, breathing organism that it is: we can witness the explosion-like dissemination of information within a society, or the clusters of individuals who share common opinions or attitudes, and map the locations of these clusters. This is an unprecedented development that broadens drastically our current geointelligence capabilities. In the remainder of this paper we focus on Twitter as a representative social media feed and discuss its potential use for geointelligence applications.

3: Geolocating Twitter feeds

Geolocation information in tweets can be provided directly by the contributing bloggers, if they decide to make this information available, or it can be deduced from IP addresses using any of the IP geolocation solutions.[13] In this paper we are focusing on geolocation information that is contributed either directly by the user or provided through the client application.

This geolocation information may be available at two different levels of granularity: either in the form of precise coordinates as shown in Figures 1 and 2, or in a descriptive manner (e.g. listing only a city name). It is typically harvested from Twitter using the capabilities provided by the communication protocol linking the client to it. For example, the World Wide Web Consortium (W3C) Geolocation Application Programming Interface (API) enables scripting code to access device information from Web browsers of any Web-capable device (e.g. a mobile phone or a laptop, see).[14] In this way information is collected in a dynamic mode, reflecting the actual location from where a tweet was sent. In addition to this, geolocation information can also be harvested from the content of users' profiles, but this is less reliable as

10. http://news.softpedia.com/news/Flickr-Boasts-6-Billion-Photo-Uploads-215380.shtml .; http://royal.pingdom.com/2011/01/12/internet-2010-in-numbers/ .
11. http://www.allfacebook.com/infographic-facebook-will-have-100-billion-photos-this-summer-2011-02 .
12. http://instagram.com/press/#.; Sapiro, G. (2011), "Images Everywhere: Looking for Models: Technical Perspective," *Communications of the ACM*, 54(5): 108-108.; http://www.youtube.com/yt/press/statistics.html .
13. Eriksson, B., Barford, P., Sommers, J. and Nowak, R. (2010), "A Learning-Based Approach for IP Geolocation," in Krishnamurthy, A. and Plattner, B. (eds.), *Passive and Active Measurement, Lecture Notes in Computer Science*, Volume 6032, Springer, Berlin, Germany, pp. 171-180. Poese I., Uhlig S., Kaafar M.A., Donnet, B. and Gueye, B. (2011). "IP Geolocation Databases: Unreliable?" ACM SIGCOMM Computer Communication Review, 4(2): 53-56.
14. Doty, N. and Wilde, E. (2010), Geolocation Privacy and Application Platforms, *Proceedings of the 3rd ACM SIGSPATIAL International Workshop on Security and Privacy in GIS and LBS*, San Jose, CA, pp. 65-69.

it is static and does not necessarily reflect user location at the moment that the tweet was sent.

The reported percentage of geolocated tweets varies, from as high as two thirds or half of the tweets having some location information in the form of coordinates or description to as low as 5 percent of the users listing actual coordinates with another 21 percent listing descriptive geolocation information.[15] In our own study earlier we had approximately 16 percent of our feeds with detailed coordinate location information, with another substantial percentage of the tweets having some geolocation information at coarser granularity (e.g. the city level). This variation in the rate of geolocated tweets can be attributed to a range of factors, such as geographic area, time and theme.[16]

For example, the seemingly high rate of 16 percent, which was observed following the 2011 tsunami and Fukushima disaster in Japan, can be attributed to the response of the Japanese population to a major event (e.g. evacuation), the increased use of mobile devices after the event, and the high penetration rate of Twitter in Japan (26.6 percent).[17]

A recent study by Leetaru et al. using Twitter's Decahose data stream has reported that even in the absence of a significant disruptive event

Figure 1

Example of a geolocated tweet (screenshot from the Twitter site) following the anti-government demonstrations of December 10, 2011 in Moscow. The message likens the events to the Decembrist anti-tsarist (anti-government) movement of 1825, reading: "Today the term was born Decembrists." A photo accompanies the tweet, and the location from which this tweet was originated is shown on a map below.

15. Hecht, B., Hong, L., Suh, B. and Chi, E. (2011), 'Tweets From Justin Bieber's Heart: The Dynamics of the 'Location' Field in User Profiles,' *Proceedings of the ACM CHI Conference on Human Factors in Computing Systems*, Vancouver Canada.; Java, A., Song, X., Finin, T. and Tseng, B. (2009), 'Why We Twitter: An Analysis of a Microblogging Community', in Goebel, R., Siekmann, J. and Wahlster, W. (eds.), *Advances in Web Mining and Web Usage Analysis, Lecture Notes in Computer Science, Volume 5439*, Springer, Berlin, Germany, pp. 118-138.; Cheng, Z., Caverlee, J. and Lee, K. (2010), 'You Are Where You Tweet: A Content-based Approach to Geolocating Twitter Users', *Proceedings of the ACM Conference on Information and Knowledge Management*, Toronto, Canada, pp. 759-768.
16. Stefanidis, T., Crooks, A.T. and Radzikowski, J. (2013), 'Harvesting Ambient Geospatial Information from Social Media Feeds', *GeoJournal*, 78(2): 319-338.
17. Kaigo, M. (2012), 'Social Media Usage During Disasters and Social Capital: Twitter and the Great East Japan Earthquake', Keio Communication Review, 34(2012): 19-35.; http://bit.ly/SO1Vlr .

Figure 2

An example of the metadata of a tweet, provided by the Twitter API. Among a variety of geolocation information we have zoomed to the actual user coordinates.

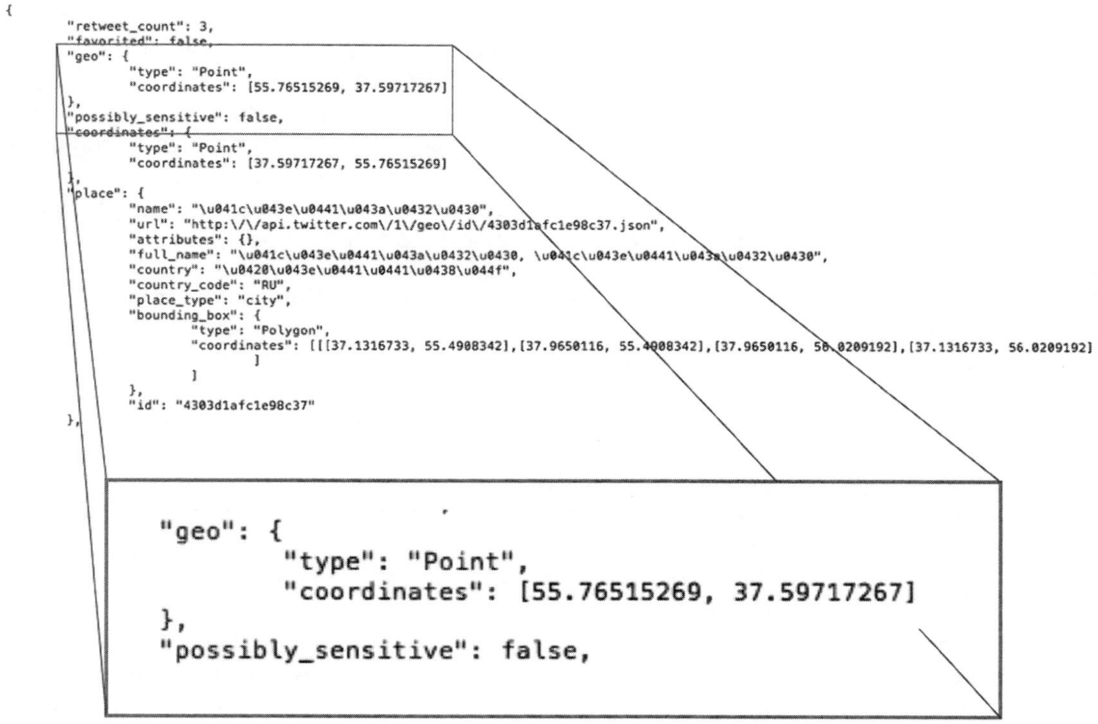

```
{
    "retweet_count": 3,
    "favorited": false,
    "geo": {
            "type": "Point",
            "coordinates": [55.76515269, 37.59717267]
    },
    "possibly_sensitive": false,
    "coordinates": {
            "type": "Point",
            "coordinates": [37.59717267, 55.76515269]
    },
    "place": {
            "name": "\u041c\u043e\u0441\u043a\u0432\u0430",
            "url": "http:\/\/api.twitter.com\/1\/geo\/id\/4303d1afc1e98c37.json",
            "attributes": {},
            "full_name": "\u041c\u043e\u0441\u043a\u0432\u0430, \u041c\u043e\u0441\u043a\u0432\u0430",
            "country": "\u0420\u043e\u0441\u0441\u0438\u044f",
            "country_code": "RU",
            "place_type": "city",
            "bounding_box": {
                    "type": "Polygon",
                    "coordinates": [[[37.1316733, 55.4908342],[37.9650116, 55.4908342], [37.9650116, 56.0209192],[37.1316733, 56.0209192]
                    ]
            ]
    },
    "id": "4303d1afc1e98c37"
    },
},
```

```
"geo": {
        "type": "Point",
        "coordinates": [55.76515269, 37.59717267]
},
"possibly_sensitive": false,
```

(e.g., a nuclear disaster) the rate of geolocated tweets may vary depending on the time of day (from 2.3 percent at 1 p.m. PST to 1.7 percent at 6 a.m. PST) or the geographic location (from 2.86 percent in Jakarta to 0.77 percent in Moscow).[18] Furthermore, it is worth mentioning that in the absence of other information, geolocation data can be obtained from IP addresses using any of the IP geolocation solutions.[19] The accuracy of this geolocated information may range from building level all the way to broader neighborhood.[20]

4: Harvesting social media feeds

Harvesting information from social media feeds involves three operations: extracting data from the data providers (various social media servers) via APIs; parsing, integrating and storing these data in a resident database; and then analyzing these data to extract information of interest.

There exist a number of tools that perform parts of these processes, such as 140kit (http://140kit.com/), or twapperkeeper (http://twapperkeeper.com/), but these are limited in their scalability

with respect to large datasets. Sites such as ushahidi (http://www.ushahidi.com/) also provide a means to collect and disseminate information over the Web. However, currently available tools offer limited capabilities to add context to content, or to support detailed analysis, thus forcing the development of custom systems to perform the above-mentioned three operations.

Original social media feeds can be retrieved from source data providers through queries. This entails submitting a query in the form of an http request and receiving in response data

18. Leetaru, K., Wang, S., Cao, G., Padmanabhan, A., and Shook, E. (2013), 'Mapping the Global Twitter Heartbeat: The Geography of Twitter'. *First Monday*, 18(5). doi:10.5210/fm.v18i5.4366.

19. Eriksson, B., Barford, P., Sommers, J. and Nowak, R. (2010), A Learning-Based Approach for IP Geolocation, in Krishnamurthy, A. and Plattner, B. (eds.), *Passive and Active Measurement, Lecture Notes in Computer Science*, Volume 6032, Springer, Berlin, Germany, pp. 171-180.

20. Poese I., Uhlig S., Kaafar M.A., Donnet, B. and Gueye, B. (2011), IP Geolocation Databases: Unreliable?, *Computer Communication Review*, 4 (2): 53-56.

in XML format (e.g. Atom or RSS). The query parameters may be, for example, based on location (e.g. specifying an area of interest to which the feed is related), time (e.g. specifying a period of interest), content (e.g. specifying keywords), or even by user handle/ID.

In response to these queries, and depending on the characteristics of the information provided by the service, we can receive from the server just metadata or metadata and actual data. A representative example of the first case is Flickr, where the query result contains exclusively metadata information (e.g. author, time and geolocation when available), and information on how to access the actual image itself. A representative example of the second is Twitter, where the data received in response to a query are actual tweets and associated metadata (e.g. user information, time of tweet publication, geolocation when available, and information on whether this particular tweet is in response to or retweet of an earlier message).

Once this information is harvested from the social media server it can be parsed to become part of a *local database* (e.g. implemented using ProstgresSQL), thus creating a local mirror of the content of the original server for the entries specified by our queries. Depending on the subject, the queries may be periodic, or may be intensified during episodes of crisis. While the information harvested from social media in this manner is not explicitly geospatial, it does include implicit geospatial content, thus rendering it suitable for novel types of geospatial analysis as we show in the following section.

5: Case studies: turning Twitter content into geospatial intelligence

Tweet content is a prototypical description of human landscape dynamics, as it includes references to geographic entities that are sociocultural hotspots at the time of the reference. It can also be analyzed to identify social dynamics within the Twitter community, in the form of complex relations and hierarchical structures among its members. In this section we provide some sample analytical processes, in order to showcase the type of geointelligence information that can be harvested through Twitter feed analysis. The experiments we present are from a system we developed in-house to collect Twitter feeds using thematic and geographic queries, and store them in a local database where they are further analyzed.

5.1 Hotspot emergence

Hotspots emerge in Twitter traffic through notable increases in the references to specific terms. This is comparable to the identification of trends in Web search engines. For example, Google is tracking through its Google Trends facility the number of searches for various terms, and analyzes the data to identify spikes in these searches. Figure 3 shows the trends in searches for the term "Tahrir Square" in 2011. The horizontal axis shows time (over a period of 12 months) and the vertical shows frequency of searches for a specific term. As we can see in this simple chart, we can

Figure 3

Google Trends: a plot of the frequency of searches for the term "Tahrir Square" in the first 11 months of 2011.

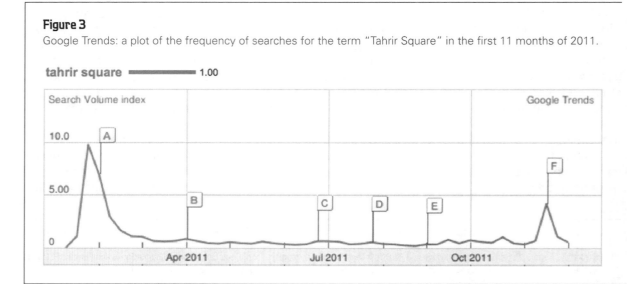

identify peaks, which indicate strong interest among the Google user community about Tahrir Square, most notably at the end of January 2011 when the anti-government Egyptian protesters started gathering there, and then again in November 2011 when pro-democracy demonstrations started again.

Trends analysis of Internet searches has been used in epidemiology to detect the outbreak of diseases (Polgreen et al., 2008; Carneiro and Mylonakis, 2009) and was also extended to address blog and Twitter content and news articles.[21] Google has even set up a corresponding website to monitor flu outbreaks through an analysis of search word patterns.[22]

A comparable analysis can be applied to Twitter data, this time searching for references to particular keywords. In Figure 4 we show, for example, an analysis of Twitter feeds originating from Cairo (based on Twitter's API location filtering) over

Figure 4

Twitter data with a Tahrir Square label, 2/25/11–3/09/11, overlaid on a map of the square. Hashtag statistics over time show how off the spike (marked by a circle) is from normal.
Source: Stefanidis et al, 2011.

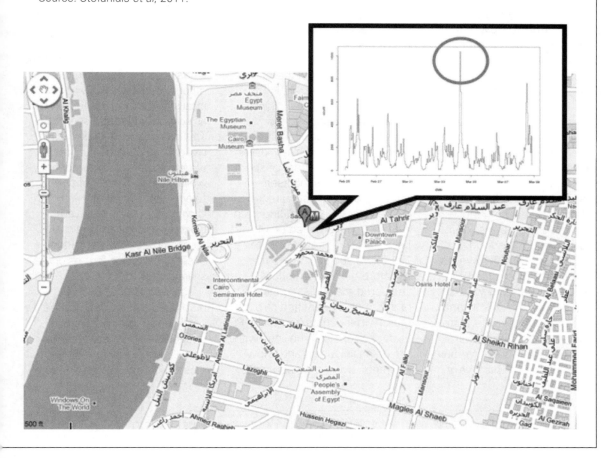

21. Brownstein J.S., Clark, C., Freitfeld, B.S. and Madoff L.C. (2009), 'Digital Disease Detection – Harnessing the Web for Public Health Surveillance', *New England Journal of Medicine*, 360 (21): 2153-2157.; Ritterman, J., Osborne, M. and Klein, E. (2009), "Using Prediction Markets and Twitter to Predict a Swine Flu Pandemic," in Carrero, F.M., Gómez, J.M., Monsalve, B., Puertas, E. and Cortizo, J.C. (eds.), *1st International Workshop on Mining Social Media*, Sevilla, Spain pp. 9-18.; Polgreen, P.M., Chen, Y., Pennock, D.M. and Nelson, F.D. (2008), "Using Internet Searches for Influenza Surveillance," *Clinical Infectious Diseases*, 47(11): 1443-1448.; Culotta, A. (2010), "Towards Detecting Influenza Epidemics by Analyzing Twitter Messages," *Proceedings of the First Workshop on Social Media Analytics*, Washington, DC, pp. 115-122.; Corley, C.D., Cook, D.J., Mikler, A.R. and Singh, K.P. (2010), "Text and Structural Data Mining of Influenza Mentions in Web and Social Media," *International Journal of Environmental Research and Public Health*, 7(2): 596-615.
22. http://www.google.org/flutrends/ .

the period 2/25/11–3/09/11, to identify ones that were labeled with the hashtag "Tahrir Square."[23] The data are shown on the upper right-hand side of the figure: a chart shows the number of tweets per hour within a 10km radius from Tahrir Square (vertical axis) over the period 2/25/11–3/09/11 (horizontal axis). Tweets are grouped hourly, and we can identify a peak (marked by a red circle) corresponding to the period 07:00-08:00 local time (UTC+2) of 3/4/11. This is actually the morning of the day when the new prime minister of Egypt eventually addressed his people at the square. Thus, Twitter traffic analysis offers an effective means to receive advance notice of this event, as people started discussing it as soon as it became known.

Figure 4 serves as an example of how spikes in references to specific terms correlate to events taking place there. The data shown in this figure correspond to approximately 38,000 tweets with a Tahrir Square hashtag reference in that two-week period, selected from among a total of 684,000 tweets from 40,000 persons with a Cairo label over that period. We have advance notice of this event, as people started discussing it as soon as it became known.

5.2 Tracing information dissemination avenues and social network structure

While hotspot detection allows us to identify locations of interest by analyzing trends in references to them, social network analysis allows us to recognize the structure of complex social groups: who is connected to whom, either directly or via common links, and how persons are clustered in groups sharing common interests.[24] This also leads to the identification of leaders and followers in social networks, and to mapping the manner in which information is disseminated within them.

In order to visualize this complex process, we collected Twitter data relating to the devastating Sendai (Tohoku-Fukushima) earthquake in Japan (3/11/11). The structure of social groups is manifesting itself through retweets and direct references. By aggregating such activities over a period of 14 hours (3/11/11, from 05:00 to 19:00) we see in Figure 5 the structure of this network. We can see some major disseminators of information identified through their Twitter names (e.g. NHK_PR, asahi_tokyo, etc.). The lines within the graph link users and show retweets: every time someone

retweets (i.e. rebroadcasts) another user's post, this person is added to the original user's cluster. This is the typical pattern of information dissemination seen within social networks.

As is common in many complex networks, this network is highly skewed in the sense that the majority of nodes have a low degree of connectivity (star-like shapes in the graph) while there are a small number of nodes which have a high degree of connectivity: these can be considered as hubs of information dispersal and to some extent key actors in the social media sphere.[25] For example, in Figures 5 and 6 we can identify NHK_PR, asahi_tokyo, and TokyoMX. The first is a national news organization, while the other two tweet mostly about local information in general, such as schools and metro services. This behavior follows power law patterns: a large number of tweeters only tweet infrequently, while a small number of tweeters tweet a lot.[26] This behavior is consistent with observed blogosphere characteristics and comparable behavioral patterns observed in online forums or file sharing sites.[27]

The network structure displayed in Figure 5 can be particularly informative in crisis situations, as it allows us to identify information dissemination routes and

23. Hashtags represent a bottom up, user-generated convention for adding content (in a sense, metadata) about a specific topic, by identifying keywords to describe content. Thus they allow easy searching of tweets and trends. Sites such as http://hashtags.org/ monitor such trends from tweets and provide relevant statistics, but only over short periods of times.

24. Simply stated social network analysis (SNA) allows us to explore how different parts of a social system (e.g. people, organizations) are linked together. Moreover, it allows one to define the systems' structure and evolution over time (e.g. kinship or role-based networks). SNA is a quantitative methodology using mathematical graphs to represent people or organizations, where each person is a node, and nodes are connected to others via links (edges). Such links can be directed or undirected (e.g. friendship networks don't have to be reciprocal).

25. Barabási, A. and Albert, R. (1999), 'Emergence of Scaling in Random Networks', *Science*, 286(5439): 509-512.; Asur, S. and Huberman, B.A. (2010), 'Predicting the Future with Social Media', *Proceedings of the IEEE/WIC/ACM International Conference on Web Intelligence and Intelligent Agent Technology*, Toronto, Canada pp. 492-499.

26. Newman, M.E.J. (2005), 'Power Laws, Pareto Distributions and Zipf's Law', *Contemporary Physics*, 46(5).

27. Shi, X., Tseng, B. and Adamic, L.A. (2007), 'Looking at the Blogosphere Topology through Different Lenses', *Proceedings of the International Conference on Weblogs and Social Media (ICWSM 2007)*, Boulder, CO.; Zhang, J., Ackerman, M.S. and Adamic, L. (2007), 'Expertise Networks in Online Communities: Structure and Algorithms', *Proceedings of the 16th International Conference on World Wide Web*, Banff, Canada, pp. 221-230.; Adar, E. and Huberman, B.A. (2000), 'Free Riding on Gnutella', *First Monday*, 5(10-2).

Figure 5

Network cores and users (nodes) retweeting. The clusters are shaded according to degree of importance (from dark for lowest, to lighter shades for highest). Source: Stefanidis *et al*, 2011.

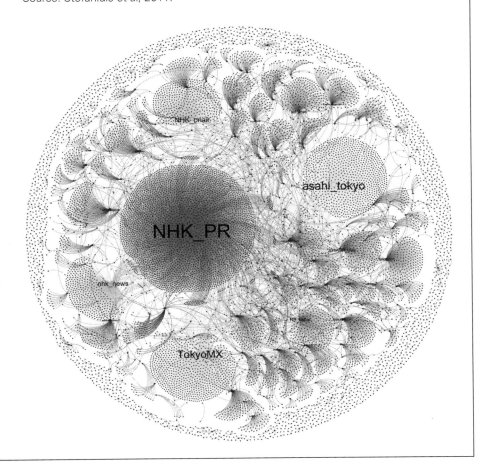

affected communities, supporting management and response. It is also important for monitoring the society, as its variations over time reveal the evolution of the human landscape, with clusters formed and broken in response to various external factors.

Furthermore, by using the geolocation information of these tweets we can map the spatial footprint of the social clusters in our area of interest, moving from the nebulous social space of Figures 5 and 6 to the geographic one as shown in Figure 7. Figure 7 shows the spatial footprint of tweet-retweet pairs in Tokyo, captured on a random instance (6/13/2011 at 8 a.m. in this case). We can see the location of the original tweeter (marked as a sitting bird next to the "source author" tag), and a link to the location of the person retweeting the original message (marked as the flying bird next to the "reTwitter" tag). These links are indicators of sociocultural kinship between their start and end node. Therefore they can be considered as sample points for the identification of socioculturally similar neighborhoods, as the places around these nodes are reasonably expected to be crowded with people who live, think and vote like the node-corresponding tweeters (Bishop, 2008). This can lead to the establishment of a human landscape reference baseline, and the monitoring of its variations over time.

Figure 6

The social network of Figure 5 at different instances during a 12-hour period after the Fukushima earthquake, as information is broadcast from the major providers to its members. At the top we see how information disseminated primarily from NHK_PR is disseminated, while at the bottom we see activity related to feeds contributed by other key nodes.

Source: Stefanidis *et al*, 2011.

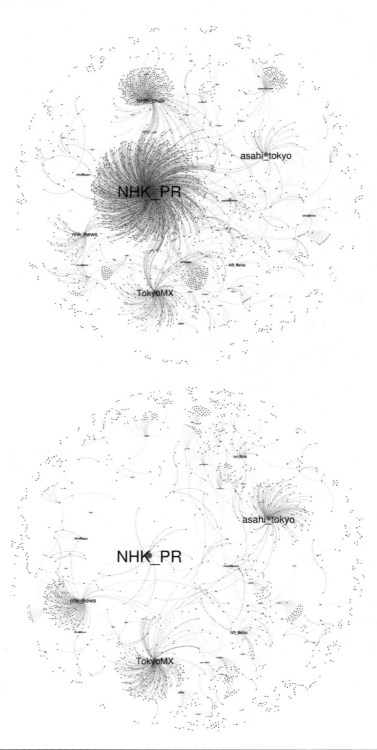

Figure 7

Geolocated pairs of tweeters and retweeters in Tokyo at the time immediately following the Sendai earthquake
Source: Stefanidis *et al*, 2011.

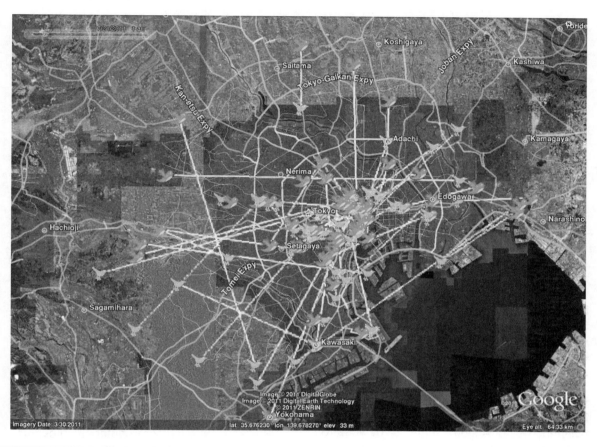

5.3 Impact area assessment following a natural disaster

In order to assess the value and use of Twitter data during natural disasters, we collected Twitter streams immediately after the 5.8 magnitude Mineral, VA earthquake of 8/23/2011. Figure 8 shows a plot of the origin locations of geolocated tweets referring to the earthquake during the first 60 minutes after the event. As we see the tweets are heavily clustered inside the impact area. It is worth mentioning that first reports of the event appeared on Twitter less than a minute after it happened, and we already had 1,000 Twitter reports of this earthquake within 5 minutes of the event. As these data were collected from a random 1 percent sample of Twitter content, one could reasonably anticipate that as many as 100,000 Twitter reports were made for this event within these first 5 minutes.[28] Actually, as early as within 5–10 minutes we have observed a good delineation of the impact area using Twitter content, with the formation of identifiable dense clusters of geolocated tweets within it.

We observe, therefore, that Twitter content serves as a timely and fairly accurate reporting system for natural disasters, with humans acting as sensors that collect and report this information. Considering the growing importance of disaster response in the geointelligence community, this is a critical advantage of social media content analysis.

28. Crooks, A.T., Croitoru, A., Stefanidis, A. and Radzikowski, J. (2013), 'Earthquake: Twitter as a Distributed Sensor System', *Transactions in GIS*, 17(1): 124-147.

Figure 8

Geolocated tweets referring to the 5.8 magnitude Virginia earthquake of August, 2011 collected during the first 60 minutes after the earthquake. The star marks the epicenter. The circle outlines the perceived earthquake impact area.

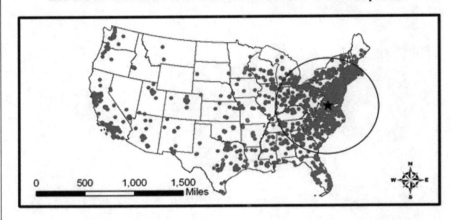

Tweets Within 60 Minutes After Earthquake

5.4 Real-time event monitoring

Social media can also aid with real-time monitoring of events, for example in Figure 9 we show geolocated tweets collected on 11/17/2011 referring to Occupy Wall Street events in New York City. This was the planned "Day of Action," with a march across the Brooklyn Bridge. We show two different instances of these data. The top view in Figure 9, is from the afternoon of that date showing various tweets contributed from Manhattan as the protesters were marching from midtown towards downtown. The bottom view in Figure 9 shows geolocated tweets harvested later in the evening as the protesters were crossing the Brooklyn Bridge.[29]

Figure 9 vividly demonstrates two facts, which are rather crucial observations regarding the use of social media feeds to gather geospatial information. Firstly, we observe that Twitter is being used to provide real-time in-situ reports from events. In this particular situation we see that people (either protesters or bystanders) are using their cell phones or other mobile devices to tweet during the march. This is consistent with the observation made in Section 5.3 where we reported the robust use of Twitter to report the impact of an earthquake, but now applies to an event of longer duration than the quasi-instantaneous earthquake. Secondly, we observe that by harvesting this information we get an excellent overview of the activities in the ground, without deploying any local sensors. With locals acting as sensors and providing steady feeds in the form of tweets we can gain remotely valuable situational awareness.

6. Outlook

Social media platforms have provided the general public with an effective and irrepressible mechanism to broadcast in real-time a variety of information, ranging from personal observations to commentaries on events of broader interest. With an already substantial and steadily increasing membership, platforms such as Twitter and YouTube serve as conduits of massive amounts of information, thus rapidly becoming essential components of open-source intelligence. The information communicated through such feeds conveys opinions, interests and links within its user community, thus revealing the complex structure of social networks.

However, this information is only partially exploited if one does not consider its

---

29. A video capturing these events and selected tweet content is available at http://youtu.be/TarIOM6eXJk. Additional examples are also provided at the website: http://www.geosocial.gmu.edu.

Figure 9

Geolocated tweets referring to the "Day of Action" events of the Occupy Wall Street movement march to the Brooklyn Bridge on 11/17/2011. Top: the march of the protesters from Union Square towards downtown. Bottom: tweets as the protesters are moving across the bridge.

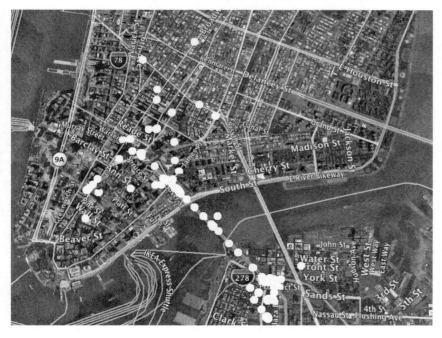

geographical aspect, such as the location from where a particular feed was contributed, or a tweet reference to a specific sociocultural hotspot. By harvesting geographic content from social media feeds we can transfer the extracted knowledge from the amorphous cyberspace to the geographic space, and gain a unique understanding of the human lansdscape, its structure and organization, and its evolution over time. This newfound opportunity signals the emergence of open-source geospatial intelligence, whereby social media contributions can be analyzed and mined to gain unparalleled situational awareness.

In this paper we presented a number of sample applications that demonstrate the geospatial intelligence value of information harvested from social media feeds. Twitter content reveals the emergence of sociocultural hotspots, and provides advanced warning of forthcoming events, as was the case with the Tahrir Square references during the Arab Spring events of spring 2011. It also offers a mechanism to obtain a rapid assessment of the impact area of natural disasters as

demonstrated by data collected during the Virginia earthquake of August 2011. It provides unparalleled situational awareness by supporting the monitoring of evolving events, as was the case with the Occupy Brooklyn Bridge experiment. Furthermore, the Sendai experiment demonstrated how Twitter data analysis allows us to identify information dissemination routes, knowledge that can be very crucial when designing emergency response plans.

These examples demonstrate the fact that humans act as hybrid sensors when using social media platforms. Unlike typical sensors that always operate on specific bands of the spectrum, or collect specific types of measurements, humans operate across a wide range of the sociocultural spectrum, commenting in one message on a natural phenomenon, and in the next on a political issue. Thus the information they provide when blogging or posting a picture has substantial intelligence value.

One could argue though that the most important information collected by harvesting and analyzing social media content is the structure and spatial

distribution of social networks, and the manner in which they evolve over time, reacting to news and events and adapting to the state of the world.

With the ability to collect such information in real-time we are now presented with an unprecedented opportunity to redefine the concept of human landscape or its various synonyms (e.g. human geography or human terrain). Our traditional approach to the problem of human terrain data collection was very static: collecting human geography data at distinct time instances through census-like campaigns, and then trying to interpret these datasets in order to identify clusters of similarly-behaving people. By harvesting information from social media feeds we are actually able to identify these relationships directly and to monitor them continuously.

Accordingly, harvesting open-source geospatial intelligence represents a transformation of our traditional operations that substantially improves our ability to analyze and understand sociocultural dynamics, and allows us to examine the human landscape as the living and evolving organism that it is.

Anthony Stefanidis is Professor in the Department of Geography and GeoInformation Science (GGS) at George Mason University (GMU), and director of Mason's Center for Geospatial Intelligence. He earned his PhD from The Ohio State University. His areas of expertise include image analysis, sensor networks and harvesting geospatial information from social media.

Andrew Crooks is Assistant Professor with the Department of Computational Social Science at GMU. Andrew's areas of expertise include GIS, creating and analyzing large spatial data sets and finding patterns and insights. He is a recognized expert on the integration of GIS and agent-based modeling.

Arie Croitoru is Assistant Professor in the GGS Department at GMU and member of Mason's Center for Geospatial Intelligence. He holds a PhD in Geoinformatics from Technion University (Israel). His research includes three interrelated research streams: geosocial analysis and location-based mass collaboration systems (LB-MCS), spatio-temporal data mining and digital image processing.

Jacek Radzikowski is Senior Researcher with Mason's Center for Geospatial Intelligence. He holds degrees in Computer Science from Warsaw University of Technology and Computational Science from Mason. Jacek's areas of expertise are database management and development, software design and systemimplementation.

Matthew Rice is Assistant Professor with the Department of Geography and GeoInformation Science at George Mason University. He conducts research in geospatial crowdsourcing, assistive geotechnology and geovisualization. Dr. Rice is a leader and contributor to the Association of American Geographers Cartography Specialty Group and the International Cartographic Association.

Toward Cybersocial Geography: Meeting the Analytic Challenge of Social Media

John Kelly

The protest events collectively known as "Arab Spring" materialized quickly. But while surprising at the time, they might have been anticipated. The U.S. government was well aware that problems of corruption, inequality, political repression and lack of economic opportunity had grown acute across the Arab world. In fact, in the months before the first spark of revolution in Tunisia, Secretary of State Hillary Clinton had strongly advocated reform to Arab leaders for just these reasons. But as the Tunisian and Egyptian governments fell, and protests grew across the region, key aspects raised eyebrows:

- the speed and scope of these movements;
- their ability to enroll formerly non-political actors, mainly youth;
- the seemingly "leaderless" origin of the protests, and degree to which established political movements and organizations struggled to keep up with events and collaborate across ideological divides to bring down ruling regimes.

Many observers lay these surprising aspects of Arab Spring at the feet of social media.

As in previous protest movements in Moldova and Iran, and in subsequent events, such as the 2011 London riots, analysts highlighted the ability of networked communications tools to spread information virally, rapidly mobilize strangers around common objectives, and facilitate tactical coordination in the midst of street battles. In the aftermath of these sometimes-called Twitter, Facebook and Blackberry Revolutions, it is clear that U.S. national interests are potentially affected as much by the actions of cyber-associated collective actors as by the actions of governments and traditional political groups.

This concern extends from rapidly organized "smart mobs" to longer-lasting and potentially more dangerous networks like Anonymous or a headless form of Al Qaeda. Consequently, government has accepted the need to develop tools for monitoring and engaging with a social media-connected global population.

For example, Defense Advanced Research Projects Agency (DARPA) recently announced a research program described by *Wired* magazine as a project to create the "Mother of All Meme Trackers." In fact, "memetracking" is good shorthand for efforts to create real time tools for monitoring what are viewed as fast-moving phenomena, to see the sparks before they ignite the forest.

The problem

Unfortunately, much of the thinking behind both government and commercial efforts to monitor social media data is misguided or incomplete. Several problems are common:

- mistaking computer science for social science;
- seeing cyberspace as "virtual" and not "real";
- analyzing Internet/social media data principally as a corpus of text;
- analyzing social network features at micro and macro levels only;
- over-emphasizing short-term phenomena.

Let us look at these briefly in turn.

First, computer science is often mistaken for social science. While generic "big data" computational capacities can produce results with almost any large data collection, having a sharp set of knives does not make one a chef. What analysts, policy makers and marketers want to discover in social media data are complicated and often subtle social facts. What is the configuration and relative strength of emerging political forces in a post-revolutionary society? What music is influential among a certain subculture of young people? Are the normally quiescent people of Ruritania on the edge of open revolt?

Because social media data sets are huge and complicated, and expertise for discovering features within massive data sets remains concentrated in computer science and the natural sciences, it has been hard to see the daylight between computational challenges and social-analytic ones.

Indeed, academic interest in "computational social science" is nascent and leading work is often accomplished by computer scientists, mathematicians and physicists who have made the attempt to cross over into sociology or political science.[1] But when the effort to exploit social media data is solely under the direction of natural and computer scientists, the wrong questions may be asked, and the wrong criteria used to judge success. Because social scientists study human collectives, they are attuned to the complexities of

behavior, culture and politics across global societies. They are experienced with interpreting weak signals in noisy data and cautious in their claims, particularly regarding prediction.

Second, online communications are thought of as "virtual," not "real." Even the term "cyberspace" suggests an abstracted plane of disembodied interactions. But in fact, actors communicating online are very much embodied (bots excepted!). They are in specific locations, and their online activity and associations are deeply interwoven with their offline lives. This abstract "cyber" conception of social media communication offers an excuse for not doing the hard work of understanding how the topologically complex fabric of online communications intersects with real-world locations, social networks and organizations.

Third, social media and other Internet data sets are too often thought of simply as text corpora, to be mined for semantic content. There are two main approaches: "pile of text" and "river of text." Search engines and document clustering engines are typical examples of "pile of text" approaches, in which messages are selected or classified based on their meaning. "River of text" approaches add the dimension of time to messages, and include "memetrackers," trend monitors, alert systems, real-time sentiment analyzers and similar "dashboard" tools. There is a powerful and growing set of tools

for semantic mining of text content, and that is a good thing.

But, in part because of the longstanding and robust academic research community and training ground for natural language processing and other semantic approaches, the view predominates that this is the primary, even only, useful way to treat social media data. When you only have hammers, it is natural to regard the world as nails. But these approaches ignore the relationships evident within social media. And often the most interesting and useful thing to discover within human communication is the structure of relationships enacted through it. The social structure is often more important than the content, and always provides key context. When looking at the river of data, "Who says what to whom?" is a better question than "What is said?"

Fourth, when structural data is analyzed, it is at the macro or micro level only. Macro-level network metrics include statistics on entire networks, as well as individual measures calculated globally (e.g., PageRank, Klout, "authority" scores). They are mainly used to assign a rank to individuals (or documents) within the entire network. Micro-level analysis looks at the neighborhood around a target individual, i.e. someone who sits close to them in the network. But global metrics make it too easy to mistake networks for hierarchies and gloss over the complexity of the cybersocial terrain, and micro-analyses miss

1. Lazer, David; Alex Pentland; Lada Adamic; Sinan Aral; Albert-László Barabási; Devon Brewer; Nicholas Christakis; Noshir Contractor; James Fowler; Myron Gutmann; Tony Jebara; Gary King; Michael Macy; Deb Roy; and Marshall Van Alstyne. "Computational Social Science." *Science* 323, no. 5915 (2009): 721-23.

the collective phenomenon which provide any individual whatever wider significance they may have. Aside from a relatively few superstars, the most important thing about any individual is what specific communities they are involved in and influential among. These communities may be very important socially or politically, even if they are small enough that prominent actors within them are all but invisible at the global level. The most valuable thing to see with network analysis of social media data are the schools of fish swimming within it, and yet all that current tools provide are a census of the ocean on the one hand, and profiles of individual fish on the other.

Finally, from commercial dashboards to advanced R&D projects, the focus is almost exclusively on identifying and measuring short-term phenomena. For analysts and decision makers, clearly the now is more important than the past. But historical data can be leveraged to vastly improve the usefulness of real time data. Regarding any particular meme, did it incubate among a known network before breaking out? Is this network part of a political movement or social interest group? Is it geographically centered? Does it represent a coordinated effort of some organization or group? Is the pattern of diffusion following well-worn paths? Is it sparking fires across previously disconnected communities? Which ones? Who are the participating influencers? Do they normally act in concert? Are they long-time influentials or did they appear out of nowhere?

Sophisticated analysis of historical data can provide a framework for understanding what is truly important about the short-term phenomena identified by memetracking tools, which otherwise raise more questions than they answer.

The solution

The dawning era of Big Data requires powerful new analytic tools. But the practical challenges of scaling storage, query and computation are often confused with the analytic challenges of extracting knowledge from the exponentially growing river of bytes. This confusion typically resolves in favor of computer (and natural) scientists, who enjoy dominion over the facilities and toolkits required to handle large-scale data. But again, what analysts and policymakers want from social media data is a feast of social facts: political, economic, cultural and biographical. And while natural/computer scientists excel at building stoves and sharpening knives, it does not follow that they have good recipes for social facts, nor that they are especially talented chefs.

In fact, most of the efforts of computer scientists working with social media data do not constitute particularly innovative social research. Rather, they focus on scaling computational resources (graph databases, massively parallel processing, etc.), in combination with incremental improvements upon and applications of established lines of research (natural language processing, entity resolution, sentiment analysis, document clustering, etc.). This is necessary tool building, but only that.

To find the kinds of insights we suspect lurk within social media data, and others we have not yet imagined, an approach is required that fuses advanced computational tools with advanced social science. In a future done right, DARPA grants related to social media will feature as many Principal Investigators (PIs) with degrees in political communication, network sociology and social informatics as in data mining and computational linguistics. Provisionally, let us imagine the establishment of a new field called *cybersocial geography*.

Why "cybersocial"? To study social media is to study social relations. These relations are enacted through mediated communications technologies, and features of these technologies are important to the shape and function of the socio-technical networks they support. Hence the "cyber." But this does not change the fact that the commanding disciplinary frame is essentially social scientific.

And why "geography"? As a metaphor, there are at least four reasons why "geography" is attractive:

- Social media networks have meaningful and somewhat stable macro-structural topologies, which constitute a kind of terrain subject to mapping and dimensional analysis. This mapped topology may be overlaid and correlated with all manner of temporal, semantic, demographic, geo-location and other data.
- Because participants in social media have physical locations, social media structural topology is inherently related to geographic topography. Some cybersocial network features are tied strongly to geographic locations, while others are not. Therefore one might view "human terrain" as organized in two intersecting planes: geographic and cybersocial.

- Geography is a model interdisciplinary field that supports rich traditions around both physical and human features, leveraging quantitative and qualitative methods for mutual advantage. Furthermore, it has successfully supported the creation of advanced computational tools and methods for storing, modeling, overlaying and analyzing diverse information types (GIS). This is what a field tasked with useful analysis of social media data must look like.
- Geography has been successfully bridged with other primary social scientific fields, like economics and sociology.

The history and evolution of geography also points to a useful distinction between the interesting work network scientists are doing now with social media data and the kinds of work cybersocial geographers will need to do.

Ancient attempts to map the known world, like those to model the heavens, suffered from a Platonic bias. Empirical observations were forced into conformity with abstract models believed to represent the beautiful and true natural order of things: e.g. the music of the spheres. Similarly, network analytic work on social media data often focuses on captivating abstractions like scale-free networks, small world properties and patterns of homophily. These efforts are theoretically valuable and intellectually stimulating, but they offer little practical insight into specific events and societies. As with the maturation of cartography, useful network analyses of social media will progress beyond abstractions toward accurate mapping and measurement of empirical particularities: specific patterns within specific societies.

What is it?

Cybersocial Geography (CSG) can be defined as the effort to extract as many kinds of social meaning as possible from social media data. Rather than focusing on a particular approach or theoretic foundation, CSG assumes that any and all tools and methods for analyzing cybersocial networks should be leveraged against one another in the service of diverse theoretical models. Furthermore, three aspects or domains of data are taken to be fundamental and interrelated:

- Relational (network) data: the social structure of cyber communications constitutes the foundational layer of analysis.
- Semantic/text data: memes, meaning and messages are analyzed within the context of network structure.
- External data: features and occurrences within cybersocial space must be correlated with data about the "real world."

From the foundational premise that cyber-relational, semantic and external data must be considered together, there are at least four maxims a good cybersocial geographer should heed:

- *Cyber reality is real reality:* Social media data represent complex interactions among real individuals, organizations and other collectives, in real places, often with non-virtual agendas and strong offline relationships.
- *Meso ≥ micro and macro:* Movements, trends, memes and emergent collective action involve communities of interest and action arising at the meso-scale, and yet most analysis is focused on individual influencers or aggregate global measurements.
- *Long-term frames short-term:* Particularly as coordinated online influence campaigns become more sophisticated, tracking and measuring short-term phenomena without the benefit of long-term context is poorly illuminating, even dangerously misleading.
- *Networks = people + culture + technology:* People participate in different communications genres for different reasons; technologies have particular affordances which constrain/enable individual and collective behavior; and different cultures use the same technologies in very different ways. All of these must be considered when designing and applying analytic tools.

Each of these deserves some elaboration.

Cyber reality is real reality

The idea that online communications constitute a "virtual" plane of interaction, apart from the "real" world, traces at least to *Neuromancer*, the science fiction novel that coined the term "cyberspace."[2] Compelling and intuitive, this view has consequences. Particularly in academia, studies often treat social media as though it were a closed system, apart from the world.

---

2.   Gibson, William. *Neuromancer*. New York: Ace Books, 1984.

An analysis might, for instance, look at how a particular meme spreads within Twitter, or how certain bloggers influence others, based on observed citation behavior. But social media systems are not closed, and particular layers of online media (such as weblogs, social network services, forums, email and microblogs) intersect not only with one another, but also with the physical world in all of its spatio-temporal complexity. Propagation patterns in Twitter often show strong signatures of external salience, with influence driven by physical events and mainstream media. Influential bloggers, from Silicon Valley superstars to Arab Spring activists, often know each other personally and have thick communication backchannels. Social media interaction often reflects social and professional relationships among actors as much as any pure form of online influence.

When we consider social media systems to be fully embedded in real life, as opposed to virtual, we can see both the greater challenge and the greater promise of deriving useful knowledge from large-scale analysis. Mapping the crossover between cybersocial terrain and spatio-temporal reality is perhaps the largest task facing future cybersocial geographers, and it is hard to foresee all the directions this effort will take. Several important directions include:

- *Mapping online actors to offline entities.* In the absence of knowledge, cyber actors (bloggers, Twitter accounts, forum participants, etc.) are usually assumed to represent individual people. Certainly most of them are, in which case it can be important to know who they are, what "real world" social ties bind them, and what agendas they may have. To adapt Miles' Law, where you stand (online) depends on where you sit (offline). But also, from phalanxes of software-controlled bots to members of organized hierarchies (Basij bloggers in Iran are a great example), large numbers of online actors do not represent individuals, but political organizations, marketing initiatives, clandestine campaigns and other collective actors.
- *Mapping the nexus of geo-location and cybersocial position.* Whether cyber actors represent real people or organizations, they can be associated with physical locations. Thus, cybersocial terrain and geo-based human terrain are related, sometimes strongly, sometimes weakly. Sometimes online communities are explicitly tied to locations, as in the case of Twitter clusters based on particular Russian cities and towns.[3] In other cases, cybersocial segments associated with locational-independent issues nonetheless have strong geographic correlations. For instance Russian-language blog clusters topically focused on professional photography and graphic design emerge around communities of arts professionals in St. Petersburg and Moscow. A common problem in current research is that physical location is often used as a filter to delimit online actors for analysis, for instance limiting an "Egyptian blogosphere" analysis to bloggers physically located in Egypt. This is the wrong approach, since cyber actors located elsewhere may in fact play key roles in Egyptian online networks. A better approach is to be mindful of the complex interaction between cyber and geo layers.
- *Correlation of offline events with cyber events.* Major news events tend to have a clear footprint across online networks, a pattern indicating widespread salience in the mainstream media and general society. Discussion of such events typically peaks quickly across online networks, and decays rapidly as well. But there are often subtle patterns around these big events, with related discussion sustaining in particular pockets of the network for days or weeks. And sometimes discussion of a major event is preceded by activity in particular network pockets, as in the case of activists planning a demonstration before it hits the streets and makes the news. These patterns are much easier to spot for large events than for small ones, but the principle is the same: offline events and online discussion are causally tied in ways that can be valuable to discern.

Meso ≥ micro and macro

Consider how much of the work of human society is accomplished at the "meso-level" of social organization,

---

3. Kelly, John; Vladimir Barash; Karina Alexanyan; Bruce Etling; Robert Faris; Urs Gasser and John G. Palfrey. "Mapping Russian Twitter." Berkman Center Research Publication No. 2012-3. (2012), http://ssrn.com/abstract=2028158.

between the scale of individuals and small groups on the one hand, and nation-states, global religions and other very large aggregations on the other. Meso-level social structures include: political parties, social movements, universities, scientific fields, innovation clusters (like Silicon Valley), corporations, issue publics, trade and professional societies, and many more of the interacting human configurations which motivate elites and move societies in one direction or another. While it is often observed that social media have changed the ways individuals communicate with friends, colleagues and other people they know, this is not why social media are having a large political and cultural impact. Their power, like the power of some other Internet communications genres, derives from their many-to-many functions. Social media are powerful because they enable meso-level networks of exchange and coordination, which previously required formal organizations to accomplish.

And yet, most modes of analyzing social media do not even consider the existence of meso-level structures of interaction, let alone offer ways to identify and measure them. Instead, metrics are either individual (Authority, PageRank, Klout, Eigenvector centrality, etc.) or global (how many people are on Facebook now). The most important phenomena present in social media data are invisible to most current analytics.

The problem of the missing

meso-level even corrupts the way individual influence is conceived of and measured. Online influencers, like political leaders, derive their power from those they influence. We often size up the qualities of a leader to construct an account of why they have achieved or lost power, without paying sufficient attention to the demand characteristics of their followers. While a sophisticated analysis of political leadership will correct this problem by looking at the leader within the context of their political base, in an analysis of online leadership this is not even possible unless online networks have been analyzed and segmented to identify key constituencies. Instead, current metrics are misleading insofar as they do not distinguish between global measures of influence and measures specific to particular segments.

Sophisticated mapping and segmentation approaches, building on a network-analytic base, can identify these meso-level online constituencies. Many of these segments represent major dimensions of interest salient in particular societies, which persist even as particular social media actors and influentials come and go.

For instance, a 2008 analysis of the Iranian blogosphere found a number of key online segments organized around major concerns within Iranian society.[4] These included concentrations of network density around opposition politics, conservative politics, politicized Shi'ism and poetry. Looking again in 2011, we discovered the network

contained the same meso-scale patterns of concentration, around the same issues, even though the vast majority of the blogs were different.

Individual fish grow and die, but the school continues. Social media analytics need to identify and track online "schools" representing persistent salient interests, not just measure individual fish.

Long-term frames short-term
Just as individual influencers must be understood in the context of a structured and segmented network space, so too must memes and other "bursty" phenomena be viewed in a historical network context. Events must be situated in the cybersocial terrain. Otherwise, it is impossible to know whether any particular short-term occurrence is a case of dog-bites-man or man-bites-dog.

An easy hypothetical example: a sentiment analysis engine camped onto the Twitter firehose detects a rapid rise in negative tweets about politician X. Should we assume that public opinion is trending against X? That is the conclusion most social media monitoring firms would push us to accept. But what if the negative sentiment is occurring exclusively in a part of the cybersocial terrain which normally opposes X and supports X's enemies? This would indicate business as usual. What if the activity were principally among X's normal supporters? Perhaps X is in trouble with the base. What if the activity is among those who do not normally

4. Kelly, John and Bruce Etling. "Mapping Iran's Online Public: Politics and Culture in the Persian Blogosphere." (2008), http://cyber.law.harvard.edu/publications/2008/Mapping_Irans_Online_Public.

behave politically at all, but rather tweet mainly about celebrities, restaurants, sports and daily life? Perhaps the general public is indeed souring on X. And what if the activity is the product of thousands of new accounts that have never before been active on any topic whatsoever? Perhaps X has been targeted by an army of bots created by an unknown domestic or foreign organization.

Modeling current behavior against historical behavior is critical for understanding what is changing, and what is remaining the same. Online networks shift fastest when huge numbers of new actors are joining (or leaving) them, i.e. when the platform itself is in a state of rapid flux. But once established, online social networks have some stability. Bloggers rarely edit their blogrolls. Social network services (like Facebook or LinkedIn) tend to connect people according to patterns that reflect their real life histories (education, workplace). Observed over time, online network structures reflect somewhat stable interests, affiliations and attitudes. Attempts to segment networks or characterize users based on short time frames risk very skewed results. Judged by data collected on Super Bowl Sunday, one would assume Twitter to be dominated by football fans.

Networks = people + culture + technology

Different modes of online discourse require different tools. For instance, the analytic

stack required to analyze threaded discussion forums is different from that required to map weblog interaction, Twitter dynamics, Facebook activity, etc. Each platform or "genre" has particular characteristics that allow certain types of interaction, and make it easier or harder to form and maintain certain kinds of relationships. Network analytic and semantic toolkits must be tailored to account for these platform and genre particularities. Anyone proposing one-size-fits all social media analytics has not spent much time analyzing different kinds of social media data.

But, differences in platform affordances are only part of the story. These systems are used by real people, who develop a great number of actual practices around them. These practices vary from society to society, and even subculture to subculture. Cultural differences affecting individual-level online behavior can have important implications for large-scale analysis. For instance, American political bloggers are very happy to pick a side, and will readily self-identify as Conservative, Progressive, etc. They also strongly prefer linking to members of their own side over linking to their ideological enemies.

Russian political bloggers do not behave in the same way. They prefer to maintain a rhetorical position of independence and eschew affiliation with specific political identities, even when it is clear to a reader that their position aligns with a known part of the political spectrum. They are much more likely than American bloggers to link to

and directly engage political opponents.[5]

These individual-level differences in behavior are manifested at the macro-structural level, with simple and strong patterns of polarization emerging in the U.S. blogosphere and far more complex patterns in the Russian one. Tools that mine network structure to estimate political biases, an increasingly common approach in research on social media in American politics, will not necessarily work the same way when applied in other societies.

Both of these issues, differences in platform affordances and cultural differences in practices, make analyzing Chinese social media systems especially challenging. Chinese platforms hybridize various social media genres within a single environment, providing blogging, micro-blogging, news aggregation, text messaging, image/video sharing and other services under a single account and login. These capabilities are engineered to be much more closed systems than their international analogs. Open Internet standards (like HTML) are used minimally, to deliver payloads of content that are much more closely tied to internal content management systems. Looking at a hyperlink to a post on a Blogspot blog, the target blog is obvious. A link to a typical Chinese blog post must be loaded and rendered from the host platform before it is clear what the target content is. The Chinese online environment is much more like the collection of "walled

5.   Etling, Bruce and Karina Alexanyan, John Kelly, Rob Faris, John Palfrey, Urs Gasser. "Public Discourse in the Russian Blogosphere: Mapping Runet Politics and Mobilization." (2010), http://cyber.law.harvard.edu/publications/2010/Public_Discourse_Russian_Blogosphere.

gardens" that existed in the U.S. before the advent of the open World Wide Web. It is as though the American online world still centered on AOL and Compuserve. Also, the Chinese government strictly limits the growth of independent sources of online content. Almost all there is to see is what is available on the major online services. Perhaps as a result, Chinese bloggers rarely embed hyperlinks. Most posts simply contain text. The thick citation networks that support vigorous emergent online communities in Russian or American weblogs do not exist in the same way in China. Online censorship is not just a matter of controlling what gets posted, it involves the deep structuring of the cybersocial terrain in ways that are invisible to standard semantic analytics.

Conclusion

The era of social media is just dawning. The transition from a society dominated by national and local mass media to one enabled by the global Internet is in its early phases, and the social and political implications of networked technologies will unfold over decades if not centuries. Likewise, the means and modes of analyzing Internet data are in the early stages of development. While computer scientists are rapidly pushing "big data" analytic capacities forward, the fruits of their labor are best viewed as tools for another class of analysts and scientists to use in answering the kinds of social questions important to policymakers, businesspeople, and academics. But no such field or discipline yet exists and so tools are presented as solutions, as though a hammer were a house.

The best way forward is to continue producing innovative and powerful computational tools, but also to begin building the social scientific layer that should operate on top of them. This would be a deeply transdisciplinary initiative, more akin to geography than to any currently recognized social scientific discipline. Like mapping the earth, mapping cybersocial terrain can be approached in a way that allows multiple domains of knowledge and information, from spatio-temporal to human cultural, to overlay and interact. This, far beyond "memetracking," is what is required to enable the next generation of actionable communications research.

John Kelly, PhD is the founder and lead scientist of Morningside Analytics and an Affiliate at the Berkman Center at Harvard. His research blends social network analysis, content analysis and statistics to solve the problem of making complex online networks visible and understandable.

Section 5

Names and Language in Human Geography

Perception and Identity in Geographical Names: The Potential for Cultural Misunderstanding

Paul Woodman

In our lives we are always seeking to make the world meaningful. We continually strive to bring a sense of comprehensible order into what can seem to be chaos, and to achieve this we first use our perception to identify the phenomena that we encounter, and then we attach labels of identity to those identified phenomena that we perceive as significant to us.

Perhaps the most obvious label of identity is the personal name. In surely all societies and cultures the individual is endowed at birth with such a label, which will be relatively exclusive within the social grouping and will furnish that individual with the crucial attribution of personal identity. Such identity is clearly necessary for an individual's self-identification, and also for each individual's specific identification by others in the same society. Personal names will usually fit into a pattern recognisably familiar to each of the individuals within that particular society, with most

people identified in the same way, such as in the format of "first name plus surname".

We are all familiar with our own society's method of establishing personal names, but as we move away into societies less well known to us, the method used for personal labelling may become unfamiliar. In an Arab Muslim society, an individual may be endowed with a personal name, plus a religious name, plus a family name, and possibly additionally a tribal or locational name. Hence the former dictator of Iraq went by the full name of *Ṣaddām Ḥusayn 'Abd al Majīd at Tikrītī*—where *Ṣaddām* was the personal name, *Ḥusayn* the religious name, *'Abd al Majīd* the family name, and *at Tikrītī* the locational element, alluding to the small town of **Tikrīt** in north-central Iraq from which the family originated. Such labelling methods can prove indecipherable for the uninitiated outsider who may be looking in vain for a familiar label such as a surname, and

as a result different outsiders may choose a different element of the name to act as their preferred single label. Thus, this particular individual was confusingly known by his personal name *Ṣaddām* in the United Kingdom but by his religious name *Ḥusayn* (usually spelled as *Hussein*) in the United States.

Even within the particular society itself, each individual may be identified by a different option, or grouping of options, from the list of available labels. In addition, within Arab Muslim society, womenfolk may habitually refer to themselves not by any of their actual names at all, but instead in an indirect manner such as *Umm Marwan*, which simply means "mother of Marwan", a label which does not represent any of the woman's actual names but is merely a partial indicator of her social place within her family. That name constitutes the woman's perception of herself within her family, but it is not a name that helps the outsider to form an objective perspective as to her identity.

Some of these characteristics of personal identity are equally applicable in the world of toponymy. Our perception of our own local landscape has become so naturally familiar to us since our earliest childhood that we scarcely give it a thought. We recognize that a particular physical feature has a specific identity as a hill or lake or forest, and that a particular cultural feature has a specific identity as a town or street. Our society shares the same perception of what we might call these constructs, and together we all agree that each such feature requires its own identifying label, its own geographical name. We also share the same perception of what does not constitute a feature deserving a label; thus (as we shall examine in more detail later) we would not normally seek to name each individual tree within a forest.

The connection between personal names and geographical names is very real. The principle in both instances is that we name only those features to which we need to attribute an identity. And with geographical names, exactly as we have seen with personal names, when we move away from our comfort zone into less familiar terrain, our outsider's application of this principle may not match its application by those who live there. As a rule, when we look at features that lie away from our familiar localities, we use a broad brush. We do not see fine detail because usually we do not need to. Yet we need to be aware that those who inhabit that terrain do need to see it in finer detail.

The Bay of Biscay provides an example of this phenomenon. It is a toponym known in many languages, yet the name does not carry the same identity across those languages. Those dwelling at some stage of remove from France or Spain can afford to regard it simply as one large feature, and accordingly languages such as English attach just one label to it. But this treatment is inadequate if those waters are on your doorstep; a greater degree of precision is then required.

In both the French and Spanish languages, the Bay of Biscay has traditionally been considered a very much smaller feature, limited to the waters right by the angle where France meets Spain. In those languages, other and different names are applied elsewhere: *Golfe de Gascogne* in the French language for the sea off France's western coast, and *Mar Cantábrica* in the Spanish language for the sea off Spain's northern coast. All of these features are covered by the English-language name Bay of Biscay; that label in that language has a much wider geographical application. There is clearly scope for misidentification and misunderstanding here, since although an English-speaker and a French-speaker will both readily understand the label Bay of Biscay/Baie de Biscaye, neither may realize that the other is attaching that label to a feature with a different scope and identity. This very obviously has potentially dangerous consequences in certain contexts such as search and rescue operations.

Cultural differences may also lead to differing perceptions of a geographical name. Consider for example the different perceptions of the celebrated waterway we know as the Bosphorus. In the United Kingdom, at least, we are customarily taught that this feature divides the continents of Europe and Asia. But the colloquial Turkish name for this feature is *Boğaziçi*, meaning "within the throat", and this name gives us our clue that Turks, who are of course on the spot, have a totally different perception of the Bosphorus— as a feature connecting rather than separating the continents of Europe and Asia, just as one's throat connects rather than separates one's head and body.

Those are some examples of just how substantially cultural perceptions of features and the labels we attach to them can differ in both reality and interpretation. So what happens when we transport our inbuilt perceptions with us into the reality of a different environment? When dropped into an unfamiliar environment our natural response is to try to make that environment fit as much as possible into our own experiences, into the environment that we do know.

Again, we are attempting to bring familiar order to what we as outsiders perceive as chaos. A good example of this is in the naming exercises undertaken by the Pilgrim Fathers and their successors on their arrival in North America. In order to bring a feeling of home into a new and uncertain environment, the settlers deployed geographical names with which they were already familiar, as the county names of Massachusetts show. Most of the counties were given names lifted straight from the old country, the first of these being Essex, Middlesex, Norfolk and Suffolk. While such an approach may be all very well for settlers with little expectation of meaningful contact with indigenous inhabitants, in other scenarios it is a dangerous attitude to carry, because if we are seeking empathy with an unfamiliar culture we need to understand its existing environment.

Arriving at such an understanding can be tricky. In a familiar European or North American forest, we know instinctively that only the forest in its entirety, or perhaps sectors of that forest, will be named. Society is most unlikely to endow each individual tree with its own toponym. But in Somalia, a single tree may represent the only significant vegetation for five miles or more in any direction. Because of this vastly different environmental context, this lone tree will be a very significant feature and accordingly its location will assuredly have a geographical name. Yet if we find ourselves in Somalia and do no more than apply the context of our outside experience, applying our inbuilt perception filters, we are very likely to say "It's just a tree; it won't be important", and we may simply pass it by unremarked. By doing so, we will have unwittingly neglected to note the one crucial toponym in an area of seventy-five square miles. Thus we cannot say as a universal rule that "a tree does not have a name". As with so much else, the reality is much more complicated and depends entirely on context.

Similarly, if we are dropped into the arid landscapes of Arabia, again our instinct will inevitably be to try to make the environment fit our experience. In this instance, our inbuilt perceptions of Arabian landscapes may lead us to expect deserts, so we arrive with that particular expectation at the forefront of our minds. Hence, when we see a suitably sandy area, our reaction— again seen through our alien perception filters—may well be along the following lines: "I know what this is; it's a desert; deserts are surely significant; it must have a name". So we ask a local inhabitant "What is the name of this desert?", and we are surprised to be met with a look of blank bemusement. The reason for this reaction is that, unbeknown to us, this is not simply a uniform desert at all, but an agglomeration of several different important features, which through inexperience we simply cannot detect. The local inhabitant, his livelihood dependent upon making sense of his environment, knows that in reality one area around where we are standing is good going for camels, another area around us is by contrast exceptionally heavy going, and yet another area nearby is renowned for bursting into floral bloom after the occasional rains. These localities, each invisible to us as outsiders, are the features that carry the geographical names because they are the features to which local people need to attribute an identity. Our question "What is the name of this desert?" has been met with bemusement because it is based on a false premise and is therefore unanswerable.

If we are properly aware of these varying perceptions and identities, geographical names can reveal a wealth of cultural information about the environment in which we find ourselves. In the Turkic and Chinese lands, for instance, it is traditional practice to use a system of color coding for the representation of compass points: black for north, blue for east, red for south, white for west, and yellow for center. This phenomenon is very often represented in geographical names. It follows that if a traveller is told that the person he is seeking resides in *Qaraqoy* (which means "Black Village"), that traveller should not necessarily seek out a village built of black stone or sited on black earth. The person sought may instead simply be living in the village just to the north. It is for this reason that Turkic languages label the Mediterranean Sea as the White Sea (*Akdeniz*), it being essentially a feature in the west as viewed from their perspective.

In Iraq, personal, religious or family names may be used by extension as geographical names, especially in those rural areas with a sedentary rather than a nomadic population, as in the countryside around Al 'Amārah and in the semi-desert area around Ṣafwān towards the border with Kuwait. Settlement around Al 'Amārah consists for the most part of isolated buildings or homesteads, and the names relevant to these locations can denote those who have possession of the homestead and its surrounding land. Some of these toponyms begin with the Arabic word *Salaf*, meaning "ancestors" or "forefathers", from which it is reasonable to infer that possession by the named family group goes back several generations. Patterns around Ṣafwān show that this type of toponym apparently relates to areas of land rather than homesteads, since there are few buildings in this area. Hence an awareness of the cultural factors within a local toponymy can facilitate an understanding of land ownership patterns.

Interestingly, too, examination of some of these personally based toponyms in Iraq may reveal them as specifically indicative of Sunni or Shia habitation.

On the island of New Guinea, villagers may not have a specific name for their own village, or for the river running nearby. These features are simply "the village" and "the river" respectively, those labels deemed sufficient within that localised environment. Similarly the Socotri language, spoken only on the Yemeni island of Socotra, contains no word to identify Socotra itself. The inhabitants have no need for such a label; to them it is simply "the island." In Pacific Ocean cultures the concept of a national capital may not refer to a built-up area; in Tuvalu the capital of the country is considered to be the natural feature of Funafuti Atoll in its entirety, not the main settlement on that atoll.

Thus, the significance of perception and identity in the world of geographical names is paramount. Recognition of this fact is vital if we are to properly understand cultures different from our own. Somalia, Iraq, New Guinea, Socotra and Tuvalu all demonstrate that in order to interpret a foreign environment successfully we need to understand its own particular physical and cultural dimensions, and the societal and environmental contexts in which these dimensions come together. If we view a landscape solely through our own cultural eyes, we do not see the features that possess local identity and therefore carry geographical names. Hence it is all too easy to start off on the wrong foot, ask the wrong questions, provoke thereby a response of bemusement, and very possibly compound it all by misconstruing this bemusement as hostility. This is of course not to claim that the methods of perception and identity used by others are superior to ours, but simply to state that they will have been designed for the local environment and will therefore be more relevant than ours to that environment. If we are ignorant of this, we blunder into that other environment at our peril.

Paul Woodman was for 30 years Secretary of the U.K. Permanent Committee on Geographical Names, and is a long-standing member of UNGEGN. He is editor of *The Great Toponymic Divide* (2012) and co-edited *Exonyms and the International Standardization of Geographical Names* (2007). He co-edits the toponymic journal *Name & Place*.

EMPIRE AND NAMES: THE CASE OF NAGORNO KARABAKH

Benjamin Foster

The area of Nagorno Karabakh, encompassing 4,400 square kilometers (1,699 square miles) in Western Azerbaijan (see Figure 1), was the site of a bloody conflict between Azerbaijan and Armenia from 1988 to 1994.[1] Both nations claim it as an inseparable part of their countries' territory, history and culture. These claims appear in bitter comments that include arguments over the origins of the area's toponyms. In Azerbaijani President Heydar Aliyev's 1998 decree declaring March 31 the Day of Genocide against Azerbaijanis, he included a description of cultural destruction that included changing of geographic names of Karabakh during the 20th century.[2]

The comment by Aliyev invokes the turbulence that has resulted in a confusing toponymic landscape for more than a century. During the second millennium A.D. numerous empires conquered the area, each leaving new toponyms that were destroyed, left alone or shared by successors. For several centuries, the Persian-Ottoman fighting in the Caucasus became such that at times, one empire or the other would pursue a "scorched earth" strategy, deporting Kurdish, Armenian or Georgian inhabitants to Tabriz or Istanbul.[3] In 1603, the Persian Shah Abbas led a massive deportation of Armenians to Tabriz. In 1796, Shusha was completely emptied of inhabitants.[4] The towns' subsequent occupiers would either not be able to decipher the foreign alphabet or simply ignore markers indicating place names, and would make up their own names for geographic objects.[5] The Russians invaded a short time later and, with the exception of regional trade or government centers such as Yelizavetpol and Alexandropol, left alone the cultural markers of the area. In other words, the Russian Empire did not project Russian culture onto the area by means of toponyms, as had previous empires. Maps published in 1915 show a Caucasus featuring mostly Turkic names with Persian elements, with the more prominent features— Yelizavetpol, the Caucasus (Kavkaz) mountain range, for example—with Russian names.

When the Soviet Union arrived in 1921, they projected cultural power in a different way. Though Russians constituted a majority in the Soviet Union, the Bolshevik leadership was clear about renouncing any legacy of Russian imperialism. The Soviets did not capture the Caucasus Republics in order to Russify them; that is, they did not do so in order to change the local national identities to match that of the conquering

---

1. A note on spelling of geographic names: due to the era researched in this project, sources were mostly Soviet and rendered in Russian. Toponyms are romanized from the Cyrillic alphabet, and may not agree with direct Romanization from the Azeri or Armenian forms. So *Nagorno Karabakh*, rather than *Yuxarı Qarabağ*, or *Artsakh*, is the form used.
2. Aliyev, Heydar. 1998. Decree of the President of the Republic of Azerbaijan on the Genocide of the Azerbaijani People.
3. Saparov, Arseny. 2003. The Alteration of Place Names and Construction of National Identity in Soviet Armenia. *Cahiers du Monde Russe* 44, 181.
4. Hewsen, Robert H. 2001. *Armenia: A Historical Atlas*. Chicago: The University of Chicago Press, 146.
5. Saparov, 182.

Figure 1

Source: United States Central Intelligence Agency

people. This avoidance of imperialist practice was intentional, and the fact that the Soviets were concerned with identities at all made them unique among previous empires in the Caucasus. While Ottomans left Turkic marks, Persians left Persian marks, and Russians left Russian marks, the Soviets *removed* Russian marks. In renaming geographic features, the Soviet policy was to shun the "imperialist" tendency of finding culturally internal names for nationally external features.

If projecting linguistic culture through toponyms was a method of past empires, the Soviet method was to project political power while preserving local cultural forms. The toponym remained a local *form*, obeying phonological and linguistic constraints of the local language, and in some cases even honored national figures or themes. The *content* of these toponyms was socialist, as the national figures honored were socialists. In addition to the content of the names being socialist, the mechanism, or bureaucratic procedure of name-changing, was unequivocally bound in the highly centralized structure of the Soviet Union.[6] Due to a law passed by the Supreme Soviet of the Union, name changes could not be carried out at the national level, but required Union-level consent. No name was approved, even a name "entirely" Armenian, Azerbaijani or Georgian, without approval by the all-Union Supreme Soviet.

As Nagorno Karabakh has been subject to such a succession of empires throughout its history, toponyms there have a very short life. An objective argument of what lands legitimately belong to which people in Nagorno Karabakh would be difficult, if not impossible, to create. Each ethnic group inhabiting the area has left a patchwork of cultural, linguistic and historical markers. In this context, assigning ethnicities to one place or another based solely on its toponym's form would be to ignore the history of the people and place of Nagorno Karabakh.

Though some have called the toponym the "most valuable source for resolving the problem of ethnic origins," there are numerous linguistic and historical obstacles to an accurate conclusion reached by this methodology.[7] Rather than follow Aliyev and the many others into the either-or argument over Nagorno Karabakh, this paper will take as given the historically heterogeneous makeup of the region as it examines Soviet toponymic practice during the 20th century.

In order to do so, the toponymic landscape of Nagorno Karabakh under Soviet rule will be examined. Sources include maps from 1915, 1941, 1979 and 1994; policy documents detailing the birth of the Nagorno Karabakh Autonomous *Oblast'* (NKAO) and toponymic guidelines; and other textual sources, such as the

Territorial'noe-Administrativnoe Deleniye Catalogs of Azerbaijan. These changes and policies enlighten as to how the Soviets made any changes to national toponyms, and how quickly the independent states "corrected" the names of Soviet-named features.

It is expected that toponyms in Karabakh from the Soviet period mixed Armenian, Azeri and "Soviet" names. If this is the case, then Soviet toponymic policy resulted in a confusing geographical landscape that has fueled local tensions since the collapse of the Soviet Union. By bringing this aspect of Karabakh's history to light, the perspective on the area will be broadened to one that considers how outside forces can antagonize local actors against each other.

The first section briefly explains the role of autonomy in the Soviet Union, and in regards to Nagorno Karabakh in more detail. The intended use of Nagorno Karabakh as an autonomous *oblast'* will allow predictions about what the Soviet toponymic practice in the *oblast'* should be, and provide a framework with which to analyze the findings of the survey of the toponyms therein. The next section looks at the ethnic makeup of the area, and the major changes that may have affected what the deciding bodies saw as the desired name for a given geographic object. The third section will present the data: the number of geographic objects catalogued; the ethnolinguistic categories the

6. Saparov, 185.
7. Geybullayev, G.A. 1986. *Toponimiya Azerbaydzhana: Istoriko-Etnograficheskoye Issledovaniye. [Toponymy of Azerbaijan: A Historio-Ethnographic Analysis.]* Baku: Academy of Sciences of Azerbaijan Soviet Socialist Republic, 3.; Geybullayev also notes that, even in antiquity, the Caucasus presented a dizzying array of languages. For example, the name Albania, from which both Azerbaijanis and Armenians draw for legitimacy, refers to places in modern-day Armenia, Azerbaijan, Georgia and even Dagestan.

names fall into; and changes to toponyms made in the Soviet era. The conclusions made therein will inform the final section, which will compare the trends to the expectations from the first section. An assessment of the legacy of Soviet toponymic practice in Nagorno Karabakh, and its effects on the ongoing conflict will conclude this study.

The role of autonomy in Nagorno Karabakh

The framers of the Soviet Constitution had evidently learned what dangers to the Union could be presented by disenfranchised nationalities. In prewar Vienna during the 1910s, Stalin observed how the Hapsburgs ascribed a separate national status to non-Austrians. He criticized the Austrian model for dividing the proletariat, preventing them from any sense of class unity.[8] He instead advocated a territorial autonomy, which, when practiced in the Soviet Union in the 1920s, would lead to the creation of non-Russian republics and autonomous regions. Within these regions, national cultures, national elites, and education were allowed to flourish.[9] Thus the Soviet Union could assert not a national supremacy of Russians, but a political supremacy of the Communist Party.

Autonomy in the Soviet Union served several purposes, though all of these purposes were ultimately subservient to winning the loyalties of non-Russian peoples. First, if the new empire was to be a force for the international movement of communism, it would not work for the borders to shrink back to a scale comparable to those of 18th century Russia. The revolution and collapse of the Russian Empire emboldened the new Turkish state, as well as western powers interested in supporting new Baltic States. Foreign troops were quick to arrive on Soviet soil, even as a civil war was raging in the new Union. The Soviets wanted to secure the allegiances and convince the indigenous people and secure their loyalty away from the advancing Turks, British and French in Anatolia and the Caucasus.

Second, autonomy for non-Russian nationalities could serve as a step in the eventual "withering away" of nations. While the nationalism of Europe sought to divide people along ethnic, linguistic and cultural lines, the Soviet Union aimed to unite people according to economic class. The hope was that by bringing about a state in which different nationalities could participate and in which economic and class development among nationalities reached a similar level, the Soviets could "drain nationality of its content while legitimizing its form, to promote long-term withering away of the nationality as a vital component of life.[10] Autonomy within the USSR would "create" nations with their own schools, educated leadership and national culture. Autonomy, however, would not be so generous as to allow separate SSRs to actually emancipate themselves from the binding socialist principles, but would only be so extensive so as to make culture serve the purposes of building socialism.

Third, autonomy served as a rhetorical tool, used to distance the new Soviet leadership from their Imperial Russian predecessors. The leadership claimed solidarity with the smaller nationalities of the empire by pointing to the similarities between the class oppression that the working class had suffered at the hands of the tsars and national oppression that the Turkic and other peoples had suffered. The minorities of the Russian Empire had been exploited and used the same way that the working class of Russia had been exploited, so the logic went. By considering minorities of the erstwhile empire as an exploited people, a sort of "national proletariat" was created. Autonomy for these peoples would include them in the "dictatorship of the proletariat."

Autonomy would be reflected in toponymy by changing geographic names to those that would agree with national forms of language, but in many cases would evoke socialist themes. Cities with tsarist content such as Tsaritsyn would become Stalingrad, Yelizavetpol eventually became Kirovabad, and in Nagorno Karabakh, Xankendi (a Turkic name meaning "the Khan's town") became Stepanakert. Elsewhere, many populated places were renamed after Lenin, but were unique in their national forms: Leningori

8. Stalin, Josef. 1913. Marxism and the National Question. *Prosveshcheniye. [Enlightenment.]* Saint Petersburg, Russia.
9. Brubaker, Rogers. 1994. Nationhood and the National Question in the Soviet Union and post-Soviet Eurasia: an Institutionalist Account. *Theory and Society* 23, 52.
10. Brubaker, 49.

in Georgia; Sovietabad in Tajikistan, or Kyzyl-Orda ('kyzyl' meaning "red") in Kazakhstan.

Nagorno Karabakh stands as a unique exception among autonomous regions of the Soviet Union. Each republic and autonomous region (from here on represented collectively by "autonomous region") was named to indicate "titular" nationalities or ethnic groups not represented in another republic or region. Nagorno Karabakh, however, was home to Azeris and Armenians, who were represented in the Union by the Azerbaijani and Armenian Soviet Socialist Republics.[11] This uniqueness provided a problem with regard to toponymy: should names be represented according to Armenian or Azerbaijani conventions?

Some characteristics of Nagorno Karabakh complicate the why and how of the *oblast's* designation. The history of the region does not provide legitimacy exclusively for any one ethnic group's claims. Its Soviet name sets it apart as the only autonomous region that does not explicitly state the ethnicity for which it was formed. While there were regions created and designated as homelands for specific groups (Adyghea, Karakalpak, Kyrghyz), each indicating with their toponym who would live there, Nagorno Karabakh contained no such explicit indication. While other autonomous administrative bodies of the Union were formed with internal stability

and preservation in mind, Nagorno Karabakh was formed with external factors in mind. The new Turkic state advanced into the Caucasus until 1920, forcing the weakened Soviet State, now in the grip of a civil war, to the Treaty of Moscow that would involve Karabakh. On the other hand, Armenians in Karabakh, reacting to the pro-Turkish conditions of the treaty, threatened internal stability.[12] At the same time, British and French forces had designs for an independent Armenia in the Caucasus.

If the Soviet Union was going to resolve the problem of Nagorno Karabakh, it needed to find a solution that satisfied various requirements. The internal conflict needed to be solved in order to assert Soviet sovereignty in the Caucasus; the external threat of the Turks needed to be removed; the ideological enemies from the west needed to be neutralized; and Armenia's allegiance guaranteed. The Soviets resolved to leave Karabakh in Azeri territory, but created an autonomous *oblast'* that would be populated by both Armenians and Azeris.[13]

Due to the mixing of ethnic groups in Nagorno Karabakh, and the official celebration of that diversity, a diverse set of toponyms is expected. The Soviets, wishing to promote solidarity between Azeri and Armenians there, would be expected to make several name-changes to represent the Armenians of

the oblast', but would retain the Turkic names as well.[14] Given the 1924 ban on name-changes without the all-Union Presidium's approval, most populated places would retain their pre-1917 names. As is consistent throughout the rest of the Union, a small percentage of names can be expected to feature a "socialist" name, though even toponyms socialist in content must contain a national (local) form. We can expect these to be shared between Azeri and Armenian forms.

Demography and toponyms in Nagorno Karabakh

As reviewed in the last section, the Soviet government and party committees who created the NKAO wrote that they did so in order to promote "brotherly solidarity" between the then-warring Armenians and Azeris who lived there. This section reviews the demographic history of Nagorno Karabakh and how it led to competing narratives about the "rightful" inhabitants of the region.

The Persian and Ottoman Empires clashed in the Caucasus for centuries, drastically changing the ethnic makeup of the area. Armenians, Kurds, Persians and Turks were exiled, relocated, and resettled. Until the systematic slaughters of the late 19th and early 20th centuries, the Armenians enjoyed a certain favored minority status in both empires. Those deported

---

11. The Karachay-Cherkessian and Kabardino-Balkarian autonomous regions were each home to two nationalities, but these nationalities had no "home" territory elsewhere, as the Azeris and Armenians did, and each ethnicity's legitimacy was confirmed in the name of the autonomous region.

12. *K Istorii Obrazovaniya Nagorno-Karabakhskoy Avtonomnoy Oblasti Azerbaidzhanskoy Sovetskoy Sotsialistikoy Republiky: Dokumenty i Materialy. [Towards a History of the Creation of the Nagorno-Karabakh Autonomous Oblast' of the Azerbaijani Soviet Socialist Republic: Docments and Materials.]* 1989. Baku: Azerbaidzhanskoye Gosudarstvennoye Izdatel'stvo, 41.

13. *K Istorii*, 155.

14. *K Istorii*, 155.

during the wars to Istanbul or Tabriz became a vital part of the commercial sectors there.[15] The Armenian land itself, however, became emptied of most Armenians. Upon repopulation by Turkish, Iranian and Kurdish settlers, the Armenian settlements lost their Armenian character and in effect became Turkish, Iranian or Kurdish, as these new settlers had no reference by which to name them with any but their own language, resulting in "the total replacement of the cultural landscape."[16]

When the Russians entered into the Caucasus at the beginning of the 19th century, the Armenians began to return. Depending on the nationality of the source, the Armenians either returned under the impression that the Russians, being Christian, would make Armenia safer for Armenians; or they were brought back by the Russians in an attempt to Christianize their newly acquired territory.[17] At any rate, the ethnological makeup of eastern Anatolia changed dramatically in the 19th century. Armenians, long since gone to Tabriz, Istanbul, or elsewhere, returned in such numbers as to render Turkish, Kurdish or Iranian towns Armenian again.[18] As many as 105,000 Armenians arrived in the South Caucasus between 1828 and 1831.[19] Even by then, half of the population of the *Armyanskaya Oblast'* including Nagorno

Karabakh was non-Armenian, but more Armenians flooded the region throughout the rest of the 19th century through 1917.[20] According to the 1926 census, Armenians constituted over 84 percent of the population of the Armenian SSR. As the Russians did not populate the area themselves, beyond the major commercial and administrative centers of Alexandropol and Yelizavetpol, the toponyms generally retained their Turkic character.[21]

Under Soviet rule the toponyms of Nagorno Karabakh became more Armenian, as over 80 changes to populated places' names were made, reflecting the mixed population of Armenians and Azeris. The Soviets desired a multiethnic NKAO, as the *oblast's* own toponym was the only one out of all of the autonomous regions not to indicate a specific ethnic group. From official documents, this intentional decision would promote goodwill among peoples of the Caucasus. Given the *korenizatsiya* practices of the 1920s and 30s, the resulting toponymy attempted to reflect the *oblast's* ethnic makeup and do away with the either-or discussion about the ethnicity of the area.

The demographic trends in Karabakh for the last 150 years have generally shifted in favor of the Armenian population. In 1845, when sources began to note significant changes in the area, Azeri Turks constituted about two-thirds of

the population there (92,000, see Figure 2). By 1897, the populations were almost equal to one another. When the NKAO was created in 1921, the Soviet census found that out of 131,500 people accounted for, 94.4 percent were Armenian, with the rest being Azeri Turk. The census did not, however, include seminomadic inhabitants, who wintered in the lowlands outside of the *oblast's* border. Even considering that Azeri Turks in Karabakh numbered as many 50,000 in the previous century, the low population density associated with seminomadic people indicates that the nearly 125,000 Armenians there still would outnumber them. Over time, the Soviet practices of urbanization, collective farming and forced emigrations led to the end of the seminomadic way of life. More Azeris were included in the 1979 census, in which Azeris numbered 37,000 (22.8 percent of the population), while the figure of Armenians living in Karabakh numbered at 123,000 (77.2 percent). Note that the Armenian figure changed little, if at all, throughout the century. The trend of Armenian growth there would continue through the end of the Soviet era, with 4,000 more Azeri Turks and 20,000 more Armenians in the *oblast'*. The beginning of armed conflict in Nagorno Karabakh can account for this, with Armenians fleeing into Karabakh, and Azeris persecuted and expelled from Karabakh.

---

15. Hewsen, 11.
16. Saparov, 182.
17. Geybullayev.; Saparov.; Yamskov, Anatoly. 1991. Ethnic Conflict in the Transcaucasus: The Case of Nagorno Karabakh. *Theory and Society* 20, 631-660.
18. Geybullayev.; Saparov.; Hewsen.
19. Yamskov.
20. Which consisted of the Yerevan (present-day Armenia) and Nakhichevan (made Azeri in 1921) provinces.
21. Saparov, 183.

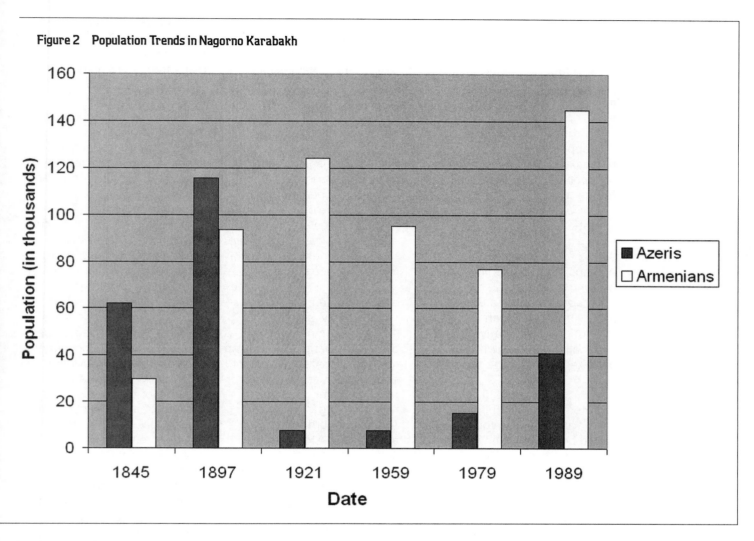

Figure 2   Population Trends in Nagorno Karabakh

Soviet-era toponyms of Nagorno Karabakh

Determining the ethnolinguistic "belonging" of toponyms in Nagorno Karabakh can appear deceptively simple. Both languages lend toponyms distinct endings indicative of one nationality or the other. These endings will indicate a given toponym's ethnicity. In addition, each language features certain letters or letter combinations that the other does not have. For example, the consonant clusters *dz* and *ts* are not part of the phonological inventory of Azeri. Toponyms with these combinations can be considered at least partly Armenian.

There are complexities, however, of determining the ethnolinguistic root of Karabakh's toponyms. These complexities are the legacy of the region's difficult history. While Armenian and Azeri are very distinct from one another, both have been heavily influenced by Persian languages.[22] Even the name *Karabakh* is evocative of Persian, as *–bağ* means garden in Persian. Therefore,

names that feature Persian characteristics could be claimed either by Armenians or Azeris. The Persian ending *-abad* appears in several toponyms, meaning one must look elsewhere for evidence of more local linguistic influences. In addition, the Turkic and Armenian cultures have mixed. Powerful Armenians under Turkic rule were given the title *Melik* (the Armenian version of *malik*, Arabic for "king"). Eventually, the title found its way into local toponymy. "Melikjanli," for example, is a town in Karabakh with a

22. Hewsen, 11.

Turkic name using an Armenian term. Some toponyms with Armenian endings use Turkic titles in the same way, such as "Mkhtarishen," which has as its root the Turkic title *muhtar*, meaning "headman."

Another phenomenon that appears in Nagorno Karabakh is the Sovietization of toponyms. These toponyms feature distinct Azeri or Armenian endings, but contain Soviet roots. Most of these toponyms are either clearly Azeri or Armenian in their endings, such as *Leninkend* or *Leninavan*, but the name *Leninabad* features a Soviet root with a Persian ending. The intended representative Soviet nationality in this town cannot be determined by the toponym alone.

In this context, the first step to determine what choices the Soviets made in toponyms would be to examine which toponyms have distinctive Armenian or Azeri elements, and to determine the types of toponyms existing in the area. Informed by the Soviet instructions for transliterating Azeri and Armenian names and Geybullayev's *Toponimiya Azerbaidzhana*, I have classified the names of Nagorno Karabakh into six categories:

1. Armenian names. Names can be identified as Armenian if they contain solely Armenian characteristics. Such characteristics include the digraphs *rr*, *dz* or *ts*, which do not occur in Azeri names; the endings -*bert*, -*van*, -*kert*, -*gyukh*, -*tag*, -*shen*, -*shat*, -*gomer*, -*dzor*, -*zur* and -*tekh*; the descriptive terms *nerkin*,

verin or *lerr*; or consonant clusters, such that appear in *Mkhtarishen*.[23]

2. Azeri names. Names can be identified as Azeri if they contain solely Azeri characteristics. Such characteristics include vowel agreement across an entire word, such that one will seldom see the letters *i* and *y* in the same word; the appearance of vowels at the end of a name; or the endings -*li*, -*ly*, -*kend*, -*bey*, -*peya*, -*gaya*, -*qaya*, -*lar*, -*lyar*, -*chi*; otherwise containing *memme*, *bazar*, *kuscu*, *guscu*, *kun*, *gu*, or *kul*; or the descriptive terms *ashaghi*, *yukhari*, *chay*, *su* or *dag*.

3. Armeno-Azeri names: toponyms featuring an Armenian root with an Azeri generic or ending, such as *Metstaglar*, from the Armenian *mets*, meaning "big"; "tag," the Armenian word for "crown"; and -*lar*, the Azeri plural suffix.

4. Azero-Armenian names: toponyms featuring an Azeri root with an Armenian generic or ending, such as *Dashushen*, from the Azeri word *dash*, meaning "stone," and the Armenian *shen*, meaning "town."

5. Sovietized Azeri names: toponyms with the form of an Azeri word, but featuring an element of Soviet culture, such as *Leninkend*, *Mir-Bashir*.

6. Sovietized Armenian names: toponyms with the form of an Armenian word, but featuring an element of Soviet culture, such as *Leninakan* or *Stepanakert*.

Maps from pre-revolutionary

Russia show that Karabakh was covered in Turkic-named settlements. General Staff maps from 1915 do not display boundaries for Nagorno Karabakh, but within the approximate area I counted 334 names, including those of settlements, mountains, passes and rivers. Thirty of these features had Armenian names, with five Azero-Armenian or Armeno-Azeri names. Existence of the latter categories indicates that adaptation of Turkic or Muslim conventions had been used to form Armenian names, in the case of *Allaberd* from *Allah* and -*berd*, meaning fortress. Armenian titles were also used in order to form Turkic names, such as the case of *Melikli*, from *melik*, the Armenian variation of the Arabic word for "king," and -*li*, a common Azeri suffix. In toponymy this denotes the inhabitants of a given settlement.[24] The majority of toponyms with Armenian elements in them were found in a North-South axis running from the town of **Ağdam** to the Akera River near the present-day border between Azerbaijan and Armenia.

Nearly all of the changes towards Armenian names took place between the founding of NKAO in 1921 and publication of the 1961 *Administrativno-Territorialnoye Deleniye* of Azerbaijan. Out of 269 toponyms listed in that publication that fall within NKAO, 82 are Armenian names, with at least nine Sovietized Armenian names, six Azero-Armenian names,

---

23. -*tag*, meaning "crown," is problematic, due to its proximity to the Turkic word and toponymic suffix *dağ*, meaning "mountain." I have refrained from using *tag* as a definitive indicator of either language and used other elements in the toponym instead. -*dağ* is considered an Azeri element.

24. Geybullayev, 36.

and one Armeno-Azeri name.[25] There are three Sovietized names which indicate no affiliation with either ethnic group, and one Sovietized Azeri name. The increase in names with Armenian elements from 35 to 95 shows a practice of name changing inclined towards creating cultural space for the Armenian toponyms at the expense of the Azeri names. It is important to note that the remaining 156 names catalogued in the publication are Azeri names without overt socialist references or Armenian elements. It appears that, from the numbers alone, toponymic practice did not coincide with the change in demography. Given the pre-Soviet state of toponymy in Nagorno Karabakh and the distance between the Caucasus and Moscow, a majority of Turkic (Azeri) names

should have been expected.

The dynamics of the features renamed show that the scales are tipped significantly in favor of Armenian names. In the list of "the most significant" name changes in the 1961 version of *Administrativno-Territorial'noe Deleniye*, four names of NKAO features are listed, and each is changed to an Armenian name.[26] The existence of more than 90 toponyms with Armenian elements in 1961, compared to less than 40 in 1915, indicates that there were more changes during this period (see Figure 3). Finding changes from Turkic name to Turkic name would be more difficult, excepting names such as Mir Bashir, Krasnyy Bazar, Leninkend, etc. Looking elsewhere in Azerbaijan, it appears that the majority of name changes removed Persian, imperial

Russian, religious, or Armenian elements, and did not change from one Turkic name to another.[27]

One must keep in mind that not all geographic objects are equally significant. In the same way, not every toponym will carry the same political significance. This phenomenon in ethnolinguistic research has been called the *incongruent* nature of languages, and it is useful to consider this phenomenon in the study of toponyms as well.[28] Therefore it is necessary here to view the *types* of objects renamed. The administrative divisions of NKAO, for example, provide an example of significant features that underwent name changes. Before the revolution in 1917, the area of NKAO lay within the province of Yelizavetpol. When the Soviets absorbed Azerbaijan (and Karabakh),

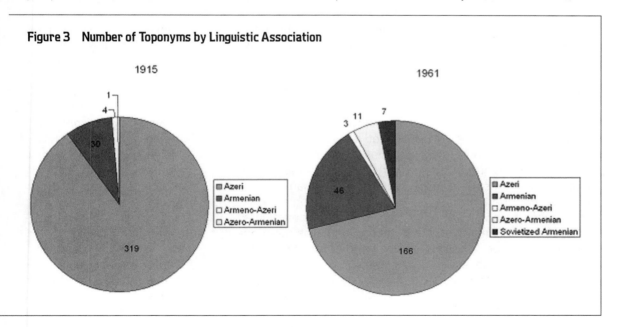

Figure 3   Number of Toponyms by Linguistic Association

25. The discrepancy between the 334 names collected from the 1915 map and the 251 collected here lies in absence of a boundary of Karabakh in the 1915 maps surveyed, so a larger area was surveyed; also, only populated places are indicated in the *Deleniye*.

26. These are Hadrut Rayon (from Dizak), Leninavan (from Margushevan), Mardakert Rayon (from Jerabert), and Martuni (from Nerkin Karanlug).

27. *Azerbaydzhanskaya SSR: Administrativno-Territorial'noye Deleniye. [Azerbaijan SSR: Administrative-Territorial Division.]* 1961. Baku: Azerbaydzhanskoye Gosudarstvennoye Izdatel'stvo.

28. Viechnicki, Peter. 2008. Language Mapping for 21st Century Intelligence Operations: a Case Study of Chitral, Pakistan. Unpublished paper.

the province and borders of Yelizavetpol were dissolved and *rayons* were created which did not include a mention of Karabakh.[29] However, when the Autonomous *Oblast'* of Nagorno Karabakh was created in 1923, each administrative division within it featured names with Armenian elements: Stepanakert, for Stepan Shahumyan, a notable Armenian communist; Mardakert, Hadrut', Shusha and Martuni. Since the dissolution of the Soviet Union, the *rayons* have been dissolved and the cities from which the administrative divisions took their names have all been renamed, with the exception of Shusha. While the majority of settlements retained Azeri names, those that were changed to names with Armenian elements carried either administrative significance or socialist themes (*Kolkhozashen*).

Conclusions

The initial hypothesis was that one would find a mix of Armenian and Azeri names in Nagorno Karabakh, due to the supposed intentions of pacifying the Turks and integrating two (or more) antagonistic ethnic groups into one region. The most precise guess was that there may be more Azeri toponyms in NKAO, but that the majority of renamings would be toward Armenian names. The actual result was that the commercial and political centers of Nagorno Karabakh were renamed to reflect the Armenian majority, while smaller settlements officially retained their Turkic names.

The initial hypothesis, and the Soviet experiment in Karabakh toponymy, both neglected a few important aspects of cultural geography. First, spatial distribution of geographic data is often the first noticed, but it was an aspect apparently ignored in Soviet toponymy. A spatial display of the categories of toponyms (see Figure 4) indicates no frontier between "Azeri" and "Armenian" cities in Soviet Nagorno Karabakh. Given the Soviets' prediction regarding nationalities, the possibility of Nagorno Karabakh becoming a nonethnic *oblast'* may have appeared viable. It became clear in 1988 that ethnicities were still very pronounced, as Karabakh's people became casualties of the non-frontier between the warring ethnicities.

Toponymy does not account for the Karabakh War. However, tensions between the two ethnic groups were exacerbated by the inconsistency created between toponymic and administrative structures: the Soviets did not rename settlements in spatial groups. Rather, towns with Armenian toponyms existed mixed in with Azeri-named towns. They even renamed certain Azeri-populated towns with Armenian names.

The second neglected aspect, that toponyms are incongruent, was mentioned above. In order to perform a significant study of toponymy in any region, a "weighting" of geographic objects will be necessary. This weighting would differ according to the political and geographic context of the region considered. In the case

of NKAO, where populated places and administrative regions constituted the majority of features surveyed, the weighting would be performed according to commercial and administrative importance, and population size.

Third, the hybrid toponyms found in NKAO provide another phenomenon seen in ethnolinguistics that applies to toponymy: the heterochthonous nature of toponyms, or the lack of linguistic purity featured in the region's toponyms. In the context of the Soviet experiment in creating a non-ethnic region in the Union, it should not be a surprise that toponyms were heterochthonous. The pre-revolution maps from 1915 showed a few hybrid names already in existence. In addition, Armenian and Turkic names—as functions of Armenian and Turkic languages, which both feature words borrowed from each other—featured political and cultural phenomena of the other culture, as demonstrated in the toponyms *Mkhtarishen* and *Melikjanli*.

The Soviet attempt to mix the toponymy of the ethnic groups was frustrated by the administrative structure, which appears to have had the intention of dividing them. The very existence of NKAO symbolically distanced the Karabakh Azeris from Baku, but divided the Armenians from Yerevan. To the Armenians and Azeris living there, it appeared as a place of limbo between the two republics, instead of an

---

29. *Azerbaydzhanskaya SSR.*

Figure 4   Spatial Distribution of Toponyms by Linguistic Association

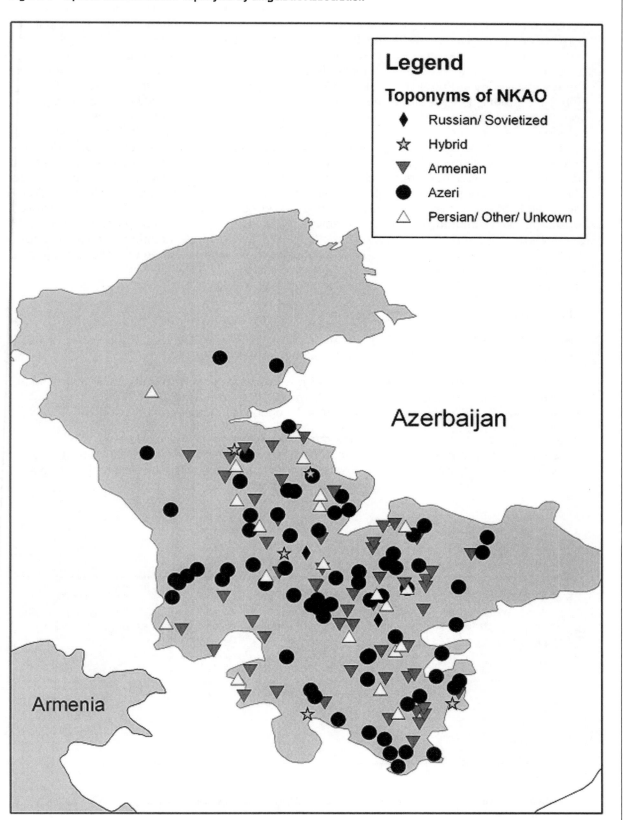

intersection of the two.[30] Administrative oversight was another difficulty. NKAO was not placed under the direct administration of a Union-level body; rather, it was placed under the administration of the Azerbaijan Soviet Socialist Republic. Armenians frustrated with leadership in Baku had no alternatives or avenues for appeal, given the Union's strictly hierarchical structure in political and economic matters. The juxtaposition of toponymic mixing and administrative division renders the prediction that the ethnic identities would wither away in favor of a universal proletarian identity disastrously inaccurate.[31] A

more critical stance would consider it a deliberate attempt to direct the smaller nations' frustrations toward each other and create conflict that only a more powerful actor could control.

In 1993, only two years after declaring independence and despite (or perhaps, because of) the Karabakh War, the government of Azerbaijan began their own renaming campaign in the region. The government renamed the *rayons* of the former *oblast'*, and dissolved the *oblast's* own boundaries. No less than 116 name changes took place within those two years.[32] Some names, however, such

as *Yekhtsaog*, an Armenian name even according to Azeri sources, were retained.[33] Others were renamed to an Azeri name, but still retained an Armenian element: the new name for the Soviet-era *Khintaglar* is **Köhne Tağlar**, from the Armenian *tag*, meaning "chief" or "head of family."[34] Toponymic homogeneity, according to internationally recognized political bodies, appeared for the first time in the region. And it coincided with the similarly homogeneous administrative structure, even if it did not agree with the demography.

Other source material

Hovannisian, Richard G. 1973. Armenia and the Caucasus in the Genesis of the Soviet-Turkish Entente. The International Journal of Middle East Studies 4, 129-147.

Instruktsiya po Russkoy Peredache Geograficheskikh Nazvaniy Armyanskoy SSR. [Instructions for Translation into Russian of Geographic Names of the Armenian SSR.] 1974. Moscow: Tsentralnyy Nauchno-issledovatel'skiy Institut Aerogeodezii, Aeros"emki i Kartografii.

Instruktsiya po Russkoy Peredache Geograficheskikh Nazvaniy Azerbaydzhankoy SSR. [Instructions for Translation into Russian of Geographic Names of the Azerbaijani SSR.] 1972. Moscow: Tsentralnyy Nauchno-issledovatel'skiy Institut Aerogeodezii, Aeros"emki i Kartografii.

Benjamin Foster currently supports the U.S. Foreign Names Committee by maintaining Russian and Caucasian names in their Geographic Names Database. He recently completed a Master's Program in Geospatial Information Systems at the University of Maryland, and now hunts for geospatial projects to create with Python or JavaScript.

30. Yamskov.
31. Brubaker, 52.
32. Permanent Committee on Geographic Names. 1993. "The Geographical Names of Nagornyy Karabakh." London.
33. Geybullayev, 119.
34. Even if it is an alternate spelling of *dağ*, meaning "mountain," it would have been very easy to remove ambiguity by naming it *Dağlar*, instead of *Tağlar*.

MINORITY LANGUAGES AND GEOGRAPHICAL NAMES IN THE CAUCASUS

Catherine Cheetham

The Caucasus region

The Caucasus is a geographical region on the border of Europe and Asia, and is bisected by the various ranges of the Caucasus mountains, most significantly the Greater Caucasus range. This impressive range, usually considered as forming a natural boundary between Europe and Asia, includes Mount Elbrus, which at 5,642 meters is Europe's highest mountain. The area to the north of the mountains lies in Russia and is divided into nine first-order level administrative units: two *krays* (territories, with a dominant Russian population): Krasnodar and Stavropol'; and seven republics (former *autonomous republics* and *autonomous regions*, each with a considerable proportion of non-Russian population, and being majority Muslim): from west to east Adygeya, Karachayevo-Cherkesiya, Kabardino-Balkariya, Severnaya Osetiya-Alaniya (North Ossetia),

Ingushetiya, Chechnya and Dagestan.[1]

The southern and larger part of the Caucasus, Transcaucasia, features a more rugged terrain crossed by chains of mountains in addition to the dominant Greater Caucasus range. This region comprises Georgia, Armenia, Azerbaijan and also part of northeastern Turkey and is bordered to the west by the Black Sea, to the east by the Caspian Sea, and to the south by Iran.

Languages and language families of the Caucasus

It is in the context of this mountainous region that the peoples, their languages and their geographical names will be considered. The Caucasian region is a rich tapestry of ethnic groups and languages: described by 10th Century Arab geographer Al Mas'udi as a "Mountain of Tongues," the region is characterized by having indigenous languages that scholars believe are not

relatable to any other language families, as well as being home to other entirely distinct language families: Indo-European and Turkic.[2]

Interestingly, perhaps due to the political structure of the region (for the most part its not having formed part of a single state), the Caucasus has not until relatively recently had a single *lingua franca*. Rather, residents have usually been bilingual or even multilingual according to necessity. As Johanna Nichols notes, geography and the size of speech community have been correlated: traditionally in highland villages many people knew the language(s) of lower villages, but not vice versa, because economic advantages such as markets and winter pasture were to be found in the lowlands.[3] Accordingly, it has tended to be the highland languages that have diminished over time. Nevertheless, some 37 indigenous Caucasian languages still exist today.

---

1. As an early note on geographical names, to be covered in more detail later, each of these republic names reflects the Russian-language short form (i.e. the name when appearing without the generic term Republic (Respublika)) romanized according to the BGN/PCGN Romanization System for Russian. The U.S. Board on Geographic Names and the U.K. Permanent Committee on Geographical Names approved the use of this system for representing geographical names written in the Russian Cyrillic alphabet in the 1940s, and it has been used by U.S. and U.K. governments since that time.
2. Jabal al Alsinah, جبل الألسنة
3. Nichols, Johanna, *An overview of languages of the Caucasus*, 1998, available at http://popgen.well.ox.ac.uk/eurasia/htdocs/nichols/nichols.html.

Scholars have long taken interest in the indigenous Caucasian languages, noting their peculiarities and searching for links to other language families outside the region. Such links have never been authoritatively proven, however, and the languages are most usually considered as isolates. The Caucasian languages are usually acknowledged as forming three language-families: South Caucasian (Kartvelian), Northwest Caucasian (Abkhaz-Adyghe), and Northeast Caucasian (Nakh-Dagestanian).[4] They are often characterized as having a rich density of consonant phonemes and corresponding paucity of vowels, but the precise relation between the three families has been much scrutinized.

The South Caucasian languages—Georgian, Mingrelian, Laz and Svan— are closely related to one another. Georgian, the national language of Georgia, is the only Caucasian language with an ancient literary tradition, and Mingrelian, Laz and Svan remain unwritten languages.

The Northwest Caucasian group consists of Abkhaz, Abaza, Adyghe, Kabardian and Ubykh. These languages have a total today of something over half a million speakers in their ancestral lands (and many more in Turkey and the Middle East). Abkhaz is spoken in Abkhazia, to the south of the Greater Caucasus mountains, and the others to the north. The Ubykh language,

however, is now extinct, its entire population having (been forcibly) migrated in 1864 as a result of the conclusion of the Russian conquest of the Caucasus; the Ubykh moved principally to Turkey, where the language has since become extinct. Abkhaz has approximately 90,000 speakers in Abkhazia. Kabardian, also known as East Circassian, has some 300,000 speakers in the republics of Kabardino-Balkariya and Karachayevo-Cherkesiya. Adghye, or West Circassian, is spoken in Adygeya by approximately 100,000 people. Approximately 30,000 Abaza speakers live in Karachayevo-Cherkesiya.

A characteristic feature of the sound systems of Northwest Caucasian languages is a very limited number of distinctive vowels, with some scholars even positing just one vowel. Conversely, these languages have a large and complicated consonant inventory, with over 80 different consonants being identified in Ubykh.

The Northeast Caucasian group consists of the Nakh and Dagestanian languages, and these similarly are characterized by their phonological complexity. Nakh languages comprise principally Chechen and Ingush, which are both written languages. Dagestanian languages are subdivided into three groups: Avar-Andi-Dido languages of central and western Dagestan and part of Azerbaijan; Lak-Dargwa languages of central Dagestan; and Lezgian languages,

principally of southern Dagestan. The Lak-Dargwa subgroup has almost half a million speakers; the Lezgian language group a few more.

The most significant of the Avar-Andi-Dido subgroup is Avar, which has over 500,000 speakers; it has literary status and has traditionally been used amongst these ethnic groups for intertribal communication.

Alongside the indigenous Caucasian languages, a significant Indo-European minority language is Ossetian; a member of the Northeastern Iranian language group with over 500,000 speakers.[5] Turkic languages are represented too: Karachay-Balkar comprises two dialects, and is an official language within both Kabardino-Balkariya and Karachayevo-Cherkesiya.

Demographics and the official status and use of indigenous languages

Given the geographical region and its indigenous languages, it is important to examine the extent to which languages are officially recognized and how widely they are spoken in the region.

A word here should be given on the geo-political context of the region. Given its strategic location linking Europe and Asia and on the important trade and oil pipeline routes from East to West, particularly today the pipelines from Central Asia and the Caspian Sea to the Mediterranean, the Caucasus has long been of interest to the powers surrounding it.

4. Readers will note the apparent discrepancy between this spelling 'Adyghe' (for the language) as opposed to the Russian romanization 'Adygeya' used for the name of the republic (as described in footnote 1). Here, and for subsequent language names, I have used the most recognisable English-language spelling for the language name (e.g. Lezgian rather than Lezgi); this usually corresponds to that used by/in: Lewis, M. Paul (ed.), *Ethnologue: Languages of the World*, (Sixteenth edition. Dallas, Tex.: SIL International, 2009). Online version: http://www.ethnologue.com/.; Comrie, Bernard, The Languages of the Soviet Union, (Cambridge University Press, 1981).
5. Woodman, P.J., *Georgia: a toponymic note concerning South Ossetia*, (Permanent Committee on Geographical Names, 2007a), available at http://www.pcgn.org.uk/Georgia%20-%20South%20Ossetia-Jan07.pdf.

The Russian conquest of the Caucasus in the 19th century significantly altered the demography of the Cacausus. In 1864, the power of the victorious Russian armies pushing toward the Black Sea provoked a mass migration of the Caucasian peoples, mostly to Turkey, Syria and Jordan. The resultant under-populated and conquered Caucasian lands in turn saw an influx of Russian as well as Georgian and Armenian migration, and it was at this time that Russian became the region's main *lingua franca*.

Twelve languages of the Caucasus region were given literary language status in the Soviet era: Georgian, Abkhaz, Abaza, Adyghe, Kabardian, Chechen, Ingush, Avar, Lak, Dargwa, Lezgian and Tabasaran. The intention of this assignment of literary status was to improve literacy; authorities believed that goal would be more easily achieved by allowing the use of native languages than by stipulating the use of just non-native Russian. This status to a degree helped to preserve the languages (in contrast to the diaspora, where the knowledge of the languages rapidly diminished). This is not to overstate the degree of their use though, and efforts to promote and preserve the languages have become more explicitly stated in the years since the Soviet Union's end.

The languages' preservation has in part been hindered by the region's demographic make-up. Kabardian is alone amongst Northwest Caucasian languages in its being the language of the ethnic majority in Kabardino-Balkariya. Kabardian and Russian are together official languages in both Kabardino-Balkariya and Karachayevo-Cherkesiya; similarly, Adyghe has official status in Adygeya. Abaza, however, does not have any official status.

Looking in more detail at Abkhazia, an area which has been ethnically diverse over centuries, since the mass migration in the 1860-70s there have been significant fluctuations in both demographic proportions and in overall population numbers. With the restoration of Georgian sovereignty in 1918, the authorities organized considerable resettlement of Georgians into Abkhazia, allocating land to the Georgian settlers. After the establishment of Soviet rule and the creation of the Socialist Soviet Republic of Abkhazia on 31 March 1921, the influx of Georgian settlers into Abkhazia was temporarily stalled. However, under Stalin, in 1931, the Abkhaz SSR was incorporated as an autonomous entity into the Georgian SSR, and an overt program of Kartvelian resettlement into Abkhazia was initiated. This 'demographic engineering', managed through the 'Abkhazpereselenstroy' resettlement department, reinforced the ethno-demographic distribution in favor of Georgians, the 1959 census recording a 39 percent Georgian and 15 percent Abkhazian population.

In the 1989 Soviet census, these proportions had widened to 45 percent and 18 percent, respectively, (with 15 percent each for Armenian and Russian) for the republic's overall population of 525,000.[6] In the years since, the most notable change has been in overall population. Now estimated at 180,000, this huge reduction has been principally a result of the 1992-93 war with Georgia. The figures drawn from the 2003 Abkhaz census (although this is widely believed to be inaccurate, and criticized even by Abkhaz officials), recorded 44 percent Abkhaz, 20 percent Georgian, 21 percent Armenian and 11 percent Russian.[7]

All these figures notwithstanding, it is very difficult to establish truths concerning the demographic history, as information is frequently inextricably laden with political bias. Both pro-Georgian and pro-Abkhazian 'proofs' on the indigenous population of Abkhazia are used to state that the non-indigenous people have less right to take charge of the territory now.[8] Similar arguments are articulated over the indigenous population of Ossetia: the Georgian contention is that Ossetians arrived in the region as immigrants in the 17th century to work as serfs; this view is manifest in the usual Georgian name of the region, Samachablo, after the princely family in whose fiefdom the Ossetians worked. This contrasts with the Ossetian view that their people are descendants of the Alans, resident in the region since the fourth century BC.[9]

What is certain is that these

---

6. Kirkwood, Michael (Ed.), *Language Planning in the Soviet Union*, (London, Macmillan, 1989).

7. Trier, Tom; Lohm, Hedvig; Szakonyi, David, *Under siege: Inter-ethnic relations in Abkhazia*, (London, Hurst and Co, 2010).

8. Trier et al., 2010.

9. Woodman, 2007a.

demographic shifts have had an effect on language. For instance, it is a predictable consequence of Abkhaz feelings of hostility toward Georgia that Georgian has become little used in Abkhazia. Moreover, though Russian continues to be the principal language of Abkhazia, Abkhazians have become determined not to lose their own language.

The 1995 Georgian Constitution granted official status to Abkhaz alongside Georgian in Abkhazia. In addition, in November 2007 the *de facto* president of Abkhazia signed a law concerning the status of the Abkhaz language, making Abkhaz a "state" language alongside Russian, and also determining that Abkhaz would become the language of official communication within the Abkhaz government by 2010 and more generally for official communications by 2015. With the shortage of both teachers and funds, these targets have been criticized as unrealistic, and there is some concern that the law might prove counterproductive.[10] The knowledge of Abkhaz has diminished among Abkhazians, and is extremely low amongst the other ethnic groups, who continue to form a majority. It should be said that Abkhaz is mainly a spoken language, and even in speaking is less widely used

than Russian.[11] Middle-aged and older Abkhazians have often not mastered Abkhaz and therefore, in spite of the desire to preserve and promote the language, its transmission to the younger generation is hampered.

In the Northeast Caucasian sphere, by contrast, indigenous people are a significant majority in Dagestan (the population being less than 5 percent Russian according to the 2002 Russian Census, while Avars formed almost 30 percent); furthermore the Russian population has become progressively smaller over the past four decades, while the overall population of Dagestan has grown consistently).[12] As we have seen, the ethno-linguistic situation of Dagestan is complicated, and Dagestan's 1994 Constitution chooses to refrain from specifying individual languages as being official, instead stating that "all the languages of Dagestan" possess official status as state languages. In spite of this lack of specific official status, the linguistic and political dominance of Avar as the prime minority language within Dagestan is widely attested.[13]

Language contact

Given the diminished knowledge of the region's minority languages, it is interesting to consider not only how they have been displaced by other languages,

but also the degree to which the languages themselves have become influenced by those around them.

Fehim Taştekin reports that the original vocabulary of the North Caucasian languages has been fairly well preserved in the modern languages, although many words have been borrowed from Arabic (through Islam), the Turkic languages, and Persian.[14] There are also loanwords that have been taken from neighboring languages (Georgian and Ossetian). However, naturally, the most significant influence on all the languages has come from Russian, which has been the major source of new words since the late 19th century. Bernard Comrie notes that this use of Russian loanwords for technological or "new" vocabulary is true all over the former Soviet Union.[15] In addition, there are considerable social motives for the move toward Russian. In an area of such ethno-linguistic diversity, any *lingua franca* takes on a disproportionate significance, and in turn this can only be to the detriment of the minority and regional languages concerned. There is some evidence of the sentiment that knowledge of the respective languages has never been of social or economic advantage, and some parents are therefore reluctant to encourage their children to follow education in their minority language.[16]

10. Anon, *Abkhaz Worried by Language Law*, (Institute for War & Peace Reporting, 21 December 07), available at http://iwpr.net/print/report-news/abkhaz-worried-language-law.

11. Trier et al., 2010.

12. *Census of Russia*, 2002, available at http://www.perepis2002.ru/index.html?id=87.

13. Woodman, P.J., *Respublika Dagestan. Land of Mountains: Mountain of Languages*, (Permanent Committee on Geographical Names, 2007b), available at http://www.pcgn.org.uk/Dagestan-Land%20of%20Mountains-2004.pdf.

14. Taştekin, Fehim, *Caucasian Languages*, available at http://www.kafkas.org.tr/english/kultur/diledebiyat.html.

15. Comrie, 1981.

16. Höhlig, Monika, *Prospects for the survival of the Adyghe Language in the Caucasus*, in *Studies in Caucasian Linguistics: Selected Papers of the Eighth Caucasian Colloquium* (Leiden, Research School of Asian, African and Amerindian Studies (CNWS), Universiteit Leiden, 1999).

Language contact occurs not only from linguistic proximity, but frequently also for political reasons, either with explicit intention, or as a tangential effect of a wider political situation. The effect and significance of the longevity of languages in Abkhazia has been much discussed. For instance, Hewitt looks at the historical etymology and evolution of the languages and at evidence of these through toponymy, and comments that the lack of Abkhaz influence on Kartvelian languages suggests that they have not been in contact for a long period (and therefore that Abkhazia was inhabited exclusively by Abkhazians).[17]

There have also been investigations of language contact between Caucasian and other language groups. For instance, Fridrik Thordarson has investigated the language contact between Ossetians and Kartvelians, noting that there have been Ossetian-speaking peoples in Georgia since at least late medieval times.[18] Ossetian as spoken to the south of the mountains has unsurprisingly taken on borrowings from Georgian in a way that northern Ossetian has not.

Toponymy

Geographical names are a gauge or outward expression of the lands they describe, providing keys to historical, political and linguistic heritage. Certainly, the Caucasus is a good example of this phenomenon, and it is unsurprising that place names have frequently been used for political motive and exploitation.

The Caucasus generally has seen successive periods of name changing activity and, to exemplify Abkhazia, these phases include the change to Russian names as a result of the Russian conquest of the Caucasus, reflecting Soviet ideology through the early years of the USSR, Georgianization through Stalin's era, some reversion to Russian and Abkhaz names post-Stalin, and then further moves towards Abkhaz names since *de facto* independence.

This last stage is seen in the decrees passed by the Supreme Council of the Republic of Abkhazia on renaming and retranscribing (i.e. "Abkhazizing") settlement names. One such decree, from September 1994, stated that "proceeding from desire of population, as well as for the sake of restoration of historical justice" a list of name changes would take effect, including transcriptional changes from Gali to Gal, Chkhortoli to Chxwartal and Okumi to Uakwÿm as well as renamings such as Repo Ets'eri to Riap, Leselidze to Gyachrÿpsh and Gantiadi to Tsandrÿpsh.[19] It is important to note, though, that whilst these Abkhaz names have taken on *de facto* significance, the international community, in not recognizing the authority of this Supreme Council, does not recognize these as the official names. There is clearly a delicate balance to be struck between practical utility and international diplomacy.

Toponymy is indeed used frequently as a means of political assertion, as demonstrated earlier by the Georgian resistance to the name "South Ossetia." For Abkhazia too there are many articles written by both Georgians and Abkhazians purportedly demonstrating the evidence through geographical names and maps that Abkhaz peoples cannot and can (respectively) be proven to be the indigenous residents of the present-day Abkhazia. We have noted one example in the previous section; a contrasting pro-Georgian viewpoint is given in an article called *Metamorphoses of the Abkhazian Toponymy*, which describes a certain 15th century Italian map showing the district of "Apsua" and the city of "Aqva" being within Samegrelo, the Mingrelian province to the southeast of Abkhazia, and using this information to extrapolate the autonomy of Georgians in Abkhazia in that period.[20]

Evidently, the choice of place names can be politically highly sensitive, and so it proved for

17. Hewitt, B. George (ed.), *Languages in contact in NW Georgia: fact or fiction?*, in *Caucasian Perspectives*, (Munich, Lincom Europa, 1992) pp 244-257.

18. Thordarson, Fridrik, *Linguistic contacts between Ossetes and the Kartvelians: a few remarks*, in *Studies in Caucasian Linguistics: Selected Papers of the Eighth Caucasian Colloquium* (Leiden, Research School of Asian, African and Amerindian Studies (CNWS), Universiteit Leiden, 1999).

19. *Decrees issued by the Supreme Council of the Republic of Abkhazia*, available at http://smr.gov.ge/uploads/file/annex/annex15.pdf.; These, and subsequent romanizations relevant to these languages, are spelled in accordance with the BGN/PCGN (2009a; 2009b; 1947) agreed romanizations for Georgian, Abkhaz and Russian, respectively. The names are given in English-language decree with the spellings: Gali/Gal, Tkhortoli/Tkhuartal, Lkumi (sic)/Uakum, Repo Etseri/Riap, Leselidze/Giarchipshch and Gantiadi/Tsandripsh.

20. Аҧсны (Apsnÿ) is the Abkhaz name for the region. In Georgian the name is აფხაზეთი, Apkhazeti and in Russian, Абхазия, Abkhaziya. Аҧсуа (Apsua) is the Abkhaz adjectival form.; Аҟәа (Aqw'a) is the Abkhaz name for the capital. In Georgian the name is სოხუმი, Sokhumi and in Russian, Сухум, Sukhum.; Nachkebia, Merab, *Metamorphoses of the Abkhazian Toponymy*, (Spekali Journal Ed. 2, Ivane Javakhishvili Tbilisi State University, 2010). Online version: http://www.spekali.tsu.ge/index.php/en/article/viewArticle/2/15/.

a high profile U.K. cartographic publisher whose atlas, in accordance with the U.K.'s position, showed Abkhazia being within Georgia, and with uniquely Georgian place names. Abkhazia's Vice-Foreign Minister wrote a letter stating:

"There is no surprise that Abkhazia was represented as part of Georgia, given the general pro-Georgian Western attitude towards my country, but what really struck me was that most of the names in Abkhazia were given in Georgian. A traveler referring to this map of Abkhazia will simply not find many of these cities and villages in Abkhazia today, since probably only members of the older generations who lived here during the period of the Soviet Union will remember such names in Georgian. Moreover, a traveler will certainly face difficulties acquiring up-to-date information on the basis of these Georgian names. Let me note that Georgianization of Abkhazia's toponymy was introduced at the time of Stalin (who, as I'm sure you know, was Georgian). This was the time of immense discrimination against the Abkhazian population and reduction of the status of Abkhazia to that of an autonomous republic within Georgia."[21]

The Soviet era produced a large number of geographical name changes, often reflecting Soviet ideology or commemorating high profile Soviet figures, and many such changes have seen either reversions to their former names, or a further change, since the fall of the Soviet Union. The Caucasus has seen a good number of these Soviet-era changes as well as changes for a number of other motives, such as the jostling for ethno-linguistic dominance. One interesting such example is a town in the region of South Ossetia: renamed Leningori, after Lenin, but in the Georgian style (with final 'i', the word 'gora' meaning hill in both Russian and Georgian), the name Ленингори is still used in Russian-language contexts today. The Georgian name, however, has reverted to its previous Georgian form: Akhalgori (ახალგორი). However, the Ossetian name remains the Ossetian-language variant (without the Georgian ending) of the Soviet name: Leningor (Ленингор). And an interesting illustration of an outside language's presence in the name-change process is the village founded as Salme by Estonian settlers in the 1880s. Itself the name of a parish in Estonia, the Russian and Georgian names of the village reflect this Estonian name (Сальме [Sal'me] and სალმე [Salme], respectively); the modern Abkhaz name for this village, as a conscious move away from the non-Abkhaz heritage, however, is Ҧсоу (Psou), after the river near which it lies (see Table 1 for more).

Treatment of geographical names by the U.S. and U.K.

The U.K. Permanent Committee on Geographical Names (PCGN) and the U.S. Board on Geographic Names (BGN) jointly agree on romanization systems to be used by official bodies in the United Kingdom and the United States for geographical names originally rendered in non-Roman scripts. Amongst the first such agreements were systems for Russian, Korean and Arabic in the 1940s and 1950s. More recently, BGN and PCGN have worked on developing systems for minority languages, many of which have a degree of official status and/or are spoken by a significant population.

The languages of the Caucasus have been amongst those recently identified as useful in this regard. Given the complicated phonetic inventories of these languages, their presentation in a romanization system so that the languages may be represented in a standard way in Roman script presents a challenge. In this digital age, it is felt to be desirable that romanization systems be reversible (so that the original script can accurately be reconstructed from its romanized form), even to the degree that this might be a computerized process. Conversely, it is desirable that the use of diacritical marks be limited in the resulting Roman form, so that the result is seen as palatable and practical for (in the case of U.S. and U.K. government) English-language users. These preferences are not easily reconcilable considering the large number of phonemes in Caucasian languages, and the conclusion in the development of these systems has been that neither could be fulfilled perfectly, but instead a balance of both attained.

---

21. Letter sent to PCGN by Abkhazia's Vice-Foreign Minister, dated 4th April 2009.

Table 1

Examples of the differing language forms for some significant features (towns unless otherwise stated) across the region are given below. It may be seen that generally the Russian forms remain quite close to the indigenous names.

IN ABKHAZIA[22]

Georgian	Georgian Romanization[23]	Abkhaz	Abkhaz Romanization[24]	Russian Romanization[25]
ახალი ათონი	Akhali Atoni	Афон Ҷыц	Afon Ch'yts	Novyy Afon
ბზიფი	Bzip'i	Бзыҧ	Bzÿp	Bzyb'
ბიჭვინთა	Bich'vinta	Пиҵунда	P'its'unda	Pitsunda
გაგრა	Gagra	Гагра	Gagra	Gagra
გალი	Gali	Гал	Gal	Gal
განთიადი	Gantiadi	Цандрыҧшь	Tsandrÿpsh	Tsandrypsh
გუდაუთა	Gudauta	Гәдоуҭа	Gwdouta	Gudouta
გულრიფში	Gulripshi	Гәылрыҧшь	Gwÿlrÿpsh	Gulrypsh
ოჩამჩირე	Ochamchire	Очамчыра	Ochamchÿra	Ochamchira
სოხუმი	Sokhumi	Аҟәа	Aqw'a	Sukhum
ტყვარჩელი	Tqvarcheli	Тҟәарчал	T'qw'archal	Tkuarchal

IN NORTH OSSETIA[26]

Ossetian	Ossetian Romanization[27]	Russian	Romanization
Беслæн	Beslæn	Беслан	Beslan
Дзæуджыхъæу[28]	Dzæudzhykh'æu	Владикавказ	Vladikavkaz
Елхот	Elkhot	Эльхотово	El'khotovo
Мæздæг	Mæzdæg	Моздок	Mozdok
Цыкола	Tsykola	Чикола	Chikola

IN SOUTH OSSETIA[29]

Ossetian	Romanization	Georgian	Romanization	Russian	Romanization
Дзау	Dzau	ჯავა	Java	Джава	Dzhava
Знауыр	Znauyr	ზნაური	Znauri	Знаур	Znaur
Квайса	Kvaysa	კვაისი	Kvaisi	Кваиси	Kvaisi
Ленингор	Leningor	ახალგორის	Akhalgori	Ленингори	Leningori
Цхинвал[30] or Чъреба	Tskhinval or Ch'reba	ცხინვალი	Ts'khinvali	Цхинвали	Tskhinvali

Table 1 continued on next page

22. Map of Abkhazia, in Abkhaz, 1:200,000, *Apsnÿ Ahwyntk'arra*, Alashara, Sokhumi (Aqw'a), 1997.; Map of Georgia, in Georgian, 1:500,000, *Sakartvelos Administ'ratsiul-T'erit'oriuli Daq'opa*, Geoland, Tbilisi, 2010.
23. Permanent Committee on Geographical Names, *BGN/PCGN Romanization System for Georgian*, unpublished, 2009a.
24. Permanent Committee on Geographical Names, *BGN/PCGN Romanization System for Abkhaz*, unpublished, 2009b.
25. Permanent Committee on Geographical Names, *BGN/PCGN Romanization Agreement for Russian*, 1947, available at: http://www.pcgn.org.uk/Romanisation_systems.htm.
26. Kasayev, A M [ed]; *Osetinsko-Russkiy Slovar'* [Ossetian-Russian Dictionary] State Publishing House of Foreign and National Dictionaries, Moscow 1952.
27. Permanent Committee on Geographical Names, *BGN/PCGN Romanization System for Ossetian*, unpublished, 2009c.
28. From 1931 to 1944 and from 1954 to 1990 this town was named Ordzhonikidze in both Russian and Ossetian.
29. Map of Georgia, 2010.; Kasayev, 1952.
30. Between 1934 and 1961, this town was named Staliniri in Georgian, Stalinir in Ossetian.

Table 1 *Continued*

IN KABARDINO-BALKARIYA[31]

Kabardian	Kabardian Romanization[32]	Russian	Romanization
Балъкъ	Balhq'	Малка	Malka (*river*)
Бахъсэн	Baḥsän	Баксан	Baksan
Дых-Тау	Dyk-Tau	Дыг-Тау	Dyg-Tau (*mountain*)
Налшык	Nalshyk	Нальчик	Nal'chik
Шэджэм	Shäjäm	Чегем	Chegem
Шэрэдж	Shäräj	Черек	Cherek
Эльбрус *or* Іуащхьэмахуэ	Äl'brus *or* 'waṣḥämakhwä	Эльбрус	El'brus (*mountain*)

AVAR NAMES IN DAGESTAN[33]

Avar	Avar Romanization[34]	Russian	Romanization
БецІгІор	Bets'ġor	Каракойсу	Karakoysu
ГІандадерил МегІер	Ġandaderil Meġer	Андийский хребет	Andiyskiy Khrebet (*mountains*)
ГІахъуша	Ġaqusha	Акуша	Akusha
Кьохь	Tl'okh	Тлох	Tlokh
ЛъаратІа	Lharat'a	Тлярата	Tlyarata
МахІачхъала	Maḥachqala	Махачкала	Makhachkala
Онсоколо	Onsokolo	Унцукуль	Untsukul'
Салатави	Salatawi	Эндирей[35]	Endirey
Хьаргаби	Khargabi	Гергебиль	Gergebil'
Яхси	Yaxsi	Аксай	Aksay

The BGN/PCGN romanization for Abkhaz was compiled in 2009, and systems for Avar and Kabardian are to be finalized for anticipated approval at a joint meeting of the BGN and PCGN in September 2011, after which time it is hoped that these systems will be used for the representation of geographical names in these languages. Also, within the Caucasus region a romanization system for Ossetian was compiled in 2009, and tables of the correspondences between Cyrillic and the occasionally-used Roman alphabets for Karachay-Balkar and Chechen compiled in 2008.

However, though the creation of these systems presents a method of representing these languages in a standard way in Roman script, the practical application of these approved systems should also be considered. Naturally for diplomatic considerations, geographical names policy for official use in the U.S. and U.K. follows the respective U.S. State Department's and U.K. Foreign and Commonwealth Office's position on the respective region. In the case of the Abkhaz system already devised, the self-proclaimed statehood of Abkhazia is not

---

31. *Kabardinsko-Russkiy Slovar'* (Kabardian–Russian dictionary), State Publishing House of Foreign and National Dictionaries, Moscow 1957.
32. Permanent Committee on Geographical Names, *BGN/PCGN Romanization System for Kabardian* [DRAFT], unpublished, 2011a.
33. Institute of Estonian Language (Eesti Keele Instituut) Place Names Database, available at http://www.eki.ee/knab/valik/index2.htm.
34. Permanent Committee on Geographical Names, *BGN/PCGN Romanization System for Avar* [DRAFT], unpublished, 2011b.
35. Formerly Andreyaul in Russian.

recognized by the U.S. or U.K. governments, and therefore for official U.S. and U.K. maps covering this area, the Abkhaz names cannot be shown in isolation, and the recognized sovereignty of the region must be acknowledged. However, for practical purposes, as we have seen, Georgian is little used and even little known in Abkhazia, and the addition, for instance on a briefing map of the Caucasus, of Abkhaz-language names is evidently of practical value for reference purposes. Given, as we have seen, that the names are frequently quite visually different in the two languages, and recalling also that the Georgian Constitution grants official status to Abkhaz in Abkhazia, it would be quite sensible for names to be shown in (for instance) the style of Sokhumi (Aqw'a); this style has been adopted where relevant in this document.

Ossetian is official alongside Russian in North Ossetia, but is not bestowed by the Georgian authorities with official status in South Ossetia; for reference purposes, however, the same presentation style would be proposed: e.g. Akhalgori (Leningor).

The presentation of names in the Russian republics is arguably less contentious; the minority languages are officially acknowledged. Of course, Russian is far more extensively used than the minority languages, so for these it would be sensible to show Russian forms primarily, with the minority form as a cross-reference where interesting or relevant: e.g Vladikavkaz (Dzæudzhykh'æu).

Writing systems

For the most part there is little literature of the minority Caucasian languages predating the late 19th century; Avar had been written in an Arabic script over some centuries, and there had been some use for other languages of both Arabic and Georgian scripts, but any such use was rather sporadic and inconsistent.

In the 1920s the USSR supported the development of Roman-script alphabets across the region, and such alphabets were devised for, amongst others, Avar, Abkhaz, Ossetian, Kabardian and Adyghe. However, these attempts were abandoned in the 1930s in favor of Cyrillic-based alphabets, with the exception of Abkhaz and South Ossetian, on which Georgian-based alphabets were imposed, until these were also returned to Cyrillic scripts after Stalin's death.

The use of Cyrillic is by no means a perfect match for the Caucasian languages: Russian's having many fewer consonant phonemes, the Russian Cyrillic alphabet is ill-equipped to capture the required sounds and the result is the frequent use of digraphs, trigraphs and even one (in the case of Kabardian, /Кхъу/) tetragraph, with the addition only of the character /I/ (called palochka). This has been avoided only in Abkhaz, where instead of using combinations of standard Russian letters, it employs 14 characters that do not appear in the Russian alphabet.

Additionally, though the script-evolutions for these languages have occurred within broadly the same timeframe, it must be noted that today's Cyrillic scripts were devised independently, and that therefore, although the languages share many phonetic characteristics, these have not been shown uniformly in Cyrillic. For instance, glottalization is marked with either /I/ or /ъ/ in Kabardian, and either of these characters or indeed /ь/ or a plain Cyrillic character denote glottal characters in Avar, while in Abkhaz glottals are most frequently represented with the single Cyrillic base character. By contrast, the BGN and PCGN development of romanization systems for a number of these languages has been undertaken in conjunction, so that the romanized results for co-occurring phonemes across languages are standard. For instance, glottalization has been marked uniformly with an apostrophe in the systems for Abkhaz, Avar and Kabardian.

Having first been written in the 1860s, Abkhaz Cyrillic was modified a number of times before a 55-character script, first utilized in 1909, was adopted for the literary language as part of the Soviet drive to eradicate illiteracy. In 1926 this was replaced by a 75-character Roman-script alphabet, itself modified in 1928. From 1938 until Stalin's death, Abkhaz was compelled to accept a Georgian-based orthography.[36] Since 1954 the present 62-character Cyrillic-based script has been in use, though this is widely felt to be both cumbersome and inconsistent.

Ossetian has principally been written in a modified

---

36. Woodman, P.J., *Abkhazia: A short toponymic introduction*, (Permanent Committee on Geographical Names, unpublished, 2008).

Cyrillic alphabet. A Roman alphabet was used between 1923 and 1938, at which point a script based on Georgian was introduced for Ossetian in South Ossetia, to emphasise its place within the Georgian SSR, while Ossetian in North Ossetia switched to a modified Cyrillic script.[37] This same Cyrillic script was subsequently imposed on South Ossetia in 1954; it contains one non-standard Cyrillic character /Æ/ and uses /ъ/ consistently to mark glottalization. The BGN/PCGN Romanization system for Ossetian, developed in 2009, is derived from the correspondences between the short-lived Roman alphabet and the Cyrillic alphabet used for Ossetian today, and modified to suit an English-language audience.

Meanwhile in Russia, Avar was written in Arabic script until 1928, before being altered to use Roman script until 1938, since which time it has used the slightly extended Cyrillic alphabet (with the *palochka*). Kabardian has been written in this same Cyrillic script since 1936, Chechen since 1938. Chechen has seen some use of a Roman-script alphabet, and correspondences between this alphabet and the official Cyrillic were agreed by BGN/PCGN as a standard for representing Chechen in Roman-script in 2008; the same is true for Karachay-Balkar.

All that said, however, perhaps due in part to the rather inadequate and inconsistent writing systems, the minority languages are infrequently written. In her research, Monika Höhlig notes that Adyghe people scarcely use the written form of their mother tongue, due to its complicated appearance and phonemic inconsistencies.[38] It is widely recognized that a language needs to be written to safeguard its use and there is discussion amongst linguists across the region of revising their existing alphabets, or of introducing the Roman alphabet. The introduction of Roman is itself an interesting question within Russia, as the Russian authorities have been changeable in their support of any script apart from Cyrillic, culminating in 2002 in a ban on the use of any other scripts. As a result, the Roman-script alphabets extant for Karachay-Balkar, Chechen and further afield, too, for instance for Bashkir, have faltered in their implementation in spite of the efforts to create a pan-Turkic alphabet.

The post-Soviet era and prospects

The combination of historical, demographic, ethnic, linguistic, economic and geostrategic factors has created a delicate situation in the Caucasus. It is interesting to note, however, that religion does not play an especially significant part. Strong support for (the mainly orthodox Christian) Abkhazians during the Abkhaz war came from there principally Muslim Kabardian and Chechen "brethren," alliances forming across religious differences.

Due to the growing importance of the Caspian oil-and-gas-producing region, the global geostrategic significance of the Caucasus has increased significantly in recent years and so the engagement from the EU and the U.S. on matters concerning the Caucasus has developed. Within the area discussed in this paper, the most notable pipeline is Baku-Novorossiysk, which runs through Dagestan; its successful transmission of oil is evidently dependent on good diplomatic relations between Russia and Azerbaijan, as well as freedom from tampering within Dagestan, both of which have hampered the pipeline in past years.

The generally rather little that the West knows of the Caucasus is perhaps characterized by the strife as a result of ethnic and religious tension in Chechnya, given the international press coverage of the Chechen Wars and continuing insurgency. Of course, this is representative, but does not convey a full picture, and political and economic discomfort is felt across the region and beyond. Russian racist groups' actions towards those of 'non-Slavic appearance' are frequently reported, with particularly ugly scenes in Moscow in December 2010; this activity has provoked a number of revenge attacks, and naturally produces ill-feeling amongst the North Caucasian minority groups.

Instability is firmly present in Georgia as well. The 2008 Georgian attempt to re-incorporate South Ossetia has resulted in Russia's more focused involvement in the region, and its subsequent recognition of both South Ossetia and Abkhazia

37. Woodman, 2007a.
38. Höhlig, 1999.

as independent states. This recognition has been followed by few others. External monitors, such as Freedom House, report that the economic situation in both territories suffers from corruption in addition to the predictable effects of the political situation.[39] Russian troops remain within both territories as peacekeepers, though this itself produces some local feelings of resentment and a perception of a return to colonialism. South Ossetia's proclaimed desire to unite with North Ossetia to form a common Ossetian land, and to create a union state with Russia, is not necessarily a goal shared by Russia.[40]

Since the end of the Soviet Union, the Abkhazian territory has endured the Abkhaz war of independence in 1992-93 and successive resurgences of hostilities. Memories of the reported atrocities by both Abkhazians and Georgians cannot be erased lightly. Abkhazians and Georgians share many elements of common culture, and had lived side by side for generations, but the war was traumatic and its legacy endures.

It is clear, then, that the problems and challenges across the region are multi-layered, in terms of political and economic factors as well as ethnic and linguistic that have been the focus of this paper. However, identification with ethnic heritage has been considerably revived, both in the region and amongst the diaspora. Almost three million people in Turkey now claim to be the descendants of Abkhaz, Circassians and Chechens. Furthermore, it is a region with considerable economic potential, thanks to its mineral and energy resources. The 2014 Winter Olympics to be held in Sochi are seen as an opportunity to draw positive international attention to the region. Observers hope that heightened international interest in the region will reduce the likelihood of renewed conflict; many challenges remain for the region, however, and the Caucasus continues to rest on the brink of instability.

Catherine Cheetham is Head of the Permanent Committee on Geographical Names advising the U.K. Government on proper writing of geographical names. Her particular interest is romanization, allowing a standardized transfer of writing systems into Roman script. She has developed systems for many languages, including recently for Caucasian languages described in this paper.

39. *Freedom House* annual *Country Reports*, available at http://www.freedomhouse.org/template.cfm?page=363&year=2010&country=7978 and http://www.freedomhouse.org/template.cfm?page=22&year=2010&country=7959.
40. e.g. from an Ekho Moskvy news agency report, 2nd August 2011: South Ossetia is ready to create a union state with Russia and Belarus but the republic does not intend to become a constituent part of Russia, South Ossetian ambassador to Russia Dmitriy Medoyev has told Ekho Moskvy radio.

HIDDEN IN PLAIN SIGHT: SOCIO-CULTURAL ANALYSIS OF THE GEOSPATIAL DISTRIBUTION OF TOPONYMIC TOKENS IN THE AF/PAK REGION

James Sater

In some ancient cultures, to know the true name of something was to have power over it. Even today, to understand the meaning and purport of a name is to be able to modify our own behavior with reference to our expectations of the named entity. For example, we may travel carefree to Springfield, but more hesitantly to Death Valley. In our own language it is easy to understand the reasons for this, but when confronted with foreign sounding names whose meanings are unknown to us, we may be left without the sensory clues, which would inform our prejudices. How should a person know if it is safer to take the road through دشت مرگو (Dasht-e **Margō**) or مني مچله (Maṉē Mēlah)?

Nowhere is the cultural gap more immediate, our understanding so stopped in its tracks, than in **Afghānistān**, where enigmatic place names provide a wealth of unexploited information. Generally not translated, originating in foreign language, foreign script and foreign culture, often phonetically transcribed by non-natives working through interpreters or roughly transliterated from a foreign script, place names are often gibberish to outsiders— الله قولی (Allāh Qōlī) may as well be كناتی (Kunāṯaī).

Place names or toponyms (from Greek *topos*, or "place" and *onym*, or "name") need not be so opaque, so inscrutable. For an analyst equipped with a few reference materials or a good guide these names can reveal much about the history or attributes of a place and/or the socio-cultural dynamics of the people who named it. The deep currents within societies can be mapped, their patterns predicted. The Desert of Death becomes more forbidding than Apple Fair and God's Valley is differentiated from Buttocks (all translations of actual place names in **Afghānistān** cited previously).

Every name tells a story. In the United States our place names speak to our origins (New York, Plymouth), our aspirations (Hope, Philadelphia), the way we organize our space (Central Park, Boston Common), the attributes of an area (Rocky Mountains, Detroit [French for *strait*], Alachua [located in Northern Florida, an Oconee or Timucua word for *sinkhole*]), which territory was influenced by other colonial powers (Florida, Illinois) and the story of what became of the first Americans (White Earth Indian Reservation). We can also see place names which are consciously suppressed or changed to move beyond uncomfortable memories, such as Danvers, Massachusetts, which changed its name in 1757 to escape its infamy as Salem Village, site of the 1692

Salem Witch Trials. In a similar manner, a focused investigation of the toponymy of a given area can yield valuable clues about the history, culture or attributes of the place in question.

Afghānistān's toponymy affords a data-rich environment to demonstrate that place names can be systematically analyzed to glean socio-cultural clues within a geospatial context. Three themes—the influence of Islām, Islamic syncretic traditions and the continuing influence of pre-Islamic cultures on the place names of Afghānistān and Pākistān have sufficient historical records to shape an experiment and then fact check the results. These themes are often woven into the identity and reputation of a place— that it is (or was) sacred, perhaps still under the spell of whatever deities the ancestors worshiped there, perhaps still reverberating with the psychic echo of a conqueror's passing or imbued with the healing powers of some saint.

The sources of raw toponymic data that could be used are many, some dating back thousands of years to the composition of the Zoroastrian *Avesta* and the Vaishnavite (Hindu) *Veda*, but for ease of repeatability, especially in short timelines, the United States Board on Geographic Names (BGN) GEOnet Names Server (GNS) provides the foundational data. While this source is far from exhaustive, it is a tool that can rapidly output large datasets based on linguistic tokens. Variant spellings based on multiple transliteration systems or phonetic values must be generated by the user and the various spreadsheets manually conflated and de-duplicated, requiring some linguistic

capability on the user's part. Conflated spreadsheets are then imported into an ArcGIS® personal geodatabase as feature classes for spatial visualization. The geospatial distribution of tokens relating to specific cultural features or activities can then be assessed for patterns which may reveal or confirm the history of a place or its inhabitants.

The difficulties inherent in linguistic analysis of place names in Afghānistān and Pākistān mean that these pulls are not exhaustive, and some features named after a particular people or cultural practice will not be recognized as such due to some ambiguity or outright butchering of some place names in the original sources. Other features which contain the linguistic token of a people or cultural practice may be homophones or homographs with unrelated meanings, but on aggregate it is likely that the bulk of the toponyms selected represent the traces of the people or cultural practices they denote or connote. Interpretation of the data presented is not exclusive, and multiple correct interpretations are possible due to source bias or analytic perspective.

It bears mentioning that the GNS entries for Afghānistān are almost entirely ultimately derived from a single series of maps produced in the mid-20th century by a government dominated by a single ethnic group making a definitive political statement. Names later entered into the database from Soviet and U.S. mapping mostly originate from the same series. Thus the GNS does not necessarily reflect the current ground truth, which may have changed over the intervening decades of war, displacement

and social upheaval.

A general understanding of south-central Asia's religious history is necessary in order to know what toponymic evidence to seek out. The further back in history one goes, especially when dealing with remote antiquity, the more contentious particular dates become; but relatively speaking the beliefs of the *Arya*, the Aryans, first embraced the fire sacrifice and demigod worship attested in the *Veda*. Later, Aryans living in modern Iran, northern Afghānistān and the central Asian states of Turkmenistan, Uzbekistan and Tajikistan adopted the fire-venerating, dualistic spiritual views of Zoroaster (Zarathustra, Zardasht) and differentiated themselves from the peoples southeast of the Paropamisus (the Hindū Kush) in what was termed "White India." Zoroaster himself is claimed to have been born in Bactria, modern Balkh. Later, Buddhist influence spread northwest from the Ganga (Ganges) valley and was the dominant religion of the Gandhāra civilization, which ruled much of the region in the first three centuries of the Common Era. These Buddhist rulers also sponsored Zoroastrian *ātash kadah* (fire temple) facilities like the one at Ātashkadah-ye Surkh Kōtal, Baghlān Province. Thus, for a time, Vaishnavism, Buddhism and Zoroastrianism were being practiced simultaneously in the area of modern Afghānistān, marking the historic high point of religious tolerance in the region.

The Islamization of the region came gradually. For example, the Buddhist monastery (and possibly a former Zoroastrian fire temple) called Nava Vihāra, modern Now Bahār near Balkh, was allowed to flourish as a *dhimmi* enclave for hundreds of years after arrival of Islām in the seventh century. The Persian Saffarid dynasty brought most of western Afghānistān under Islamic dominance by the ninth century and by the 11th century Maḥmūd of Ghaznī defeated Jaī Pāl, the Hindū Shāhī king of Kābul, ushering in the period of general Muslim dominance. The final and best recorded episode of Islamic conquest occurred in 1896 when Amīr 'Abd ur Raḥmān compelled the non-Muslim peoples of the mountains east of his kingdom, but within the Durand Line, to accept his sovereignty and convert to Islām. Thus the Land of the Infidels, Kāfiristān, became Nūristān, the Land of Light.

In 1890–1891 the British military surgeon Sir George Scott Robertson had direct observation of these non-Muslim peoples prior to their forced conversion. He left a few clues as to the toponymy of the area prior to conquest, so some record of changes exists. A variety of English-language primary sources from the 19th century provide a record of toponymic shifts throughout the Afghānistān, India, Pākistān and Īrān (Persia) regions prior to the creation of Islamic states in the latter two countries. British Survey of India (later Survey of Pākistān) mapping and Afghān native mapping carried out by Fairchild Aerial Surveys (a Los Angeles

based firm) and Teknoeksport (a Soviet company) provide a wealth of datapoints for analysis of toponymic artifacts relating to the spread of Islām across the receding borders of classical civilization.

Zoroastrian influence on regional toponymy

Zoroastrian religious practice is characterized by the conspicuous presence of fire altars, often an outdoor ceremonial center on high ground with a large stone on which a sacred fire burns (see Figure 1). Place names such as Sang-e Ātash ("fire stone") hint at a historical Zoroastrian connection to the areas in western and

Figure 1

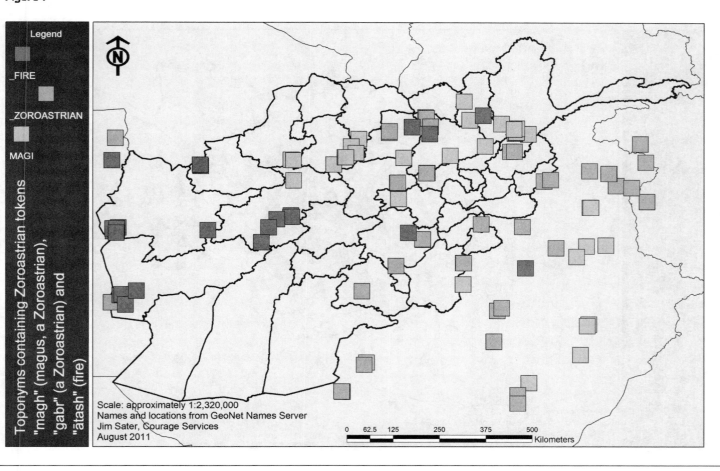

Legend
_FIRE
_ZOROASTRIAN
MAGI

Toponyms containing Zoroastrian tokens "magh" (magus, a Zoroastrian), "gabr" (a Zoroastrian) and "ātash" (fire)

Scale: approximately 1:2,320,000
Names and locations from GeoNet Names Server
Jim Sater, Courage Services
August 2011

0   62.5   125   250   375   500
Kilometers

northern **Afghānistān**. Northern **Afghānistān** was the early homeland of Zoroastrian practice, so the lingering echoes of their presence in names like **Kōh-e Gabarī** ("Zoroastrian mountain") and **Maghān** ("magi") is unsurprising; less expected, however, are the number of names south of the **Hindū Kush** (i.e. Gabar Algad, Maghband Algad—both in **Pākistān**) which indicate similar influence.

The name of a Zoroastrian (and Hindu) demigod, Mithra, appears in its modern Persian form *Mehr* in such place names as Band-e Sang-e Mehr, **Badakhshān** Province and **Mehrābād**, **Nangarhār** Province. Persian heroes from the Zoroastrian period

such as Rustam and his son **Suhrāb** are remembered in many place names, including Takht-e Rustam, a plateau immediately west of **Aībak**, the provincial center of **Samangān** Province. This location contains the ruins of a Buddhist *vihāra* (monastery) and a *stūpa* (a ceremonial mound or tower with a hemispherical top) carved out of the rocky plateau.

Buddhist influence on regional toponymy

Under the Kushan empire (1st–3rd centuries C.E.), imperial capitals were established at Mathura (northern India), **Purūshapūr** (modern **Peshāwar**, **Pākistān**) and near **Bagrām**, **Afghānistān**. The ruins of major Buddhist centers cluster in

the **Swāt Valley** (over 1,400 Buddhist sites are said to be located there), the trans-**Peshāwar-Bagrām** corridor and the **Hazārah Jāt** (see Figure 2).

In contrast to the Zoroastrian use of natural features as places of worship, the Buddhists under the Kushan empire built extensive monastery complexes (विहार – *vīhāra*) and ritual mounds (see Photograph 1), known in English by their Sanskrit name (सतूप – *stūpa* – a tuft of hair, crown of the head, a mound), from which derived the **Pāli** term (थुप – *thūpa*), from which the modern regional term for a rounded mound, *tōp* takes its root. This latter term is of some interest, as **Pashtō** dictionaries and most Persian/

Figure 2

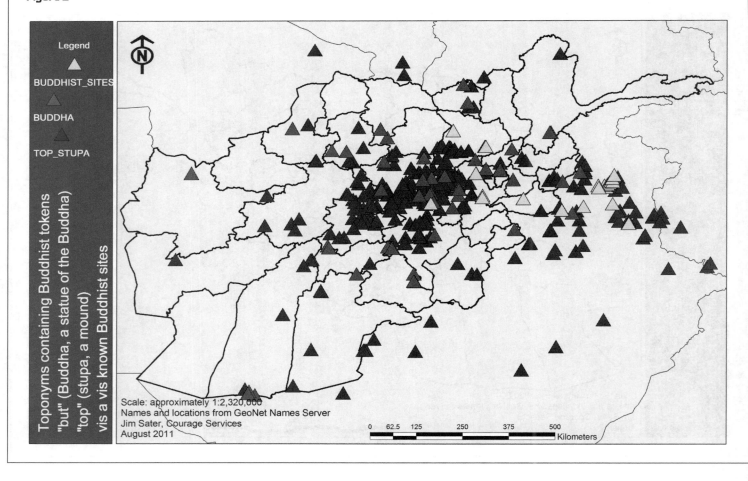

Toponyms containing Buddhist tokens "but" (Buddha, a statue of the Buddha) "top" (stupa, a mound) vis a vis known Buddhist sites

Legend
△ BUDDHIST_SITES
△ BUDDHA
△ TOP_STUPA

Scale: approximately 1:2,320,000
Names and locations from GeoNet Names Server
Jim Sater, Courage Services
August 2011

0   62.5   125   250   375   500
                                                    Kilometers

Photograph 1

Farsi dictionaries only provide the meaning of "a rounded mound" for the term with absolutely no reference to its other meaning as a Buddhist monument. To find this other definition, one may look to a 19th century lexicon of Anglo-Indian terminology (generally native terms such as *bungalow* or *thug* for which English had no equivalent and were thus absorbed into English language texts by colonial authors), which describes "tope" as "an ancient Buddhist monument in the form of a solid dome."[1] One may also look to the term's contextual usage in historical documents such as an 1846 account of a British mission to **Kābul** by Sir Alexander Burnes in which the excavation and plundering of numerous "topes" in the **Kābul** and **Jalālābād** areas is described in some detail by his interpreter, Mohan Lal. The account points out that locals were digging and finding gold and "idols" (which they promptly destroyed "in the excitement of their foolish prejudices") near **Bālā Bāgh** in the **Surkh Rōd** valley at a place called Behar (possibly an ancient *vihāra* or monastery, given the similar V/B shift at Now **Bahār**), which has since fallen off the map. Writing in 1842, Charles Masson (a pseudonym for James Lewis, who deserted the East India Company to write extensively of his travels in Asia), described and sketched numerous "topes" from **Rāwalpindi** to the **Bagrām** plain including the very well preserved one at **Tōp Darah** which is noted on **Afghān** maps as an anonymous tower (see Figure 3).[2]

1.   Yule, Henry and Burnell, A.C., *Hobson-Jobson: The Anglo-Indian Dictionary* (Ware: Wordsworth Editions Ltd., 1996) 934.
2.   Masson, Charles *Narrative of Various Journeys in Balochistan, Afghānistān and the Panjab Vol. 3* (London: Oxford University Press, 1842) 165.

Figure 3

Afghān native map showing symbology for graveyards, shrines and an anonymous tower.
Inset: Masson's sketch of the stupa at Tōp Darah.
Source: Fairchild Aerial Surveys 1:50,000 TLM Sheet 510-A-I. (1960).

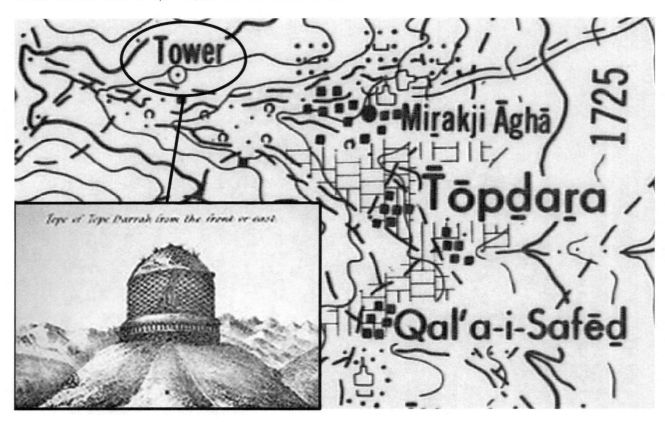

The treatment of toponyms and pre-Islamic cultural features in the native mapping of **Afghānistān** highlights an aspect of the national character of **Afghānistān**. Why would a mapping project so meticulous about showing cultural features such as graveyards, shrines, mosques, mills, nomad encampments and ruins go to such lengths to obfuscate or completely turn a blind eye to large and or prominent structures which may serve as important local landmarks? Maps are not impartial—they always carry the bias and values of their compilers. The Muslim, **Pashtūn** dominated government of **Zāhir Shāh** [reigned 1933–1973] which produced the first native series of 1:50,000 scale topographic line maps for **Afghānistān** was creating a national narrative and stood to gain little by putting pre-Islamic features on the map.

The **Afghān** nation has long struggled with their pre-Islamic past (which is referred to as *jahiliyah*—the time of ignorance). To this day many **Afghāns** will say, and honestly believe, that their ancestors were Jews or even Christians, anything but idolaters or fire worshipers. This extraordinary discomfort manifests in a measure of denial, which can be verified by the number of known *un-named* or omitted features on **Afghān** maps. It may also be the case that many pre-Islamic features were simply forgotten, their significance unrecognized as noted by Henry Bellew (with a dash of imperial judgment) in 1880 when he told an anecdote about a Buddhist relic residing in a Muslim shrine near **Kandahār**:

"Its history is forgotten, and, like that of the infidels connected with it, is an utter blank to the fanatic Musalmán of the present day."[3]

Masson noted how many of the mounds near Kābul had been purposely filled and covered with dirt by the Hindū population as Maḥmūd of Ghaznī, an iconoclastic warrior king who harnessed the license of Islām to raid the temples of India and destroy the material artifacts of un-Islamic religious culture, set his sights on Kābul, that

they might be overlooked and perhaps one day recovered.[4] They were never recovered, but fortunately for history many have remained overlooked and may be located near features with names containing the token *tōp*.

Masson also explains that the area east of Kābul known as But Khāk takes its name from the memory of Maḥmūd breaking the famous deities of Somnāth on that spot.[5] From these clues one could expect that toponyms containing the token *but* may refer to either Buddhist sites or any site that is related to anthropomorphic statues.

Hindū influence on regional toponymy

The Vedic or Hindū culture of central and south Asia occupies such a deep stratum and has remained a part of ongoing cultural shifts that it can be difficult to sift specifically Vedic tokens (see Figure 4) from tokens representing Buddhist, Zoroastrian or Muslim syncretic traditions. Many locations that carry the token "Hindū" received the name after the coming of Islām, but reflect a more tolerant social condition than places carrying the token "kāfir" (infidel).

Figure 4

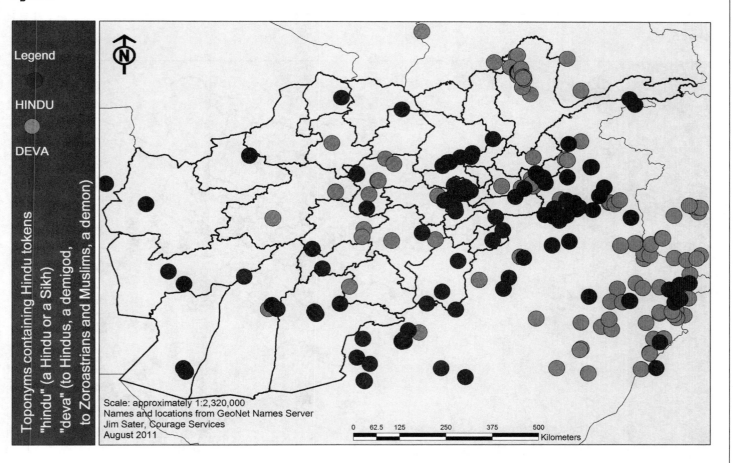

Legend

HINDU

DEVA

Toponyms containing Hindu tokens
"hindu" (a Hindu or a Sikh)
"deva" (to Hindus, a demigod,
to Zoroastrians and Muslims, a demon)

Scale: approximately 1:2,320,000
Names and locations from GeoNet Names Server
Jim Sater, Courage Services
August 2011

0   62.5   125   250   375   500
Kilometers

3. Bellew, Henry Walter *The Races of Afghānistān* (Calcutta: Thacker, Spink and Co., 1880) 22.
4. Masson, Charles *Narrative of Various Journeys in Balochistan, Afghānistān and the Panjab Vol. 3* (London: Oxford University Press, 1842) 95-96.
5. Masson, Charles *Narrative of Various Journeys in Balochistan, Afghānistān and the Panjab Vol. 3* (London: Oxford University Press, 1842) 175.

One term of interest, which originates in the Vedic period but carries through to modern day, is *dēvah*. In the Veda this refers to a demigod, but Zoroaster rejected myriad demigods and painted them as demonic adversaries of mankind. Today's Muslim Afghāns, if they know of them at all, know them as powerful spirits like the *jinn* (genie) or the *parī* (linguistic and semantic cognate to English faerie) mostly inhabiting mountains and alpine valleys especially in Badakhshān and Hazārah Jāt. In these areas the token is fairly clearly used by this meaning in toponyms like Dēw Khānah (house of the *dēw*). Closer to India they retain the original meaning and tend to occur in unambiguously Hindu place names like Mahādev (a name for Lord Shiva). In between, in the areas once populated by the Sīāh Pōsh Kāfir (the ancestors of today's Nūristānīs) the particle is attached to the end in a way that reflects Vedic naming practices, for example Ghālishdēw resembles names like Mahādev.

Unfortunately, many of the place names in the greater Nūristān area were poorly recorded by the Afghān government, making their meaning less transparent. Some pre-Islamic toponyms are known to exist, however. The mountain of Amrōdak takes its name from Imrā or Imrō, one of the main deities of the pre-Islamic pantheon thought to be identifiable with the Vedic demigod Indra.

The impact of Islām on regional toponymy

Generic terms like river, village, mountain, etc., aside, nothing affected regional toponymy more than the coming of Islām (see Figure 5). Every name with an Arabic word in it was a

Figure 5

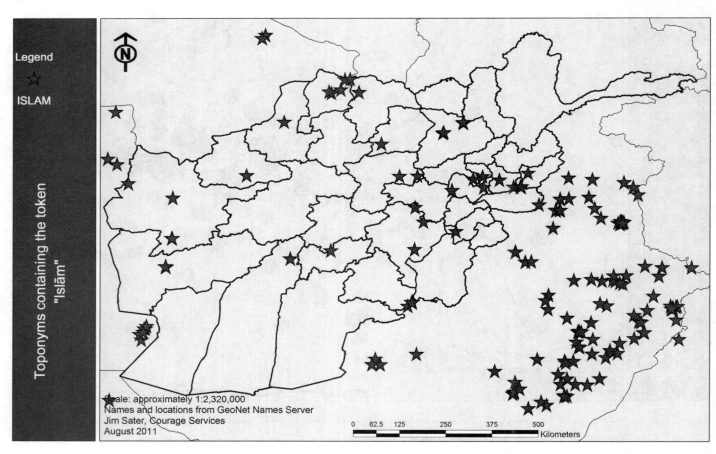

Legend

☆ ISLAM

Toponyms containing the token "Islām"

Scale: approximately 1:2,320,000
Names and locations from GeoNet Names Server
Jim Sater, Courage Services
August 2011

0   62.5   125   250   375   500
Kilometers

product of or changed by Islām. Even many old generic terms for village like *pūr* or *dēsh* were replaced with Arabic terms like *qal'ah* or *ābād* by those embracing a new faith.

Some tokens tell the story of the Islamic conquest of Central and South Asia. Central Asia did not face the kind of military onslaught that Sindh and the Punjab did, and this is borne out by the lack of toponyms

containing the token *ghazī*, which is defined in Arabic as an aggressor, an Islamic raider or conqueror, though it is sometimes loosely interpreted as "defender of the faith" in the same way that *mujāhid* gets interpreted as "freedom fighter." Names containing this title of Islamic conquerors cluster along ancient battle lines, Islamic frontiers and areas that experienced heavy

fighting between Muslim and Hindū populations (such as Kābul, Peshāwar and Swāt) (see Figure 6).

The Islamic conquest did not always entail conversion by the sword. The toponymic evidence of willing conversion is everywhere, often carrying the token *shaykh*. In Arabic it means an elder or a respected gentleman, but in south Asia it was often given as a title to

Figure 6

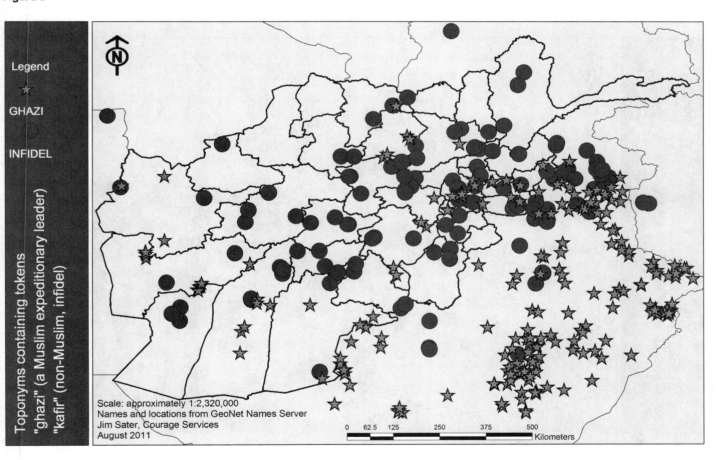

those who converted to Islam, particularly when they did it ahead of their peers. These conversions may not have been coerced, but judging by the spatial coincidence of *ghazī* tokens and *shaykh* tokens one could reasonably suppose that not everyone wanted to wait for a conqueror's ultimatum (see Figure 7).

The high level of respect that Islām accorded its converts was likewise accorded to those who died to spread or defend the faith as attested by the volume of toponyms containing the token *shahīd* (see Figure 8). Modern governments in the region often apply the term to soldiers killed in the line of duty whether or not what they were doing when they died was a faith-based initiative (or even when fighting other Muslims), while extremists use the term for terrorists who kill innocent Muslims praying in the mosque. This liberal application of the term somewhat dilutes its significance and makes interpretation still more complex. One can certainly conclude that many people in the region have perished in conflicts with religious overtones, especially in the appreciably dense clusters between Kābul and Swāt and along the borders of the current Islamic states.

The recent decades have produced many more martyrs, as well as named shrines, graveyards and monuments

Figure 7

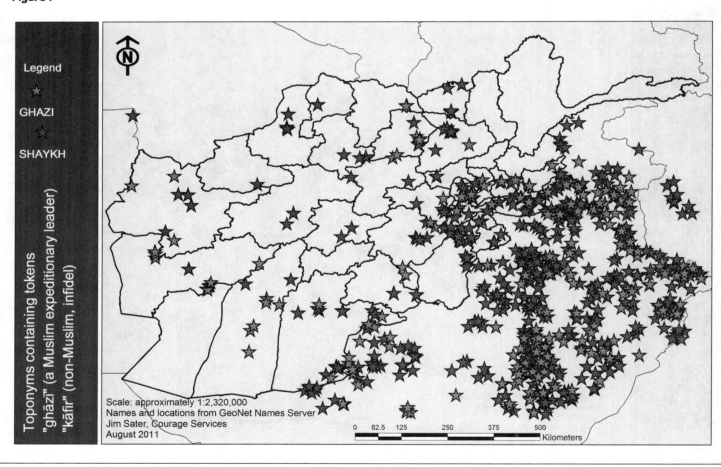

Legend

☆ GHAZI

☆ SHAYKH

Toponyms containing tokens
"ghāzī" (a Muslim expeditionary leader)
"kāfir" (non-Muslim, infidel)

Scale: approximately 1:2,320,000
Names and locations from GeoNet Names Server
Jim Sater, Courage Services
August 2011

0   62.5   125   250   375   500
Kilometers

Figure 8

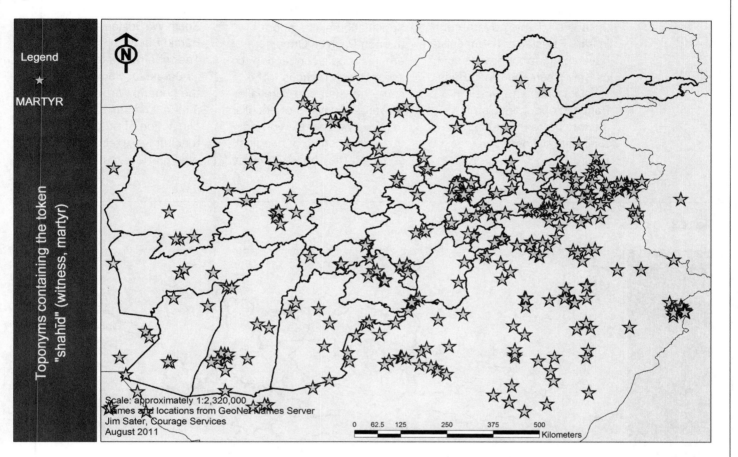

Scale: approximately 1:2,320,000
Names and locations from GeoNet Names Server
Jim Sater, Courage Services
August 2011

to them, but these are not reflected in the GNS because they have not yet been mapped.

Recent Islamic governments in Īrān, Pākistān and Afghānistān have changed toponyms such as Kāfir Chāh and Hindū Bāgh to Islām Chāh and Muslim Bāgh to reflect an Islamic identity more in keeping with their national narrative (see Figure 9).

Syncretic religious traditions reflected in regional toponymy

Speculation exists about the non-Pashtūn Ōrmur ethnic group's connection to Zoroastrian practices.[6] The name translates to "fire killer" (relating to rumors of peculiar religious practices involving the extinguishing of candles), and itself may be an exonym

put on them by the Pashtūn tribes which surround their dwelling places in Kāniguram, South Wazīristān Agency and Bārakī Bārak, Lōgar Province.[7] The tribe refers to themselves as Bārakī (or Būrkī, following the general Wazīrī vowel shift ā to ū), and has the dubious distinction of producing a revolutionary religious leader who grafted *vedic* beliefs

Figure 9

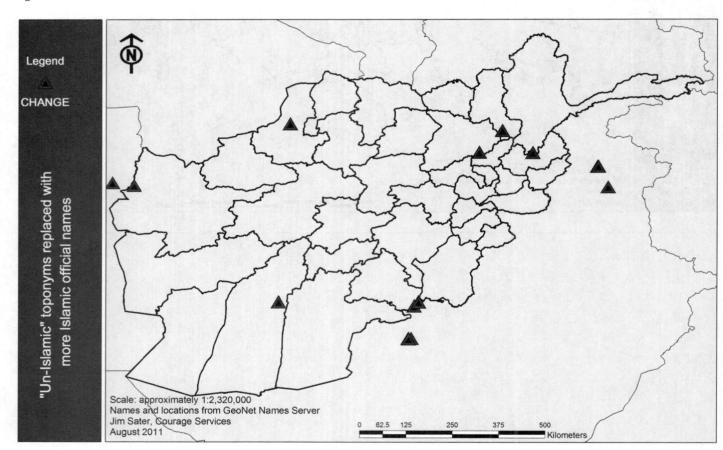

Legend

 CHANGE

"Un-Islamic" toponyms replaced with more Islamic official names

Scale: approximately 1:2,320,000
Names and locations from GeoNet Names Server
Jim Sater, Courage Services
August 2011

0   62.5   125   250   375   500
Kilometers

6.   Bellew, Henry Walter *The Races of Afghānistān* (Calcutta: Thacker, Spink and Co., 1880).
7.   Bellew, Henry Walter *The Races of Afghānistān* (Calcutta: Thacker, Spink and Co., 1880).

about reincarnation and the transmigration of souls onto the frame of Islamic practice. As much as half the Pa<u>sh</u>tūn nation may have embraced the beliefs espoused by Pīr Rō<u>sh</u>ān (the illuminated teacher, also known as Shaykh Bāyazīd; see Figure 10) in the 16th century, though later Muslim scholars branded his teachings a heresy and called him "Pīr Tarīq" (the teacher of darkness).[8] To this day, near Kāniguram, the neighboring Ahmadzaī Wazīr tribe of Wāna has a subtribe and associated localities named after him—Shaikh Bazid.

The center of gravity for the Rō<u>sh</u>āniyah movement was the modern Federally Administered Tribal Areas, particularly the Tīrah valley, but also Mohmand Agency and Wazīristān, especially among the Karlā<u>n</u> and Durānī Pa<u>sh</u>tūn tribes. From this base of operations the Rō<u>sh</u>āniyah movement launched a failed revolution against the Moghul emperor Akbar. After this, the movement gradually lost momentum, but tantalizing evidence of a connection to the movement exists in toponyms located far from the FATA, in areas that were once hotbeds of Zoroastrian practice.

Taşawuf or Şūfī spiritual practice exhibits many behaviors that originate in Vedic practices. For example, Şūfī spiritual masters called *pīr* initiate disciples called *murīd* into an unbroken chain of disciplic succession called a *silsilah* (see Figure 11). This is exactly the methodology when a *guru* initiates his *shishya* into the *parampara*. The *pīr* performs many of the same functions as a *guru*—teaching, guiding and interpreting religious information for his disciples and leading ecstatic congregational call and response chanting (*qawwālī* for

Figure 10

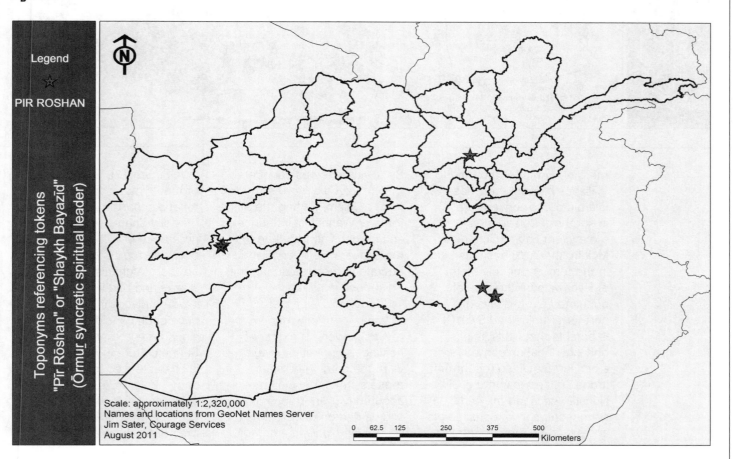

Legend

☆ PIR ROSHAN

Toponyms referencing tokens "Pīr Rōshan" or "Shaykh Bāyazīd" (Ōrmur syncretic spiritual leader)

Scale: approximately 1:2,320,000
Names and locations from GeoNet Names Server
Jim Sater, Courage Services
August 2011

0   62.5   125   250   375   500
Kilometers

8.   Census of India, volume 17, 1901 p. 147.

Figure 11

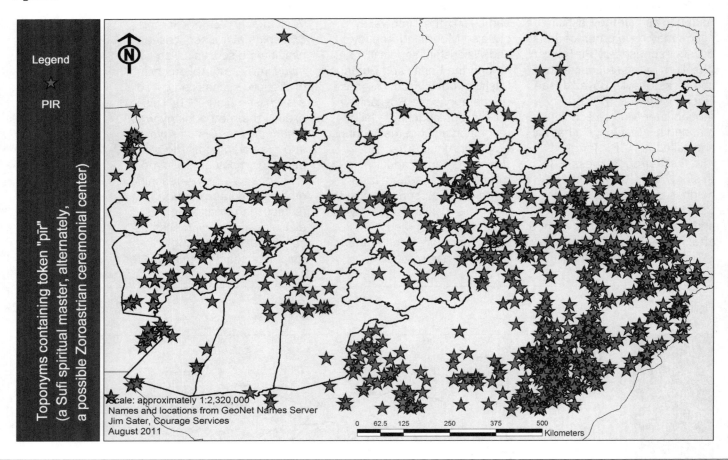

Legend

⭐
PIR

Toponyms containing token "pīr"
(a Sufi spiritual master, alternately,
a possible Zoroastrian ceremonial center)

Scale: approximately 1:2,320,000
Names and locations from GeoNet Names Server
Jim Sater, Courage Services
August 2011

0   62.5   125   250   375   500
Kilometers

the Şūfī, *kirtan* for the Hindū).

Places named after these Islamic *gurus* concentrate in southern Punjab (near the ancient city of Uch, near Multān, the "city of saints" and in the former princely state of Bahāwalpūr), the densely populated river valleys of northern Punjab and Swāt. It is notable that Nūristān has only one location named after a *pīr*, and that is so recent that it does not appear in the GNS. Nūristān escaped the early conquests, conversions, saints and syncretic movements.

By the time it was conquered they received a more orthodox form of Islām, setting the stage for later Wahhābist influence and perhaps contributing to the appearance of an Islamic emirate in the area during the Soviet occupation.

South Asia has a history of wandering holy men with mystic powers, the gifts of healing, prophesy or magic. With the coming of Islām these ascetic mendicants adopted Muslim trappings and carried on under names like *malang*, *qalandār* or *faqīr*

(see Figure 12). The absence of toponyms containing these tokens in northern Afghānistān may say something about the difference in cultural practices between the Turkic peoples of northern Afghānistān and the Wazīrs and Saraikis of Pākistān.

Some places in South Asia have been considered sacred since time immemorial. Shrine culture in Afghānistān is characterized by a variety of symbols, from stone cairns topped with flags or goats' horns on a hilltop or the petrified remains of a

Figure 12

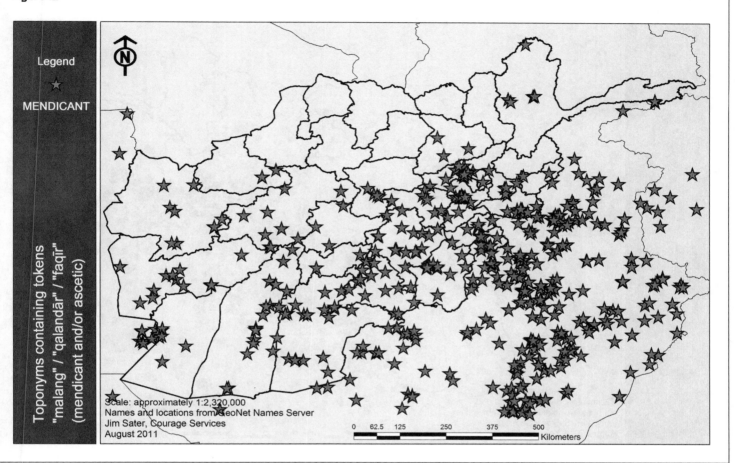

Legend

☆ MENDICANT

Toponyms containing tokens "malang" / "qalandār" / "faqīr" (mendicant and/or ascetic)

Scale: approximately 1:2,320,000
Names and locations from GeoNet Names Server
Jim Sater, Courage Services
August 2011

0   62.5   125   250   375   500
Kilometers

dragon said to have been slain by the caliph 'Alī. Like Catholic shrines, some are dedicated to saintly individuals or mystics whose blessings or intercession the faithful seek. They are credited with contributing to the productiveness of towns, curing infertility or any number of other supernatural qualities.[9] They appear to cluster most densely in the northern FATA and around Kābul (see Figure 13).

Taking these various layers of syncretic tradition together and comparing them with the locations of known Buddhist sites (a readily identifiable layer of significant religious activity in the distant past), a picture begins to emerge of a region and a people who have always held deeply religious convictions and maintained a strong religious practice no matter what the *de jure* religious paradigm is. In the density of points one can also almost make out the areas of predominantly Pashtūn population and some possible differences between the Saraiki-speaking Punjabis in the southern Punjab and their kin in the northern Punjab.

It may not be the purity of orthodox Islamic practice but rather the composite strength of syncretic traditions which so informs the Pashtūn religious mindset, the willingness to take on the greatest powers of any age, Moghul, British or American. The toponymy yields valuable clues about whence this courage emanates, both spiritually and geospatially.

9.   Masson, Charles *Narrative of Various Journeys in Balochistan, Afghānistān and the Panjab Vol. 3* (London: Oxford University Press, 1842) 198.

Figure 13

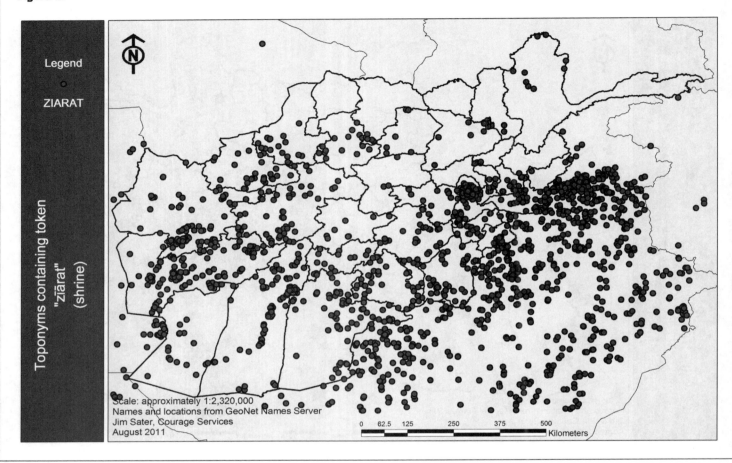

Legend

 o ZIARAT

Toponyms containing token "zīārat" (shrine)

Scale: approximately 1:2,320,000
Names and locations from GeoNet Names Server
Jim Sater, Courage Services
August 2011

0   62.5   125   250   375   500
                                    Kilometers

Conclusion

The geospatial distribution of toponymic tokens relating to the influence of Islām, Islamic syncretic traditions and the continuing influence of pre-Islamic cultures on the place names of Afghānistān and Pākistān (see Figure 14) are just a few themes that could potentially be systematically analyzed for a long term perspective on regional history and current cultural norms. The utility of this process is to inform the observer about potential hot spots of activity rooted in socio-cultural practices that are often hidden in plain sight in the name—untranslatable, set just beyond the bridgehead of understanding between two cultures in the dim twilight where no commensurable alternative of the same standing exists in our own language. Our own Western ordering of reality confronts the yawning chasm of understanding at the foreign place name and proceeds no further until some bridge is formed by careful study. Such study is worthwhile, providing a foundational knowledge without which costly, avoidable errors of judgment may occur—like taking a wrong turn into the Valley of the Shadow of Death. Similarly, a working knowledge of the spatial distribution of socio-cultural tokens may illuminate areas of opportunity where a given message might resonate—like preaching to the choir. The breadcrumbs are there waiting, strewn across the map waiting for recognition.

Figure 14

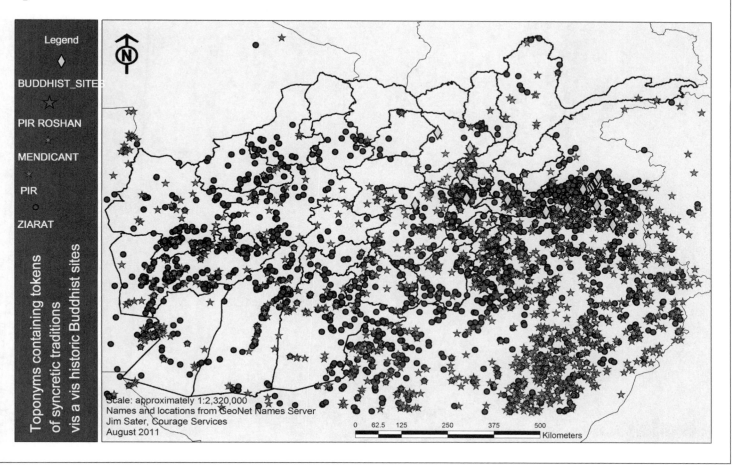

Legend

◇ BUDDHIST_SITES

☆ PIR ROSHAN

✦ MENDICANT

✶ PIR

○ ZIARAT

Toponyms containing tokens of syncretic traditions vis a vis historic Buddhist sites

Scale: approximately 1:2,320,000
Names and locations from GeoNet Names Server
Jim Sater, Courage Services
August 2011

0   62.5   125   250   375   500
Kilometers

James Sater works with the Department of Defense as a subject-matter expert on Afghan geography and Pashto language. His professional work has included toponymic, socio-cultural and human terrain analysis within the Intelligence Community. He has also written for the Society for Indian Philosophy and Religion and Hindu Human Rights.

THE ENDONYM: NAME FROM WITHIN A SOCIAL GROUP

Peter Jordan

Introduction

Place names are not just attached to certain features of the geographical space, they are not just—colloquially speaking—"hanging around" in space, but they are also attached to a certain social group in the sociological sense, i.e. in the sense of a number of people characterised by mutual relations and a common culture (ranging in size from a family or a couple of friends to a nation). They have in fact been created and are applied by a certain group.[1]

This is the very reason and justification for dividing place names into endonyms and exonyms. An endonym is, under this aspect, a name applied by a social group permanently residing in a certain section of the geographical space for geographical features within this section, as opposed to an exonym, which is a name used by another social group not residing in this section of the geographical space and not corresponding to the endonym.

This concept coincides with the new UNGEGN definitions of the endonym and the exonym.[2] These definitions do not, however, mention the social group as a factor in this context.

This concept is also not opposed to the assumption that every place name—endonym as well as exonym—refers always to a geographical feature in its entirety, even if this feature crosses language boundaries and extends across the area settled by a social group, i.e. is a transboundary name according to the UNGEGN Glossary.[3]

English *Alps* and English *North Sea*, e.g., are certainly the names for the whole feature. German *Alpen* and German *Nordsee* refer to the whole feature as well, not only to the German-speaking sections of the Alps, but also to the Alps in France, Italy, and Slovenia; and not only to the coastal waters of Germany, but also to parts of the North Sea, where it washes the coasts of Great Britain or Norway.

This continues a discussion in the UNGEGN Working Group on Exonyms.[4] Some say that this discussion was over-sophisticated and had no practical meaning. But to the contrary: It affects the basics of the naming process and we will not arrive at a

---

1. The social group creating and applying place names is not necessarily the same. But if a social group applies place names created by another group, it has appropriated these place names and has made them lexicographically part of its own language.
2. Woodman P. (2007), The UNGEGN definitions of endonym and exonym. In: Jordan P., Orožen Adamič M., Woodman P. (eds.), Exonyms and the International Standardisation of Geographical Names. Wien—Berlin, pp. 81-87.; Kadmon N. (2007), Glossary of Terms for the Standardization of Geographical Names: Addendum (UN document ST/ESA/STAT/SER.M/85/Add.1, 07-60262, dated 16 November 2007).; **Endonym:** Name of a geographical feature in an official or well-established language occurring in that area where the feature is situated. Examples: Vārānasī (not Benares); Aachen (not Aix-la-Chapelle); Krung Thep (not Bangkok); Al-Uqşur (not Luxor).; **Exonym:** Name used in a specific language for a geographical feature situated outside the area where that language is widely spoken, and differing in its form from the respective endonym(s) in the area where the geographical feature is situated. Examples: Warsaw is the English exonym for Warszawa (Polish); Mailand is German for Milano; Londres is French for London; Kūlūniyā is Arabic for Köln. The officially romanized endonym Moskva for Москва is not an exonym, nor is the Pinyin form Beijing, while Peking is an exonym. The United Nations recommends minimizing the use of exonyms in international usage (Kadmon 2007, p. 2).
3. Kadmon, 2007.
4. Jordan P. (2009), What is an endonym—Still a question after decades of standardization. WP 32, 25th UNGEGN Session, Nairobi.; Woodman P. (2009), The Nature of the Endonym. WP 1, 25th UNGEGN Session, Nairobi.

proper understanding of the meaning of place names in the social context if we do not carry this discussion to a final clarification.

The discussion is also fundamental for the endonym/exonym divide: If we accept that a place name can be called an endonym also outside the area where its language is spoken—where this language is official or well-established, and where the social group to whose language it corresponds permanently resides—then we soften the divide between endonym and exonym and make this divide meaningless. If we accept that place names of social groups are endonyms

also outside their area of residence, we also risk stirring up all kinds of political disputes.[5]

It is rather surprising that this discussion was not conducted much earlier, but emerges only after decades of place-names standardization, long after a comprehensive glossary of terms in toponymy has been developed and after definitions of the endonym and the exonym have been formulated and revised.

This contribution presents a closer look at the roles of social groups in the naming process before it arrives at conclusions as regards the endonym/exonym divide.

Roles of social groups in the naming process

Role description

The factors involved in the naming process and shown in Figure 1 are (1) geographical space, (2) social groups and (3) place names.

Geographical space is inhabited by social groups of all kinds, sizes and levels. Social groups have developed a certain culture, which includes a certain language—a standard language, variant language or dialect—as an element of this culture.

Social groups classify and subdivide geographical space into geographical features according to their needs and

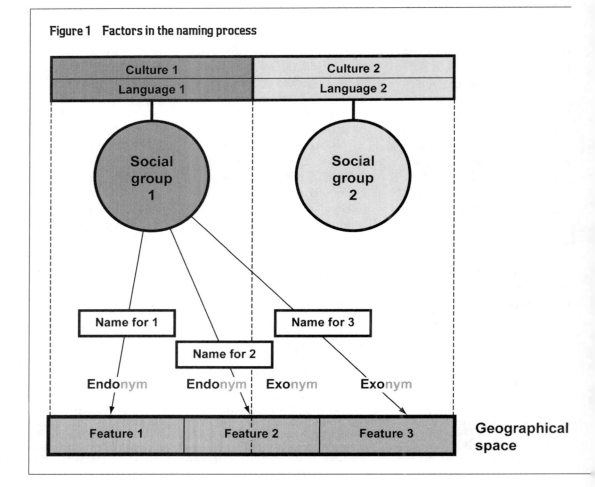

Figure 1   Factors in the naming process

cultural backgrounds. These geographical features (e.g. mountains, valleys, plains, seas, bays) then constitute subunits of geographical space. Classification and subdivision by different social groups may result in different classifications of the same geographical space due to their divergent cultural backgrounds and divergent views on reality they may have.

As an element of language the social group then attributes a place name to a feature.[6] For features totally outside the territory inhabited by a certain social group, especially for more remote features, a social group and its language have names only for more important features or features of special interest for the group. They may also have a name only for the more comprehensive concept of a feature, not for its subunits (e.g. for a mountain range, not for individual peaks).

What is important to stress here is that in the naming process the factors "name," "language" and "feature" are not the only ones to play a role, as it was frequently argued and is highlighted by the current UNGEGN definitions of the endonym and the exonym. The principal factor, in fact the exclusive agent, is the social group. The social group:

- elaborates a certain culture including language and place names;
- classifies and subdivides geographical space, i.e. complex spatial reality, into

geographical features;
- attributes place names to them.

Without social groups place names simply would not exist. This is an almost trivial finding, but far from being adequately recognized in our ongoing discussion on the "nature of the endonym" and even less by the UNGEGN definitions already mentioned.

Meaning of these roles for the endonym/exonym divide

Social groups have usually a *stable location in space*, they reside more or less permanently in certain places, transform them and leave a certain cultural footprint, which is partly visible and insofar termed "cultural landscape" by geographers.

Social groups receive in turn a part of their identity from their relation to places—from the cultural landscape they inhabit and to which they have developed emotional ties.

Such emotional ties are composed of various ingredients, among which certainly memories of places, persons and events play a prominent role. However, place names are also important here. Memorizing, mentioning or reading the place name may stimulate a whole set of feelings for a person having emotional ties to a place.

It is not by chance that emigrants occasionally carry the place name of their former home to their new destination in order to preserve the

memory of the former place, but also to make the new place more familiar. New Amsterdam and New York are prominent examples. Photograph 1 presents a current signpost in front of a village in Canada, which may have been founded by German emigrants from Breslau [Wrocław] in Silesia [Śląsk].

Place names mark space-related identity and ties to places on the one hand and support them on the other. "Naming turns space into place," as Bill Watt explains.[7]

Another characteristic of social groups (and individuals) relevant in our context is that they discern between "self" and "the other," between what is theirs and what is the others. This attitude is unavoidable to preserve (group) identity, although it may look anachronistic in our globalizing world.

It is in fact practised at all levels and with all size categories of social groups: Even within the closest personal relationship partners will try to preserve their own personality (although it is also true that some older couples become more similar), to keep some secrets and to have at least some place to store their very own belongings; at work we prefer to have our own office with a door-plate indicating that it is ours; we draw fences around our houses—state borders are just the consequent extension of these attitudes

---

6. It may be argued that in fact individuals and not social groups attribute place names to features, i.e. decide which names are actually attributed. But it has also to be taken into consideration that they act according to rules, regulations or traditions of their social group and that their naming occurs under the control of the social group. If the name was not accepted by the social group or at least by the dominating force in it, the name will soon be removed.

7. Watt B. (2009), Cultural aspects of place names with special regard to names in indigenous, minority and regional languages. In: Jordan P., Bergmann H., Cheetham Ch., Hausner I. (eds.), Geographical Names as a Part of the Cultural Heritage. (Wiener Schriften zur Geographie und Kartographie, 18). Institut für Geographie und Regionalforschung der Universität Wien, Kartographie und Geoinformation, Wien, pp. 21-24.

Figure 2 Signpost nearby Kitchener in Ontario, Canada[8]

to one of the (by size) higher levels of social groups.

Differentiation between "self" and "the other" or between "ours" and "the others" is implemented and exerted by the definition of a territory as described previously, by attributing a collective name to all the others (as it was with many national/cultural and religious groups in the past and still is with some up to the present day) or by highlighting

certain elements of culture (like a certain language, denomination, mode of dining and clothing, music) as specific for a group. Social groups organised in administrative units exert some sort of jurisdiction over the territory and the population of this unit.

And also in this context place names play a role. Place names in a group's own language—let us call them endonyms—are (among other means) markers of the group's own territory.[9]

Social groups claim to be entitled to have the primary name for features of their own territory, since naming is a symbol for appropriation. Who owns a feature usually has the right to name it. Who has the power to attribute the primary name usually also has the power over this feature or has at least responsibility for it. This is all but an antiquated, anachronistic concept—it vigorously persists up to now, shows itself in many recent

8. Jordan 2008.
9. In cases of cohabitation of more than one social group in an area (in minority situations) every cohabitating group may, of course, have its own names—endonyms—for features in this area.

and current examples and helps us to understand why place names—and names in general, but place names in particular—have always and inevitably had a political dimension.[10] Social groups organised in administrative units (from municipalities upward) are usually also attributed the power to standardize names.[11]

Under normal circumstances a social group would never claim the right to attribute the primary name to features outside its own territory. It does so only when it is aggressive and expansive.

This also affects features located only partly in the territory of the social group, but expanding its boundaries, i.e. transboundary features. The right to impose the primary name is always conceived to be confined to this part of the feature that is on the group's own territory.

This statement is primarily based on my personal experience from my home valley in the mountains of Austrian Carinthia close to the Italian border, but has so far only been confirmed by many additional—certainly less profound—experiences during my research as a cultural geographer in the eastern part of Europe. In my home valley, the local name for the mountain range marking both country border and language boundary—although conceived as valid for the range as a whole including peaks and slopes down to the valleys on both sides—is never conceived to be the local name, the endonym, also beyond the border. Dwellers of the other side are not even expected to know it!

Indeed, a social group would feel offended if another group would claim to have the primary name, the endonym, for features (or portions of features) on its territory. The strength of this feeling is perhaps a function of spatial distance and historical relations between the two groups involved. While it may indeed affect Czechs not too much, if English-speakers call their name *Ore Mountains* an endonym alongside with Czech *Krušné hory*, this would very likely be different if Germans claimed the same status for their name Erzgebirge also for the Czech side of the border.[12] While the English are perceived as distant and not at all threatening, the Germans are close and historical relations were not always unproblematic.

In contrast to the endonym, the exonym does in principal not express ownership or an attitude of responsibility. In contrast to the endonym, the exonym is not the primary, but a secondary name, not imposed on the feature by the receiver (exonym) community, but just received by it.

Usually it is a derivate of the endonym shaped by translation or linguistic (phonetical, morphological) adaptation to the receiver language. Sometimes it corresponds to or is a derivate of an older version of the endonym from times when the feature became important or when the receiver community first came into contact with it. Rather frequently the current exonym was an endonym in a historical period, when the receiver community had a share in the local population of this feature or was politically dominating it.

10. Brozović-Rončević D. (2009), Croatian place names as a reflection of regional and national heritage and identity. In: Jordan P., Bergmann H., Cheetham Ch., Hausner I. (eds.), Geographical Names as a Part of the Cultural Heritage (Wiener Schriften zur Geographie und Kartographie, 18). Institut für Geographie und Regionalforschung der Universität Wien, Kartographie und Geoinformation, Wien, pp. 117-123.; Dutkó A. (2009), Changes of Hungarian place names in a political context. In: Jordan P., Bergmann H., Cheetham Ch., Hausner I. (eds.), Geographical Names as a Part of the Cultural Heritage (Wiener Schriften zur Geographie und Kartographie, 18). Institut für Geographie und Regionalforschung der Universität Wien, Kartographie und Geoinformation, Wien, pp. 129-132.; Hrytsenko P., Sossa R., Syvak N. (2009), Preservation of geographical names in Ukraine. In: Jordan P., Bergmann H., Cheetham Ch., Hausner I. (eds.), Geographical Names as a Part of the Cultural Heritage (Wiener Schriften zur Geographie und Kartographie, 18). Institut für Geographie und Regionalforschung der Universität Wien, Kartographie und Geoinformation, Wien, pp. 159-162.; The large number of place names changes under Communism in Eastern Europe and the prompt renamings after the fall of Communism (as described a.o. by Brozović-Rončević 2009 for Croatia, Dutkó 2009 for Hungary or Hrytsenko, Sossa and Syvak 2009 for Ukraine) can be interpreted as an expression of the dominating force in society to demonstrate its domination and to leave its cultural imprint. Kladnik and Pipan's 2009 description of the names conflict accompanying the conflict between Croatia and Slovenia over the Bay of Piran is another most recent example.
11. Boháč Pavel (2011), Why do transboundary features cause a real problem in exonymy? Remarks on the relation feature vs. Name. In: JORDAN Peter, BERGMANN Hubert, BURGESS Caroline, CHEETHAM Catherine (eds.), Trends in Exonym Use. Proceedings of the 10th UNGEGN Working Group on Exonyms Meeting, Tainach, 28-30 April 2010. Hamburg 2011, pp. 4.; Standardization adds to the social and political connotations of place names also a juridical and underlines in this way the endonymic quality of a name by a normative act resulting in upgrading and selection. The well-established term *standardized endonym* (Kadmon 2002, p. 10) may thus well be regarded as the highest distinction of an endonym. But also a non-standardized endonym is still an endonym with all the other connotations mentioned earlier. The endonym/standardized endonym divide is therefore not suitable to replace the endonym/exonym divide as suggested by **Pavel Boháč** in this volume.
12. Český statistický úřad: http://vdb.czso.cz//vdbtab/uvod.jsp (last accessed 25/12/2010).; The endonym status of German *Erzgebirge* also on the Czech side of the mountain range may, however, be justified by splinters of German minorities there (Český statistický úřad).

It is this latter case that is politically sensitive, since the social group currently dominating this feature may feel reminded of the former domination, when the exonym is used. It may indeed also suspect that the exonym is used at least in a nostalgic sense, if not in the sense of a latent or actual claim on the feature. Honestly speaking it can also not be denied that this is sometimes true.

All the more it is important to stress that exonyms must not be interpreted as claims for possession or domination and to emphasize the basic difference in this respect between endonym and exonym, primary and secondary name. It is also all but helpful in this context, when the divide between the two categories is smoothed. This will only prompt misinterpretations.

What exonyms really do is reflect the pattern of external features important for a social group or language community.[13] The formation of an exonym means the appropriation of the name, not of the feature. The name is incorporated into the social group's own language and culture. Simultaneously the feature marked by the name is integrated into the cultural sphere of the group. Using an exonym means making the strange familiar, transcending language and cultural boundaries, emphasizing the importance of international relations.

It should be stressed that the benefits of exonym use are effectuated mainly in communication between speakers of the same language, while they decline significantly in international communication, except in air traffic or when corresponding endonyms are not available (e.g. for high seas or historical features).[14] Guidelines for the use of exonyms under elaboration by the UNGEGN Working Group on Exonyms will offer advice how and in which areas endonyms or exonyms provide for the more efficient communication.

Intermediate conclusion, discussion of counter-arguments and questions still to be answered

It may be impossible to regard the name/language/feature relation apart from the social group and its relations to territory and features. It is in fact the relation between social group and feature that is the most crucial. And this means in turn that the difference between "self" and "the other," between "our own" and "theirs," with all its sociological, political and juridical implications remains essential and has to be considered when we talk about place names. We simply cannot escape it as long as we wish to preserve our personal and group identities.

This difference between "self" and "the other" is also the very reason why we feel the need to discern between endonyms and exonyms. The endonym is under these auspices the name a feature receives from the social group by which it is owned, i.e. the primary name. An exonym is the name for a feature used by an external group, i.e. a secondary name. Would an external group claim to have the endonym, the primary name, for a feature, this would imply also a claim on the feature, and the local group would rightfully feel offended.

It may be argued that our personal sphere of interest usually exceeds the territorial limits of our social group and that we have multiple identities, among which the identity of a *global citizen* may even be the prevailing one. We may then, with some justification, also argue that as global citizens no feature on this globe leaves us (or should leave us) unaffected and that we were in fact related to all features everywhere. This point of view elevates all place names to the status of endonyms, i.e. primary names. But it makes at the same time the endonym/exonym divide meaningless. All place names are, therefore, endonyms.

But this stage of human development—i.e. that all people on Earth conceive themselves as global citizens, as parts of a homogenous social group with the same culture and the same interests, and as nothing else—is not yet achieved. And it is a question whether it is desirable to have it achieved—taking into account all the social, political and juridical consequences, and also how much we like to experience

---

13. This pattern is, however, not reflected precisely. It is distorted by the fact that a need for an exonym is much less felt when the endonym corresponds to an educational or trade language in frequent use with the receiver community or when the endonym is easily pronounceable.

14. Jordan P. (2000), The Importance of Using Exonyms—Pleading for a moderate and politically sensitive use. In: Sievers J. (ed.), Second International Symposium on Geographical Names "GeoNames 2000" Frankfurt am Main, 28-30 March 2000 (Mitteilungen des Bundesamtes für Kartographie und Geodäsie, 19). Frankfurt am Main, pp. 87-92.

other cultures as tourists.

And even if our personal space-related identity is this one of a global citizen and if we personally disregard our national, regional, local and other group identities completely, we still have (or should still have) to accept that others have a rank list different from ours and feel primarily or at least additionally attached to smaller social groups.

It should also be noted that the acceleration of globalisation processes in recent decades has prompted various reactions in the opposite direction. Especially regional and ethnic identities are booming in various parts of the world. Also city branding—mainly for commercial reasons, but not the least also to intensify the identification of citizens with their place—is very much on the agenda.[15]

It is therefore necessary to count on the reaction of other social groups when we claim to have endonyms—names from within, primary names—for features, to which they feel closer and more attached. There is always and everywhere a social group in place that is not only—as we necessarily are—a temporary and occasional visitor in this place, but inhabits it permanently and has (as a rule) developed much closer ties to it than we have. It would be an offence to this group to deny its right on the primary name and to claim it for ourselves.

It is still another question up to where a social group's attitude of feeling responsible and emotionally attached

extends. Where exactly is the line drawn between "one's own" and "the other's"?

This question is relatively easy to answer at the level of nations, at least regarding land surface. The limits of responsibility and attachment of a nation are usually quite clearly defined by country borders. However, if a nation has minorities outside the borders of its nation state, if the "ethnic territory" is larger than the nation state, the nation state would be inclined to define (standardise) the place names of its minority also there.[16] But competencies are neatly defined in this respect, and to standardise place names outside its area of legislation is not within the competence of a "mother country." And this regulation is certainly in the interest of avoiding permanent conflict.

No definite answer can be given regarding seas. Is the high sea—far beyond the horizon from the coast—still conceived as "ours" by a coastal dweller community? Does this feeling even include coastal waters at the opposite coast?

The answer is almost as indefinite when we turn to the subnational level, at least with culturally heterogeneous countries inhabited by several subgroups—e.g. linguistic minorities. Is the unpopulated mountain range, the (naturally) unpopulated lake, the unpopulated desert, or the unpopulated swamp nearby and at the edge of a minority's settlement area still part of the "ethnic territory" of the minority?

Has a minority perhaps even some share in the capital of a country, even if the capital itself has no minority population— simply due to functional relations between minority citizens and the state capital?

All these questions are also relevant in our context, but would need a much more detailed discussion than is possible here.

Endonym and exonym are status categories of place names

From the fact that a name is always bound to a social group and not only to a geographical feature, results that endonym and exonym are accidental status categories of geographical names— subject to change in space (synchronically, horizontally) and time (diachronically, vertically) depending on the spatial relation between feature and social group.

In space—i.e. synchronically, horizontally—status changes at language boundaries, when a geographical feature crosses a boundary. The German name *Donau* for the river Danube, e.g., shifts from endonym status to exonym status, when the Danube crosses the Slovakian border (but remains the name for this feature elsewhere, as well).

The Italian name *Mar Adriatico* loses the status of an endonym, when it is used not to mark Italian territorial waters, but the high sea or Croatian territorial waters. There, in Croatian territorial waters, the Croatian name

---

15. Weichhart P., Weiske Ch., Werlen B. (2006), Place Identity und Images. Das Beispiel Eisenhüttenstadt [Place Identity and Images. The example of Eisenhüttenstadt] (Abhandlungen zur Geographie und Regionalforschung, 9). Institut für Geographie und Regionalforschung der Universität Wien, Wien.

16. As a sign of mental reservation the term is set in quotes here, since—although frequently used—it corresponds to a nationalist view. It suggests that land surface is neatly subdivided among nations and ethnic groups from the beginning of history up to its end. This means much more than the claim of social groups to own and be responsible for a territory temporarily (for the time they reside there).

Jadransko more assumes the status of an endonym.

Over time—i.e. diachronically, vertically—status changes, when social groups disappear from an area where features were bearing their names. This can happen almost overnight as it was with Germans in parts of modern Poland or Czechoslovakia after World War II. The social group using names for this area, the Germans, left and was replaced by speakers of other languages. This meant that the status of the German names changed from endonym to exonym almost overnight.

Another example illustrating status change, but rather in the course of a longer span of time, are larger parts of the Eastern Alps on the territory of modern Austria. They had in the sixth and seventh centuries been settled by a Slavonic population. These Slavonic speakers had their place names—and had many of them as research has very well proved. The largest part of this former Slavonic settlement area, however, has later, already from the early Middle Ages onward, been settled by Bavarian/German speakers. They assimilated the Slavonic population, and only in southern Carinthia [Kärnten] and in some border regions of Styria [Steiermark] some Slavonic (later called Slovene) speakers are left. In this case place names have changed in status from endonym to exonym, however just gradually, due to the gradual linguistic assimilation of the relevant social group.

The Slavonic names were originally, and for a longer span of time, indeed endonyms, i.e. names attributed and used by the local social group, but turned in the largest part of the Eastern Alps (not where Slovene is still actively spoken) later into exonyms used by the remains of Slovene speakers in Austria, Slovenia and elsewhere.

It may be justified to term these current exonyms as "historical endonyms." But this choice moves us onto rather slippery ground—not in the case mentioned previously, where settlement history has been made transparent enough by research, but in many other cases—since settlement history is a favourite topic of antagonistic national historiographies and may give reason to political dispute.

In many cases the question would arise, who, the speakers of which language, had once inhabited a certain territory, perhaps in a distant past, and can thus claim to have "historical endonyms" for it.

Conclusion

This contribution has tried to show that social groups are fundamental factors and even the exclusive agents in the naming process. Having a relatively stable location in space and the attitude of discerning into "self" and "the other" as well as regarding features—including geographical features—as either "ours" or "the other's," they are the very reason for the endonym/exonym divide. In turn, this divide must take into account sociological, political and juridical aspects, that it can be problematic if external groups claim to have an endonym, and that *endonym* and *exonym* are status categories of a name, subject to change in space and over time. Only a globally homogenous society and a well-developed feeling that we are all global citizens (and nothing else) would allow the removal of this categorization.

Peter Jordan is a geographer and cartographer. He edits a map series on Eastern Europe at the Austrian Academy of Sciences and teaches in Vienna, Klagenfurt and Cluj-Napoca. His other positions include chair, Austrian Board on Geographical Names; convenor, UNGEGN Working Group on Exonyms; and chair, ICA Commission on Atlases. Jordan researches cultural geography of Southeast Europe, toponomastics and thematic cartography.

LANGUAGE, CULTURE AND HUMAN GEOGRAPHY: DECODING THE NARRATIVE ON THE GROUND

Douglas E. Batson

Reacting to Charlemagne's quote, "To have another language is to possess a second soul," Jason Teshuba, CEO of Mango Languages, a firm that develops online language-learning products, gushes, "When I speak another language, I take on many of the characteristics of native speakers of that language including hand gestures and body language. I feel like a new person. I feel like a different person. I feel like a person with a second soul."[1] The 34-year-old entrepreneur, proficient in five languages, continues:

"Language provides us with a way to organize and symbolically represent all of the experiences and cultural influences that define who we are. When we acquire another language something amazing happens. We open up wonderful opportunities that would have never been available to us in the past. ... We learn to think in new ways thereby deeply enriching our lives with new and amazing experiences. This fresh way of thinking is uniquely born from understanding a new language and culture."[2]

Rather than a polemic bemoaning the dearth of foreign language and culture knowledge in the U.S. Armed Forces and the 16-agency U.S. Intelligence Community (IC), this article's polestar is toponomy, the study of place names of a region or a language. The naming of places is a social process that reveals subtle elements of a given culture. Thus, toponomy is an unsung tool with which to decode socio-cultural narratives. This singular human geography discipline is oft underappreciated, but is as vital to geospatial intelligence as it is to other human-earth dimensions: trade and tourism, environmental planning, property rights and disaster response.

Toponomy may lack university chairs, nevertheless it is "located at the intersection of several acknowledged disciplines: notably linguistics, geography and cartography, but also historical, cultural and juridical research."[3] In their book series titled Name and Place, Peter Jordan and Paul Woodman seek to raise the academic status of toponomy and attract young researchers to present theses and dissertations:

"Toponyms are symbols, like flags and coats of arms, and as part of the intangible cultural heritage they possess—in addition to their more practical functions of identification and orientation—also hold a political significance. At the symbolic level they can often represent conflicts with deep roots in society."[4]

Capturing place names and rendering them with standardized spellings has been the hallmark of the

---

This chapter references authors and chapters included in this volume.

1. Jason Teshuba, "New Language, New Perspective on Life," interview from 31 March 2011 http://www.mangolanguages.com/tag/second-soul/.
2. Ibid.
3. Name and Place: Contributions to Toponymic Literature and Research. Working Paper No. 67. United Nations Group of Experts on Geographical Names, 26th Session, Vienna, Austria, 2-6 May 2011. 2. http://unstats.un.org/unsd/geoinfo/UNGEGN/docs/26th-gegn-docs/WP/WP67_Name%20&%20Place.pdf.
4. Ibid.

United States Board on Geographic Names (BGN) for over a century. The BGN is the interagency organization established in 1890 to maintain uniform geographic name usage throughout the United States Government (USG). It develops principles, policies and procedures governing the spelling, use and application of both domestic and foreign geographic names. Its decisions enable federal users to apply geographic names uniformly across all official products. A small cadre of toponymists at the National Geospatial-Intelligence Agency (NGA) practices a tradecraft steeped in research and analysis of foreign languages and cultures.

The criticality of toponymic tradecraft

For example, NGA toponymist Charles Eng wrote a paper for the BGN and its United Kingdom counterpart, the Permanent Committee on Geographical Names (PCGN), in response to false alarms that new military units were springing up in China. While skill in Mandarin Chinese is highly desirable for intelligence analysts, inferences based solely on reading proficiency led to false conclusions. Eng elucidates on the cultural reasons for this. A term, often attached to a specific number written in Chinese characters as labeling of a populated place and that has appeared in increasing numbers is "dadui" 大队 or sometimes "dui" 队. Because the word dadui has multiple meanings and is translated in dictionaries

as battalion, brigade or production brigade, there had been speculation that those names could be identifiers of military units. Even though production brigades have been disbanded for some 25 years, it appears some villages are still attached to the dadui name. Because it is impossible to trace the origin of every name to see if some of these places are truly former production brigades or villages that simply decided to nostalgically name themselves brigades, a suitable standard is to collect names with dadui, dui or zhongdui as farm villages. Any conjecture that dadui, or brigades, could have military significance is undoubtedly wrong.[5]

In "Perception and Identity in Geographical Names," Paul Woodman, former PCGN Secretary, notes that the native Turkish word *Boğaziçi* (Bosporus to the English-speaking world) reflects a spatial concept indiscernible from an entry in a gazetteer alone. Woodman further warns that toponyms are a vital component of social identity and thus are ripe with the potential for cultural misunderstanding. He explains that without proper cultural awareness, blunders and even perils can arise from our natural human response to attempt to make sense of a foreign cultural environment via our no-less-culturally-learned spatial and temporal experiences.

NGA toponymist Benjamin Foster's study of place names in a small corner of the Transcaucasus echoes a history of successive civilizations and conquests. In "Empire,

Names and Renaming: The Case of Nagorno-Karabakh," he observes that the Ottomans left behind Turkic names, Persians left Farsi names, and Czarist Russians left Slavic names, and notes a more recent exception that has backfired.

The Soviet Union actually removed Russian place names upon establishing regional hegemony in the 1920s, and encouraged national languages in an effort to forge a perception of Kremlin benevolence. Foster's excellent analysis on Soviet cultural "terraforming," the willful socio-geographic engineering in the former Nagorno-Karabakh Autonomous Oblast (NKAO), does much to explain the intractability of the frozen conflict between Azerbaijan and Armenia. Soviet toponymic reshaping in the NKAO has resulted in a human disaster more pronounced and perpetual than the forced deportations and colonization carried out elsewhere in the former USSR. The differences between the organic borders between ethnic nations and the territorial borders drawn by the Soviets in Nagorno-Karabakh have produced a two decades-long stalemate with global consequences. Oil and gas transit routes from the Caspian Basin to Europe have had to be circuitously rerouted. Political rapprochement between Turkey and Armenia, so significant for regional stability, remains sadly mired.

The 2014 Winter Olympic Games will be hosted by the Russian city of Sochi, near the border with the Republic

---

5. Charles Eng. *China: Treatment of Production Brigades,* unpublished paper presented at the 26th Joint Conference of the United States Board on Geographic Names and the U.K. Permanent Committee on Geographical Names, Royal Geographical Society, London, 5-9 July 2010.

of Georgia. Yet most Abkhaz people across the border in Georgia boast Russian passports, they do not speak the Georgian language. As a result, Abkhaz youth grapple with the tentativeness of their own cultural narrative. Catherine Cheetham of the PCGN broadens and deepens regional analysis in her treatise, "Minority Languages and Geographical Names in the Caucasus." She probes the other frozen conflicts in the region, the ongoing attempts in Abkhazia and South Ossetia to break away from Georgia.

Cheetham relates how the opposing factions have cited a plethora of geographical names and maps in an effort to "prove" that the current populace in the disputed areas can or cannot be an indigenous people, and thus possess certain inalienable rights. She also highlights the ongoing collaboration between the BGN and PCGN to develop Romanization systems for Abkhaz, Ossetian and other languages of this polyglot region. Her tables of side-by-side Romanization comparisons are those only a toponymist can love. In fact, commenting on the local languages so rich in consonant phonemes at the expense of vowels, the 10th century Arab geographer, Al Mas' udi, declared the Caucasus to be a "Mountain of Tongues!" Centuries earlier Pliny the Elder had named the area in Greek as the *Kaukhasis* from a similar Scythian word for mountain.[6] Let us have faith that the 2014 Olympic Games will engender the desired

international goodwill to move the regional actors to thaw the destabilizing frozen conflicts. It was, after all, a contemporary of Pliny's who said that faith can move a mountain.

A decade of U.S. engagement in Afghanistan has added yet another chapter to that nation's woeful history of warfare. Because Afghan place names often reflect local history, AF/PAK maven Jim Sater states that those names may contain tactically significant information. Since native tactics are often tied to terrain, and Afghans have repeatedly used the same terrain in similar ways over time, that information has enduring relevance and can aid the analyst or warfighter in describing today's battlespace. This information is evident to those with a nuanced understanding of Afghan generic terms for terrain and cultural features.[7]

Sater proves that toponymic studies in conflict zones do not lend themselves to traditional sourcing. His fascinating study "Socio-Cultural Analysis of the Geospatial Distribution of Toponymic Tokens in the AF/PAK Region," expands on his earlier MCIA product with analysis borne by his linguistic training, academic study and theatre exposure. Sater masterfully queries the NGA-hosted GEOnet Names Server (GNS) to chart more than three millennia of Afghan religious history via toponymic signposts. His map graphics depict successive waves of Zoroastrian, Buddhist, Hindu and Islamic influences. Many

Afghan place names denote some memorable event useful in fashioning a terrain narrative. Not all place-naming in Afghanistan belongs to antiquity, however. In his MCIA product, co-authored by Wayne Yunghans, Sater documented how "new spatial references are made almost daily that do not make it into official records but that may appear in reporting ... because such names often do not appear on maps, the places they reference may require some analytic effort to locate on the ground."[8] Scores of IC analysts over the past 11 years would call that an understatement. In a word, toponomy is indispensable to socio-cultural analysis: it can preclude misinterpretations of indication and warning signs and make sense of cultural concepts of place. Toponymic insight into successive waves of cultural hegemony has helped decrypt recent battlefields and explains the tentative nature of political sovereignty in foreign lands.

Toponymic technicians, tyrants and toadies

Peter Jordan of the Austrian Academy of Sciences Institute of Urban and Regional Studies affirms that place names are invariably attached to a social group. Each group reflects a certain culture that classifies and subdivides geographical space before naming a feature. Once confined to a particular culture, this eons-old social process now has instant global reach via 21st century information and communications technology

---

6.   Pliny the Elder. Natural History, book six chapter XVII. http://dictionary.reference.com/browse/Caucasus.

7.   Jim Sater and Wayne Yunghans. "What's in a Name? The Tactical and Cultural Significance of Afghan Place Names," U.S. Marine Corps Intelligence Activity Product MCIA-2630-AFG-211-11. 26 July 2011: 1.

8.   Ibid. 2.

with the potential to both confound and inform the IC. A century of BGN-approved names and spellings, "the only toponymic game in town," now has competition from crowd-sourced, on-line geographic names databases. Dr. Michael Goodchild, emeritus professor of geography at the University of California, Santa Barbara, explains the trend. "The modern era was an era of the expectation that every feature should have a single name, and a top-down authority would determine that … I think we're moving past that with digital technology," and "government data collection efforts like the census are in decline all over the world."[9]

A brief history of USG toponymy is warranted here. For decades the BGN published paper gazetteers with alphabetical listings of place names and associated information. Beginning in the 1990s, digital U.S. and foreign place name databases supplanted the paper products, making online gazetteers accessible to the general public. Domestic toponyms are searchable via the Geographic Names Information System (GNIS), hosted by the U.S. Geological Survey website at http://geonames.usgs.gov/domestic.[10]

The work of the BGN expanded to foreign place names during WWII. In 1947, Public Law 80-242 reorganized the BGN into its present form, and established the Board's Foreign Names Committee (FNC). This Act of Congress,

reinforced by the 2002 Director of Central Intelligence's Guidelines for Uniform Spelling of Foreign Place Names, mandate adherence to the BGN-approved toponyms on all USG maps and products. The FNC carries out the BGN's foreign names standardization programs, with support from NGA, part of the U.S. Department of Defense. By working with geographic naming authorities in foreign countries and the United Nations Group of Experts on Geographic Names (UNGEGN), and coordinating its activities with the PCGN, the FNC determines policies for the treatment of foreign names, including systems for rendering geographic names in non-Roman scripts such as Arabic and Korean. The official BGN repository foreign place name information is the GNS, hosted by NGA technicians at http://earth-info.nga.mil/gns/html/. This searchable database contains 8.5 million place names and locations for over 5.5 million foreign geographic features, including BGN-approved, English language conventional, and variant names.[11] The GNS logged a record 19 million visitors in 2010. Recent GNS enhancements are toponyms written in native (non-Roman) scripts and displays in MapQuest and Google Maps.

"Just five years since the release of Google Maps and Google Earth, the corporation may well be the world's most important mapmaker. More than 600

million people around the world have downloaded Google Earth. But Google is also intent on upending our very notion of what a map is. Instead of producing one definitive map of the world, Google offers multiple interpretations of the earth's geography. Sometimes, this takes the form of customized maps that cater to the beliefs of one nation or another. More often, though, Google is simply an agnostic cartographer—a peddler of "place browsers" that contain a multitude of views instead of univocal, authoritative, traditional maps."[12]

In "The Endonym—Name from within a Social Group," Jordan confronts enterprising toponymic tyrants by asking, "What are the global security implications when a non-governmental entity that enjoys some limited legitimacy and access to the Internet, but possesses no actual authority, caters to the beliefs about geographic names and space of one society over another?" A case in point is Google Earth's ill-timed data update in August 2010 that transformed Indian place names in the **Arunāchal Pradesh** state bordering China (Tibet) to Mandarin ones. This incident took place only hours prior to sensitive bilateral negotiations on a long-standing border dispute between the two mega-nations, prompting many Indian nationals to suspect a conspiracy and outright collusion between Google and

9. John Gravois, "The Agnostic Cartographer: How Google's open-ended maps are embroiling the company in some of the world's touchiest geopolitical disputes," *Washington Monthly*, July/August 2010 http://www.washingtonmonthly.com/features/2010/1007.gravois.html.
10. Marc Wick. About Geonames. 2011. http://www.geonames.org/about.html.
11. The US BGN: An Introduction. Leaflet available from the National Geospatial-Intelligence Agency. 2009.
12. Gravois.

Beijing.[13] While Google may be guilty of commercializing toponomy in order to endear itself to a preferred customer, other non-state actors have ideological or sectarian motives for projecting a worldview on the global stage. Via social media and Internet websites, their selection of place names has an agenda.

An episode from the U.S. Army Command and General Staff College's (CGSC) is troubling for its implications of competing online, toponymic databases for U.S. military and intelligence operations. Granted, many U.S. military members and USG officials are uninformed about the mandate to use only BGN-approved place names. Media outlets exercise very creative licenses in transliterating foreign place names into English.

For instance, no fewer than 15 different spellings have been tallied from the Perso-Arabic script for the Pakistani city of **Muhammadābād**. Thus, education was one of my tasks as a geographic advisor to the week-long CGSC Division Exercise event. The reluctance I observed on the part of the participating Army officers to query the GNS was in no way catering to any social-political persuasion. In fact, little or no thought was given that place names from Soviet-era maps might be totally different over their notional Area of Operation (AO) in Azerbaijan, for 20 years an independent nation populated by non-Russians. However, international peacekeeping forces, especially, are at peril, as is the entire mission, should the

intervening actors be viewed by the population as toadies to a particular faction.

The following incident illustrates: Curious about how the U.S. Army officers would respond, I inserted place names into a scenario different from the names on their maps. Undaunted, they promptly queried online media outlets that guided them to the location's correct coordinates with no regard for conflicting place names. In this case, in their reports, the officers used the names from their Common Operating Picture—30-year-old topographic maps. If unauthorized toponyms from cyber sources with perceived legitimacy (Google Earth) are tempting to use in the classroom, then it stands to reason that even less thought is given to correct place names during high-tempo field operations.

The officers had no reason to believe that they had not flawlessly completed their mission; moving material from Point A to Point B with remarkable precision as far as physical geography is concerned. Yet they were totally unprepared for the human backlash following their public statements about the city of Pushkino as it appeared on their Joint Operational Graphic (JOG). **Biləsuvar** is the correct native, BGN-approved name for the town (see Table 1). Pushkino, in memory of the 19th century poet Alexandr Pushkin, a Bolshevik favorite, had been the Soviet era name forcibly applied to the town.

Regional reporters reacted

with consternation when this politically-charged toponym was unwittingly and repeatedly invoked at a notional "CNN-like" press conference. The quarreling among the journalists over the number of "martyrs" who had lost their lives in **Biləsuvar** while ousting the former Soviet overlords ended only when they united to criticize American insensitivity to have uttered the "P-word" in the first place.

In terms of human geography, the Army officers had committed a cultural blunder that completely overshadowed the success of their humanitarian mission.[14]

Toponomy in cognitive and slum maps

Language and cultural insights are inherent in the human geography sub-discipline of toponomy, which helps decode the cultural narrative in foreign areas of the world. I agree with Teshuba that "this fresh way of thinking is uniquely born from understanding a new language and culture."[15] Yet a prerequisite to learning other cultures is to first recognize how culturally-laden our own cognition is.

To train military members how to query the GNS with the aim to close socio-cultural intelligence gaps, I compiled Turkic toponyms into a 20-word dictionary. The soldiers quickly solved the problem that involved translating the Turkic adjective for the color green, *Yeşil* or *Yashil*. However, when I inserted the Persian word for green, *Sabzī*, none could solve the same problem. The centuries-long Persian influence over that area was

13. Gravois.
14. Douglas Batson. *Overseas Contingency Operations: Cultural Perceptions in Place Names Ground Truth*, unpublished paper presented at The Conference of Army Historians, Crystal City, VA, 28 July 2011.
15. Teshuba.

Table 1 GeoName Search Results

A GNS query result for Pushkino reveals that the BGN-approved name is **Biləsuvar**.

Total Number of Names in query: 11   Records 1 through 11

The geographic names in this database are provided for the guidance of and use by the Federal Government and for the information of the general public. The names, variants, and associated data may not reflect the views of the United States Government on the sovereignty over geographic features.

Name		Country	ADM1	Latitude/ Longitude	Feature Type
Biləsuvar Rayonu	(Approved)				
Bíläsuvar	(Short)				First-Order
Rayonu	(Generic)	Azerbaijan	**Beləsuvar**	39° 30′ 00″ N	Administrative
Belyasuvarskiy Rayon	(Variant)			048° 25′ 00″ E	Division
Pushkin Rayonu	(Variant)				
Pushkinskiy Rayon	(Variant)				
Biləsuvar	(Approved)			39° 27′ 30″ N	
Pushkin	(Variant)	Azerbaijan	**Beləsuvar**	048° 32′ 42″ E	Populated Place
Pushkino	(Variant)				
Pushkino	(Unverified)	Azerbaijan	**Beləsuvar**	048° 33′ 23″ E	Airfield

of little account; many class members thought it was unfair of me to impose a foreign word on them not included in their dictionary. Cries of foul quickly subsided after I explained that the same toponymic phenomenon occurs in the United States. The Green Mountains are not just located in Vermont. Due to early French influence that state's name literally is "green mountain," though most Americans are oblivious to the word's French origin and meaning.

Social scientists have long examined human speech and cognition, perception and identity, and the geographic extent of a social group's influence. Lera Boroditsky, professor of psychology at Stanford University and editor-in-chief of *Frontiers in Cultural Psychology*, is as exuberant as Teshuba about foreign language acquisition. But her research suggests that the cultural constructs of space and time are further construable via language. For example, she relates how an Australian aboriginal community does not use terms like "left" and "right" to interpret space:

"Instead, everything is talked about in terms of absolute cardinal directions (north, south, east, west), which means you say things like, "There's an ant on your southwest leg." To say hello … one asks, "Where are you going?" and an appropriate response might be, "A long way to the south-southwest. How about you?" If you don't know which way is which, you literally can't get past hello."[16]

Boroditsky opines that speakers of such languages just might outperform Special Operations Forces in land navigation skills. "They perform navigational feats scientists once thought were beyond human capabilities."[17] She then notes, "differences in how people think about space don't end there. People rely on their spatial knowledge to build many other more complex or abstract representations including time, number, musical pitch, kinship relations, morality and emotions."[18]

This chapter underscores that the naming of places is a social process that we must study, ergo toponymy, if we are to understand a given culture. Not all non-state

---

16. Lera Boroditsky. "Lost in Translation," The Wall Street Journal, 24 July 2010.
     http://online.wsj.com/article/SB10001424052748703467304575383131592767868.html?mod=wsj_share_digg.
17. Ibid.
18. Ibid.

actors harbor nefarious toponymic motives. Twenty-first century information and communications technology has empowered civil society organizations to map communities long-neglected by their government.

Kibera in Nairobi, Kenya, was a blank spot on the map until November 2009, when young Kiberans created the first free and open digital map of their own community (see Figure 1). Map Kibera has now grown into a complete interactive

community information project.[19]

Kibera, a notorious Nairobi slum teeming with a population upwards of 250,000, is subdivided by walls, alleys and drainage ditches into many neighborhoods, each with a

Figure 1

This Map Kibera product includes neighborhood names, their spatial extents, and associated security warnings.

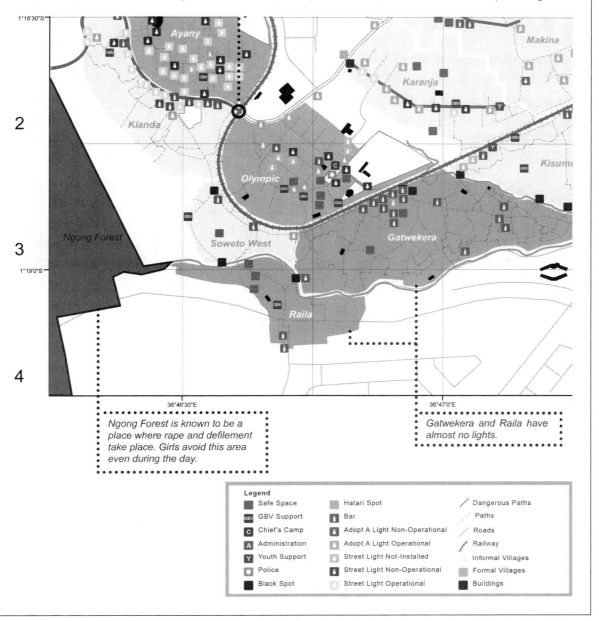

Ngong Forest is known to be a place where rape and defilement take place. Girls avoid this area even during the day.

Gatwekera and Raila have almost no lights.

Legend

■ Safe Space	■ Hatari Spot	/ Dangerous Paths			
GBV GBV Support	🍺 Bar	⋰ Paths			
C Chief's Camp	Adopt A Light Non-Operational	/ Roads			
A Administration	Adopt A Light Operational	Railway			
Y Youth Support	Street Light Not-Installed	Informal Villages			
Police	Street Light Non-Operational	Formal Villages			
■ Black Spot	Street Light Operational	■ Buildings			

19. Map Kibera. www.mapkibera.org, 2012.

name not found on any official map. What if a pandemic breaks out among the tens of thousands of people in Gatwekera? What if rumor, propagated by Twitter, has it that the disease has spread to Kianda? Crisis response will be anything but timely and effective if these toponyms remain unknown and/or spatially undefined. The toponymic technicians of Map Kibera, who, via self-help publish a variety of community information, do themselves, and indirectly, their country and international actors, a proud service.

Conclusion

Woodman and Jordan aptly state that toponomy, like other human geography subsets,

is located at the intersection of several acknowledged disciplines, notably linguistics, geography and cartography. If finding the intersection were a mere matter of calculating cartographic coordinates, then there would be no need for a Carolingian Renaissance in the IC. Population-centric operating environments, by definition, are not soulless; they cannot be analyzed from technical platforms, textual reports in English and databases alone. Understanding this, Lieutenant General Michael Flynn's, (current Director, Defense Intelligence Agency), et al., forceful "Fixing Intel" report makes a case for a rebirth of the IC:

"Having focused the

overwhelming majority of its collection efforts and analytical brainpower on insurgent groups, the vast U.S. intelligence apparatus is unable to answer fundamental questions about the environment in which U.S. and allied forces operate and the people they seek to persuade."[20]

Undoubtedly, improved use of toponomy, that is, applying foreign language and cultural knowledge to decode the narrative on the ground, benefits intelligence analysis. It goes at least a furlong toward what the IC requires for a renaissance, and that is a second soul. Just ask Chuck, a.k.a. Charlemagne.

Douglas Batson joined the National Geospatial-Intelligence Agency (NGA) as a toponymist in 2004. He earned the Deutsches Sprachdiplom des Goethe-Instituts and a diploma with honors in Turkish from the Defense Language Institute. He has been twice selected an Office of the Director of National Intelligence Exceptional Analyst Research Fellow.

20. Michael T. Flynn, Matt Pottinger, and Paul D. Batchelor, "Fixing Intel: A Blueprint for Making Intelligence Relevant in Afghanistan" Center for a New American Security. January 2010. 7. http://www.cnas.org/files/documents/publications/AfghanIntel_Flynn_Jan2010_code507_voices.pdf.

Section 6

Policy and Governance in a World of Experts: Harnessing Socio-Cultural Dynamics for Global Security

BUILDING AND USING SOCIO-CULTURAL DYNAMICS ANALYSIS CAPABILITY

Nathan Hamm

Introduction

The idea that socio-cultural knowledge can equip warfighters and policy makers with the ability to make better decisions has become increasingly accepted over the past decade. Socio-cultural analysis capabilities have now been built to not only serve Special Operations Forces (SOF) customers and forces in Iraq and Afghanistan, but also to support the needs of strategic missions and national policy. In all of these environments, groups have faced challenges in putting together teams with the right mix of skills, ensuring the right data inputs and sticking to charters to provide unique forms of analysis that provide game-changing insights and visualization of complex socio-cultural dynamics.

Companies have been founded with the purpose of serving the socio-cultural data and analysis needs of warfighters, the intelligence community and policy makers. Analysts have served in many of the socio-cultural capabilities established in the U.S. government over the past decade. While we analysts do not claim to have the final word

on best practices or human capital requirements, this experience does give us some lessons learned regarding desirable skills and use of socio-cultural analysis teams that those who are establishing new socio-cultural capabilities and refurbishing existing ones can use to avoid repeating the community's missteps.

Identifying socio-cultural analysis

While socio-cultural analysis is a type of all-source analytical output, an all-source capability simply given a socio-cultural or human geography portfolio will almost certainly fail to produce analysis of social groups that provides unique, game-changing decision advantages to warfighters and policy makers. Socio-cultural analysis adds powerful weapons to the decision maker's arsenal when it answers questions about social groups with more than just "who," "what" and "when," but also "how" and "why."

The socio-cultural and human geography teams in which our analysts have worked have been called upon to answer a wide range of questions for SOF, conventional, policy,

operational and strategic customers. Most all-source analysis capabilities can answer straightforward questions like "Where are the bazaars?" and "Who is the leader of the tribe?" Regardless of the customer, we have found that successful socio-cultural analysis teams are able to provide rich, descriptive answers about society. However, they also layer explanatory and predictive analysis on this descriptive foundation that adds value not only to the original requestor but also to analysts and decision makers in other organizations. Such products provide consumers with frameworks for independently contextualizing and acting on new data and scenarios.

Skillsets

In order to produce valuable descriptive, explanatory and predictive analysis of human groups, a socio-cultural team needs the right blend of skills. Advocates of socio-cultural analysis have recognized that experts are needed to augment more traditional intelligence functions. The value of expertise is uncontroversial, but what kind of expertise is actually needed? Different organizations have taken their own approaches, with some showing preference for holders of advanced social science degrees and area specialists, some preferring those with expertise in geospatial and social network analysis methodologies, and still others trying to bring in a range of people with diverse skill sets.

Expertise is scarce, expensive, and easy to misapply. Not every socio-cultural or human geography analyst will be an expert at each skill. Every mission has unique needs, but in the varied settings in which we have performed socio-cultural and human geographic analysis, we have identified several lessons for applying expertise as well as qualities that should exist among the members of a successful socio-cultural analysis team.

Area expertise

In every setting in which our analysts have tackled socio-cultural and human geography problem sets, regional expertise has been critical. It allows analysts to more immediately support their organization's mission without having to build a baseline of area knowledge, learn the information environment for the area of responsibility, or build a network of relationships with other practitioners inside and outside of government. An area expert can immediately act as a multiplier, amplifying the quality and quantity of work that traditional all-source analysts, geospatial analysts and social network analysts on the team are producing.

Area expertise is not uniform, however. Because regional expertise is scarce, especially for the conflict-wracked

denied areas for which the U.S. government needs expert assistance, organizations building socio-cultural analysis capabilities should be cautious to hire experts that meet their particular needs.

Natives of a country or region of interest provide an attractive pool of area expertise. Over the last decade, Afghans and Iraqis living in the United States or recruited from within their respective countries have played important roles as interpreters and cultural advisors to warfighters.

As socio-cultural analysis capabilities were built at various organizations, they were added to these new teams to play a similar role. They provide skills and perspectives almost impossible to replicate. Not only are they native speakers of languages few Americans know, but they also are "native practitioners" of the society and culture that is the team's analytical target. They are especially helpful in quickly answering questions calling for descriptions of social and cultural beliefs and practices. These skills are particularly useful in a direct support cultural advisor role or on teams providing descriptive answers in support of operational customers.

Native language capabilities are critical for navigating the news and social media environment and for accessing primary sources in their original language. Additionally, language abilities and deep cultural familiarity are a boon to geospatial socio-cultural output as they provide insights into toponyms, administrative and socially constructed geographic organization, land use patterns and exploitation of foreign-language map and geographic data sources. These attributes

can be useful in any socio-cultural analysis setting, but are particularly so in organizations mainly interested and willing to invest in gaining insights from open sources.

However, relying too heavily on natives involves an element of risk. Particularly high among these risks is that the credibility they gain as natives can blind their analytical teammates and customers to problems in the information and analysis they provide. Native biases can be as dangerous to socio-cultural analysis as ignorance because of the confidence usually placed in natives' accounts.

In Afghanistan, the prejudices of the population have manifested in the information and analysis provided by local counterparts serving socio-cultural capabilities. Some biases (one Pashtun's claim that Hazaras are sorcerers, for example) are easy to identity, but many others are harder to catch. For example, in the former Soviet republics of Central Asia, Slavs and Russophone Central Asians—who typically live in urban centers—often present history, especially regarding the Soviet period, very differently than do rural residents.

Native biases can also surface when they identify cultural traits as essential qualities of a social group. Many natives of Kyrgyzstan's capital, Bishkek, for example, view natives of rural Kyrgyz—especially those from southern Kyrgyzstan—as uneducated, violent, religious zealots, thereby overstating the similarities among rural Kyrgyz and the extent to which this identity drives behaviors.

A related form of native essentialism exoticizes and fetishizes traits of a social or cultural group. An example of this is an Uzbek who earnestly reported that

Uzbek men squat by the side of the road and stare because the Uzbek people are deeply contemplative and philosophical. Native exoticization can in fact be indistinguishable at times from non-native varieties.

Both Afghans and other U.S. counterparts—both customers and socio-cultural analysts—have overstated the role of Pashtunwali in Afghanistan, sourcing it as everything from the reason Pashtuns typically live in walled compounds to being the reference manual to which Pashtuns refer before acting. More care is needed to temper such claims from the native perspective because of the weight and authority customers are likely to give to indigenous input.

Organizations building socio-cultural analysis capabilities can also find regional expertise and field experience among non-natives. We have found that area experts (both native and non-native) who provide the greatest value to socio-cultural analysis organizations have language skills, field experience, and a network of contacts and resources on the region.

Language skills should, at minimum, provide the ability to read news articles. This is sufficient to provide added value at organizations with a strategic mission; additional fluency can provide significant value, but is not absolutely necessary as an in-house capability. Higher-tempo organizations in direct support of SOF, serving a cultural research and advisory role directly to operational units, and especially organizations seeking to exploit foreign language sources such as social media see significantly greater returns from in-source

language fluency.

Many U.S. citizens with overseas experience as development professionals, businesspeople and academics have a wealth of language skills and experience operating in foreign cultures. Care should be given to determine the nature of the field experience, however. Especially with overseas government, military and business experience, there are reduced chances for independently navigating society and building the language skills and network of relationships that allow for deep insight.

Successful regional experts in socio-cultural analytic capabilities have one or both of two kinds of networks that they can leverage. Though Operational Security (OPSEC) concerns may limit or prohibit its use, many area experts, especially natives, have a network of in-country contacts—friends and relatives—to whom they can reach for additional perspectives and insight. Because most socio-cultural and human geography teams operate within the intelligence community, it is rare that this kind of network is leveraged, especially for quick-turnaround products. However, some organizations such as the Human Terrain System, through its reach-back cell of Iraqi and Afghan analysts, have been able to take advantage of these networks.

More common are networks consisting of colleagues who also share a professional or academic interest in the target region. These kinds of networks are most common among those with academic or professional experience in the region. Through their regional experts, socio-cultural

analysis teams can leverage these networks to survey the field to find existing research on particular subjects, to vet analysis, and discover new datasets. In settings where we provided support to both strategic and operational customers and did not routinely face deadlines shorter than seven days, our analysts consistently leveraged their professional and academic networks to obtain open source data and existing research that answered customers' needs, saving time and money.

Typically, individuals with both on-the-ground experience in the region and an academic background with an area studies component provide the full complement of desired area-expertise attributes. While both are useful in all settings, socio-cultural teams that routinely provide quick responses to customer requests or serve in cultural advisor capacities will probably see more benefit from field experience. Capabilities in strategic settings and that have longer timelines for producing analysis benefit more from attributes of an expert with an academic background, though again, field experience will also be beneficial.

Technical and methodological skills

Regional expertise begins to transform an all-source analysis team into a socio-cultural analysis team by orienting it toward and providing context to the data inputs the team needs to analyze the population of a target area. With this alone, a team is likely fairly well outfitted to provide qualitative, textual answers to socio-cultural requests from customers in a wide range of settings. A team outfitted with the right technological and methodological skills can do much more. Typically, these skills include geospatial sciences and technologies and a broad range of social science methodologies and perspectives. Combining tools and methodologies add depth and confidence to a socio-cultural analysis team's output and also open the door to producing a much wider range of products and datasets.

Geospatial sciences and technologies have been a core component of most socio-cultural analysis teams. For many in the community, the use of geographic methodologies and GIS tools distinguish human terrain analysis or human geography on the one hand from socio-cultural analysis on the other. Geospatial sciences and technologies complement all-source analysts and area experts by adding another dimension for storing, navigating, analyzing, and presenting data both for analysts and end-customers. Geospatial methodologies and technologies have been most powerfully used in environments where geospatial analysts are true experts with strong geographic information system (GIS) data management skills, working knowledge of the theories and methodologies of human geography, and familiarity with an array of tools for analyzing geospatial data. Some organizations have gone light on geospatial skills and still been able to meet most of their customers' needs. However, when requested to provide geospatial output, they had difficulty meeting customers' needs as adequately as socio-cultural analysis teams with robust capabilities.

Social science methodologies have been recognized as an important part of socio-cultural analytic processes, though there has been little offered to more narrowly define which are most useful. Discussions on the subject have defined social science extremely broadly, as something the military already does, and as something used "to understand the environment on the ground." Unfortunately, experienced socio-cultural analysts have failed to arrive at a narrow definition.

Quantitative social science methodologies, often used for analysis of survey data, have proven beneficial, especially in strategic settings. Anthropologists and sociologists have typically added more value than qualitative social scientists from other disciplines. However, it is rare that a social-science methodology has been explicitly inserted into any organization's analytical processes.

Many of the benefits from the social sciences come when the data's reliability is assessed and it is contextualized for use in analysis, or when processes are created for ongoing data creation and analysis tasks. Those using these skills often do so as second nature. And because the concentration of analysts with substantial backgrounds in formal social science disciplines in most organizations is small, the processes that these analysts use to assess reliability of data and incorporate it into analysis have gone uncatalogued.

It is likely that social science methodologies will continue to be used as they have been. While waiting for the community to identify the methodologies that

have been most important to analysis and the creation of analytical processes, organizations can narrow their human capital search focus by seeking social scientists who possess the skills to execute the organization's mission. Organizations interested in public opinion will want to find candidates with strong backgrounds in statistical analysis and survey design methods. Meanwhile, organizations doing qualitative, face-to-face interviews will want social scientists familiar with methods for conducting and analyzing anthropological interviews. Analytical teams that create and analyze geospatial data require analysts with methodological backgrounds to make responsible and reliable decisions about how data should be presented and caveated. In these cases, like almost all socio-cultural analysis questions, analysts are dealing with probabilities and uncertainties that will force them to make assumptions. Social scientists add value by increasing the objectivity of the assumptions and the responsible handling of data in analytical processes.

This value added by the methodological contributions of social scientists is closely tied to an organization's core mission and the types of data the socio-cultural analysis team will be handling. Teams charged with the production of geospatial datasets and multi-layered geospatial analysis of population groups require a member with a solid grasp of the theories and methodologies of geography as an academic discipline. Conversely, teams serving in a more advisory and information capacity to operational units will find few opportunities to formally employ social-science methodologies.

The technologies and methodologies described are certainly not an all-inclusive list of required or even the only useful ones available. Many organizations have used social network analysis methodologies and tools in limited capacities to great effect. Others have experimented with methods for aggregating and analyzing social media as well. While the book is still being written on this subject, organizations should take care to align the inclusion of social science skills to their core missions and to handling the types of data the analytical team will handle. There will be gaps and unanticipated needs. However, structuring the team in ways described next and fostering innovation encourages experimentation with new technologies and methodologies that can help bridge skill gaps.

The -INTs: The many intelligence (INT) disciplines and how they relate to socio-cultural analysis

Socio-cultural analysis teams have derived notable value by including intelligence-discipline specialists, though many teams have not explicitly sought to include such specialists. Signals intelligence (SIGINT) specialists have been especially useful to socio-cultural analysis teams that support targeting missions. The SIGINT analyst's skills have proven versatile and important for teams performing other missions as well. These analysts have proven critical to mapping ethnic or religious groups in certain areas, and they have used link and nodal analysis skills

to serve as their teams' social network analysis experts. Analysts with backgrounds in Human Intelligence (HUMINT) collection and counter-intelligence have proven broadly valuable to organizations that both actively drive socio-culturally focused HUMINT collection, and analyze large amounts of HUMINT data. Because most organizations use maps to display and analyze data, GEOINT (Geospatial Intelligence) too has proven extremely valuable to a large number of organizations.

Skillsets from each of these INTs are a valuable component in any organization; GEOINT and SIGINT are critical capabilities for teams robustly supporting targeting with link and spatial analysis.

Few organizations have in-sourced OSINT skills beyond including them under the All-Source Intelligence umbrella. The reason for this is unclear. This might be a result of the combination of a lingering bias against "unreliable" open-source reporting in favor of "reliable" classified intelligence reporting and poor experiences with OSINT support elements. This is unfortunate because the socio-cultural analysis missions for most regions of the world necessarily rely on open-source reporting the way that the Afghanistan socio-cultural analysis mission, for example, relies on HUMINT.

Going forward, organizations building socio-cultural analysis capabilities will want to examine finding ways to bring OSINT onto the team either by in-sourcing the skills through including an OSINT specialist on the team or by integrating more closely with OSINT analysis support teams.

Mindset skills

In addition to the types of formal skills and regional expertise described previously, successful socio-cultural analysts have a variety of skills that likely already exist among the cadre of all-source analysts. The importance of many of these behavioral, communication, and attitudinal skills to the success of any analytical team is self-evident. For example, the abilities to structure data, understand one's audience, think critically and clearly communicate ideas should be qualities of any experienced analyst. In the context of socio-cultural analysis there are skills especially important for the team to have or to cultivate.

The ability to think flexibly and spatially about socio-cultural data and problems drastically increases the effectiveness of human geography and socio-cultural analysis teams. Flexibility includes the ability to incorporate multiple layers of data to discover and display geospatial, temporal and network relationships. However, thinking flexibly also means adapting analytical processes to incorporate new types of data and to respond (and even anticipate!) customer needs.

We have found that especially for socio-cultural analysis organizations that serve both strategic and operational customers and are responsible for multiple countries, it is critical that both all-source and geospatial analysts be creative in regard to what is possible with data on their regions and adapt processes to maximize the extent to which they exploit these data. Additionally, it is important that as many analysts as possible on the team be able to think about spatial aspects of socio-cultural problems. Not every problem calls for it, but adding geospatial dimensions to socio-cultural analysis enhances the value of products and datasets, making them useful to a broader customer base by allowing them to lead to more insights. Either by incorporating geospatial analysts throughout the analytical production process or fostering this awareness in every member of the team, awareness of geographic approaches to socio-cultural questions dramatically increases the team's ability to serve its customers.

As discussed previously, networks of colleagues and experts on the team's region of responsibility enhance effectiveness. Equally important, however, is to network, reach out and collaborate to improve analysis. These behaviors can be encouraged, and some organizations even have formal steps in their analytical processes in which analysts are called upon to reach out to counterparts and/or experts. We have observed that it can be difficult to get every analyst to do this as a matter of course, and that those analysts who do collaborate in such a way often routinely contact only a few names from their list of contacts. There are no obvious solutions to solving these problems or cultivating these behaviors. Logistical, technical and legal barriers, and short production windows can even make inter-agency collaboration and networking difficult.

External collaboration is even more problematic. Typically, the way to ensure that this behavior occurs within a

team is to make sure that at least some analysts have demonstrated networking and collaboration skills, or have access to robust networks. It is also essential to create an environment that fosters collaboration.

Sourcing the skills

Organizations building socio-cultural analysis capabilities should keep the previous points in mind when sourcing their human capital. Skill gaps exist on every team, and given the need for security clearances in most environments, even external sources are unlikely to fill every need. That said, most organizations will likely benefit tremendously from composing a team of formally trained all-source analysts; geospatial analysts, especially those with graduate degrees in geography or geographic sciences; and regional experts with experience living in foreign cultures. Those individuals with a focus on an area of interest, language skills for the area of interest (or the languages in which research on the area is written, and access to a robust professional network will be particularly beneficial to the team.

Structuring/using the team

A socio-cultural analysis team can have all the right people and skills, yet still fail as a result of poor structure, leadership and processes. No organization has established best practices, and one is likely to find a wide range of opinions on how socio-cultural analysis teams should be structured and operate. Many of these opinions are likely informed by individual organizations' needs and concerns. However, the areas in which our analysts

have achieved success or met failure as a result of structures and procedures suggest lessons that organizations building socio-cultural analysis capabilities should keep in mind.

First, structuring the team rigidly and hierarchically can have significant drawbacks, even for large teams. Hierarchy and rank creates problems on teams with a large number of people who have strong backgrounds in the social sciences, but little to no experience in the military or intelligence community.

This cuts both ways. Social scientists leading organizations in which they have little to no experience are likely to require significant hand-holding from their teammates and may diminish customers' confidence in the entire team. On the other hand, experienced area experts and social scientists may chafe at being assigned the rank of entry-level analysts in organizations that do not have separate labor categories or functional roles for different kinds of all-source analysts.

Flattening hierarchy and rank also allows the entire team's expertise to attack every analytical product. In one organization, almost every product went before all of the analysts who happened to be in the office at the time, and was thoroughly worked over. Because everyone, even the senior analysts, went before the "firing squad" on every product, analysts felt more comfortable offering their viewpoints on all incoming requests for information. Because the team's backgrounds were diverse, this resulted in far more robust products. This model is unlikely to be replicable everywhere, but efforts by leaders to include a broad swath of analysts on products that might be in one or two analysts' normal lane can replicate some of these benefits.

There is a tendency to structure socio-cultural analysis teams geographically like their political-military counterparts. While this is understandable, it often is described as if it leads to analysts achieving expertise. This author has never actually witnessed this happen, especially when analysts are assigned to sub-national regions.

A lawyer who studied Spanish as an undergraduate may learn a mountain of facts about the Gadabuursi of Adal in Somalia, but mastery of trivia is not expertise. This same analyst, however, may excel at analyzing legal and administrative issues and at structuring analytic arguments. Some degree of geographic organization may be appropriate, especially in organizations responsible for regions with very different problem sets. However, it is important to keep in mind that defining analysts' portfolios as functionally identical, but geographically focused, defeats the purpose of hiring a specific blend of skills and characteristics and almost certainly prevents cross-regional functional expertise from emerging.

Second, socio-cultural analysis teams need access to outside expertise, data and resources. Financial limitations, legal restrictions, and OPSEC concerns all prevent socio-cultural analysts from operating at full capacity by limiting their ability to access external resources. In many environments, socio-cultural analysis relies heavily, if not exclusively, on unclassified data gathered from open sources. Hurdles that prevent analysts from reaching these data exist for valid and understandable reasons, but organizations seeking to extract full value from their socio-cultural analysis teams need to put effort into building processes that result in data getting into analysts' hands.

Access to library resources has been a recurring problem for analysts in several organizations. Books, journals, rare maps and unique reference materials are especially critical sources for teams with a deficit of subject matter expertise and for answering requests for information with descriptive analysis. Large datasets such as gazetteers and censuses, critical for creating human geography datasets, are also found in libraries with specialized collections.

Similarly, data residing on the Internet is critical for analysts. Foreign media, governments and social media sites all house data important for understanding socio-cultural dynamics and for creating geospatial datasets. However, in many organizations, analysts are blocked from accessing these sites with Web filtering or OPSEC rules.

No organization has found universal solutions for removing analysts' obstacles to accessing data, though some have cobbled together partial solutions. Meanwhile, analysts and private contractors have filled some gaps on their own, obtaining resources with their own funds and on their own time. Though no solution can be confidently offered here, the widespread nature of this problem does suggest that building a socio-cultural analysis team composed of quality analysts cannot achieve full performance without strong partnerships with private industry or counterpart organizations elsewhere in government to access external resources.

Finally, the right leaders are necessary for socio-cultural analysis teams to thrive. Because socio-cultural analysis in many organizations is often seen as competition by geospatial analysis and traditional all-source analysis teams, socio-cultural analysis teams—especially when establishing themselves—need advocates. Senior leaders advocating the creation and enhancement of socio-cultural analysis capabilities need to be visionaries willing to invest in a team whose true value may not emerge for several years.

The team also benefits from being led by an aggressive, articulate leader. This leader preferably should have both traditional intelligence analysis and socio-cultural analysis experience. She or he should also be able to clearly communicate how socio-cultural analysis complements peer analysts' production and enhances customers' abilities to execute their missions. The team leader needs to aggressively seek access to the unique resources socio-cultural analysts require to succeed. In some organizations, battles to outfit teams with the technical capabilities to more efficiently store and serve geospatial data have been ongoing for years. In many cases, however, full operational capability remains on the far horizon. However, tenacity and persistence have achieved partial victories and enhanced team function. These traits may not be necessary in all organizations, but in some they can mean the difference between success and failure of the socio-cultural analysis capability to perform at full function.

Conclusion

Socio-cultural analysis is a field that continues to develop rapidly. Therefore, by the time this article is in print, new technologies and methodologies will already be extending our ability to leverage geospatial and temporal analysis to visualize complex socio-cultural processes. Meanwhile, new sub-fields such as social media analysis are just emerging, with methodologies and technologies that are now in their infancy. As the field grows and matures, and especially as it tackles new environments such as Africa, Iran, Russia and the Asia-Pacific, analysts and leaders will learn new lessons.

With the security transition completed in Iraq and projected to be complete in Afghanistan in 2014, socio-cultural analysis missions will begin to change. Therefore, now is a good time to reflect on what has been learned to date. The lessons shared here will help those establishing new socio-cultural analysis teams to build on the foundations already laid by the community.

Nathan Hamm is a specialist in Central Asian culture and politics and human geographic analysis. He has led socio-cultural analysis teams for the U.S. Army and Central Command. His well-known Central Asian affairs website, Registan, has been an important voice discussing policy in the region since 2003.

REFINING THE INTELLIGENCE PROCESS: ADAPTING TO AN ERA OF POPULATION-CENTRIC SECURITY CHALLENGES

Daniel T. Maxwell
Christopher K. Tucker

Deconstructing the intelligence cycle for sensemaking

Treverton's "Real" Intelligence Cycle (see Figure 1) has much in it that can be debated.[1] Yet, it offers a rather granular deconstruction of the traditional intelligence cycle of Tasking, Collection, Processing, Exploitation and Dissemination (TCPED) processes (see Figure 2), which may serve as a useful foil in understanding how existing processes might be adapted to better support sensemaking about complex and rapidly evolving socio-cultural dynamics facing our national security community around the world. The utility of this foil is that it forces us to explore a more highly articulated set of intelligence related functions than the five outlined in the TCPED concept, or the traditional intelligence cycle. Ideally, such an understanding will allow for

the development and execution of a better informed and more cohesive change management strategy across the research, material acquisition, process improvement, human capital and organizational dimensions that must be addressed if change is to be successfully managed.

"Make things as simple as possible, but not simpler," Einstein has been paraphrased as saying. While the traditional cyclic process description is simple to understand and easily explained, it is not consistent with the reality of how intelligence activities are usually accomplished, especially given the changes and pressures already described. Moreover, there are ambiguities in how different elements of the community define these steps. These inconsistencies between how Intelligence Community members

describe their processes and how the work of intelligence is actually accomplished have deleterious effects on the whole community's ability to evolve toward more efficient and effective practices. The Intelligence Community faces and will always face monumental challenges trying to make sense of huge quantities of uncertain and ambiguous data. It really can't afford to handicap itself by attempting to organize around a set of overly simple, ambiguous and inconsistent models of intelligence processes.

The goal of intelligence is to reduce uncertainty for some decision maker or set of decision makers, or to help them understand a situation and the range of uncertainties where they are irreducible. To accomplish this, any useful intelligence product needs to answer two critical questions:

---

1. Treverton, G. (2001). *Reshaping National Intelligence for an Age of Information*, Cambridge University Press, Cambridge.

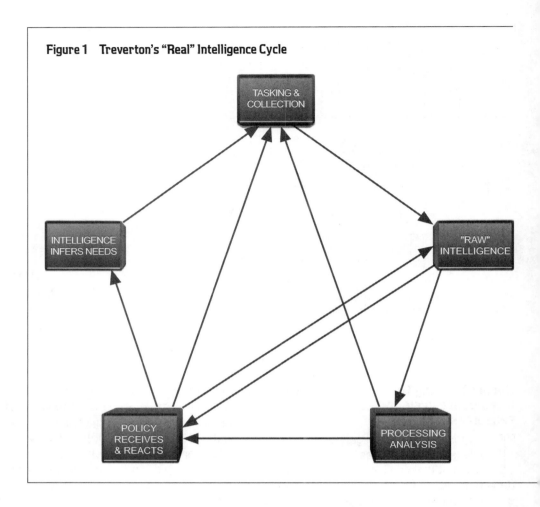

Figure 1   Treverton's "Real" Intelligence Cycle

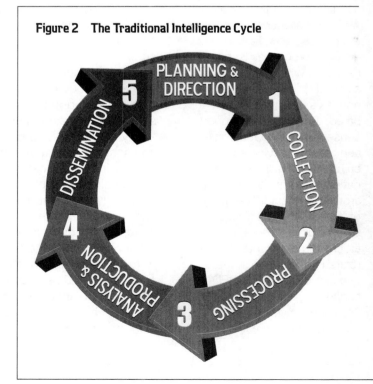

Figure 2   The Traditional Intelligence Cycle

Figure 3   Goals of PED

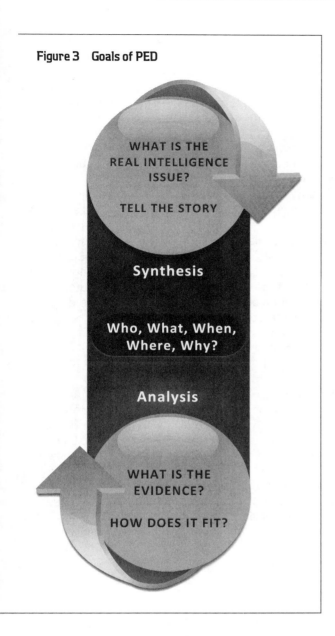

WHAT IS THE REAL INTELLIGENCE ISSUE?

TELL THE STORY

Synthesis

Who, What, When, Where, Why?

Analysis

WHAT IS THE EVIDENCE?

HOW DOES IT FIT?

1) What is the real intelligence issue?, and 2) What evidence and critical thinking exist that supports the conclusions? To answer these questions, intelligence analysts need to iterate between systematically analyzing the data they have collected and synthesizing it into a "story" that is both relevant to the decision situation under study and understandable to the decision maker(s) being supported (see Figure 3). Moreover, it should clearly communicate the five w's (who, what, when, where, why), supported by the evidence they have collected, assumptions that have been made and the uncertainty that remains in the situation.

For a meaningful intelligence process that stands the test of time, and the test of changing personalities and organizational dynamics, these stories must be managed as a set of narratives that coalesce our understanding of the world. Critically, these overarching narratives must fundamentally be grounded in real world geography and a concrete understanding of the temporal dimension if the constant onslaught of new information is to be rapidly marshaled in search for contrast with the existing accepted narratives.

Complex intelligence questions fraught with uncertainty may indeed require that competing narratives are maintained in order to properly convey the stories that engaged expert analysis and operational experience lead us to. Yet, without a concerted effort to continually condition the sensemaking process within a disciplined set of overarching narratives supported by consistent data, the intelligence process becomes untethered and ultimately fails to serve the decision maker.

The specifics of these intelligence questions and the relevant time horizons differ depending on the situation. At the tactical level, the time horizon might be minutes to hours, informed by a few key sources, with the relevant intelligence questions focused on immediate threats to warfighter safety or operational success. At the other end of the spectrum, strategic intelligence might be looking months to years in the future, conducting deep and detailed research, informing broad policy decisions. The common theme across all levels of decision makers is that intelligence must be timely and as informative as possible; assessing what is known, what is believed but uncertain and what is unknowable.

The threads connecting synthesis and analysis, the five w's (who, what, when, where, why), are the primitive elements of both storytelling and intelligence. It is this set of questions and answers that flow through the intelligence process and provide the building blocks for finished intelligence products. And, just as the world is changing, the nature of the questions is changing as is the type of data that will most effectively answer those questions.

Data regarding complex, ever evolving socio-cultural dynamics has become critical. Understanding the cultural/ linguistic frames and the narratives that actors adhere to and seek to recreate is essential. And, "where" and "when" have become elevated in status within the 5Ws, because location and time offer a central organizing logic for bringing together all relevant information

sources and characterizing uncertainties in a time dominant fashion. In short, no narrative can be formed that provides useful intelligence to the decision maker without grounding socio-cultural dynamics geospatially and temporally. For it to be useful, it must be actionable. And, as has been said many times, all actionable intelligence exists in space and time.

Intelligence professionals, whether they are analysts, executives or collection managers, know that the intelligence cycle is not a cycle at all, but is a highly interactive network of manual, semi-automated and automated activities with the goal of producing one key output: information that reduces uncertainty and illuminates decision situations. This process must aid decision makers in their process of sensemaking, by offering fact-based stories that through both their newly harvested facts and uncertainties offer conformance or contrast with the narrative that has accumulated from previous intelligence- and experience-based sensemaking. This is true for virtually all intelligence organizations; government and commercial.

Figure 4 gives us an opportunity to appreciate the broader range of intelligence functions and their complex interconnectedness and offers what we believe is crisp and rich enough to support meaningful introspection of existing processes, simple enough that it can help explain intelligence requirements to interested outsiders, and generic enough that it is applicable from the tactical to the strategic levels. Moreover, this model provides

a foundation for making the investments in people (education and development), process and organizational change, and infrastructure (especially technology) that can lead to an even more effective intelligence enterprise in the future.

We have broken down the intelligence process into a set of 10 interconnected activities. Each of these processes can be thought of as existing across the issue spectrum from tactical to strategic and as having human and automated components to some degree. The 10 activities are described as follows:

1. Develop goals and objectives

Goals and objectives are the seminal input to the intelligence process. These are provided in the form of intelligence questions asked by decision makers ideally with some set of relative priority. As previously stated, these have evolved from nation-state, military centric questions to questions attempting to gain understanding of more amorphous socio-cultural issues.

2. Plan and direct

Planning and direction are critical activities that begin to operationalize the goals and objectives. A first activity at this stage of the process is to develop baseline metrics at the outset of an intelligence activity. These can provide some insight into the completeness and effectiveness of various intelligence activities related to the prosecution of the goals and objectives defined by decision makers. Historically, planning has focused on collection planning, usually

Figure 4   The Actual Intelligence Process

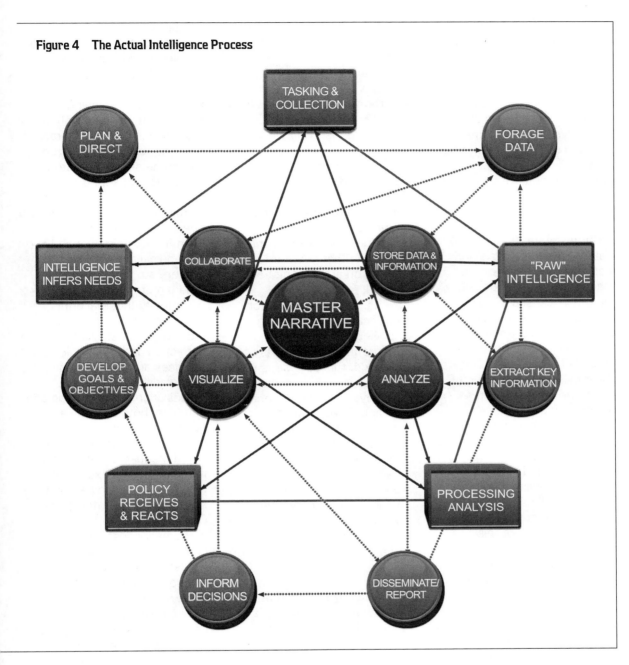

with a preference for classified technical and covert collection, with effectiveness measures that involve counting what is collected (e.g., outputs). The National Academy of Sciences highlights the importance of evaluation for the Intelligence Community (IC).[2] Rather than focus on counting quantities of collected information, they stated, "… the IC should carry out its evaluations in a way that focuses on systemic learning rather than on the assessments of individual analysts. Evaluation should be seen as a positive factor for the community—a process that will enable the entire IC to become more effective—rather than as a punitive process to be dreaded and, if possible, avoided. Effective evaluation, reflection, and continuous improvement are the underpinnings of organizational

2.   National Academies of Science (2011). INTELLIGENCE ANALYSIS FOR TOMORROW: Advances from the Behavioral and Social Sciences, National Academy Press, Wash. D.C.

learning, innovation, and agility.

The IC, like any organization or group, must decide how to balance process evaluation (how well correct procedures are followed) and outcome evaluation (the quality of the analyses)." Structured planning techniques, informed by metrics developed that emphasize outcome measures as an integral part of the planning process are essential.

3. Harvest data

Data to inform analysis and insight is available from many sources. Traditionally, the term "collection" has been used, breeding a bias toward technical and human collection systems that were designed and operated by the Intelligence Community. Given the changing nature of intelligence questions the modern environment presents and the vast amount of data available from open, commercial and gray sources, we have seemingly become data rich and insight poor, since we are not organized to harness much of this information.[3] This has been magnified with sources from geographies dominated by cultural and linguistic idioms with which much of our analytic workforce is unfamiliar.

There will always be a requirement for active collection via technical means and intelligence "tradecraft," but many of the questions now posed are better and more cost-efficiently answered using unclassified sources. As an example, we seek to understand human behavior that is inherently

tied to critical factors in the natural environment such as freshwater resource dynamics, domesticated crops/livestock, the environment and weather/climate. Most of this information is available in the open literature and is often more complete, current and accurate than the data collected and vetted via traditional intelligence channels.

Additionally, much of the basic data that governments depend on are administratively derived, either through census, land administration, identification provisioning or polling/surveying for sentiment. In many parts of the world, this data does not exist and is a serious challenge for analysis and operational planning. These data are absolutely critical to the success of population centric operations. Consequently, new approaches to collection are required if this data is to be successfully harvested from known sources, let alone foraged from the complex and ever changing information marketplace.

4. Extract key information

Human working memory is provably limited to about seven elements, plus or minus two.[4] The human grasp of remote geographies at heterogeneous and overlapping timescales is similarly known for its limitations. And, too often, the language skills and cultural fluency of our analysts are incomplete or insufficient. This means that it is essential that information technology

be applied as a supplement to human intuition to ensure that all relevant data is considered and potentially made available to analysts and decision makers. Accomplishing this means that key information must be extracted from raw data and reduced/organized into some set of consistent elements that support both machine reasoning and search by humans. This has historically been a near impossible task, even for very experienced and methodical analysts.

There are technologies emerging from the research community that make this vision possible. Advances in areas of automated information extraction and the ontological sciences are very promising, as are advances in the organization of knowledge and narrative, both spatially and temporally. That said, these only become useful if some set of standards that support meaningful data exchange is consistently applied among the members of the Intelligence Community.

The national security community's commitment to foster and apply Open Geospatial Consortium (www.opengeospatial.org) interoperability standards has been a good start, though too often this has been limited to traditional geospatial data.

A competent grasp of the socio-cultural dynamics that challenge us today require that these standards also be applied to the entity and transactions/events data that have been extracted from unstructured data sources, as well as the larger structured

3.   Hall, D.L., Jordan, J. M. (2010). *Human-Centered Information Fusion.* Boston: Artech House.
4.   Miller, G.A. (March 1956). "The magical number seven plus or minus two: some limits on our capacity for processing information." *Psychological Review* 63 (2): 81–97.

intelligence data systems, all of which should manage their holdings with an acute eye for their geospatial and temporal dimensions, as well as a representation of their credibility and uncertainty.

5. Store data and information
Much has been said about the promise of the "cloud" for the storage of massive data. Certainly, massive data is becoming more accessible than at any time in history. Perhaps the larger challenge is the ability to access that data in a manner that is analytically useful.

The collected and structured observations of human behavior and social change require data that is at a human scale, in terms of spatial and temporal resolution. That implies a need for analysts to flexibly access (query) structured data along these dimensions and to reach all the way back to source data if they have questions or want to manually evaluate its relevance and provenance. The challenge is further exacerbated by the fact that the bounding criteria of a search are often unclear. An informational search by an analyst (or analytic team) is not geographically constrained. The activities of transnational threats as well many socio-cultural phenomena are not bounded by the borders of a state, or a COCOM.

Perhaps more important than storing data so that the analyst can find it is managing data such that the "data can find the data," and relevance can find the user, such that computers can do what they do well, tipping and cueing the analyst, so that the analyst can be left to do what he or she does well.[5]

6. Analyze
"The IC has a long track record of successfully applying a wide variety of approaches to its tasks. It has, however, made limited use of behavioral and social sciences approaches used by other professions that face analogous problems. Those neglected approaches include probability theory, decision analysis, statistics and data analysis, signal detection theory, game theory, operations research and qualitative analysis."[6]

This observation by the National Academy of Sciences is a recurring theme in the area of intelligence analysis. Rob Johnston is more pointed in his review of the situation, stating "Community members quite often used the word "tradecraft" to describe intelligence analysis. ...The obvious logical flaw with adopting the idea of tradecraft as a standard of practice for analytic methodology is that, ultimately, analysis is neither craft nor art. Analysis, I contend, is part of a *scientific* process."

The emphasis on past tradecraft often blinds analysts to methods, tools and talent available from other disciplines that have the potential to provide many of the insights analysts seek. For too long, geospatial analysis (and spatio-temporal analysis) tools and methods have been relegated to a niche, excusing the wide range of analysts from the imperative to think spatially and temporally, as they stick slavishly to their tradecraft. Some specific analytic perspectives that are beginning to show potential are operations research, probability statistical modeling and decision analysis.[7] But, so too are the wider range of academic social science disciplines, which arguably, are only now being rediscovered by the national security community, after long neglect. All of these quantitative and qualitative techniques can become even more powerful if effectively coupled with advances in the geospatial sciences, allowing analysts and decision makers a crisper understanding of the implications of time and space.

7. Collaborate
Modern intelligence questions tend to be extremely complicated. Intelligence issues are often transnational, multi-cultural and multi-dimensional. Developing meaningful insights has become a team sport. Storytelling has become a communal process. Hackman says, "diverse groups offer at least the possibility that members will draw on their differences to produce some magic, producing some thing of extraordinary quality that would not have been generated by any one member acting alone."[8] Particularly

5. Jonas, Jeff and Lisa Sokol (2009). "Data Finds Data," *Beautiful Data: Stories Behind Elegant Data Solutions*, ch. 7, by Toby Segaran, Jeff Hammerbacher, O'Reilly Media.
6. National Academies of Science.
7. Riese, S; Hanson, M.; Seton, J. and Maxwell, D, (2012). "MORS and Intelligence Community Conduct Transnational Threats Workshop," Phalanx, March 2012.; National Academies of Science.
8. Hackman, J.R. (2011) *Collaborative Intelligence: Using Teams to Solve Hard Problems*, Berrett-Kohler Publishers, San Francisco.

when grappling with complex socio-cultural challenges, an effective team will need to be a multi-disciplinary team, capable of developing and capitalizing on the creative tension that is characteristic of professionals with differing perspectives and skills (see Figure 5). Hackman's research is further reinforced by the National Academy of Sciences, which states,

"A good rule of thumb is the 'law of requisite variety': a group's heterogeneity should match the complexity of the problems it is tasked to solve.

With heterogeneous teams, process losses can outweigh the benefits of collaboration for simple problems, with the balance shifting for complex problems. Of course, this principle is easier to advocate in the abstract than to execute in the world of imperfect perceptions, incomplete knowledge, and limited time."[9]

When thinking about how we can better collaborate within the analytical side of the intelligence process, the role of the spatio-temporal Common Operating Pictures (COP) in operational collaboration becomes critical. While experts from different academic and professional disciplines tend to be bound by different jargons and methodologies, space and time can serve as that anvil on which a common understanding can be forged. But, there are other concepts and technologies emerging that are focused on improving collaboration and group effectiveness. For example, collaborative crowd sourcing strategies have been demonstrated by programs such as the Aggregative Contingent Estimation (ACE) project at IARPA and the DARPA MoreEyes program, broadening the knowledge base of a very loose team

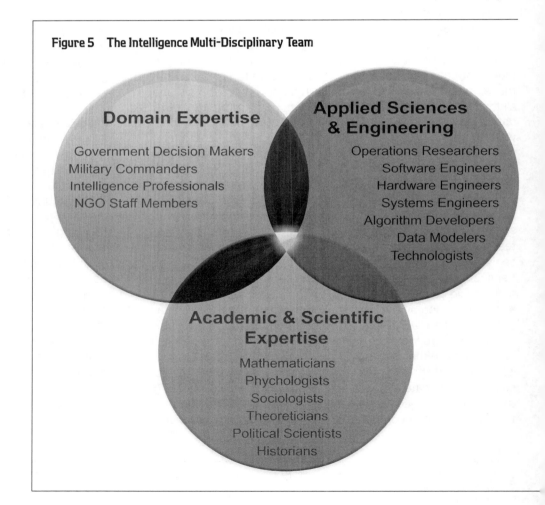

Figure 5   The Intelligence Multi-Disciplinary Team

Domain Expertise

Government Decision Makers
Military Commanders
Intelligence Professionals
NGO Staff Members

Applied Sciences & Engineering

Operations Researchers
Software Engineers
Hardware Engineers
Systems Engineers
Algorithm Developers
Data Modelers
Technologists

Academic & Scientific Expertise

Mathematicians
Phychologists
Sociologists
Theoreticians
Political Scientists
Historians

9.   National Academies of Science.

and subsequently improving the Intelligence Community's ability to forecast.[10] Additionally, many software environments are emerging that promise to support distributed collaboration.

8. Visualize

People extract meaning from what they see. The effective visualization of complicated concepts, whether it is raw data or analysis results is essential to improving the intelligence process. And, dynamic socio-cultural data, as it is arrayed across place and time could not be more complicated. Visualization is the means by which information is transferred from a computing environment to analysts for interpretation and subsequently from analysts to decision makers for decision support. The visualization of socio-cultural data comes in many forms, as it relates to the statistical, social network, spatio-temporal and other dimensions of this data. Visualization can be powerful if it reinforces well-informed analysis or dangerous if it misrepresents what the research, data or analysis can support.

Visualization is particularly vulnerable to the effects of cognitive biases and ignorance of the underlying logical models. As mentioned in previous sections, particular challenges exist in the representation of uncertainty, especially in the area of the geospatial representation (to include more recent sources such as Full Motion Video, Wide Area Persistent Surveillance, and Activity Based Intelligence) and network modeling of socio-cultural dynamics, as well the communication of credibility and (un)certainty of the underlying data. As an example of the challenge, many of the network analysis tools use frequency counts of entities or events extracted from text. These counts rarely make allowance for the quality or source of the data behind the network visualization. Using these types of models as a key piece of information, contained in only one source, would very likely be overwhelmed by the massive data and missed by an analyst.

While fraught with challenges, visualization capabilities are essential to making sense of complex socio-cultural dynamics, and should play a prominent role in both the analytical process and the synthetic process of telling the story. Visualization is a powerful approach to determining where new insights fit, or do not fit, into the existing master narrative.

9. Report and disseminate

There has been a tremendous emphasis in recent years on the need for improved information sharing among intelligence organizations as well as with the decision makers and operational personnel who would benefit from access to the information. Sometimes the focus on the dissemination of "reports" has worked at cross-purposes with this goal, leading to vast volumes of atomic level observables that come with little context. With complex socio-cultural data, which often lacks the concreteness of something like order of battle data, important observations can often be lost in such a reporting structure. This overload can be combated through use of a combination of reporting and dissemination processes and tools that encourage analysts, operators and decision makers to subscribe to tailored information feeds that update the stories and master narratives most relevant to them. These stories and narratives will evolve over space and time.

Similarly, maintaining living spatio-temporal COPs where complex socio-cultural data is communally curated over particular geographies enables understanding and sensemaking to be passed on during military Relief in Place / Transfer of Authority (RIP/TOA) processes, and the equivalent, inevitable "billet churn" experience across the larger analytic workforce. However this is done, it must be done with an eye toward time dominant conveyance of information that lets decision makers make sense of complex situations in a way that is easy to execute and informs their decisions.

10. Inform decisions

The whole point to the intelligence process is to provide integrated intelligence that supports decision making, informing decisions on an ongoing basis through the sophisticated and sustained interplay of evidence-based analysis and storytelling that effectively communicates uncertainties at play. It is the

---

10. Hickey, J. (2011). "Intel site tests crowdsourcing's ability to predict future," *Government Computer News*, Jul 15, 2011
http://gcn.com/articles/2011/07/15/intell-crowdsourcing-forecasting-ace.aspx.

"output" of the intelligence system. We have discussed the many ways in which complex socio-cultural dynamics complicate various steps in the intelligence process, and how their constant change over time and space challenges us to reimagine the intelligence process. For decisions and actions to be informed, particularly as they relate to population-centric challenges, all information and every intelligence discipline must be integrated into a common spatio-temporal framework that can amply communicate the story to and maintain the master narrative for decision makers.

Sensemaking across domains

With this deconstruction of the intelligence process into this inter-related web of intelligence functions, we are freer to think about how they might be better organized and institutionalized so that we can better cope with the fast changing socio-cultural dynamics that are at the heart of many of our most vexing national security problems. We will conclude with a short reflection on the technological and human capital dimensions to this organizational challenge.

First, let's revisit an earlier point having to do with the technological fabric in which the intelligence process is inextricably woven. The intelligence process, or more aptly, the inter-related web of intelligence functions discussed previously, spans multiple security domains, and as a result, it can be severely disjointed and even myopic. Too many analysts' work is highly constrained to data coming across a given classified network within a single INT stovepipe. For

the overwhelming majority of analysts and operators, seamless access to relevant information sources from across the different security domains does not exist. The result is intelligence reporting that can be stilted, which fundamentally fails to take into account much of the open information that is actively foisted upon decision makers by the outside world, often in a more time dominant fashion. In a fast changing world characterized by complex socio-cultural dynamics, the hard work and dedication of analysts is being actively undermined by the failure of the technical infrastructure to enable sensemaking across the collection and security domains. (The current vision for this is called "integration.") As such, decision makers are being underserved.

Second, ensuring that the technological infrastructure is in place for cross-domain, spatio-temporally enabled inter-disciplinary intelligence is critical, but it is not enough. Investments in people are needed.

If we are to demand that analysts and operators grasp the wide world of information sources that pertain to the missions they are working, we must teach them how to forage for and through the universe of information sources and information communities available to them, and must provide them with the language skills and cultural proficiency that they need to make sense of them. If we are to demand that analysts and operators understand, make sense of and find meaning in change over time within specific geographies, we must ensure that spatial

and spatio-temporal thinking become a fundamental part of their education. If we are to demand that they grasp the complex socio-cultural dynamics at the heart of our priority national security missions, we must ensure that they have some education in a pertinent assortment of social sciences.

In conclusion, in order to re-imagine the intelligence process so that analysts and operators can better support decision makers, we must begin to explore opportunities for process and organizational change. Too many analysts see the day to day of their careers trapped within functional stovepipes, and are disconnected from the priority intelligence requirements of any given customer.

In addition, too many analysts are consigned to a mid 20th century factory workflow, generating reports without the ability to help tell a story for decision makers or to contribute to a larger, curated narrative that guides future intelligence efforts.

The re-emergence of dynamic socio-cultural challenges has demonstrated the insufficiency of current process and organizational forms within the Intelligence Community. Yet, we should view this as an opportunity. By freeing the Intelligence Community from the shackles of the traditional formulations of the intelligence cycle and TCPED, we have an opportunity to achieve efficiencies, remove latencies, deepen understanding, enable sensemaking, anticipate threats and create a more effective intelligence enterprise in the future.

Daniel Maxwell is President of KaDSci, LLC. Maxwell served as U.S. Army MP and operations research analyst, and on the DSB Task Force on Intelligence and MORS Board of Directors. He holds a PhD in information technology from George Mason University. His research emphasizes decision analysis, simulation and C4ISR modeling.

Dr. Christopher K. Tucker thinks and works at the intersection of technology, strategy, geography and national security. Tucker manages a portfolio of social ventures and technology companies across the domains of international affairs, defense/intelligence and academe. He serves on a variety of government, private sector and non-profit boards.

A Brief Overview of Activity Based Intelligence and Human Domain Analytics

Mark Phillips

Inbound, on a helicopter over Angola: A combined team of Special Operations, Civil Affairs and Army Corps of Engineers personnel prepares to enter a village to work with the villagers and to build a well. Based on an assessment of the patterns of life in the village, they understand how the village shifts and moves. They understand the identity of its leaders and the activities and transactions in which they engage. And they understand the local culture, beliefs and history, which provide context to the village's activities.

Activity Based Intelligence and Human Domain Analytics have combined to give the team the information they need to make the mission a success.

Introduction

Since 2010, when the Office of the Under Secretary of Defense for Intelligence (OUSDI) released the first two strategic guidance papers on Surveillance for Irregular Warfare and Understanding the Human Dimension, much has been written about the new discipline of intelligence called Activity Based Intelligence. Activity Based Intelligence (ABI) is defined as a discipline of intelligence where the analysis and subsequent collection is focused on the activity and transactions associated with an entity, a population or an area of interest. The Human Domain, or Human Dimension, which is a vital and integral part of ABI, is defined as the presence, activities (including transactions—both physical and virtual), culture, social structure/organization, networks and relationships, motivation, intent, vulnerabilities and capabilities of humans (single or groups) across all domains of the operational environment (space, air, maritime, ground and cyber).

The ABI multi-Intelligence (multi-INT) approach to analysis has grown in popularity and number of practitioners based on the necessities born from numerous and significant changes. These include changes in warfare, changes in the makeup of the challenges facing the U.S. and U.S. interests, the increasing flood of sensors and the resulting data growth, and the technological improvements that enable this type of analysis. Multiple intelligence agencies as well as several service components are beginning to explore the value of institutionalizing ABI within their work forces. The National Geospatial-Intelligence Agency (NGA) is at the forefront of the ABI push within the Intelligence Community. The ubiquitous nature of geospatial intelligence (GEOINT), coupled with Human Domain Analytics (HDA), forms the true foundation of ABI.

This chapter is intended to give the reader an appreciation of ABI: its origins, its contributions to analysis and its future. The concepts of HDA, which include the field of Human Terrain Analysis, are essential to ABI and will be explored in that context. Finally, a look into the future will include a brief examination of key enablers, existing policies and burgeoning career fields for analysts.

ABI is at an exciting point in its development with much refinement and evolution in its future; this is an ideal time to form an understanding of this nascent discipline of intelligence.

Historical context

In his 2009 book, *Intelligence for an Age of Terror*, Dr. Gregory Treverton discussed the shift of intelligence problems from "puzzles" to "mysteries."[1] According to Dr. Treverton, puzzles address *known* problems; a question where a new piece of information will solve the puzzle. Mysteries, on the other hand, are about *knowable* problems, which usually involve people; an analyst cannot necessarily know the answer but might know what events or activities to look for and try to figure out how they relate. In other words, in the past an analyst worked to solve a puzzle; today analysts work on mysteries and don't even know if there is a puzzle to be solved.

It is against this backdrop that ABI tradecraft was forged. The formalization of ABI as a discipline of intelligence by the Under Secretary of Defense for Intelligence (USDI) was the result of successes of activity-based practices in three disparate arenas: the military efforts in Iraq, law enforcement and those establishments under the purview of the Nevada Gaming Commission. Each arena's problems were driven by a scarcity of meaningful data and a low signal-to-noise ratio, i.e., the "bad" elements looked and acted much the same way as the "good" elements and both co-existed within their respective environments.

In Iraq, the Intelligence Community was tasked with finding terrorists and insurgents bent on harming U.S. Forces and their interests. These terrorists or insurgents rarely performed activities that were dissimilar from non-terrorists (especially in the planning phases). In terms of Iraqi mysteries, the questions were "Will something happen?" and "How can we predict it and prevent it?" Analysts began to develop techniques to address these mysteries using any means at their disposal to aggregate these activities, assess transactions and develop networks of interest.

It is interesting that the ABI approach discovered by the intelligence analysts in Iraq shares a good deal of commonality with practices traditionally used in law enforcement. Law enforcement must deal with those who would violate the law, and try to prevent them from doing so. Similarly, criminals are often indistinguishable from the normal populace. Law enforcement must assess the activities of the populace, factor in the nature of the surrounding Human Domain, and then discern abnormal or criminal activity. Of note, there is a new trend in law enforcement called "Intelligence-Led Policing," which brings to bear resources from the Intelligence Community in further addressing the activities and transactions of the populace.[2]

Finally, the Nevada Gaming Commission is responsible for the regulation of the casinos in Nevada. The principal issues facing casinos are fraud, cheating and the corruption of employees. Casinos are constantly on the lookout for activities that are out of the norm and which bear additional surveillance. They gather information on known entities and try to discern the activities of unknown entities. As the movie *21* illustrated, cheaters look just like the non-cheaters; the effort to understand the activities and transactions within a casino or group of casinos, or searching for abnormalities is clearly a mystery. Today's casinos use activity-based assessments to identify potential issues and to assess historical trends to focus in on abnormal behavior.

All of these arenas face the problem of a mystery, finding "unknown unknowns." The analyst, whether a GEOINT analyst in Iraq, or the surveillance "boss" in a casino, must decide if something warrants investigation; if additional information can crystalize the picture, and if he or she can extract the significant (the signal) from all the noise. This was the pressure cooker that necessitated a new multi-disciplinary approach to intelligence and its resulting new analytical workflows, new thought processes, new tradecraft and specialized training.

USDI formalizes ABI

OUSDI sought to codify the best practices associated with collections and analysis, and in 2010 formalized and defined ABI and HDA. OUSDI promulgated the concepts

---

1. *Intelligence for an Age of Terror*, Dr. Gregory F. Treverton, Cambridge University Press, New York, 2009, pages 146-147.
2. *Intelligence-Led Policing: The New Intelligence Architecture*, U.S. Department of Justice, Office of Justice Programs, Bureau of Justice Assistance, NCJ 210681, Marilyn Peterson, September 2005.

of ABI and these concepts formed the basis of the evolution of the discipline of ABI across the Intelligence Community. OUSDI formally defined ABI in a way that led analysts, based on activities and transactions, to drive collection. OUSDI also formally defined activities and transactions, the building blocks of ABI. The Human Domain model, which will be discussed later in this chapter, was also proposed and codified. Finally, ABI was defined in terms of multi-INT tradecraft in contrast to All Source analysis. This work by the USDI staff led the Under Secretary to state that ABI would form the intellectual underpinning of how we will conduct intelligence in the future.

ABI principles

ABI is truly a different approach to analysis. It invokes different tradecraft, data processing, technology and thought processes. Although ABI was originally conceived to assist in finding criminals or terrorists, the principles of ABI allow it to also be used, in a very real sense, with those mysteries that involve no "bad guys."

The purpose of ABI has been expressed in numerous forums and can be summarized in the following five elements:
- Collect, characterize and locate activities and transactions;
- Identify and locate actors and entities conducting the activities and transactions;
- Identify and locate networks of actors;
- Understand the relationships between networks;
- Develop patterns of life.

An examination of this list proves quite instructive.

There is no mention of adversaries (criminal or otherwise). There is an underlying current that the analyst will discover something of significance in the data and potentially be "surprised" by the data. Recall that the analyst is not cued or focused on a specific target, but rather is informed by the data as it is being presented. By examining and integrating the data before it has been exploited, one is able to discern important information about the activities and transactions of the area of interest, leading to understanding the Human Domain under observation.

Additionally, unlike many analytic efforts, the intention of ABI is to develop the patterns of life, to determine which activities and transactions are abnormal, and to seek to understand those patterns to develop courses of action. It is focused on understanding relationships between various entities and their activities and transactions. These activities and transactions are not necessarily just tied to geospatial actions, but also apply across the cyber, social, financial and commercial domains, to name a few.

The goal of ABI is to enable focused intelligence analysis on hard problems with critical timelines, such as irregular warfare, counter-terrorism, counter-insurgency, and counter-weapons of mass destruction. But of additional importance, ABI is valuable in understanding the environment, even if there are no anticipated direct hostile actions. Preparation of the environment, support to stability operations and Civil Affairs operations all benefit from characterizing and understanding the patterns of life in an area of interest and exploiting that knowledge.

Throughout the discipline of ABI there are certain principles or pillars to which the analysts adhere and that form the basis of ABI tradecraft.

First and foremost is the concept of "geo-reference to discover." All collected data should be indexed to a spot on the earth, which is known as geo-referencing. Within the ABI workflow, geo-referencing is the first step in the workflow rather than the last. This is especially important and necessary in those cases where data is sparse, and it is only through geo-referencing all the available multi-INT data that the analysts have enough information to begin their workflows. This enables discovery and integration of activities and transactions across a variety of data types and allows analysts to focus their analysis.

Closely tied to the "geo-reference to discover" concept is that of data integration and association *before* data exploitation. By exploring the relationships within the geo-referenced data, the analyst can "see" activities and transactions and begin to relate them. Often, in other analytical workflows, the data is exploited first and *then* the analyst looks for relationships, not realizing that some information may have been lost in the exploitation.

The "integration before exploitation" principle supports the assertion that ABI is a multi-INT analysis as opposed to All Source Analysis. In All Source Analysis the All Source analyst works with finished products to begin his fusion and reach his ultimate analytical conclusions. In ABI, the analyst uses multi-INT data at its most discoverable level to begin her analysis; the integration and "fusion" occurs long before a finished product is formed.

The third principle of ABI is data neutrality. Data neutrality simply means that all data and data sources are potentially equally viable for ABI analytics. All data can be geo-referenced to comprise the body of information for a given area. As part of the ABI process, the analyst must understand the pedigree and confidence level associated with the data; in other words, how reliable the data is and how much error it contains. By accepting all data as the basis of ABI analytics, issues such as non-spatial data, less reliable or accurate data, and fleeting data sources can be overcome.

The final principle of ABI is sequence neutrality. Its central tenet is that the importance of data on hand (or being collected) is often not understood until the analyst gets more information. Conversely, an analyst may find the answer to a current question by drawing in and geo-referencing information that was collected in the past.

Another way of explaining sequence neutrality is that the data often holds the answer to a question that has not been asked before. As analysts are trained in ABI tradecraft, one of the most important things they learn is to explore the data on hand as well as the current collection. Analysts approach the data not knowing what they will find; they are not simply completing a puzzle. They are looking for a needle in a stack of needles to find an unidentified special needle that has some significance. This is another case of letting the data surprise you.

Focus on the HDA and ABI

It is evident that understanding the Human Domain is the underpinning of ABI analytics. ABI is focused on understanding entities that do not have signatures in any single sensor phenomenology; understanding these entities at the human level is essential. The importance of understanding the Human Domain has increased significantly over the past decade and a half. There has been a shift from concentration on nation-states, to smaller organizations, to individuals. The impact of a single individual can be experienced globally; today, an individual sitting in a cave with a video camera and a laptop computer can have worldwide impact.

Looking at Afghanistan helps us to recognize the impact of the Human Domain on understanding the region. In Afghanistan, U.S. interests are not threatened by the government of Afghanistan, nor are our interests necessarily protected by the Afghan government. Rather, the rule of the land is tribal, with individuals possessing significant power and influence; enough to shape U.S. action within a region. Understanding the tribal relationships, knowing the leaders in a community, and understanding the beliefs and culture (such as Pashtunwali, the cultural code of the Pashtun people) continues to be vital to the success of the region.

Although the following quote from a recent Defense Science Board pertains to Counter-Insurgency Operations (COIN), its conclusion applies across the spectrum of U.S. involvement across the world. It conveniently invokes the fundamental ties between ABI and HDA.

"Unlike traditional ISR, where the focus typically is on the location of an anticipated activity, ISR for irregular warfare must focus on discovering the unknown activity of an adversary, characterizing it, and exploiting it. For support of COIN operations it also requires a clear and sustained focus on population-centric activities such as governance, development, and local population—sometimes before the start of hostilities. This demands a thorough understanding of historical, socio-cultural, economic, educational, and environmental aspects of the area of operations in addition to political and military factors and trends. This in turn requires more basic or fundamental intelligence as well as associated social, behavioral, and political sciences information."[3]

Human Domain analytical model

To paraphrase the definition of the Human Domain used earlier in the paper, HDA is the global understanding of anything associated with people. This includes organizations and affiliations,

---

3. Report of the Defense Science Board Task Force on Defense Intelligence Counterinsurgency (COIN) Intelligence, Surveillance, and Reconnaissance (ISR) Operations, February 2011, page 29, Approved for Public Release.

culture, relationships, social structure, motivation, etc. The Human Domain, and its resulting analytics, is not a replacement for other domains (air, sea, land, space, cyber); rather it is a lens through which the environment can be viewed, which spans across all the other domains. The significance of the Human Domain to ABI is unparalleled; it provides the context and understanding of the activities and transactions and allows, in some cases, for predictive intelligence, i.e., forecasting activity.

In order to quantify the analysis needed in the Human Domain, and to lay the groundwork for automating the collection and association of Human Domain data, OUSDI created an HDA model. The USDI divided the Human Domain into four data categories, which summarize what can be captured or collected about people.

The first category is biographical information, or "who you are." This is the most obvious of all the knowledge types, since it is information directly associated with an individual. The second data type is activities information, or "what you do." This data category associates specific actions to an individual as well as interactions with other individuals. The third data category is relational information, or "who you know." This is the individual's web of relationships: family, friends and associates. The final data category is contextual information, which is information about the context or the environment in which the entity is found. Examples include most of the information found within the socio-cultural/human terrain studies. Importantly, like any other form of data that feeds

intelligence processes, this data is not static, but changes and shifts radically over short timeframes. Therefore a model of the past is truly insufficient in aiding analysis of today.

Taken in total, these data categories support ABI analysts in the analysis of entities, identity resolution of unknown entities, and emplacement in a social context. It is revealing to examine the breadth of information within each data category. For the biographical data category, analysts will collect information about name, address, gender, biometrics, language, Facebook page, etc. For activities, the collected information will include travel, communications, financial transactions, movement of physical assets, etc. The relational information includes family, friends, associates, membership organizations, community involvement, etc. Finally, the contextual data type will include demographics, political environment, cultural norms, social interactions, tribal customs, religion, etc.

It is important to note that much of the work within the field of Human Terrain or Human Geography analyzes the information contained within the contextual data category.

Analysis in the Human Domain

Analysis in the Human Domain in support of the multi-INT tradecraft of ABI is bound by the same fundamental principles as ABI (geo-reference to discover, sensor neutrality, and sequence neutrality). However, for HDA to be productive, it must encompass the breadth and complexities of the four data types. The various types of data vary widely as do their granularity. Much of the information in the

Human Domain has a great deal of inherent uncertainty, as many times it is the entities themselves or their families that are self-documenting their data. HDA requires analytical methods that support multi-INT, unstructured and subjective data. Finally, the geospatial location of the entities present in the data is often unidentified at the outset, which may add complications based on legal jurisdictions.

Within the HDA endeavor are two distinct classes of analysis: find the entity (in a sea of data about innumerable entities) and characterize the entity (filling in the various knowledge types on an entity).

It is the first class of analysis that is most tightly coupled to ABI and exhibits similar tradecraft. The analyst works with multiple data types to geo-reference information with known activities and transactions. Correlating across those data types geospatially, temporally and logically (for instance how entities are related even if they have never been observed involved in a transaction), adds to the context and resolution of the entities involved in ABI.

In the second case, characterizing the needle, the analyst again brings together all available information within the various data types to characterize and understand the known entity of interest. The fact that it is a known entity, about which the analyst is building a profile, is perhaps an easier task and falls into the category of "completing a puzzle." It is also the logical follow-up to finding the needle; once the needle is found and identified, it is essential to characterize it as much as possible, using all available information.

Key ABI enablers

There are several key enablers that must be in place to support future ABI endeavors. These key enablers are necessary for not only the automation of the processing and integration, but also to ensure that the analysts performing ABI analysis have what they need to complete the mission.

First of all, there must be common, searchable databases for housing ABI data. These must include the Human Domain data, which is frequently sequestered behind law enforcement or privacy rules.

Policy must also extend to permitting the exploitation of the vast amounts of information that exist in the unclassified public arena. The rapidly approaching "cloud" architectures being developed by industry as well as the government lend themselves well to the storage and processing of immense quantities of information. Enabling the data in the cloud requires that all data have associated metadata that is tagged, searchable and accessible by analysts who have access to the tools to permit exploitation and analysis.

At this point a word about the metadata associated with ABI analysis as well as the foundational HDA is in order. The amount of data present in any phenomenology-based data set is enormous. However, when adding the four data types of the Human Domain, the wealth of information is unimaginable and in many cases so vast as to be of no use. Automation to aid analysts and focus their time and attention is vital to the ABI tradecraft. An ABI needs-driven metadata standard, whereby all necessary information about entities, their activities and their relationships can be captured, is a key enabler and an absolute essential. OUSDI has provided within the Human Domain Data Model the scope of the metadata needs for the Human Domain. The remaining ABI supporting data (time, location, nature of the activity, etc.) must still be categorized and formalized. It is only through a robust metadata standard that algorithms can be developed to associate information and thereby entities, reducing the data to a set that can be exploited and then analyzed.

Finally, the realization that ABI is a new multi-INT discipline of intelligence with its own tradecraft and processing needs drives the requirement for new, formalized training tailored to ABI. The analysts can never be removed from the analytical process and therefore their training must teach them how to approach data, integrate geo-referenced data, discover what is interesting in the data, and finally perform the required multi-INT analysis.

The future of ABI

The need for the new tradecraft and mindset of the ABI analyst continues to grow over time. The emphasis on individual entities or small units has emerged as a dominant concern for the analytical community. Major intelligence agencies such as NGA will begin to place more and more emphasis on the ABI and HDA tradecraft to solve the mysteries that all know are present.

ABI and HDA are not the answer to every intelligence problem; they are merely new arrows in a quiver of capabilities. But in the words of Director Clapper when he served as Under Secretary of Defense for Intelligence, these "arrows" will "form the intellectual underpinning for how we conduct intelligence in the future."[4]

Mark Phillips is Senior Principal Systems Engineer for Integrity Application Incorporated. Phillips was lead author of an Activity Based Intelligence (ABI) strategy papers series published by the Office of the Under Secretary of Defense for Intelligence. He currently serves as an ABI Subject Matter Expert within the Intelligence Community.

4.   The Honorable James Clapper, Under Secretary of Defense for Intelligence, TECHINT Symposium, Washington DC, December 2009.

EPILOGUE

Robert R. Tomes

Human dynamics and national security

Understanding human dynamics is essential for effective national security decision making. As discussed earlier in this volume, "human dynamics" was one of many terms that emerged to improve understanding of contemporary national security challenges by focusing on the underlying actors, groups, behaviors, ideologies and motivations driving security affairs. Examples of other terms include human geography, human domain awareness, socio-cultural intelligence, human socio-cultural behavioral modeling, human terrain analysis, pattern of life analysis and, most recently, activity based intelligence.

The recent emphasis on activity based intelligence (ABI) solutions, arguably, highlights the need for additional study on what this volume has broadly defined as socio-cultural dynamics. ABI is essentially an innovative category of human dynamics analysis dominated by "big data," multi-INT fusion and advanced analytic capabilities used to identify and correlate signatures for key events, actors and relationships regardless of their spatial or temporal coincidence (or proximity).

Today's imperative is to institutionalize, integrate and continue to grow expertise across the government in the disciplines and application of analytic methods that cut across all of the areas this volume aggregates into the umbrella category of socio-cultural analysis. These capabilities are critical to improve our capacity to anticipate and mitigate future crises, to enable proactive whole-of-government approaches to complex national security challenges, and to sustain investments in the collection, knowledge management, and analytic activities that provide timely, relevant and actionable information to decision makers.

The intent of this volume was to provide a representative cross-section of methods, analytic approaches and ways of thinking about national security issues that emerged from several years of working groups sponsored by the U.S. Geospatial Intelligence Foundation (USGIF) with participation from dozens of government agencies, academic institutions, and commercial firms all experienced in integrating social science methods into government decision processes. This epilogue sets the stage for continued discussion on the need to improve our understanding of human dynamics across the international security decision-making community.

Socio-cultural dynamics and U.S. national security policy making

For much of the past decade, debates on and discussions about U.S. national security have been dominated by the wars in Afghanistan and Iraq. In both conflicts, after struggling to design and implement an effective strategy, a people-centric counter-insurgency strategy was adopted and deep understanding of "patterns of life" became a priority. This population-centric approach required "whole of government solutions" integrating defense, diplomacy, development and other domains across strategy, policy formulation and execution phases. As was also the case in the global war against terrorism—another security area requiring a population-centric approach to address radicalism and the conditions giving rise to terrorism—success depended upon the ability to understand human geography and to leverage that understanding.

Adopting a population-centric approach as the overarching strategy to prevail in Afghanistan and against violent extremists (terrorists) was not easy. It just wasn't a natural approach or orientation for the legacy intelligence and information support activities that underpin the defense, diplomacy and development arms of the broader national security community.

The organizational and institutional memory required for a population-centric war strategy did not exist. Cold War expertise in socio-cultural intelligence collection and analysis, including efforts to understand Soviet proxies and leftist movements, were all but lost during the budget cutbacks of the 1990s. Military and defense strategy did not address occupation duties, much less a prolonged counter-insurgency war or nation-building missions. A post-Vietnam antipathy to low intensity conflict prevailed; the first Gulf War solidified an approach to combat that emphasized quick victory and limited deployments. The intelligence community, meanwhile, emphasized technical collection and support to precision targeting.

Adopting a population-centric war strategy as

a national security policy imperative required changing how resources were allocated, what equipment was procured, how people were trained and evaluated, and how the interagency would collaborate to form whole-of-government solutions. Population-centric war planning also altered expectations for the length of U.S. (and Coalition forces) deployments, changed the rules of engagement for counter-terrorism and other operations, and shifted how U.S. forces engaged with and related to the local population. More important for thinking about the future of human domain analysis were changes required inside the U.S. national security community with respect to thinking about the two ongoing wars, the larger concept of a war on terrorism and how to improve complex problem decision making in the face of great uncertainty. Adopting population-centric strategies required fundamental changes in measures of effectiveness and in the very types of information and intelligence required to inform policy, decision making and operations.

Indeed, when it appeared the prevailing approach was not working in Iraq and that a "surge" was needed, human geography or human domain awareness programs were funded, made a national security priority, and the imperative to understand patterns of life and the ideational and motivational underpinnings of foreign leader and group behaviors brought social science methods and analytic approaches into the mainstream of the national security decision-making process.

Meanwhile, the fight against terrorist and insurgent networks required the U.S. government to build a stronger interagency, whole-of-government "network" able to share information and expertise at the level of detail and in the timelines required to degrade adversary networks. Sustaining constant pressure on insurgent and terrorist networks in Iraq and Afghanistan required deep insight into local (including tribal) politics, how local politics related to political dynamics in Kabul and Baghdad, how politics in both capitals were being influenced by regional and international actors, and the myriad activities and events that influenced support for the government as well as for anti-regime forces.

The decision to focus on the human domain for the conflicts in the U.S. Central Command's area of responsibility and at the highest levels of national strategy for the global war on terrorism is one of the most significant changes in U.S. national security decision-making since the end of the Cold War. It is unclear whether this will last in light of budget cuts and waning support for continued emphasis on counter-insurgency doctrine. The historical record, moreover, suggests that our capabilities to understand socio-cultural dynamics and to apply that understanding to policy-making may once again atrophy in a post-conflict environment as priorities shift and budgets decline.

Proteus or Sisyphus? Preparing for an era of persistent conflict

This is not the first time in American history that national security planners and strategists have "discovered" the importance of social science methods and approaches to improve understanding of the human domain. In World War II, for example, programs like the Human Relations Area Files at Yale University, the use of anthropologists, and other programs informed planning and operations. This included informing operations to support insurgents, partisans and guerillas against the Axis powers during the war and to support occupation and reconstruction programs in Europe and Japan after the war. What we call human dynamics analysis today directly informed World War II operations, including those of the Office of Strategic Services (OSS). The OSS was created to provide unique capabilities deemed essential to the larger war effort and was much more than a forerunner to today's special operations forces and clandestine human intelligence and psychological warfare operations.

OSS operations relied on anthropologists and other social scientists. Social science expertise was essential to both strategic and tactical levels of operations. As authors Max Boot, David Kilcullen and others have argued, the underlying model for the OSS as an interagency, strategic services organization should be considered for adoption as a supplement to the expansion of special operations forces (SOF). While rightly considered a legacy of the famed OSS units, today's SOF are not chartered or authorized to wage strategic warfare as an interagency activity in the same fashion that were the civilian and military elements of the OSS. Information operations and the ability to focus "strategic services" on the human domain are critical to resolving 21st century security challenges.

During the early Cold War, what in today's parlance are called human security issues (part of the Human Domain) deeply influenced the Central Intelligence Agency's (CIA) assessments of stability in postwar Europe. The

CIA concluded that poverty and the underlying social conditions of post-colonial areas and in some of the devastated cities rendered them susceptible to Soviet influence, especially in areas where leftist or socialist sentiments existed. Consideration of the human dimensions of the emerging, ideological-driven Cold War factored heavily in President Truman's request to Congress for funds for Greece to fight communist insurgents and to prevent the expansion of Soviet influence into Turkey. His March 12, 1947 speech requesting aid, dubbed the "Truman Doctrine," was followed a month later by the unveiling of the Marshall Plan at a Harvard commencement by Secretary of State George Marshall.

Today's approach to pattern of life analysis (also part of the Human Domain) had its roots in Vietnam, including the human domain analytics in Operation Cedar Falls, which identified enemy dispositions and behavior in the Iron Triangle area near Saigon. Continued debate ensues about the success of Cedar Falls and its follow-on Operation Junction City; however, historians widely agree on the intelligence preparation involved, especially the layered, multi-dimensional application of human domain analysis.

Through the Vietnam Conflict, which until Afghanistan had the distinction of being America's longest war, the human domain remained an important aspect of national security decision making. After Vietnam, however, national security priorities no longer required expertise and capability for pattern of life analysis and these skills and expertise atrophied. Post-Vietnam national security decision-making imperatives actually reversed the learning curve for American intelligence agencies when it came to human dynamics. Intelligence and information collection, analysis and reporting processes gradually shifted to technical collection methods.

After Vietnam, the military revamped its doctrine and planning to wage combined arms warfare against the Warsaw Pact. An aversion to military interventions went much deeper than avoiding another small war. U.S. defense strategy was fundamentally altered to focus almost exclusively on countering the Soviet threat to NATO in Europe and on modernizing the nuclear force. The U.S. military purged counter-insurgency doctrine, training and force structure from its approach to preparing for war.

By the 1980s, Army infantry officers received only the most simplistic introduction to counter-insurgency principles and doctrine during their officer basic and advanced courses. Intelligence capabilities were retooled, shifted from insurgency and winning the hearts and minds of local populations with boots on the ground to tracking Soviet military forces and waging a different type of strategic information warfare against global communism. Military doctrine barely addressed counterinsurgency operations. The only real planning or doctrine for urban warfare, moreover, focused on armor and mechanized infantry forces bypassing cities, with limited planning doctrine written or considered for operations in "urban terrain."

In the 1990s, lessons learned from intervention in the Balkans, Iraq and Somalia emphasized airpower, precision strike and rapid decisive operations to overwhelm and defeat adversaries in combat without the need for post-conflict occupation and nation-building forces. These trends would not be reversed until after the first battle of Fallujah, which forced U.S. planners to realize they may lose the strategic battle for the future of Iraq.

Unlike the post-Vietnam environment, the United States cannot shift its defense, diplomacy and development strategies away from insurgency, terrorism and hybrid warfare. Understanding human dynamics is not simply about gathering ethnographic, demographic or other information about groups, peoples or cultures. Such understanding comes only from the systematic analysis, synthesis and integration of human-centric thinking into national security decision making processes.

American national security planners and strategists have a mixed record when it comes to predicting and preparing for future conflicts. Too often we prevail through brute force and the capacity to expend significantly more resources than our adversaries. But this model may be passé. It worked very well in the industrial age of World War I and in the mechanical age of warfare in World War II. We prevailed in the nuclear age through the illogic of nuclear annihilation and, perhaps, through the foresightedness of early Cold War leaders like Truman, Eisenhower and Kennedy.

Sadly, we seem destined to fall into a Sisyphean cycle when it comes to creating and maintaining effective human dynamics programs to support national security processes. During strategic crises, like the one we faced at the highest levels of insurgent attacks against Americans in Iraq during the mid-2000s, we tap into one of our own cultural strengths:

innovation and adaptability to overcome adversity. We become Proteus, although we revert back to being Sisyphus soon after each crisis passes. In an era defined by severe budget cuts at home and persistent crisis and hybrid wars abroad, however, we no longer have the time nor flexibility to pause, revamp our doctrines and forces, and pour enormous sums of money into innovation when a crisis emerges. Moving forward, we must sustain our commitment to understanding human dynamics and to furthering the integration, adoption and adaptation of social science methods and analytic approaches in our national security decision-making processes.

Sustaining emphasis on socio-cultural dynamics

The international security environment of the 21st century is defined by identity-related problems, the countervailing pressures of globalization and anti-modernization, and the expansion and penetration of new forms of communication that simultaneously inform citizens, mobilize political action, awaken aspirations and create new forms of activism that change the pace and scope of political behavior. At no time in American national security has it been more crucial to understand the human domain of global politics.

The contributors to this volume provided a sampling of the analysis and approaches available to inform national security policy and operations. Looking forward, it is important to understand the dimensions of the human security landscape that will shape 21st century national security challenges and why we must continue to improve our understanding of the human domain.

The global population increases at a daily rate of around 200,000 people with the fastest growth occurring in the 50 least developed, poorest countries that collectively account for or enable a large percentage of the world's current security challenges. For the first time in human history over 50 percent of the world's population lives in cities. There are some 500 cities with populations over 1 million people with a projected doubling of the global urban population every 35 to 40 years. Soon, 60 percent of the global population will reside in cities, with most of these cities in the poorest, least-developed countries and over 30 of the cities categorized as mega-cities (having a population of 10 million or more).

These are not the kinds of cities Americans are used to visiting. They lack levels of governance, justice, police, sanitation, medical or other services to which we are accustomed. Life is cheap in many countries, with human trafficking, child labor, crime and corruption dominating urban existence. In addition, over one-sixth of the world's population lives in shantytowns or slums, a population that is growing more rapidly than the overall growth of cities. Slums breed crime, violence, disease and other problems that amplify regional security challenges. Cities and slums are the ungoverned spaces of the future—the places where terrorists and anti-Western extremists will find sanctuary and plan the next 9/11 attacks on America. As discussed in this volume, water scarcity and conflict over natural resources (including diamonds, oil, natural gas and minerals) will continue to promote a vicious cycle of violence, corruption and human exploitation.

Many of the world's fastest growing nations are, politically and economically, the weakest, the most prone to internal violence and the most likely to spark larger regional problems due to human security deficits related to religious or sectarian strife, water and food security, or frustration over the lack of opportunities for educated, alienated youth. Nearly half of the world's fastest growing countries are majority Muslim populations or are over 30 percent Muslim, adding a religious dimension to political and economic affairs that many Americans struggle to comprehend. For some observers, the Arab Spring was a harbinger of coming instability.

Instability seems imminent in any state where more than 50 percent of the population is under 30 years of age, educated, increasingly aware of their poverty and lack of opportunities, resents government corruption and can be mobilized into political action using new, pervasive social media and personal communication networks.

For the foreseeable future, local and regional instability related to a global economic contraction, climate change, water and food shortages, urbanization and other socio-economic problems will trump efforts to counter the effects of failed and criminalized states, criminal syndicates, and other malign transnational actors. As the West retrenches to deal with fiscal crises at home, much of the developing world seems destined for new waves of violence that will, inevitably, compel the United States to act. As this volume demonstrated, the research provided by human geographers and other social scientists are critical for understanding international security challenges in the coming decades.

At the very least, the interdependence of global affairs requires American national security planners to improve their ability to anticipate, understand and mitigate the consequences of regional instability. This requires sustaining the level of support for innovation in human domain analytics (including social media analysis), continued support for experimentation using interagency, multi-intelligence (multi-INT) approaches that remove barriers to information sharing, and recognition that emerging or future national security challenges will require as much or greater capacity than we currently possess to understand the human domain of global affairs.

For students of American defense strategy and foreign affairs, mapping the future of U.S. national security requires gaining additional perspective on the nature of the emerging era of persistent conflict. In nations like Afghanistan, the only historical memory is one of war, occupation, violence and a government that is either an oppressive religious ideology or a corrupt, warlord-based government. In nations as diverse as Afghanistan, Iraq, Pakistan, Libya, Egypt, Mali, Nigeria, Somalia and Yemen the realization of American policy and security objectives are entirely dependent on 1) the U.S. government's ability to understand complex social and cultural dynamics, 2) avoiding the problem of mirror-imaging (assuming they view problems or solutions similarly to the U.S. government), and 3) creating long-term stability and security solutions by working with and through local leaders who may have different long-term objectives than the United States.

The United States must have the capability to develop deep, sustained understanding of local politics, perceptions and behaviors at the level of detail required to identify, understand and influence local leaders and actors. As the contributors to this volume demonstrate, sustained emphasis on social science research and analysis within the national security community, especially from senior policy makers, is critical to help shape research agendas and to preserve government engagement with academic and research communities.

Interaction between senior policy makers and social scientists dwindled in the immediate aftermath of Vietnam as many academics were discouraged by their peers from participating in government-sponsored research programs. After a decade of war, many of these aversions have been replaced by new partnerships that must be retained and matured to institutionalize and expand the support social scientists provide to policy makers.

Indeed, opportunities abound for increased partnerships between social scientists and policy makers. Even in countries like China, with its continued population growth, "graying" population and skewed male-to-female population ratio (due to the one child per family policy), understanding human dynamics is a prerequisite to understanding Chinese national decision making, economic policy and foreign policy. For example, there are indications of increased violence among China's male youth, increased nationalism and militarism among an ascendant economic class, and increased tensions between internal and coastal population over the distribution of state resources. An increasing number of Chinese are challenging local and national policies. Pollution, corruption, income inequality and forced land acquisition and housing destruction are all issues that contribute to some 300,000 local events and demonstrations against the government each year.

In addition to these challenging demographics, a generational change in Chinese state leadership is shifting the calculus of Chinese strategic culture in important areas that require deeper understanding of leader perceptions, intent and motivations. Two decades after the Tiananmen crackdown, after which the government adopted a strategy of "stability maintenance" (*weiwen*), debilitating strikes at major factories, widely covered worker suicides and mass demonstrations point to a coming wave of instability. China already spends more on stability operations internally than it does on healthcare, regulating the finance and banking communities, and foreign affairs. The central government reportedly pays for over 85 percent of the costs incurred by local authorities to maintain stability, contain demonstrations and monitor dissent. The explosion in online "netizen" protests and movements is much more difficult to contain as more Chinese take to the Internet, finding subtle ways to challenge the state despite oppressive Internet controls.

Even seemingly subtle changes in things like dietary preferences have larger implications for global affairs. For example, a Chinese dietary preference shift to higher protein coupled with an increased use of biofuels has created policies stressing the importance of Chinese agricultural production, which simultaneously jeopardizes the water table under the North China Plain that provides half of China's wheat and one-third of its corn, and has created conditions for the largest country in the world to become a net importer of food.

Food prices and the stability of the global food market directly influence internal politics when governments are forced to adapt policies or quell internal dissent over food shortages, prices or growing awareness of food inequalities. Climate change is also an important factor influencing human security problems, with rice, corn and wheat yields estimated to fall 10 percent with every one-degree rise in temperature.

Many food exporters have already banned some exports during food crises, leading to trade and diplomatic retaliations by nations facing political unrest when domestic food prices surge in response to global food shortages. Food shortages are also causing international crises over access to some 30 contested fisheries, concerns with illicit over-fishing, and the merging of conflicts over territorial rights and possessions with conflicts over energy, food and water resources. An important area of research is the analysis of "spatial inequalities," which involves understanding how geographic, social and political conditions create unequal access to food, water and energy resources and how these inequalities are controlled or manipulated.

Changes in global immigration and migration patterns are also critical to understanding global affairs. For the foreseeable future over 2 million people will migrate annually from underdeveloped to developed nations, many illegally, creating new diasporas that are more connected politically and economically with their home countries than any other time in history, with the flow of remittances back to their home nations becoming an important dimension of the global economy. Migrations, especially forced migration due to war, famine, disease or other human security deficit, continue to disrupt patterns of political and social life.

Even in Western Europe, migration and immigration patterns have altered domestic politics, sparked riots and violence, and created international crises in the case of perceived mistreatment of migrant workers. As this book goes into production, Europe is experiencing another wave of mass protests and violence over failed economic policies and proposed austerity provisions, with hundreds of thousands of people protesting across the continent. In this environment, political movements fueled by nationalism, Islamism, socialism, anarchism and other "-isms" are disrupting political processes. Understanding the interplay of social, political,

economic and ideological dynamics is critical to understanding and anticipating the regional crises likely to face Europe in the years to come.

There are few opportunities to fix the U.S. national security planning process. It is very difficult to adapt and reform processes that are always operating at or near capacity. There is precious little lag or downtime for national security decision makers, many of whom work long hours every day in a seven-day work week and become "burned out" after a year or two in their positions. The pace and stresses involved are not the only factors preventing reform. It is hard to enact reforms, or to "rebalance" resources, to borrow from former Secretary of Defense Robert Gates, if one does not know the appropriate place to apply leverage.

Certainly, the United States will not engage in another significant military intervention in the foreseeable future on the scope and scale of the Afghanistan and Iraq conflicts. Some students of American national security policy may assume that the strategic "pivot" toward the Pacific Basin to deter Chinese militarism reduces requirements for understanding human geography and human dynamics in other parts of the world where the United States is withdrawing forces. Yet the opposite is true. Not only will the coming decades require sustained, perhaps even expanded, efforts of collection and analysis of the human dimensions of national security challenges in the Middle East, South Asia and Northern Africa, the strategic pivot to the Pacific mandates that the United States understand the human domain in much greater breadth and depth in China, Indonesia, the Philippines and other nations.

Thoughts on ABI

The chapter on ABI in this volume provides some insight into the origins and current thinking about ABI in the intelligence community. Yet the intelligence community has not provided a conclusive definition on what constitutes ABI for the broader U.S. national security community. Debate remains about the methods and practices to be included in what many see as a new analytic discipline. Early ABI programs, nonetheless, have demonstrated unique capabilities to integrate huge volumes of data from many sources and leverage metadata standards, advanced processing and visualization tools, and access privileges to unique, multi-INT data sources in ways that point to new capabilities to find "unknown unknowns" that analysts would not find using existing methods and to also drive collection activities.

ABI programs have captured, for the moment, the attention and imagination of senior leaders across the intelligence community. While few agree on the definition of ABI or what problems best warrant investing in ABI solutions, there is wide agreement on the basic promise of ABI processes and analytics to improve performance in important areas. ABI solutions garner widespread support from analysts and policy makers only when they integrate and automate analytic processes that help us understand human behavior. ABI is not about wide area persistent surveillance data, voluminous signals intelligence sources, or large amounts of unstructured data. ABI is about socio-cultural dynamics and the analysis of the human dimension at the level, scale and sophistication of today's advanced analytics solutions.

Debate over ABI and what constitutes ABI methods highlights the challenges and opportunities available for those seeking to fully integrate socio-cultural dynamics in support of national security decision making. Lamentably, the amount of energy put into creating and debating the merits of labels to describe roughly equivalent needs outpaced efforts to institutionalize a robust capability to provide the information, analysis and insight required.

Mainstreaming human domain awareness and research on socio-cultural dynamics

To understand the full range of requirements for human domain analysis we must do more than "map" the human terrain. As one contributor to this volume observed, the metaphor of mapping the human terrain under-emphasizes the level of analysis required to fully understand the complexity of human behavior and fails to convey the sophistication of the methods required to support decision making and operations.

We are adding more and more capacity to map the human terrain, exacerbating the "big data" problem and its inherent challenges of managing and efficiently using data collected. We also now have the capabilities to leverage surveillance systems that capture millions of tracks a day, including dismounted objects (pedestrians), create national biometric databases accessible to police and tactical units with real-time biometric and facial recognition technology, and to provide very accurate geo-location on almost anything that emits a signal, connects to a cell tower, or touches the Internet. We are collecting huge amounts of data that can

provide enormous insight when combined with appropriate methods.

Understanding how to leverage all of this data, to what effect, and for what users is not a new problem. At least the challenge of knowledge management solutions for big data is not a new problem. What is new, perhaps, are orders of magnitude increases in the expectations we now have on fusing or integrating all of this data in a fashion that satisfies requirements for accelerated timelines, more detailed and accurate predictions about complex events or trends, and for more automation in analytic workflows to enable analysts to spend more of their time doing analysis and less time finding and retrieving relevant information from disparate databases.

Conceptually, the ABI capabilities discussed previously are really what you might consider context engines. ABI capabilities find relevance in data and bring relevance to analysts through processing and visualization solutions designed to lower the noise in the ambient environment around important pieces of data. They provide a lens for analysts that refract relevant data— sometimes anomalies or relationships—that focus attention and further analytic processes. ABI solutions are context engines because, once relationships and seemingly disparate pieces of data are correlated, ABI analytic tools and visualization software enables analysts to locate seemingly random or spurious "outlier" data within one or more meaningful contexts.

What is important here is that all of these contexts are fundamentally about human dynamics and how we seek to understand them. As we develop ABI and other solutions that leverage our ability to ingest and extract more sophisticated levels of meaning from big data we must avoid the temptation to focus only on sensors and collection systems as inputs or data sources. We must also integrate our understanding of societies, cultures and groups across the full range of data available from socio-cultural dynamics research.

Another area requiring focus is on the design of analytic offices and teams. Many of the most important analytic success stories over the past decade emerged from joint or interagency organizations that existed at the seams of traditional intelligence organizations. They operated with special authorities and by design broke established procedures and even rules. Extraordinary information sharing and collaboration processes, and sometimes access to compartmented (highly classified) data, helped these special organizations build efficient, adaptable, and successful analytic teams. Because these teams were integrated with operations and embedded within "mission" cultures, they developed different rhythms and practices than more traditional organizations. Of note is the fact that most of the success stories for human domain analysis involved multi-INT teams that were able to share information with few constraints internally, and they also found ways to share relevant information quickly outside of their organizations at lower levels of classification.

The only impediments to replicating the spirit of innovation and "mission" focus from these organizations are policy and procedural ones. Advancing our understanding of human dynamics requires more than hiring social scientists or collecting more data from field surveys. It also requires leadership commitment to organizational change and revamping legacy Cold War information sharing and knowledge management practices. The advent of the highly touted "cloud architecture" for modernizing the intelligence community's information infrastructures provides the opportunity to end data ownership debates and create

identity-based information access protocols that automatically link analysts to relevant data. Indeed, activity based intelligence and other human domain approaches to analysis cannot achieve their full potential if analysts are constrained in their analysis and reporting duties by artificially imposed barriers and boundaries to realizing the "context engine" construct discussed previously.

In the current budgetary environment, it is important to consider one of the most enduring and perhaps tragic "lessons learned" from U.S. history: we do not internalize what we have learned about the need for human domain knowledge and programs. Many of the most important and productive human dynamics, human geography, or "patterns of life" activities have been funded through supplemental budgets for Afghanistan or Iraq and have not been transitioned into baseline budgets where they can mature as formal programs.

We invite the reader to continue following the human geography discussion at **usgif.org** or become involved directly in the conversation by joining USGIF as a member and participating in one of the many working groups that touch the human geography element.

Dr. Robert R. Tomes is President of The MapStory Foundation, serves as an adjunct professor at Georgetown University and is BAE System's Director of Tradecraft Advancement. A former NGA senior manager and founder of Liminal Leadership™, he authored *US Defense Strategy from Vietnam through Operation Iraqi Freedom* and co-edited *Hybrid Warfare and Transnational Threats*. He earned his doctorate from the University of Maryland.

INDEX

An italicized *f*, *n* or *t* following a page number indicates a figure, footnote or table, respectively.